BEDLAM

IS EVIL JUST SOMETHING YOU ARE
OR SOMETHING YOU DO?

1

VOLUME

IMAGE COMICS PRESENTS

STORY
NICK SPENCER

ART

RILEY ROSSMO

COVERS
FRAZER IRVING

COLORS
JEAN-PAUL CSUKA

LETTERS
KELLY TINDALL

DESIGN
TIM DANIEL

IMAGE COMICS, INC.

Robert Kirkman - chief operating officer   Erik Larsen - chief financial officer   Todd McFarlane - president

Marc Silvestri - chief executive officer   Jim Valentino - vice-president   Eric Stephenson - publisher   Ron Richards - director of business development

Jennifer de Guzman - pr & marketing director   Branwyn Bigglestone - accounts manager   Emily Miller - accounting assistant

Jamie Parreno - marketing assistant   Jenna Savage - administrative assistant   Kevin Yuen - digital rights coordinator   Jonathan Chan - production manager

Drew Gill - art director   Tyler Shainline - print manager   Monica Garcia - production artist   Vincent Kukua - production artist   Jana Cook - production artist

www.imagecomics.com

1
CHAPTER

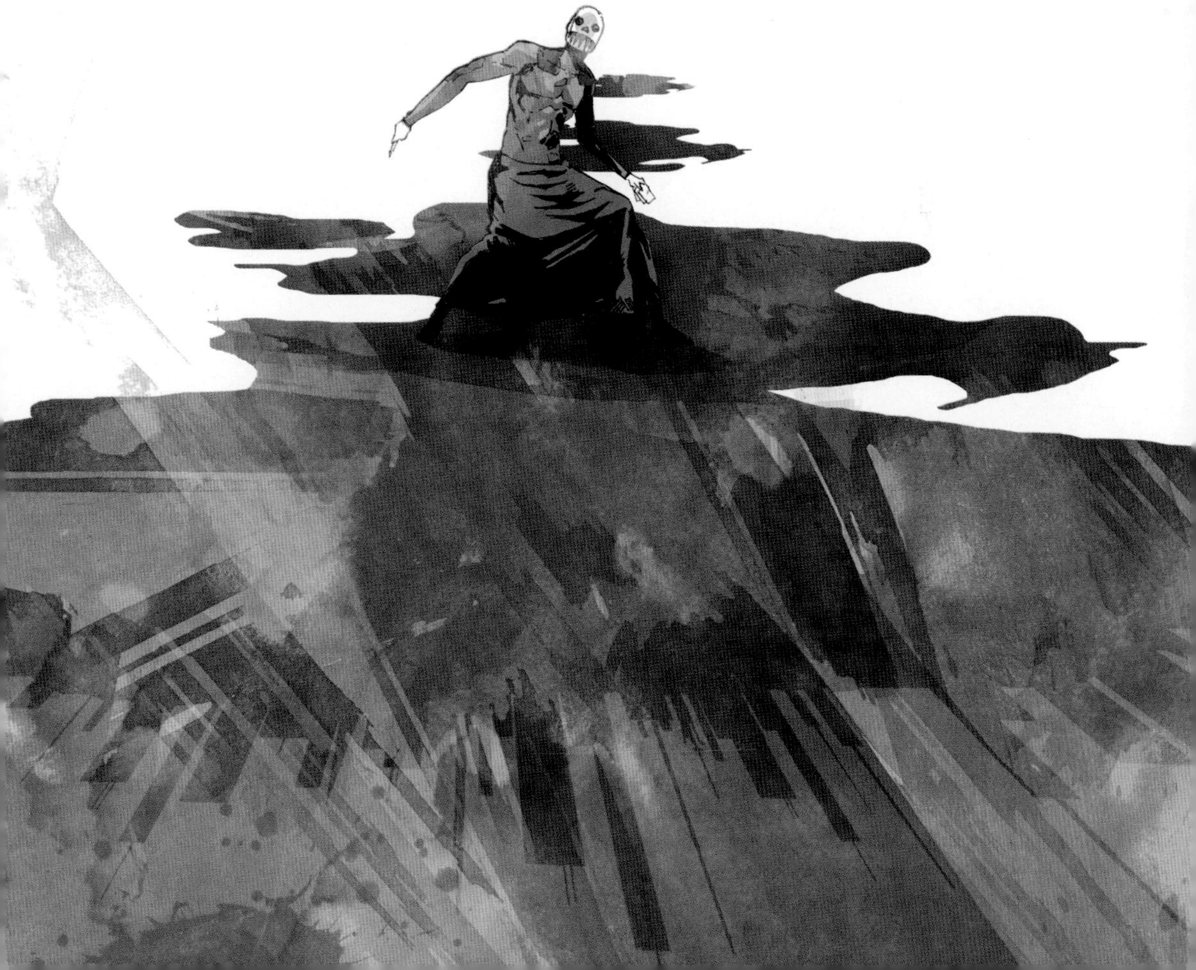

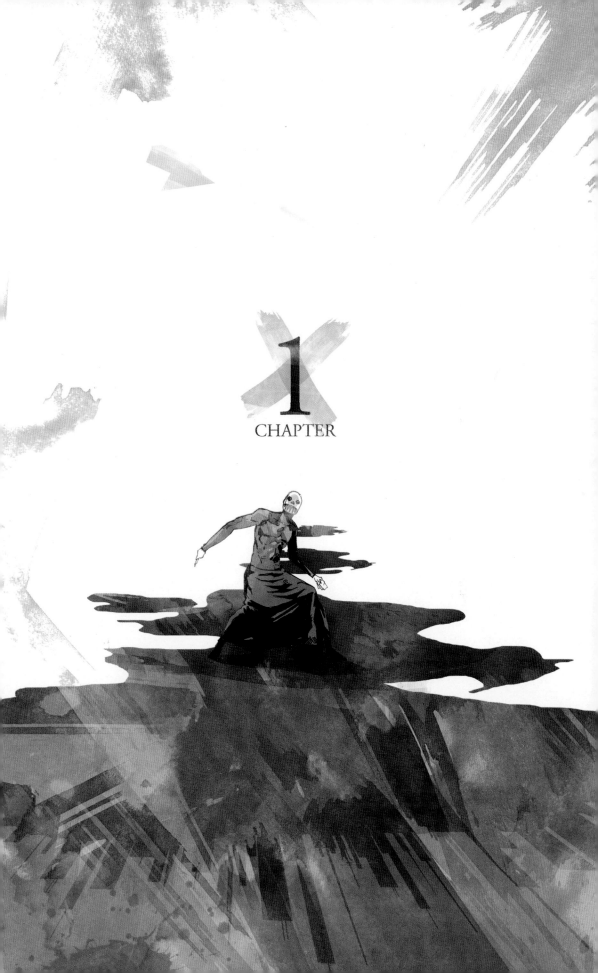

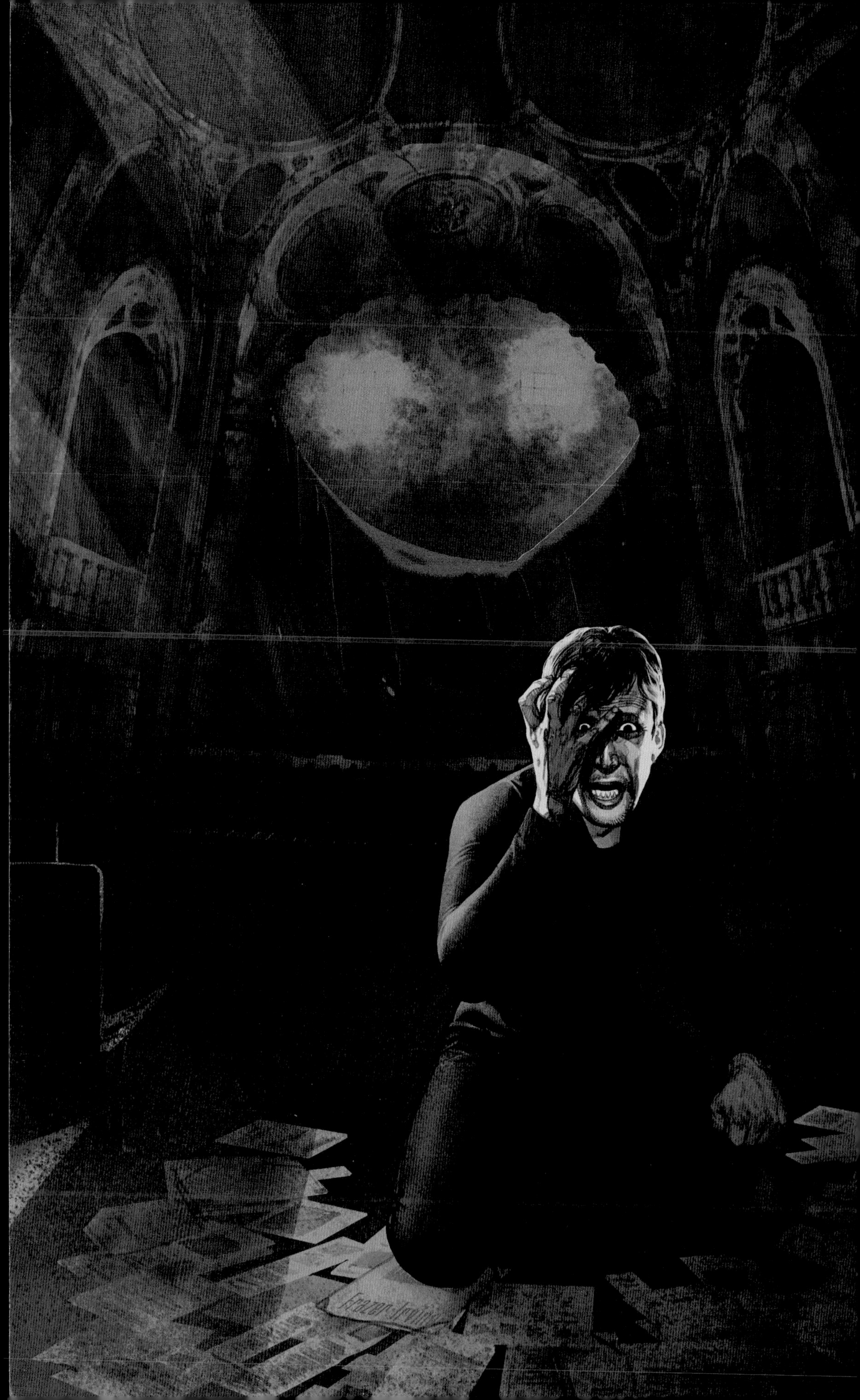

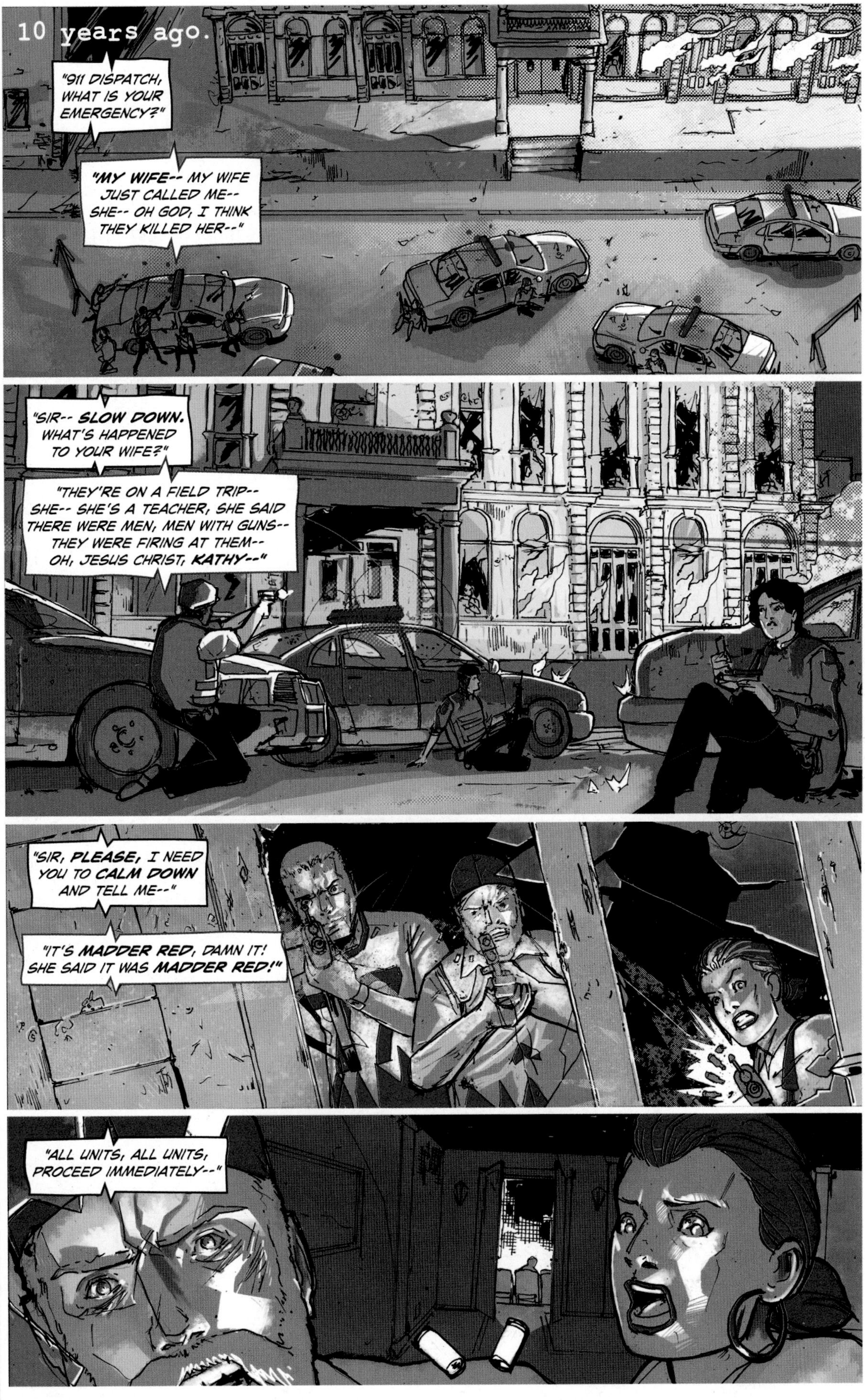
10 years ago.
"911 DISPATCH, WHAT IS YOUR EMERGENCY?"
"MY WIFE-- MY WIFE JUST CALLED ME-- SHE-- OH GOD, I THINK THEY KILLED HER--"
"SIR-- SLOW DOWN. WHAT'S HAPPENED TO YOUR WIFE?"
"THEY'RE ON A FIELD TRIP-- SHE-- SHE'S A TEACHER, SHE SAID THERE WERE MEN, MEN WITH GUNS-- THEY WERE FIRING AT THEM-- OH, JESUS CHRIST, KATHY--"
"SIR, PLEASE, I NEED YOU TO CALM DOWN AND TELL ME--"
"IT'S MADDER RED, DAMN IT! SHE SAID IT WAS MADDER RED!"
"ALL UNITS, ALL UNITS, PROCEED IMMEDIATELY--"

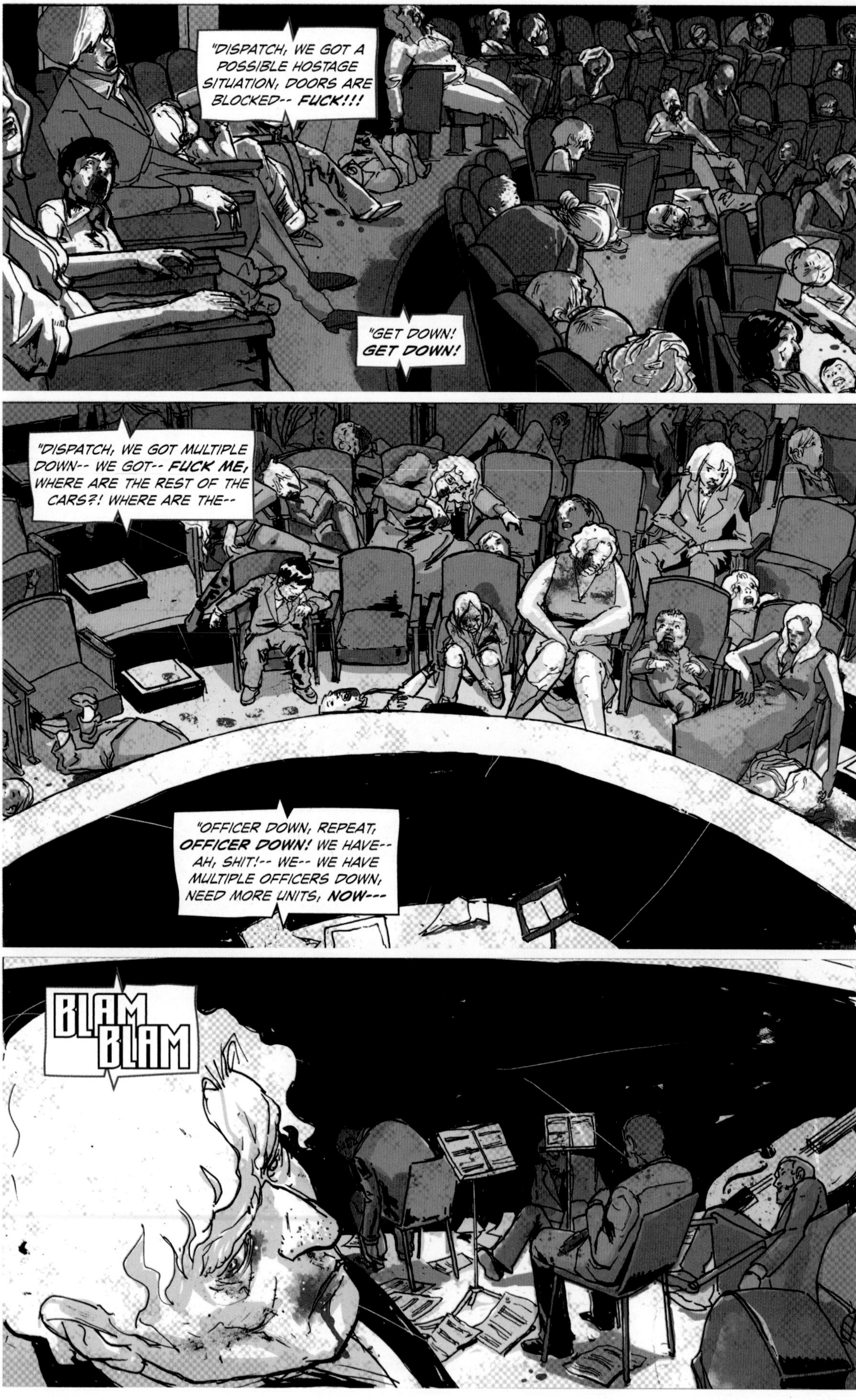
"DISPATCH, WE GOT A POSSIBLE HOSTAGE SITUATION, DOORS ARE BLOCKED-- FUCK!!!
"GET DOWN! GET DOWN!
"DISPATCH, WE GOT MULTIPLE DOWN-- WE GOT-- FUCK ME, WHERE ARE THE REST OF THE CARS?! WHERE ARE THE--
"OFFICER DOWN, REPEAT, OFFICER DOWN! WE HAVE-- AH, SHIT!-- WE-- WE HAVE MULTIPLE OFFICERS DOWN, NEED MORE UNITS, NOW---
BLAM BLAM

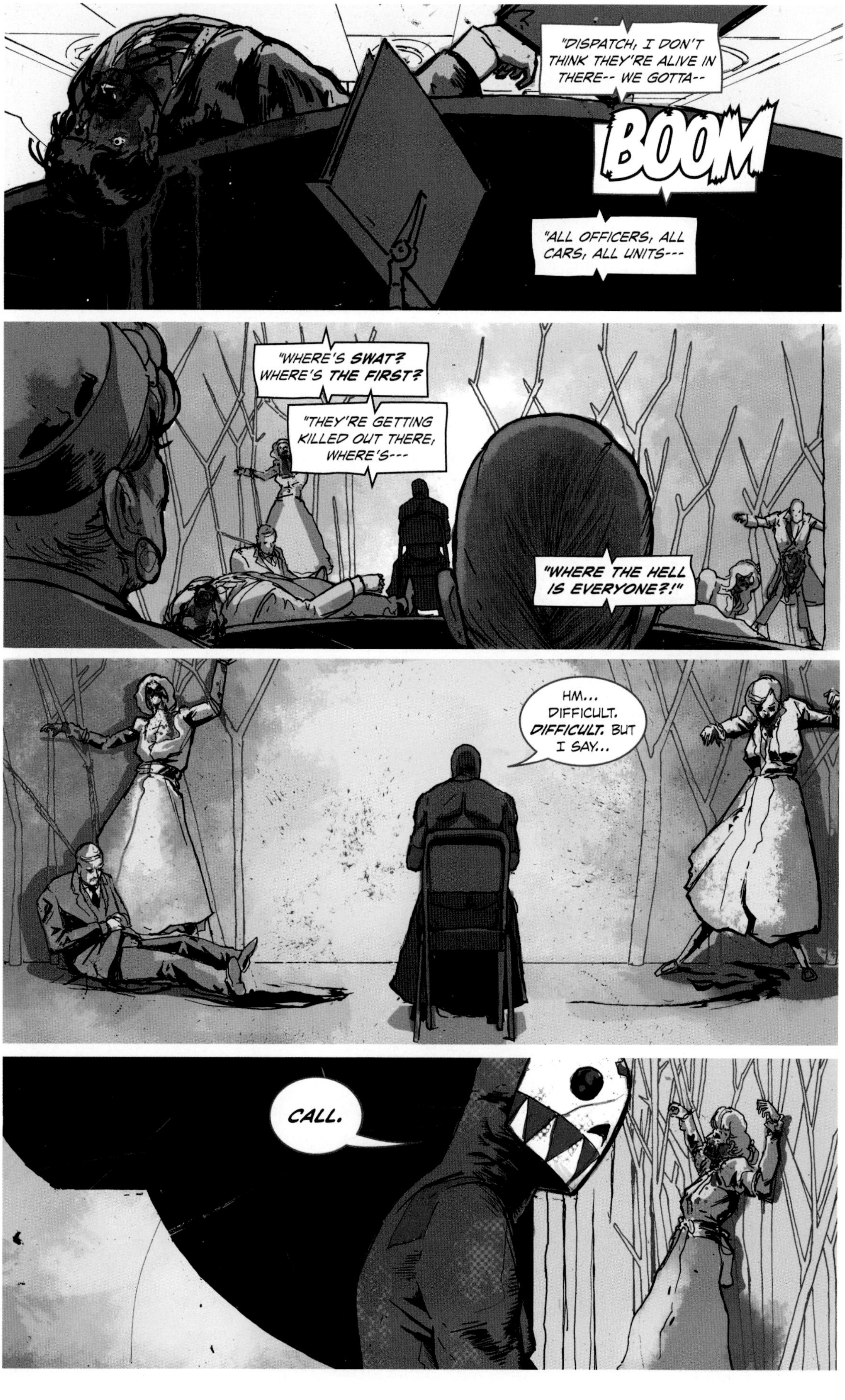
"DISPATCH, I DON'T THINK THEY'RE ALIVE IN THERE-- WE GOTTA--
BOOM
"ALL OFFICERS, ALL CARS, ALL UNITS---
"WHERE'S SWAT? WHERE'S THE FIRST?
"THEY'RE GETTING KILLED OUT THERE, WHERE'S---
"WHERE THE HELL IS EVERYONE?!"
HM... DIFFICULT. DIFFICULT. BUT I SAY...
CALL.

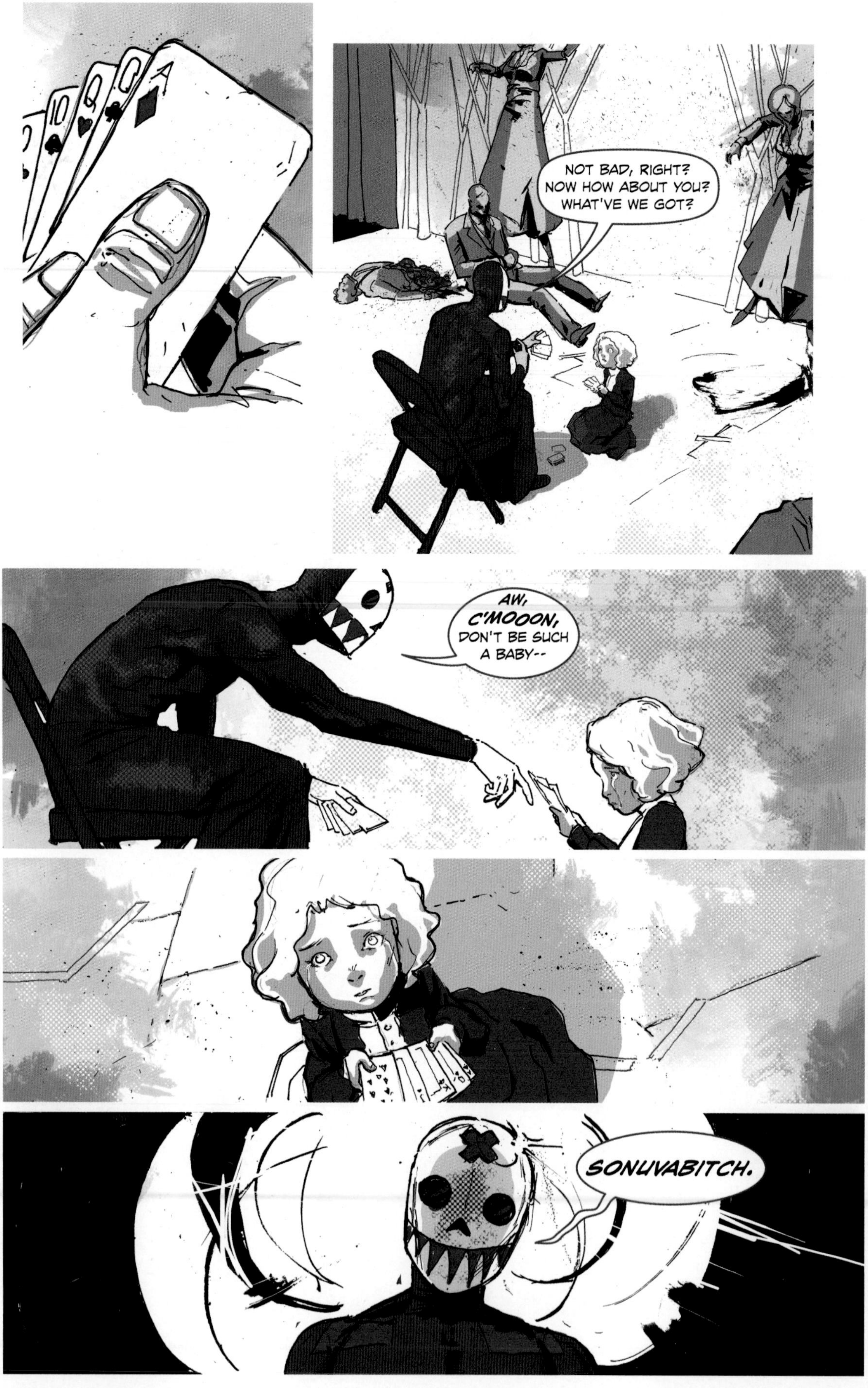
NOT BAD, RIGHT? NOW HOW ABOUT YOU? WHAT'VE WE GOT?
AW, C'MOOON, DON'T BE SUCH A BABY--
SONUVABITCH.

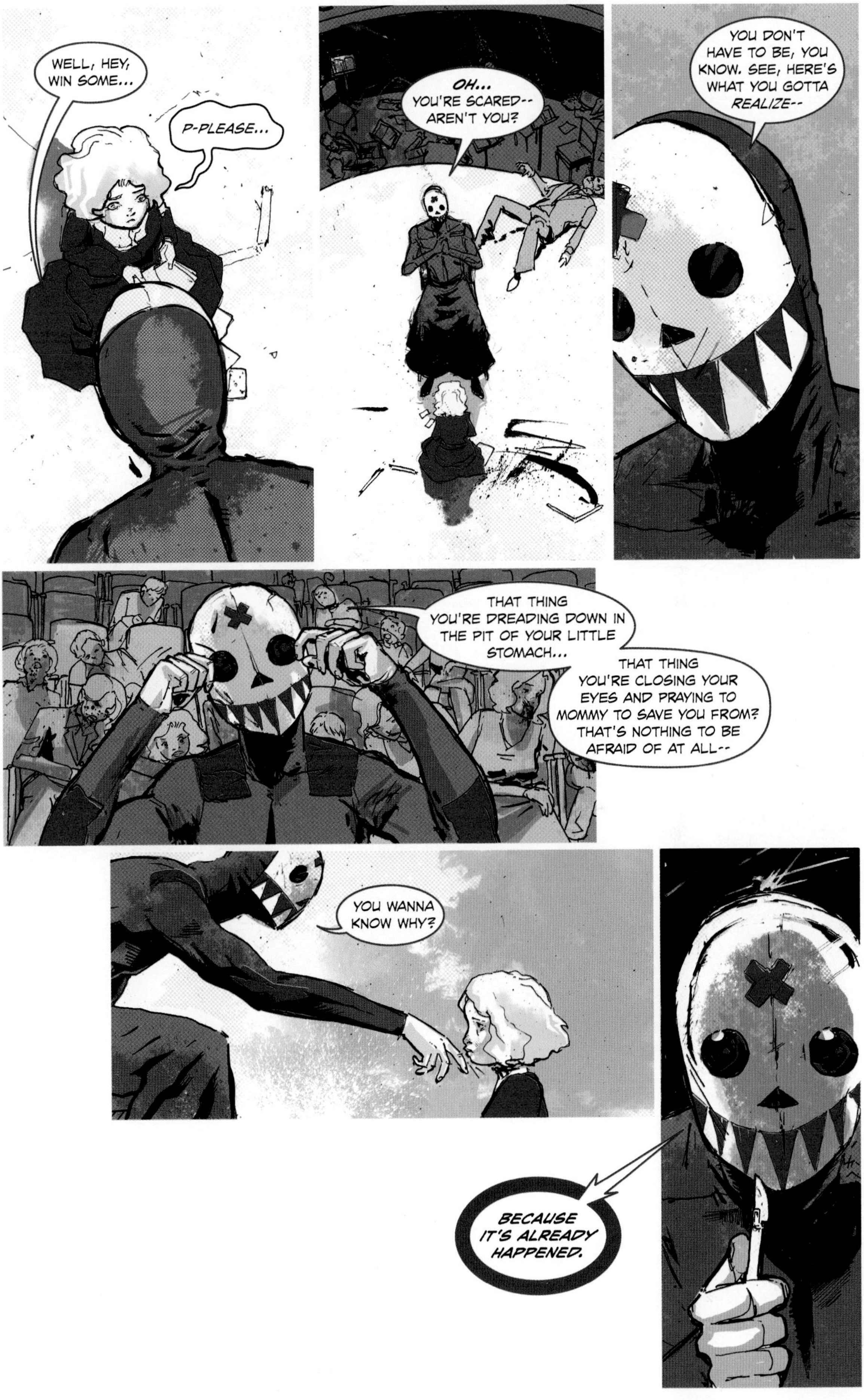
WELL, HEY, WIN SOME...
P-PLEASE...
OH... YOU'RE SCARED-- AREN'T YOU?
YOU DON'T HAVE TO BE, YOU KNOW. SEE, HERE'S WHAT YOU GOTTA REALIZE--
THAT THING YOU'RE DREADING DOWN IN THE PIT OF YOUR LITTLE STOMACH...
THAT THING YOU'RE CLOSING YOUR EYES AND PRAYING TO MOMMY TO SAVE YOU FROM? THAT'S NOTHING TO BE AFRAID OF AT ALL--
YOU WANNA KNOW WHY?
BECAUSE IT'S ALREADY HAPPENED.

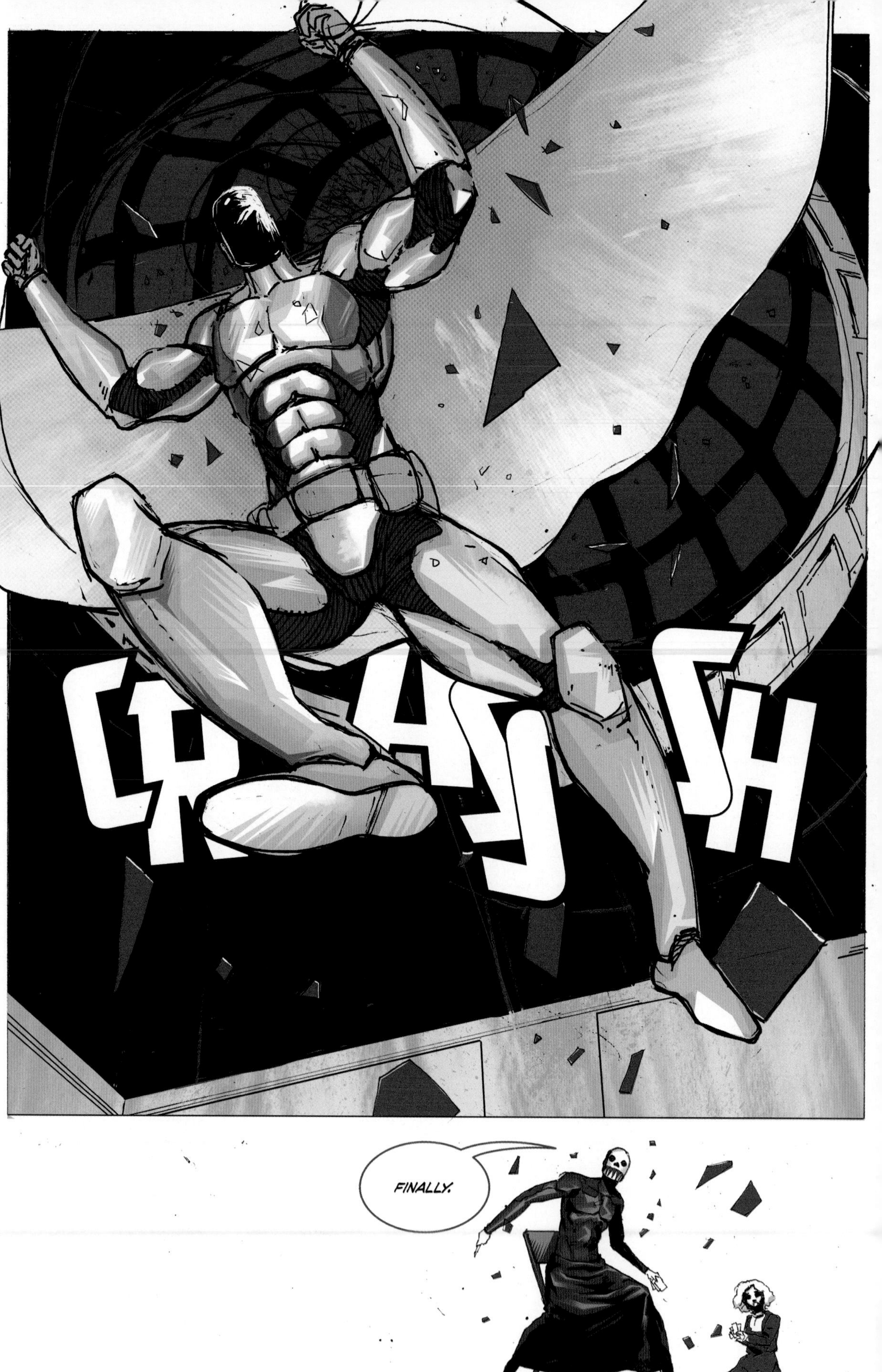
FINALLY.

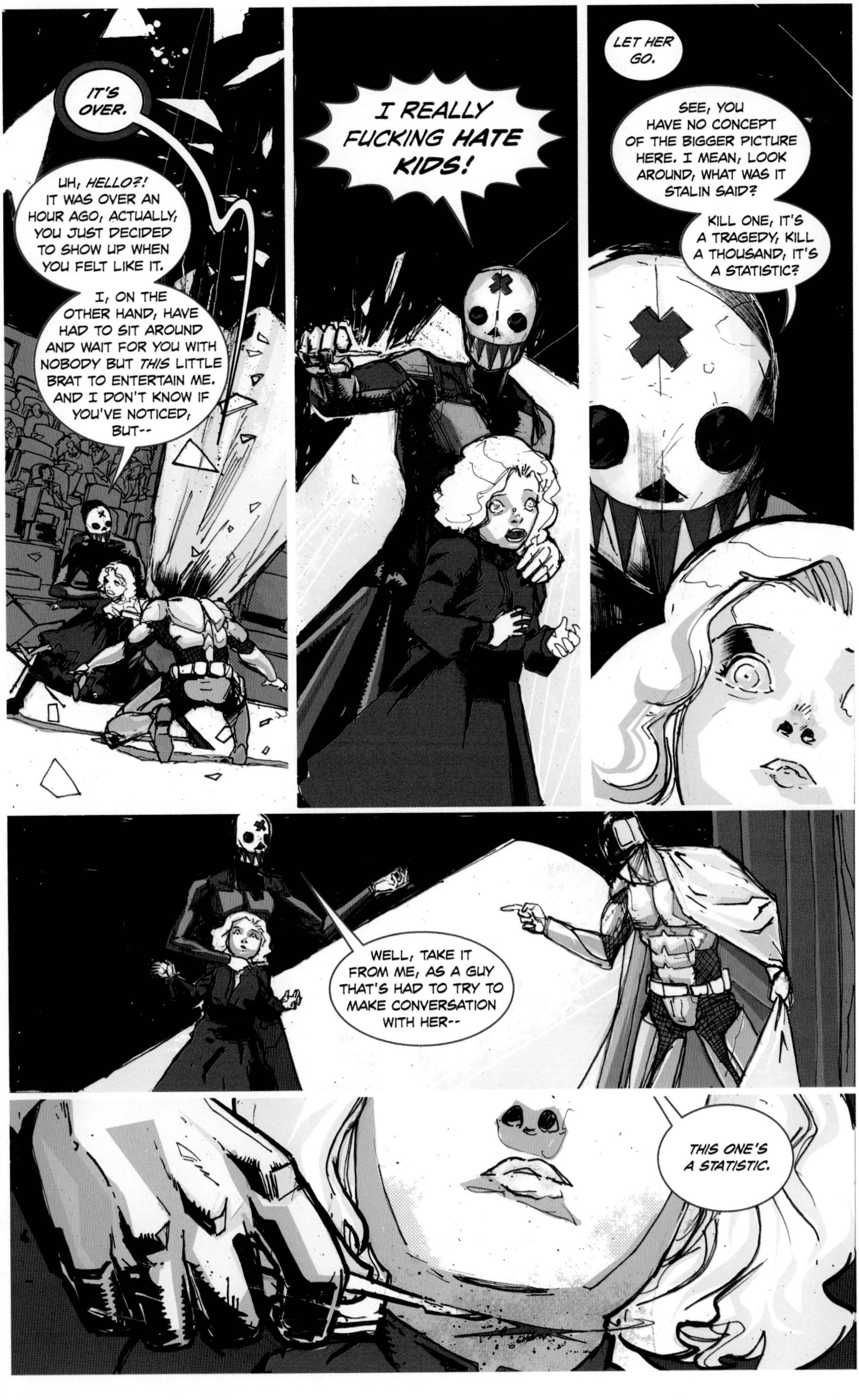
IT'S OVER.
UH, HELLO?! IT WAS OVER AN HOUR AGO, ACTUALLY, YOU JUST DECIDED TO SHOW UP WHEN YOU FELT LIKE IT.
I, ON THE OTHER HAND, HAVE HAD TO SIT AROUND AND WAIT FOR YOU WITH NOBODY BUT THIS LITTLE BRAT TO ENTERTAIN ME. AND I DON'T KNOW IF YOU'VE NOTICED, BUT--
I REALLY FUCKING HATE KIDS!
LET HER GO.
SEE, YOU HAVE NO CONCEPT OF THE BIGGER PICTURE HERE. I MEAN, LOOK AROUND, WHAT WAS IT STALIN SAID?
KILL ONE, IT'S A TRAGEDY, KILL A THOUSAND, IT'S A STATISTIC?
WELL, TAKE IT FROM ME, AS A GUY THAT'S HAD TO TRY TO MAKE CONVERSATION WITH HER--
THIS ONE'S A STATISTIC.

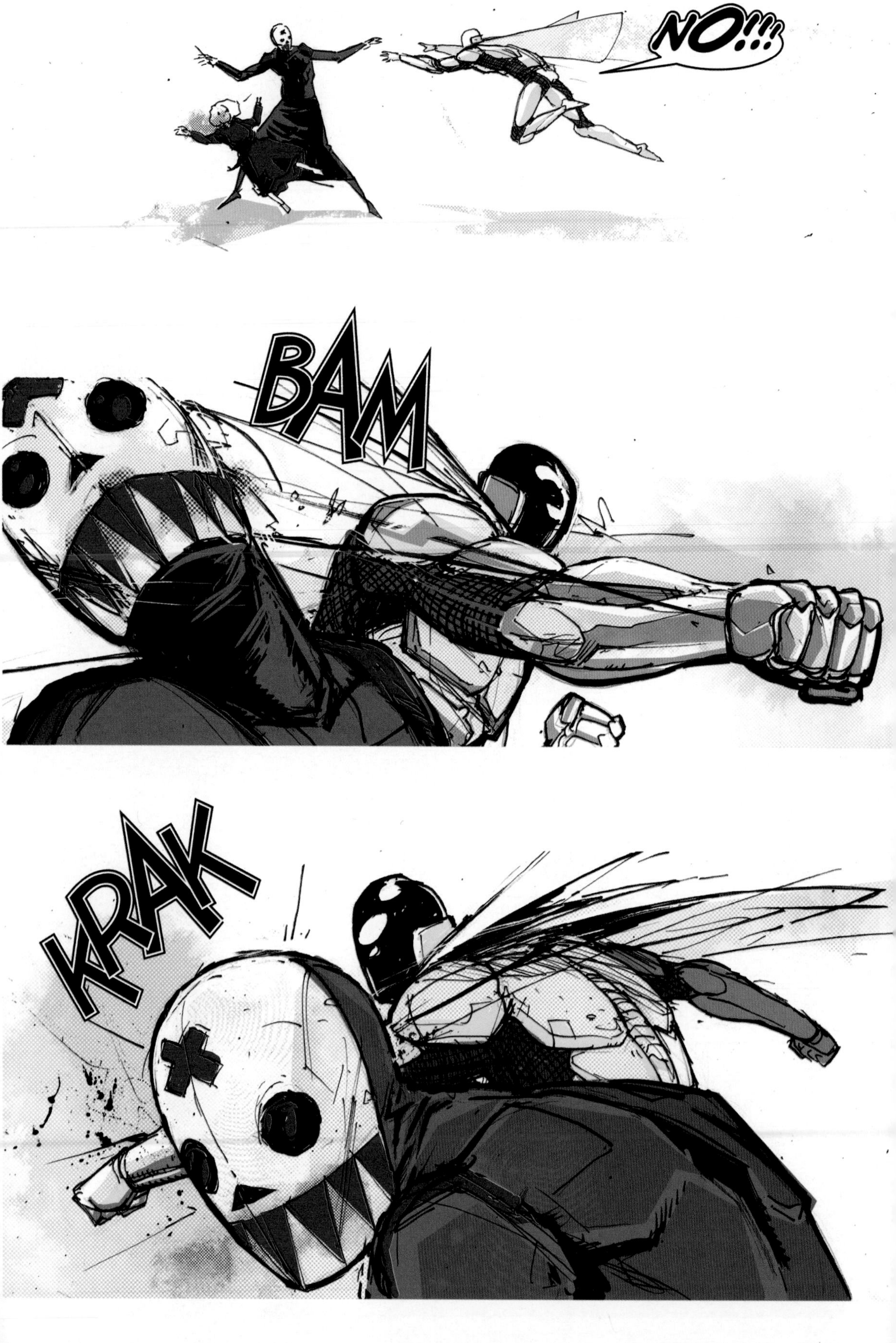
NO!!!
BAM
KRAK

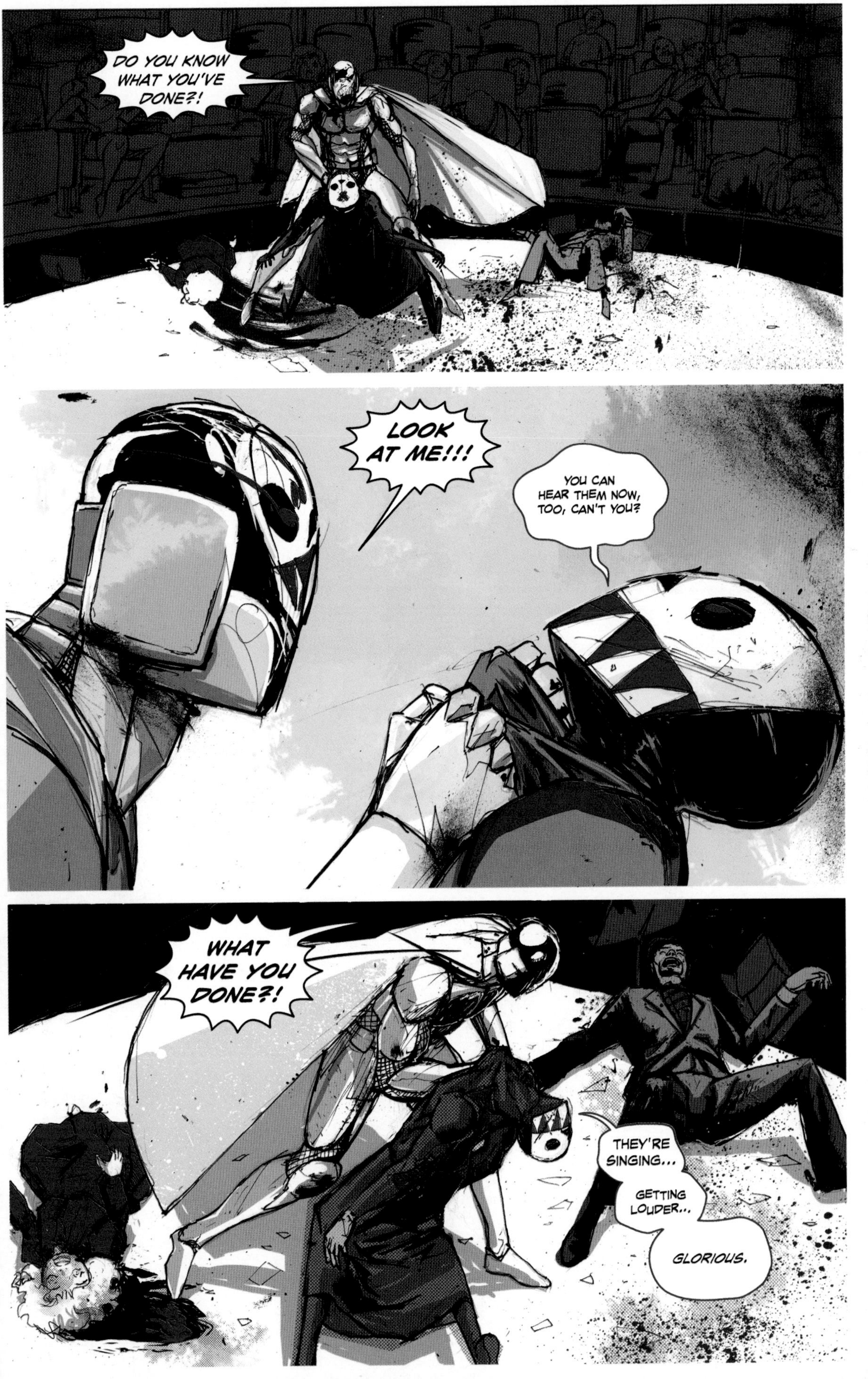
DO YOU KNOW WHAT YOU'VE DONE?!
LOOK AT ME!!!
YOU CAN HEAR THEM NOW, TOO, CAN'T YOU?
WHAT HAVE YOU DONE?!
THEY'RE SINGING...
GETTING LOUDER...
GLORIOUS.

CHAPTER ONE
THE END OF EVERYTHING GOOD

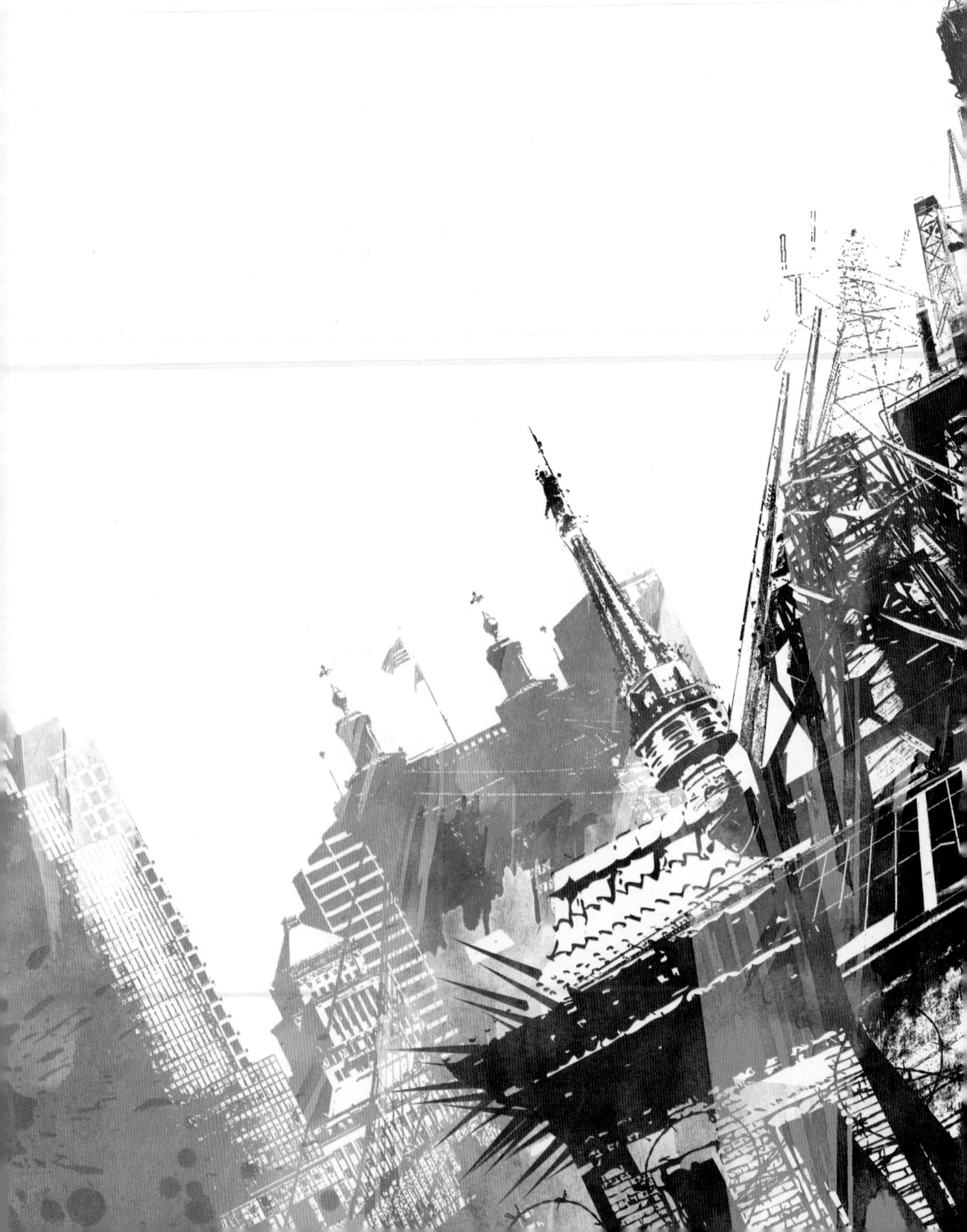

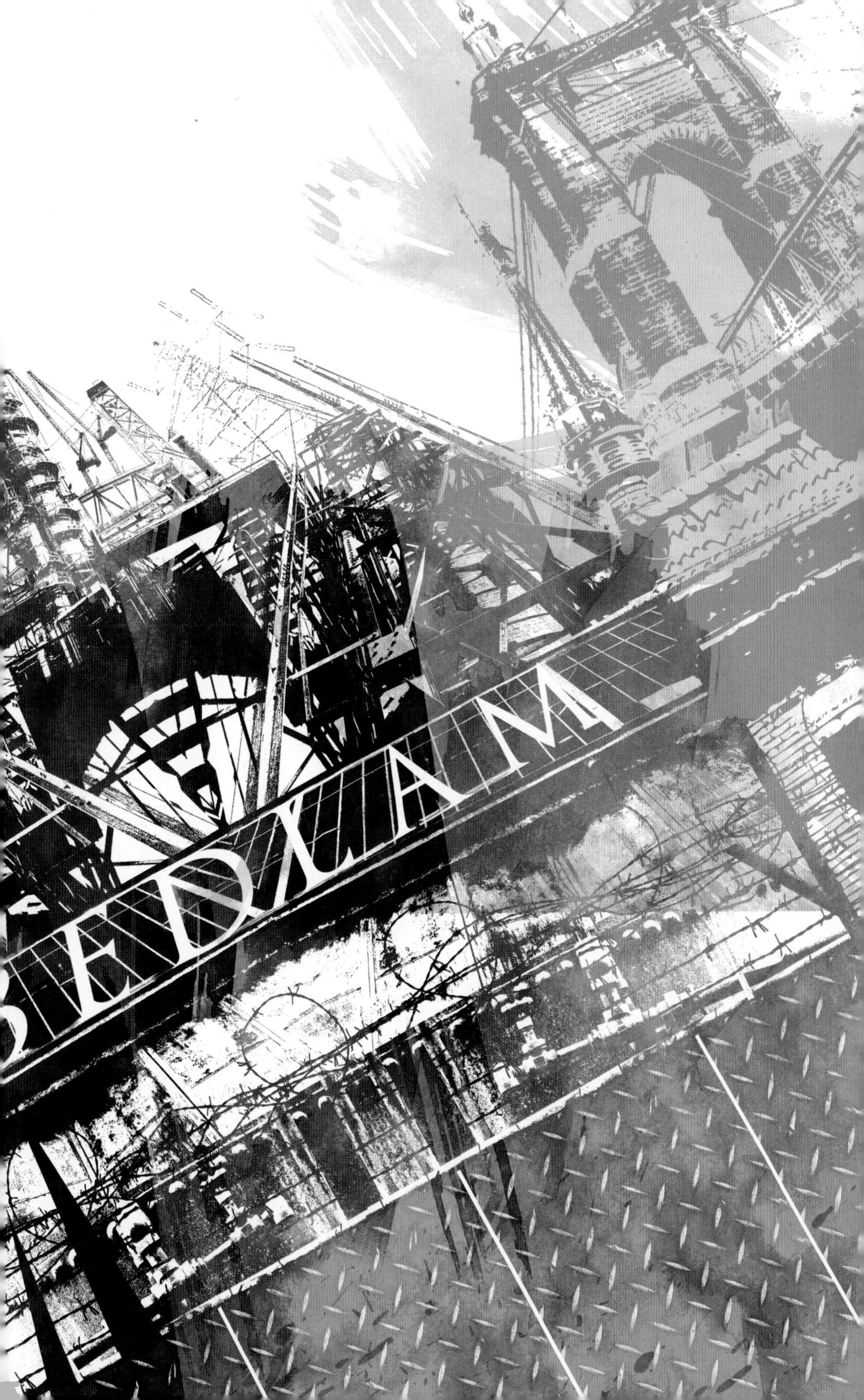
BEDLAM

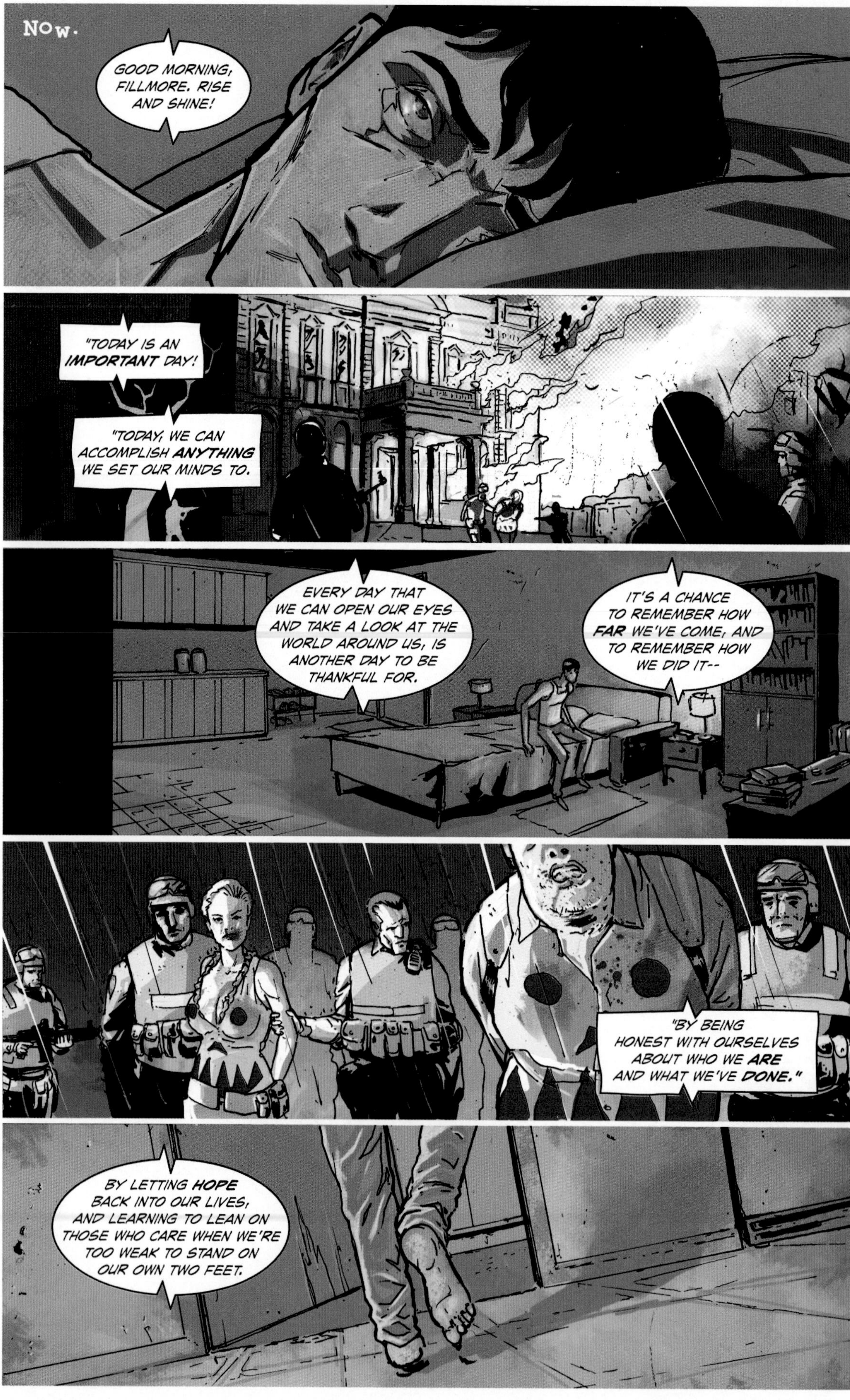
NOW.
GOOD MORNING, FILLMORE. RISE AND SHINE!
"TODAY IS AN IMPORTANT DAY!
"TODAY, WE CAN ACCOMPLISH ANYTHING WE SET OUR MINDS TO.
EVERY DAY THAT WE CAN OPEN OUR EYES AND TAKE A LOOK AT THE WORLD AROUND US, IS ANOTHER DAY TO BE THANKFUL FOR.
IT'S A CHANCE TO REMEMBER HOW FAR WE'VE COME, AND TO REMEMBER HOW WE DID IT--
"BY BEING HONEST WITH OURSELVES ABOUT WHO WE ARE AND WHAT WE'VE DONE."
BY LETTING HOPE BACK INTO OUR LIVES, AND LEARNING TO LEAN ON THOSE WHO CARE WHEN WE'RE TOO WEAK TO STAND ON OUR OWN TWO FEET.

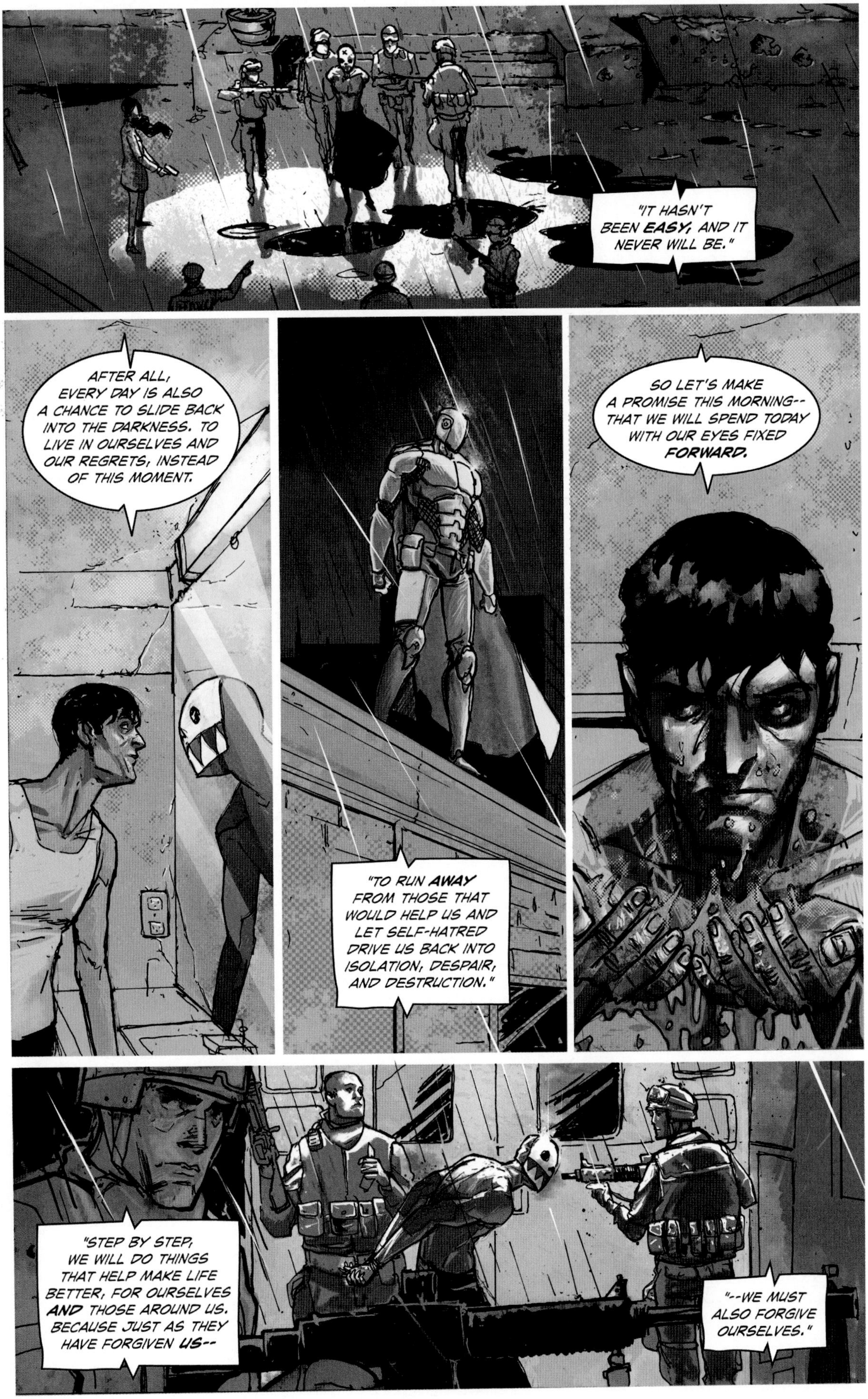
"IT HASN'T BEEN EASY, AND IT NEVER WILL BE."
AFTER ALL, EVERY DAY IS ALSO A CHANCE TO SLIDE BACK INTO THE DARKNESS. TO LIVE IN OURSELVES AND OUR REGRETS, INSTEAD OF THIS MOMENT.
"TO RUN AWAY FROM THOSE THAT WOULD HELP US AND LET SELF-HATRED DRIVE US BACK INTO ISOLATION, DESPAIR, AND DESTRUCTION."
SO LET'S MAKE A PROMISE THIS MORNING-- THAT WE WILL SPEND TODAY WITH OUR EYES FIXED FORWARD.
"STEP BY STEP, WE WILL DO THINGS THAT HELP MAKE LIFE BETTER, FOR OURSELVES AND THOSE AROUND US. BECAUSE JUST AS THEY HAVE FORGIVEN US--
"--WE MUST ALSO FORGIVE OURSELVES."

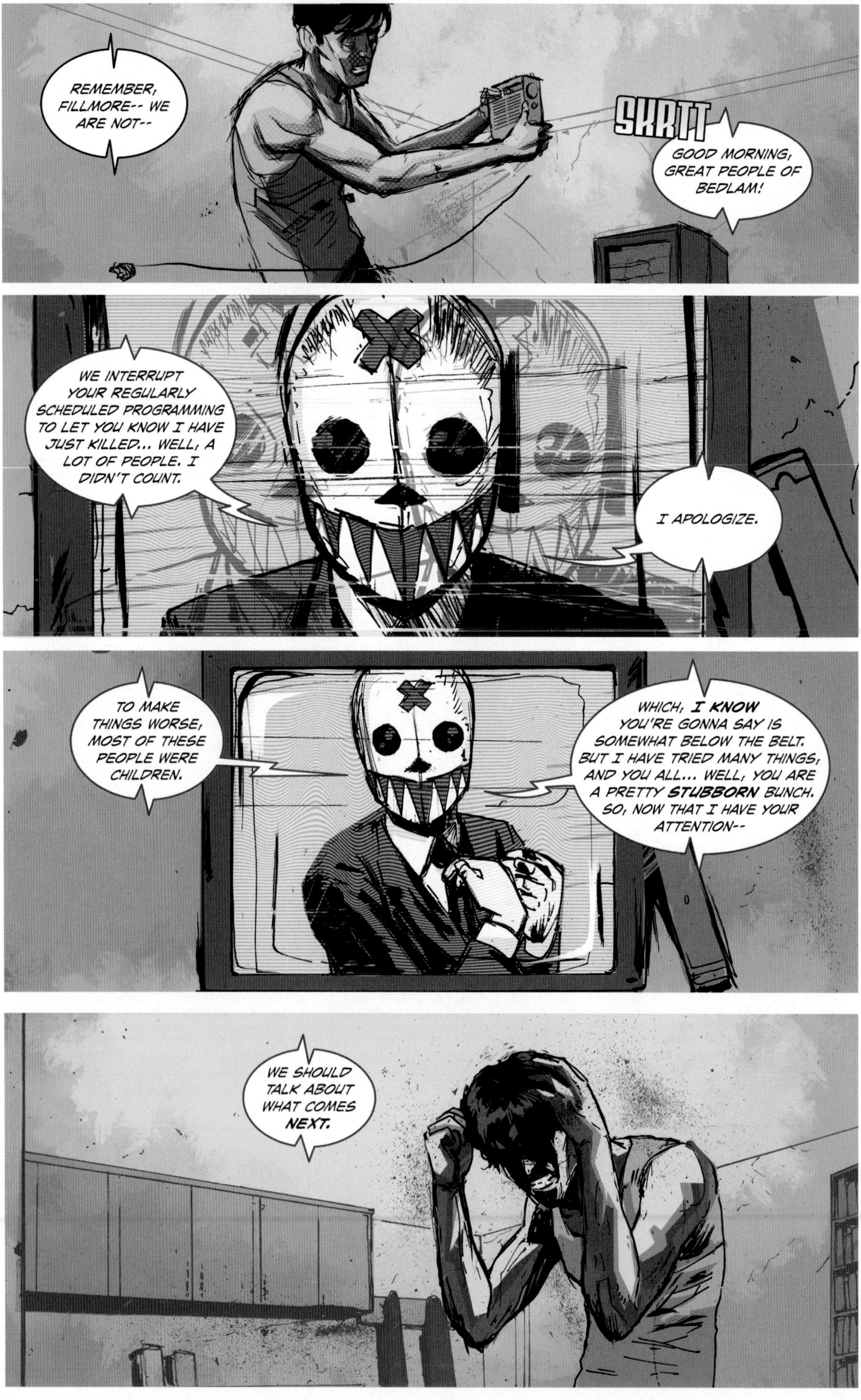
REMEMBER, FILLMORE-- WE ARE NOT--
SKRTT
GOOD MORNING, GREAT PEOPLE OF BEDLAM!
WE INTERRUPT YOUR REGULARLY SCHEDULED PROGRAMMING TO LET YOU KNOW I HAVE JUST KILLED... WELL, A LOT OF PEOPLE. I DIDN'T COUNT.
I APOLOGIZE.
TO MAKE THINGS WORSE, MOST OF THESE PEOPLE WERE CHILDREN.
WHICH, I KNOW YOU'RE GONNA SAY IS SOMEWHAT BELOW THE BELT. BUT I HAVE TRIED MANY THINGS, AND YOU ALL... WELL, YOU ARE A PRETTY STUBBORN BUNCH. SO, NOW THAT I HAVE YOUR ATTENTION--
WE SHOULD TALK ABOUT WHAT COMES NEXT.

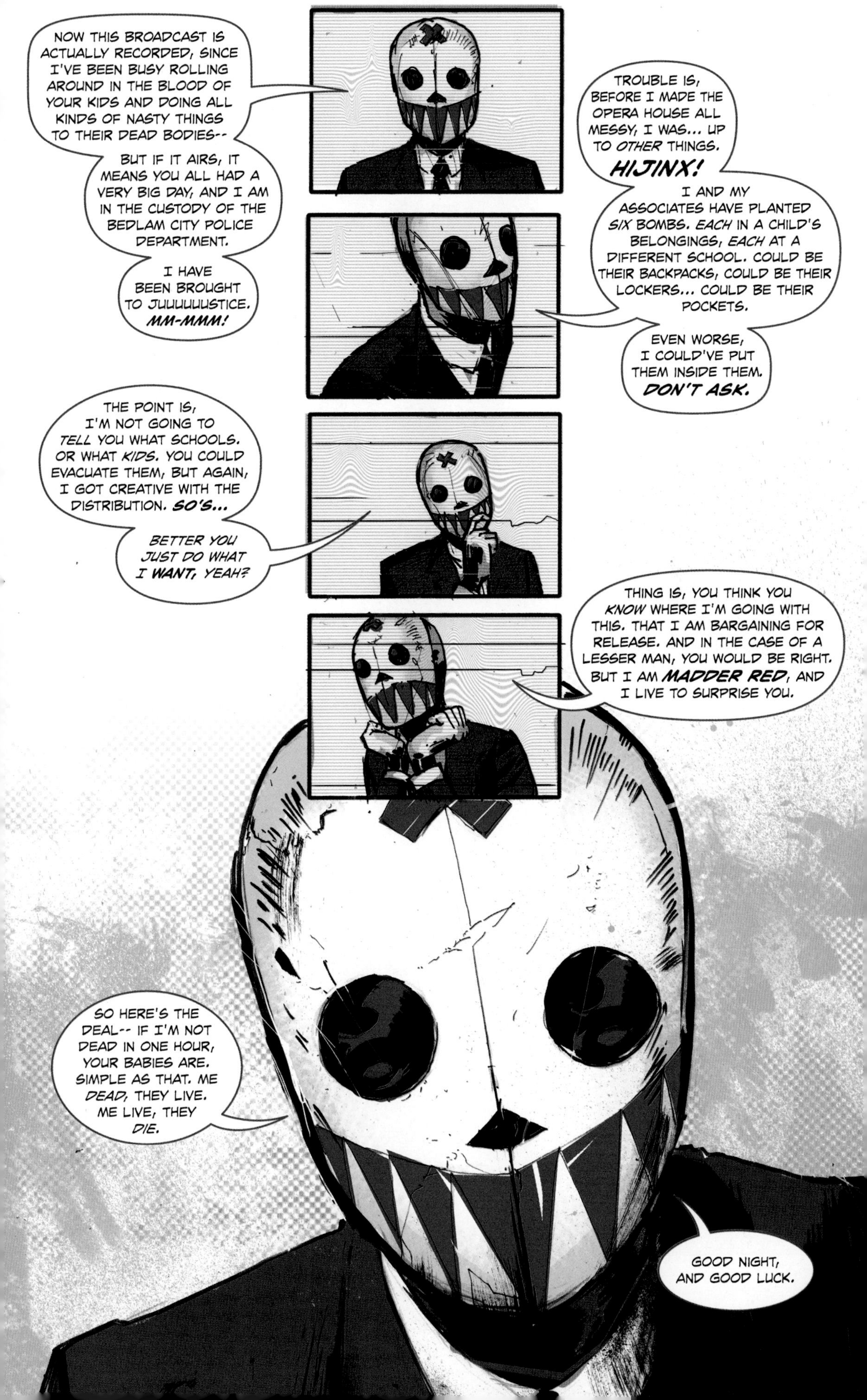
NOW THIS BROADCAST IS ACTUALLY RECORDED, SINCE I'VE BEEN BUSY ROLLING AROUND IN THE BLOOD OF YOUR KIDS AND DOING ALL KINDS OF NASTY THINGS TO THEIR DEAD BODIES--
BUT IF IT AIRS, IT MEANS YOU ALL HAD A VERY BIG DAY, AND I AM IN THE CUSTODY OF THE BEDLAM CITY POLICE DEPARTMENT.
I HAVE BEEN BROUGHT TO JUUUUUUSTICE. ***MM-MMM!***
TROUBLE IS, BEFORE I MADE THE OPERA HOUSE ALL MESSY, I WAS... UP TO *OTHER* THINGS. ***HIJINX!***
I AND MY ASSOCIATES HAVE PLANTED *SIX* BOMBS. *EACH* IN A CHILD'S BELONGINGS, *EACH* AT A DIFFERENT SCHOOL. COULD BE THEIR BACKPACKS, COULD BE THEIR LOCKERS... COULD BE THEIR POCKETS.
EVEN WORSE, I COULD'VE PUT THEM INSIDE THEM. ***DON'T ASK.***
THE POINT IS, I'M NOT GOING TO *TELL* YOU WHAT SCHOOLS. OR WHAT *KIDS*. YOU COULD EVACUATE THEM, BUT AGAIN, I GOT CREATIVE WITH THE DISTRIBUTION. ***SO'S...***
*BETTER YOU JUST DO WHAT **I WANT**, YEAH?*
THING IS, YOU THINK YOU *KNOW* WHERE I'M GOING WITH THIS. THAT I AM BARGAINING FOR RELEASE. AND IN THE CASE OF A LESSER MAN, YOU WOULD BE RIGHT. BUT I AM ***MADDER RED***, AND I LIVE TO SURPRISE YOU.
SO HERE'S THE DEAL-- IF I'M NOT DEAD IN ONE HOUR, YOUR BABIES ARE. SIMPLE AS THAT. ME *DEAD*, THEY LIVE. ME LIVE, THEY *DIE*.
GOOD NIGHT, AND GOOD LUCK.

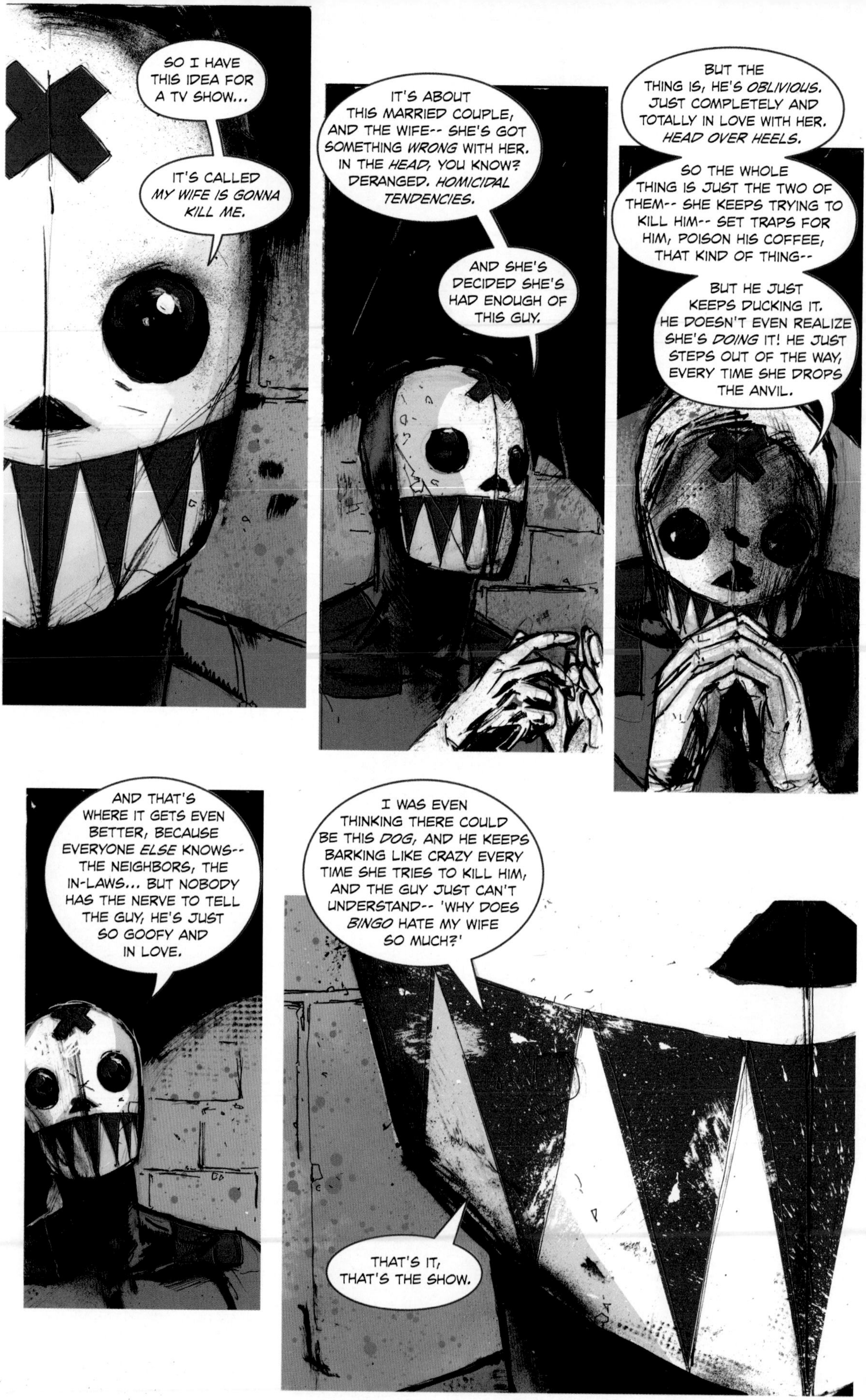

SO I HAVE THIS IDEA FOR A TV SHOW...
IT'S CALLED *MY WIFE IS GONNA KILL ME.*
IT'S ABOUT THIS MARRIED COUPLE, AND THE WIFE-- SHE'S GOT SOMETHING *WRONG* WITH HER. IN THE *HEAD,* YOU KNOW? DERANGED. *HOMICIDAL TENDENCIES.*
AND SHE'S DECIDED SHE'S HAD ENOUGH OF THIS GUY.
BUT THE THING IS, HE'S *OBLIVIOUS.* JUST COMPLETELY AND TOTALLY IN LOVE WITH HER. *HEAD OVER HEELS.*
SO THE WHOLE THING IS JUST THE TWO OF THEM-- SHE KEEPS TRYING TO KILL HIM-- SET TRAPS FOR HIM, POISON HIS COFFEE, THAT KIND OF THING--
BUT HE JUST KEEPS DUCKING IT. HE DOESN'T EVEN REALIZE SHE'S *DOING* IT! HE JUST STEPS OUT OF THE WAY, EVERY TIME SHE DROPS THE ANVIL.
AND THAT'S WHERE IT GETS EVEN BETTER, BECAUSE EVERYONE *ELSE* KNOWS-- THE NEIGHBORS, THE IN-LAWS... BUT NOBODY HAS THE NERVE TO TELL THE GUY, HE'S JUST SO GOOFY AND IN LOVE.
I WAS EVEN THINKING THERE COULD BE THIS *DOG,* AND HE KEEPS BARKING LIKE CRAZY EVERY TIME SHE TRIES TO KILL HIM, AND THE GUY JUST CAN'T UNDERSTAND-- 'WHY DOES *BINGO* HATE MY WIFE SO MUCH?'
THAT'S IT, THAT'S THE SHOW.

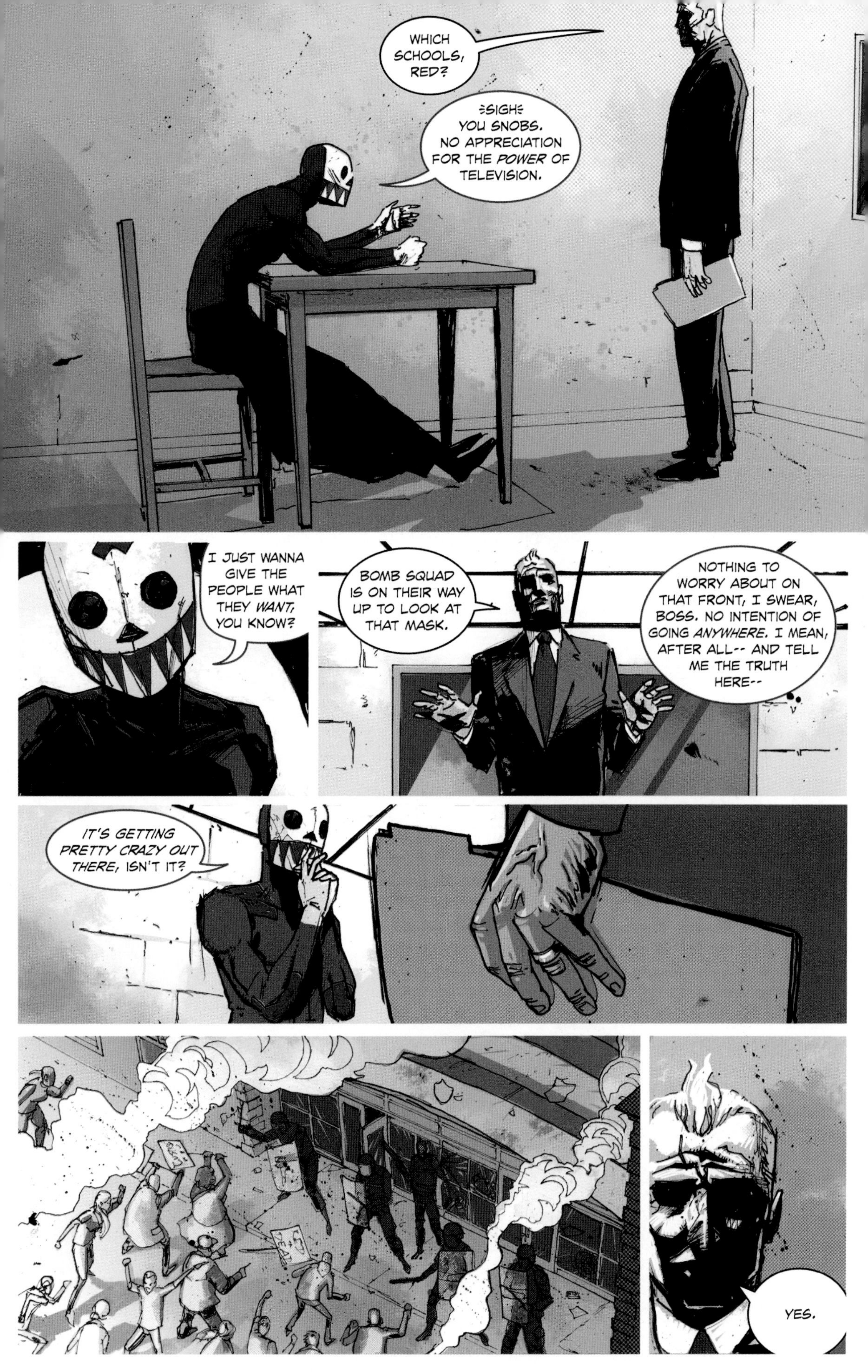
WHICH SCHOOLS, RED?
=SIGH= YOU SNOBS. NO APPRECIATION FOR THE *POWER* OF TELEVISION.
I JUST WANNA GIVE THE PEOPLE WHAT THEY *WANT,* YOU KNOW?
BOMB SQUAD IS ON THEIR WAY UP TO LOOK AT THAT MASK.
NOTHING TO WORRY ABOUT ON THAT FRONT, I SWEAR, BOSS. NO INTENTION OF GOING *ANYWHERE.* I MEAN, AFTER ALL-- AND TELL ME THE TRUTH HERE--
IT'S GETTING PRETTY CRAZY OUT THERE, ISN'T IT?
YES.

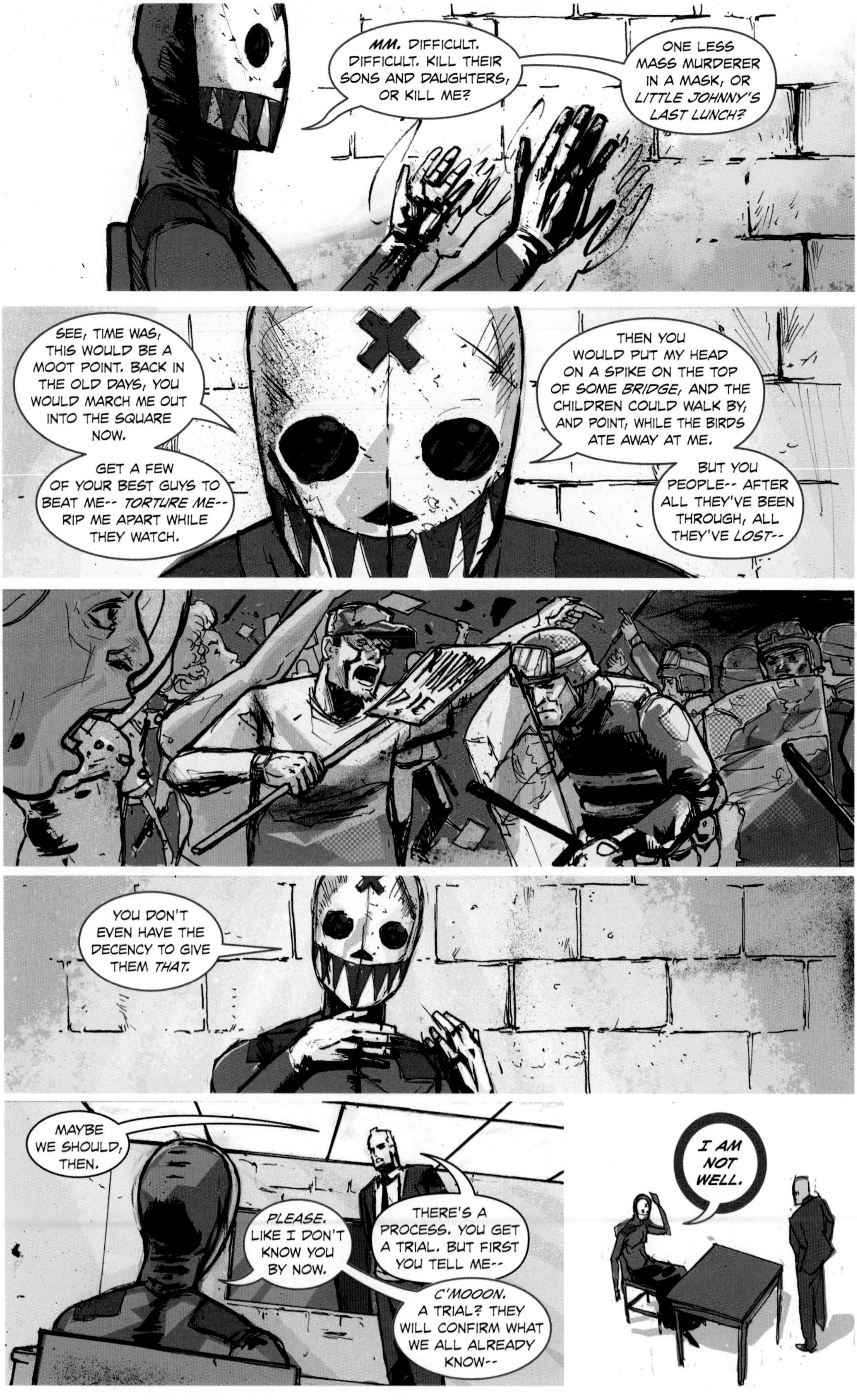
MM. DIFFICULT. DIFFICULT. KILL THEIR SONS AND DAUGHTERS, OR KILL ME?
ONE LESS MASS MURDERER IN A MASK, OR LITTLE JOHNNY'S LAST LUNCH?
SEE, TIME WAS, THIS WOULD BE A MOOT POINT. BACK IN THE OLD DAYS, YOU WOULD MARCH ME OUT INTO THE SQUARE NOW.
GET A FEW OF YOUR BEST GUYS TO BEAT ME-- TORTURE ME-- RIP ME APART WHILE THEY WATCH.
THEN YOU WOULD PUT MY HEAD ON A SPIKE ON THE TOP OF SOME BRIDGE, AND THE CHILDREN COULD WALK BY, AND POINT, WHILE THE BIRDS ATE AWAY AT ME.
BUT YOU PEOPLE-- AFTER ALL THEY'VE BEEN THROUGH, ALL THEY'VE LOST--
YOU DON'T EVEN HAVE THE DECENCY TO GIVE THEM THAT.
MAYBE WE SHOULD, THEN.
THERE'S A PROCESS. YOU GET A TRIAL. BUT FIRST YOU TELL ME--
PLEASE. LIKE I DON'T KNOW YOU BY NOW.
C'MOOON. A TRIAL? THEY WILL CONFIRM WHAT WE ALL ALREADY KNOW--
I AM NOT WELL.

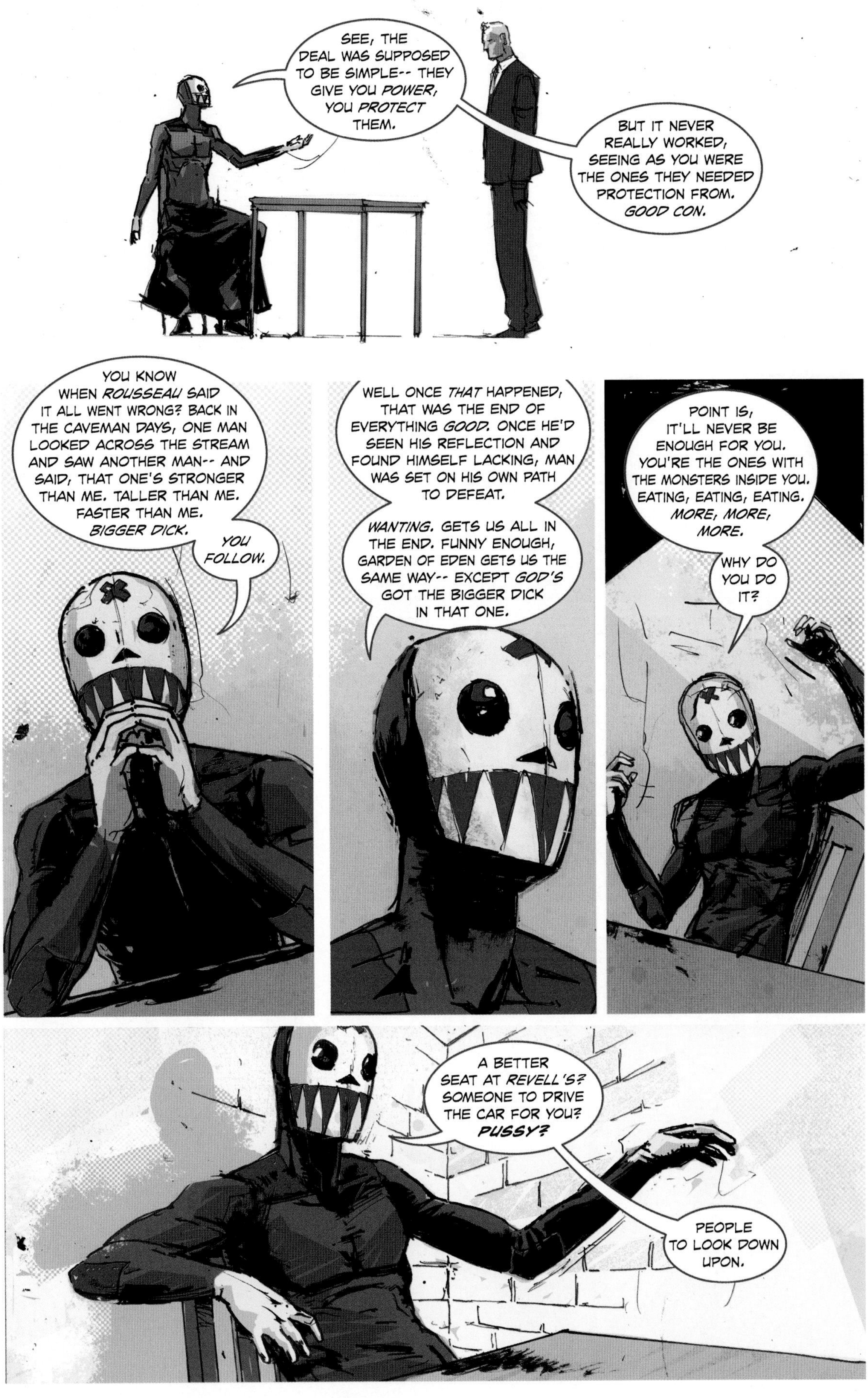
SEE, THE DEAL WAS SUPPOSED TO BE SIMPLE-- THEY GIVE YOU *POWER*, YOU *PROTECT* THEM.
BUT IT NEVER REALLY WORKED, SEEING AS YOU WERE THE ONES THEY NEEDED PROTECTION FROM. *GOOD CON.*
YOU KNOW WHEN *ROUSSEAU* SAID IT ALL WENT WRONG? BACK IN THE CAVEMAN DAYS, ONE MAN LOOKED ACROSS THE STREAM AND SAW ANOTHER MAN-- AND SAID, THAT ONE'S STRONGER THAN ME. TALLER THAN ME. FASTER THAN ME. *BIGGER DICK.*
YOU FOLLOW.
WELL ONCE *THAT* HAPPENED, THAT WAS THE END OF EVERYTHING *GOOD*. ONCE HE'D SEEN HIS REFLECTION AND FOUND HIMSELF LACKING, MAN WAS SET ON HIS OWN PATH TO DEFEAT.
WANTING. GETS US ALL IN THE END. FUNNY ENOUGH, GARDEN OF EDEN GETS US THE SAME WAY-- EXCEPT *GOD'S* GOT THE BIGGER DICK IN THAT ONE.
POINT IS, IT'LL NEVER BE ENOUGH FOR YOU. YOU'RE THE ONES WITH THE MONSTERS INSIDE YOU. EATING, EATING, EATING. *MORE, MORE, MORE.*
WHY DO YOU DO IT?
A BETTER SEAT AT *REVELL'S*? SOMEONE TO DRIVE THE CAR FOR YOU? ***PUSSY?***
PEOPLE TO LOOK DOWN UPON.

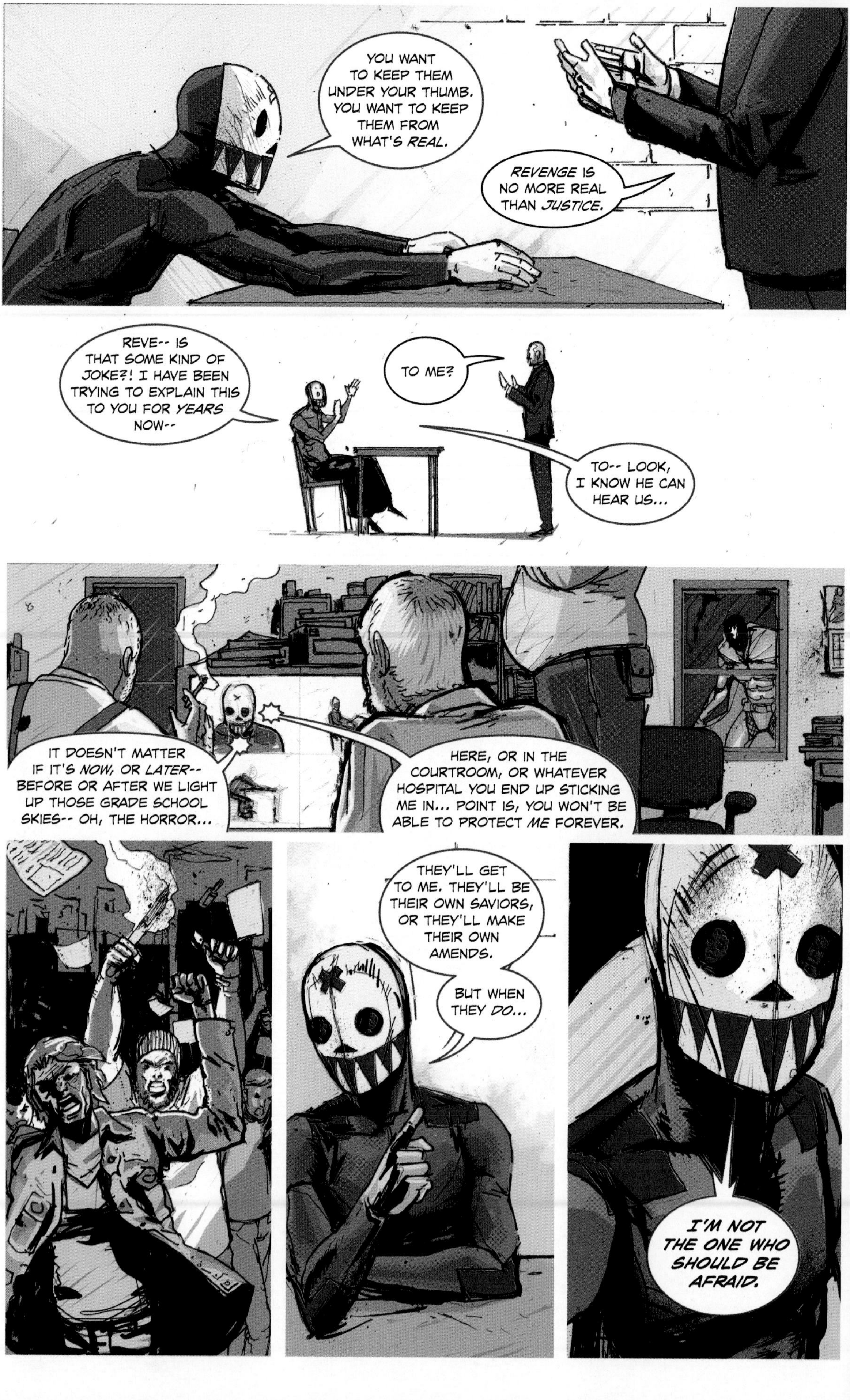
YOU WANT TO KEEP THEM UNDER YOUR THUMB. YOU WANT TO KEEP THEM FROM WHAT'S *REAL*.
REVENGE IS NO MORE REAL THAN *JUSTICE*.
REVE-- IS THAT SOME KIND OF JOKE?! I HAVE BEEN TRYING TO EXPLAIN THIS TO YOU FOR *YEARS* NOW--
TO ME?
TO-- LOOK, I KNOW HE CAN HEAR US...
IT DOESN'T MATTER IF IT'S *NOW*, OR *LATER*-- BEFORE OR AFTER WE LIGHT UP THOSE GRADE SCHOOL SKIES-- OH, THE HORROR...
HERE, OR IN THE COURTROOM, OR WHATEVER HOSPITAL YOU END UP STICKING ME IN... POINT IS, YOU WON'T BE ABLE TO PROTECT *ME* FOREVER.
THEY'LL GET TO ME. THEY'LL BE THEIR OWN SAVIORS, OR THEY'LL MAKE THEIR OWN AMENDS.
BUT WHEN THEY *DO*...
I'M NOT THE ONE WHO SHOULD BE AFRAID.

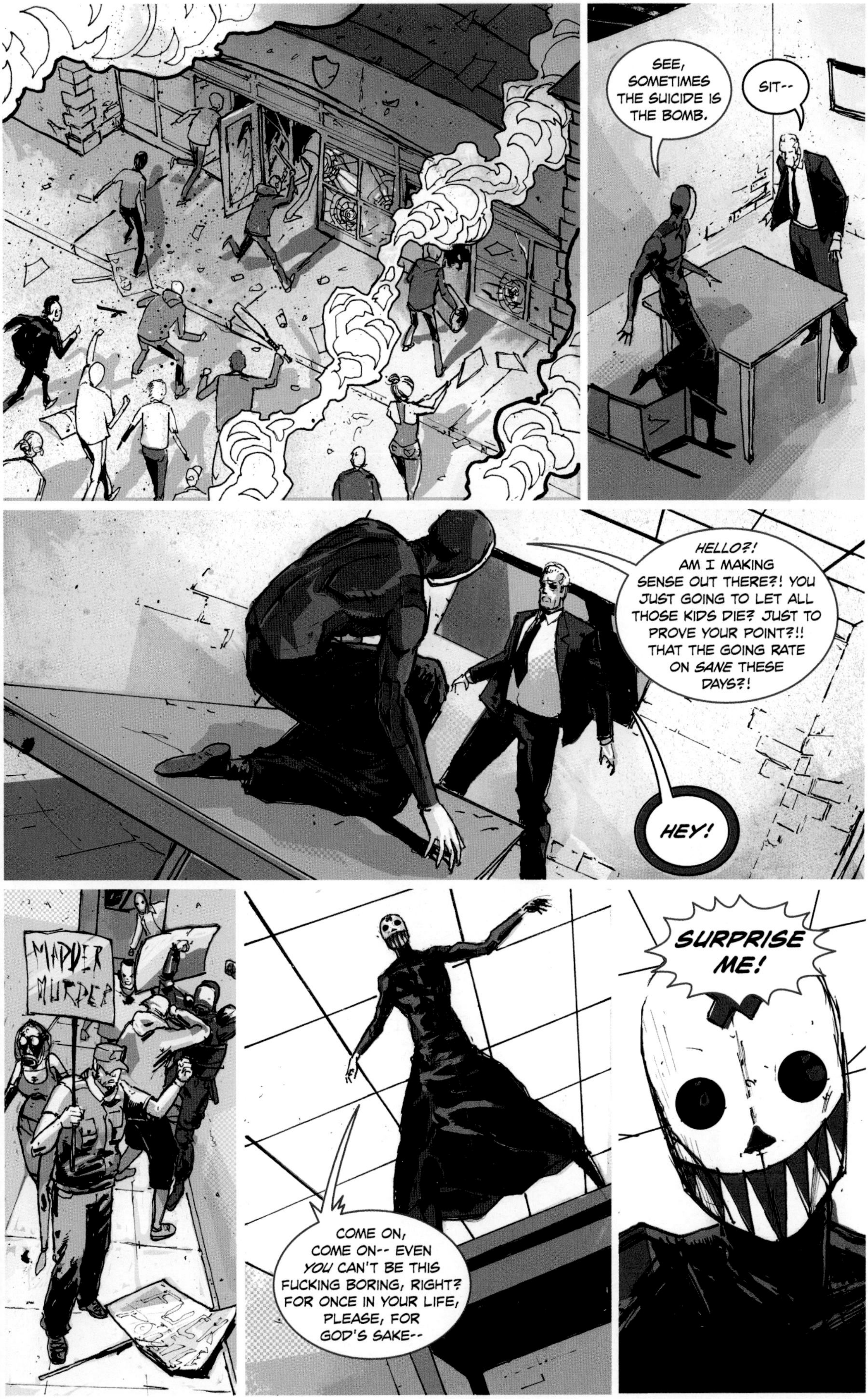
SEE, SOMETIMES THE SUICIDE IS THE BOMB.
SIT--
HELLO?! AM I MAKING SENSE OUT THERE?! YOU JUST GOING TO LET ALL THOSE KIDS DIE? JUST TO PROVE YOUR POINT?!! THAT THE GOING RATE ON SANE THESE DAYS?!
HEY!
COME ON, COME ON-- EVEN YOU CAN'T BE THIS FUCKING BORING, RIGHT? FOR ONCE IN YOUR LIFE, PLEASE, FOR GOD'S SAKE--
SURPRISE ME!

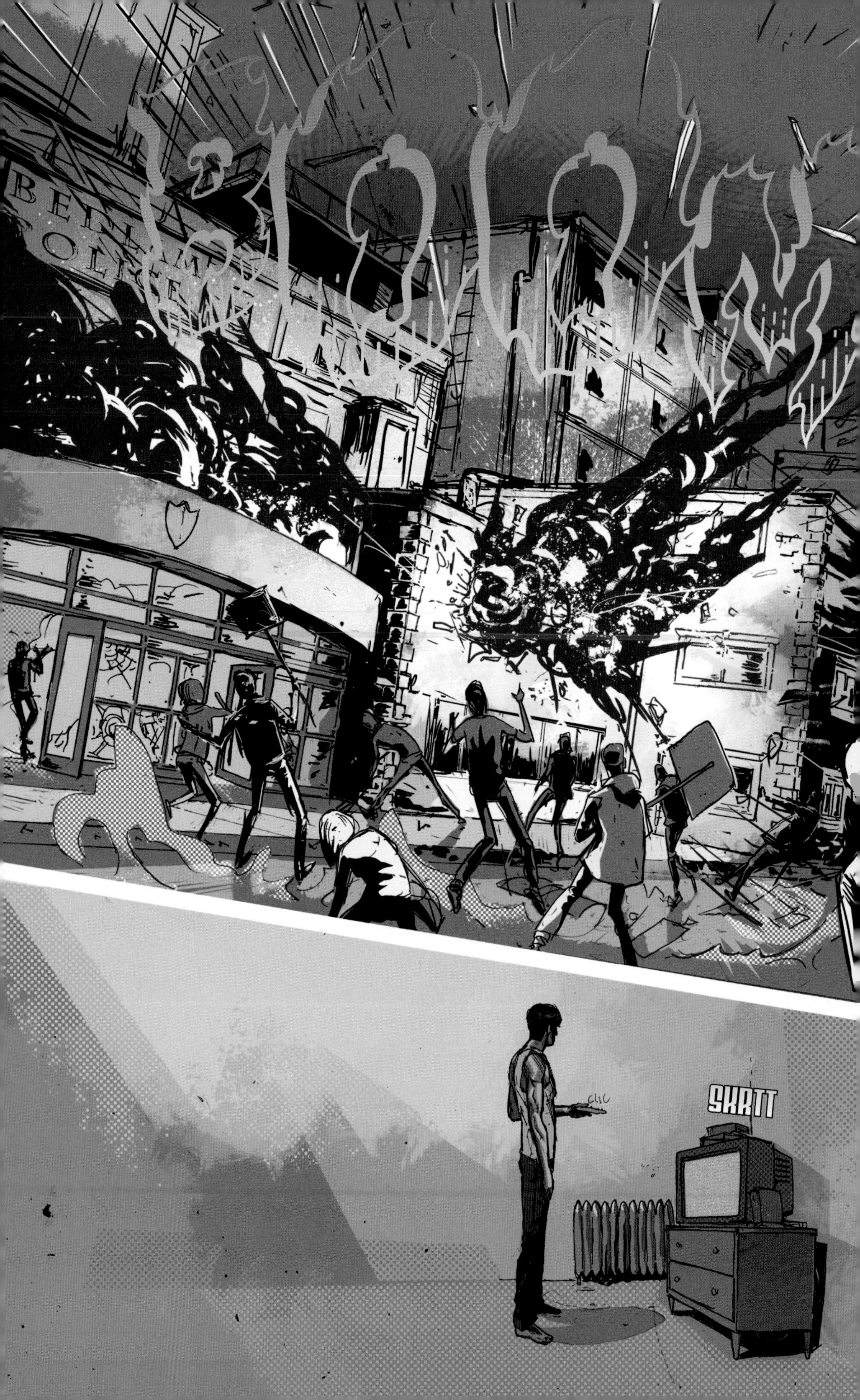
CLIC
SKRTT

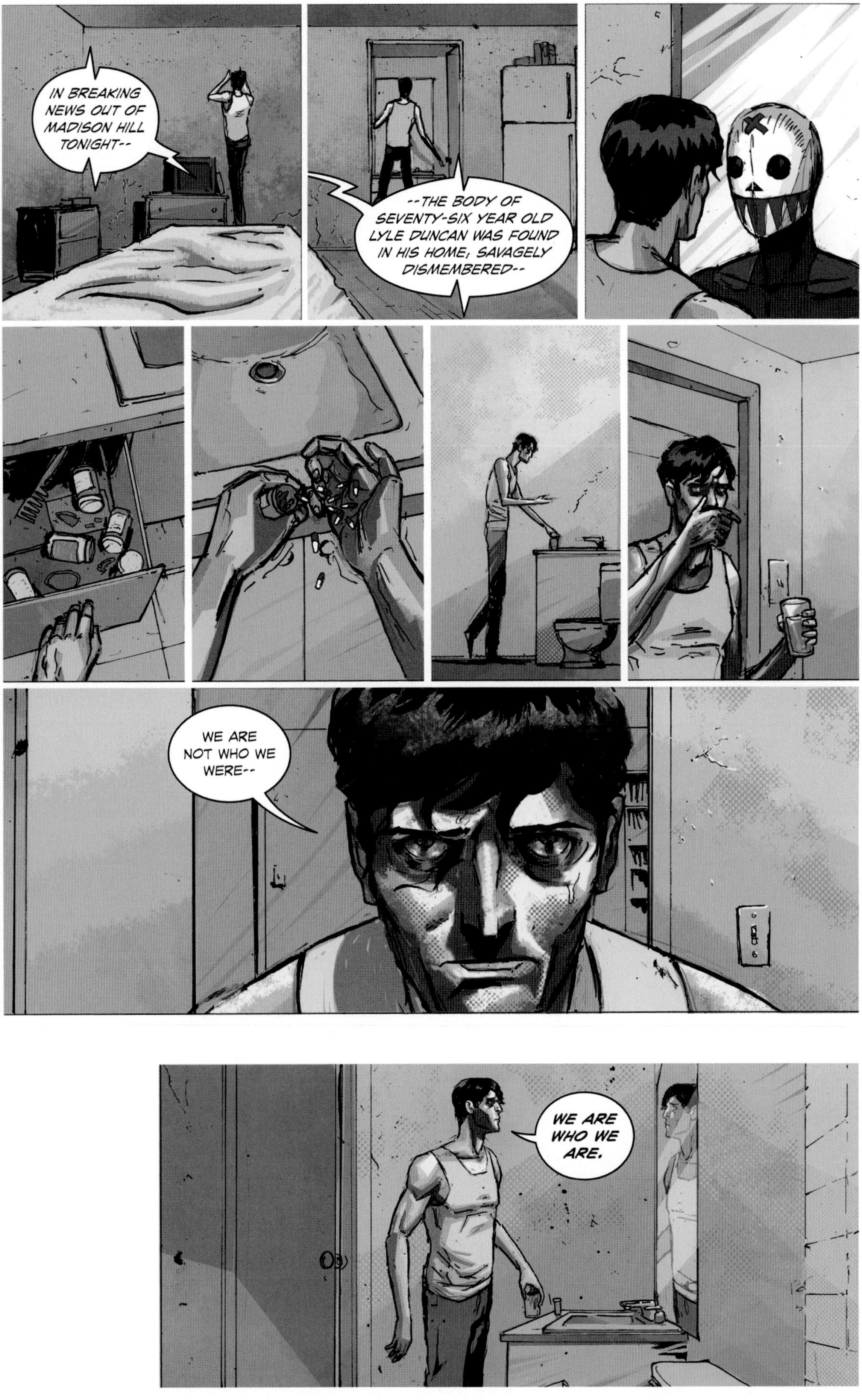
IN BREAKING NEWS OUT OF MADISON HILL TONIGHT--
--THE BODY OF SEVENTY-SIX YEAR OLD LYLE DUNCAN WAS FOUND IN HIS HOME, SAVAGELY DISMEMBERED--
WE ARE NOT WHO WE WERE--
WE ARE WHO WE ARE.

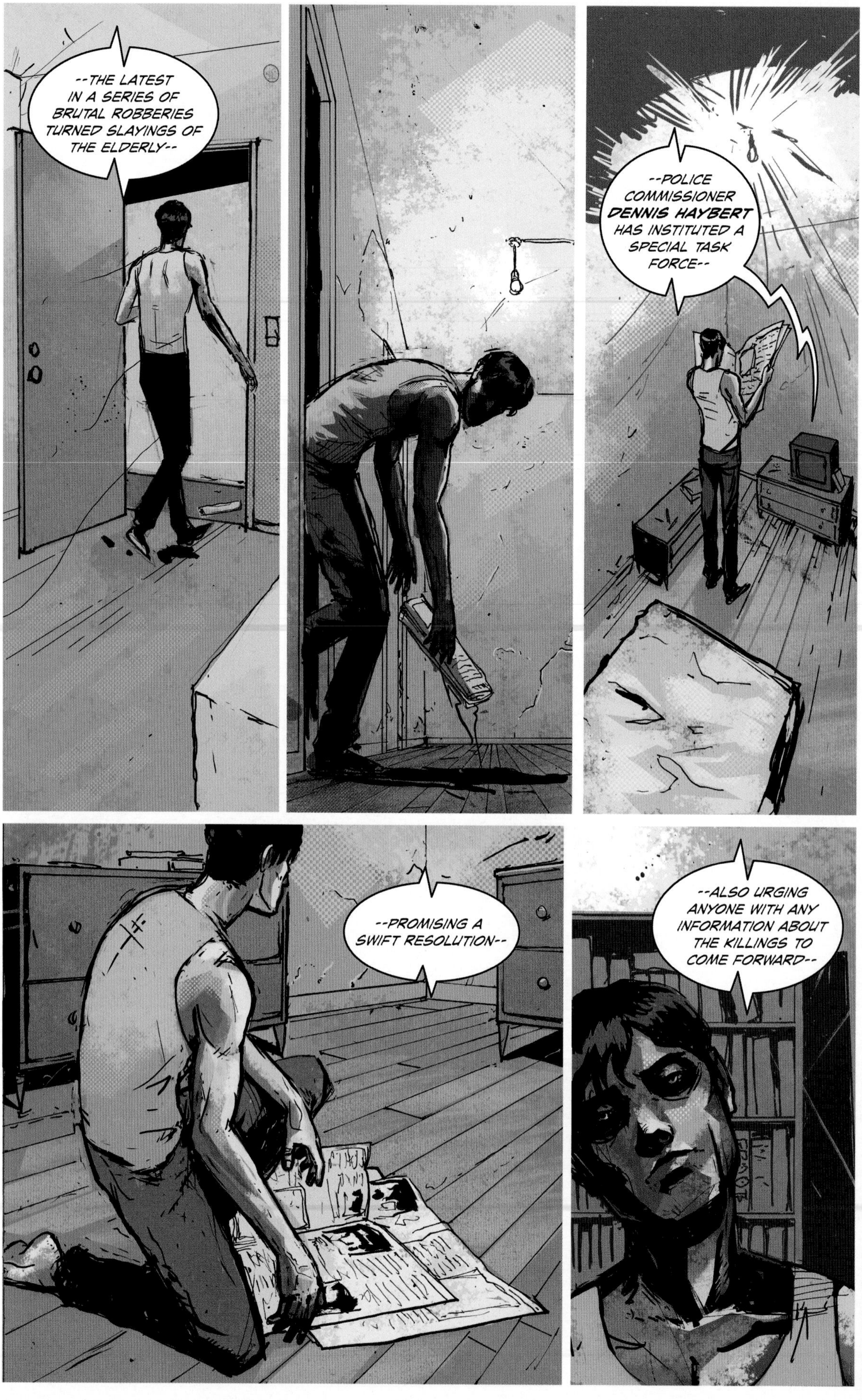
--THE LATEST IN A SERIES OF BRUTAL ROBBERIES TURNED SLAYINGS OF THE ELDERLY--
--POLICE COMMISSIONER DENNIS HAYBERT HAS INSTITUTED A SPECIAL TASK FORCE--
--PROMISING A SWIFT RESOLUTION--
--ALSO URGING ANYONE WITH ANY INFORMATION ABOUT THE KILLINGS TO COME FORWARD--

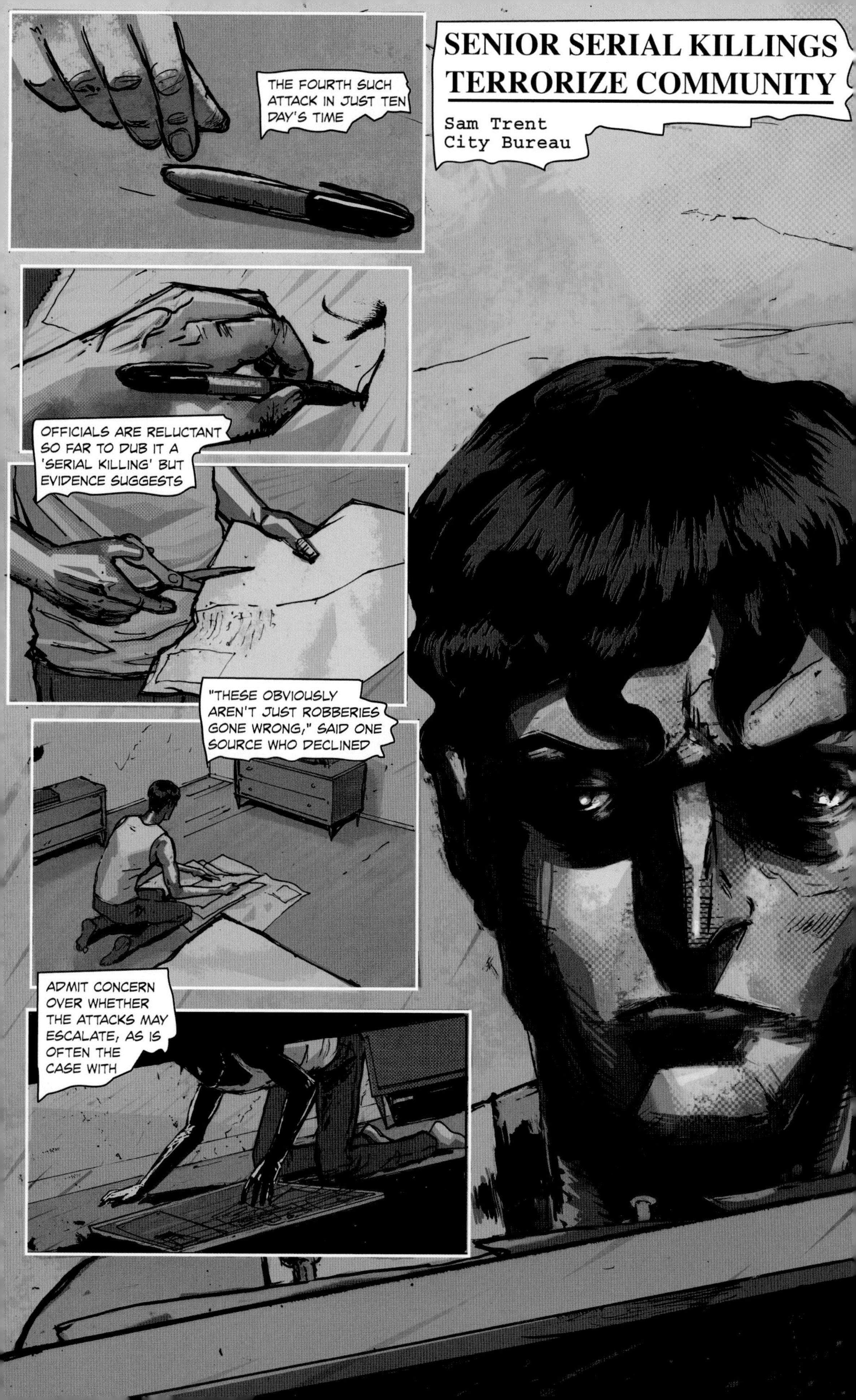
THE FOURTH SUCH ATTACK IN JUST TEN DAY'S TIME
SENIOR SERIAL KILLINGS TERRORIZE COMMUNITY
Sam Trent City Bureau
OFFICIALS ARE RELUCTANT SO FAR TO DUB IT A 'SERIAL KILLING' BUT EVIDENCE SUGGESTS
"THESE OBVIOUSLY AREN'T JUST ROBBERIES GONE WRONG," SAID ONE SOURCE WHO DECLINED
ADMIT CONCERN OVER WHETHER THE ATTACKS MAY ESCALATE, AS IS OFTEN THE CASE WITH

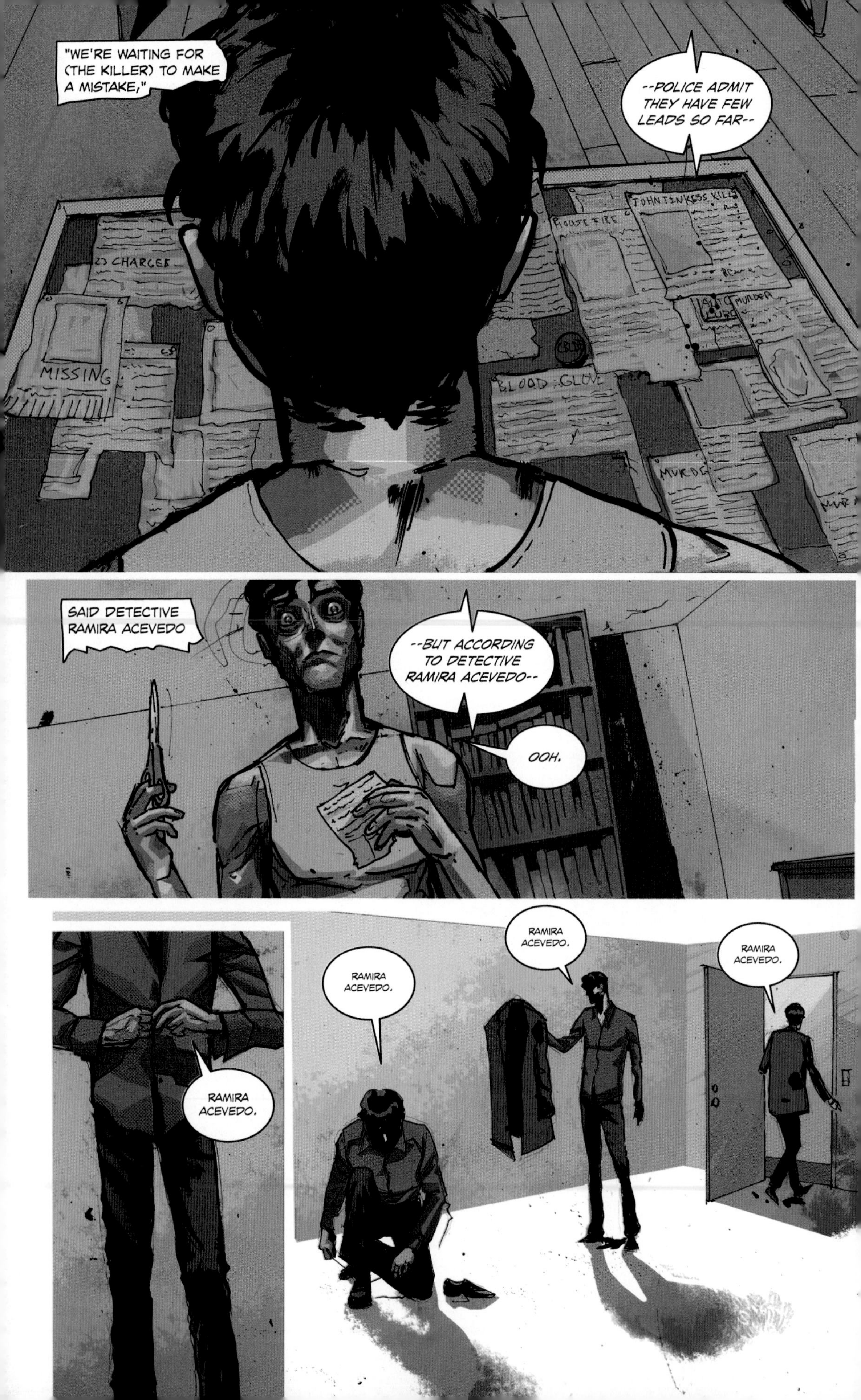
"WE'RE WAITING FOR (THE KILLER) TO MAKE A MISTAKE,"
--POLICE ADMIT THEY HAVE FEW LEADS SO FAR--
SAID DETECTIVE RAMIRA ACEVEDO
--BUT ACCORDING TO DETECTIVE RAMIRA ACEVEDO--
OOH.
RAMIRA ACEVEDO.
RAMIRA ACEVEDO.
RAMIRA ACEVEDO.
RAMIRA ACEVEDO.

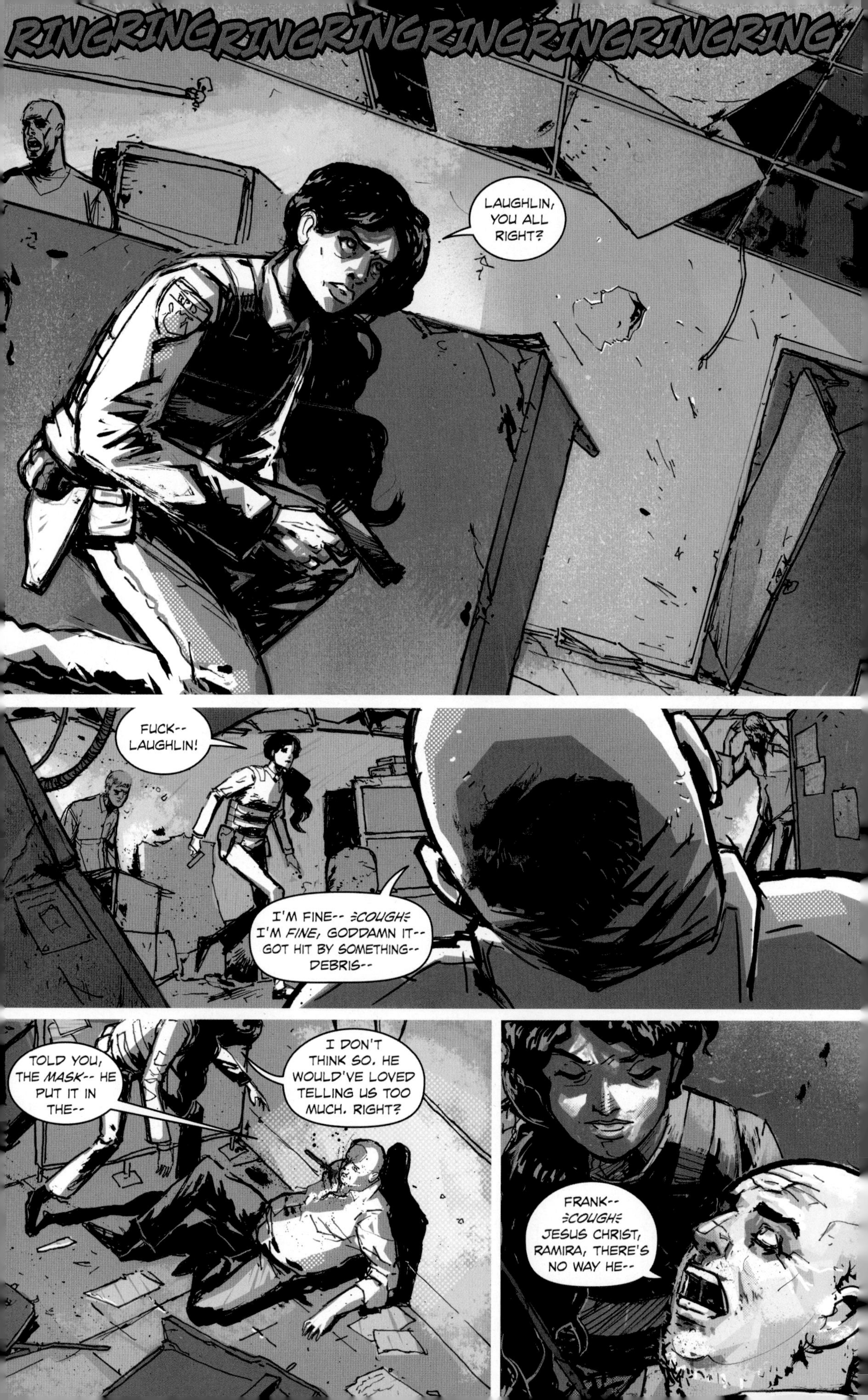
RINGRINGRINGRINGRINGRINGRINGRINGRING
LAUGHLIN, YOU ALL RIGHT?
FUCK-- LAUGHLIN!
I'M FINE-- =COUGH= I'M *FINE*, GODDAMN IT-- GOT HIT BY SOMETHING-- DEBRIS--
TOLD YOU, THE *MASK*-- HE PUT IT IN THE--
I DON'T THINK SO. HE WOULD'VE LOVED TELLING US TOO MUCH. RIGHT?
FRANK-- =COUGH= JESUS CHRIST, RAMIRA, THERE'S NO WAY HE--

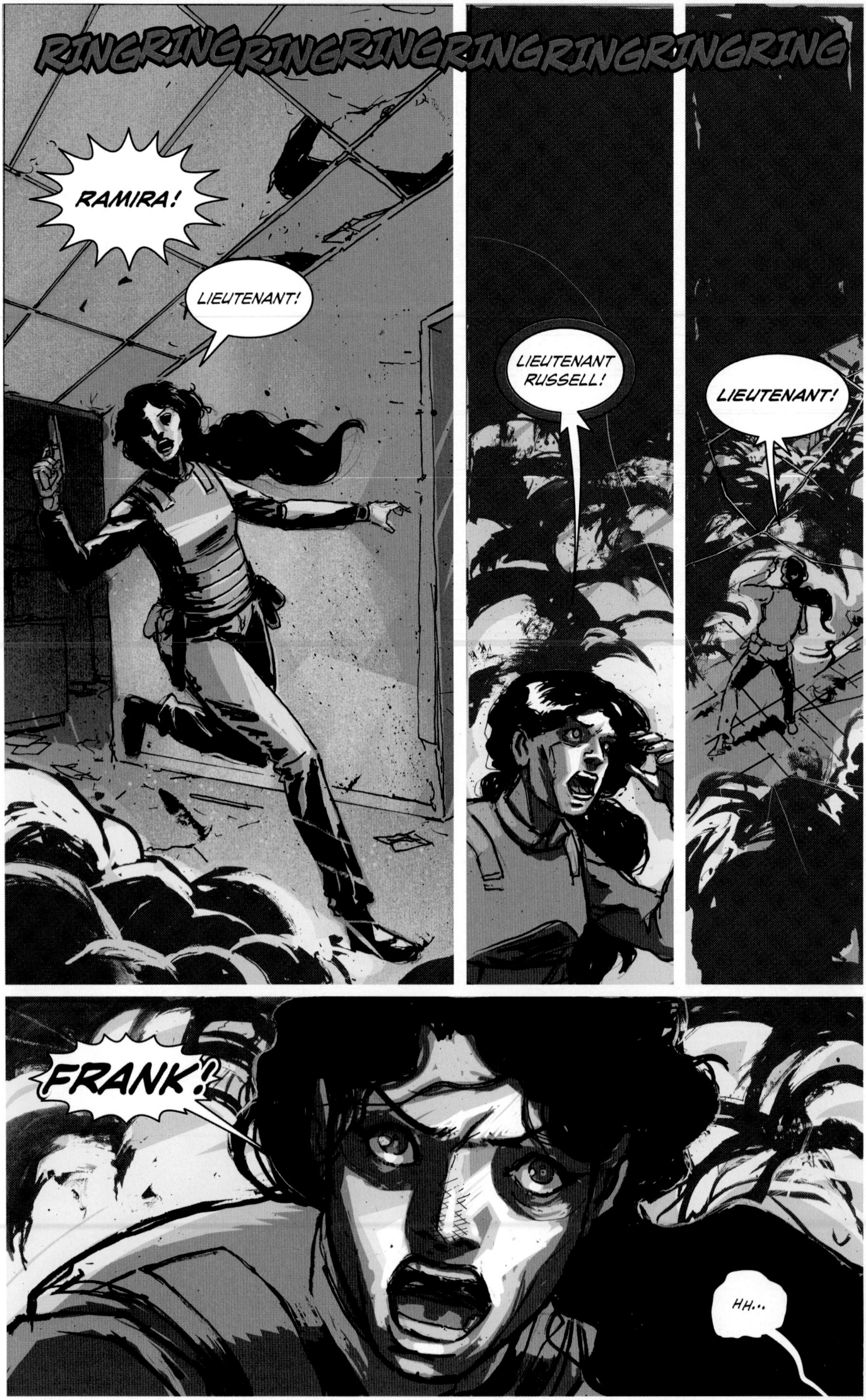
RINGRINGRINGRINGRINGRINGRINGRINGRING
RAMIRA!
LIEUTENANT!
LIEUTENANT RUSSELL!
LIEUTENANT!
FRANK!?
HH...

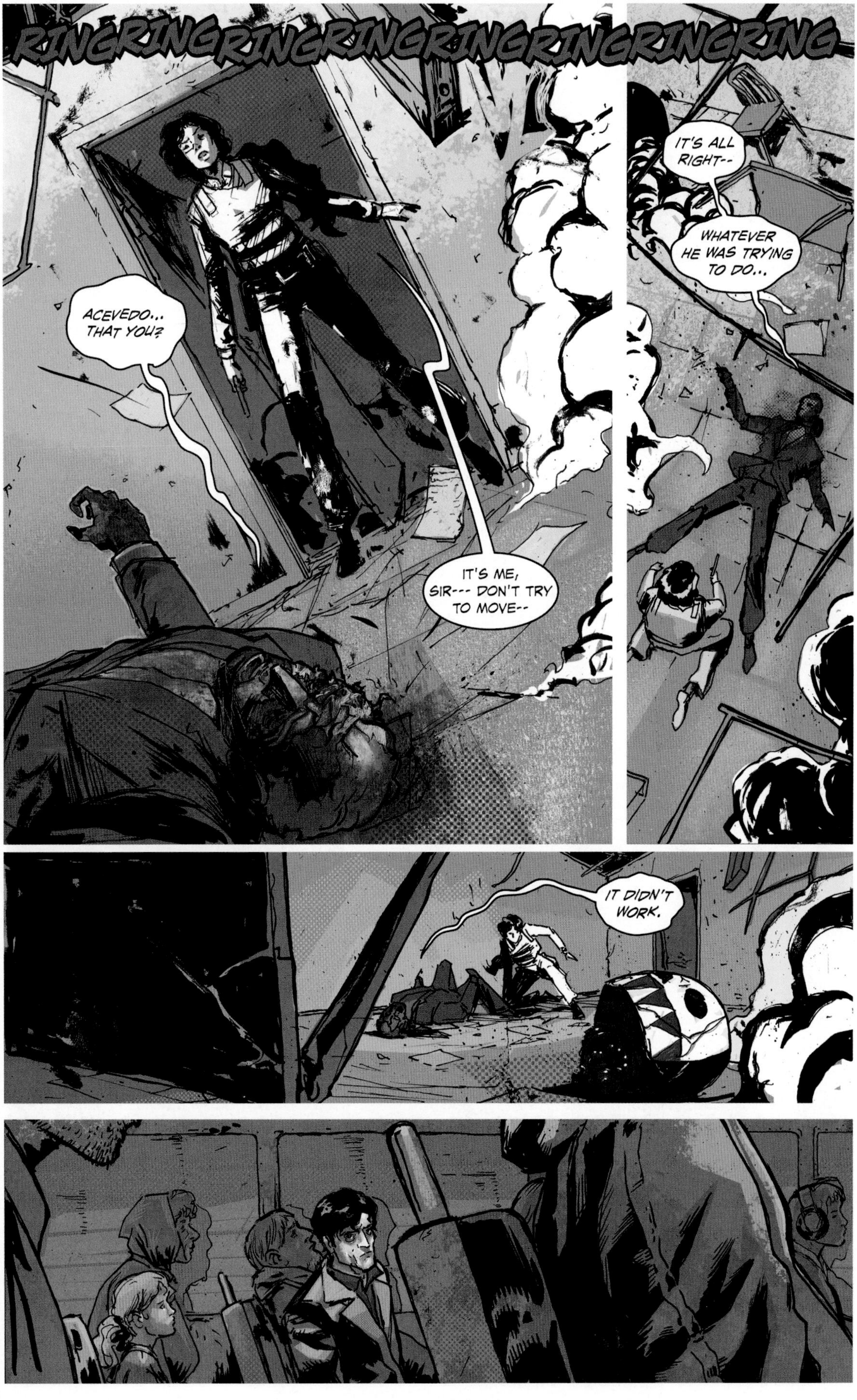
RINGRINGRINGRINGRINGRINGRINGRING
ACEVEDO... THAT YOU?
IT'S ME, SIR--- DON'T TRY TO MOVE--
IT'S ALL RIGHT--
WHATEVER HE WAS TRYING TO DO...
IT DIDN'T WORK.

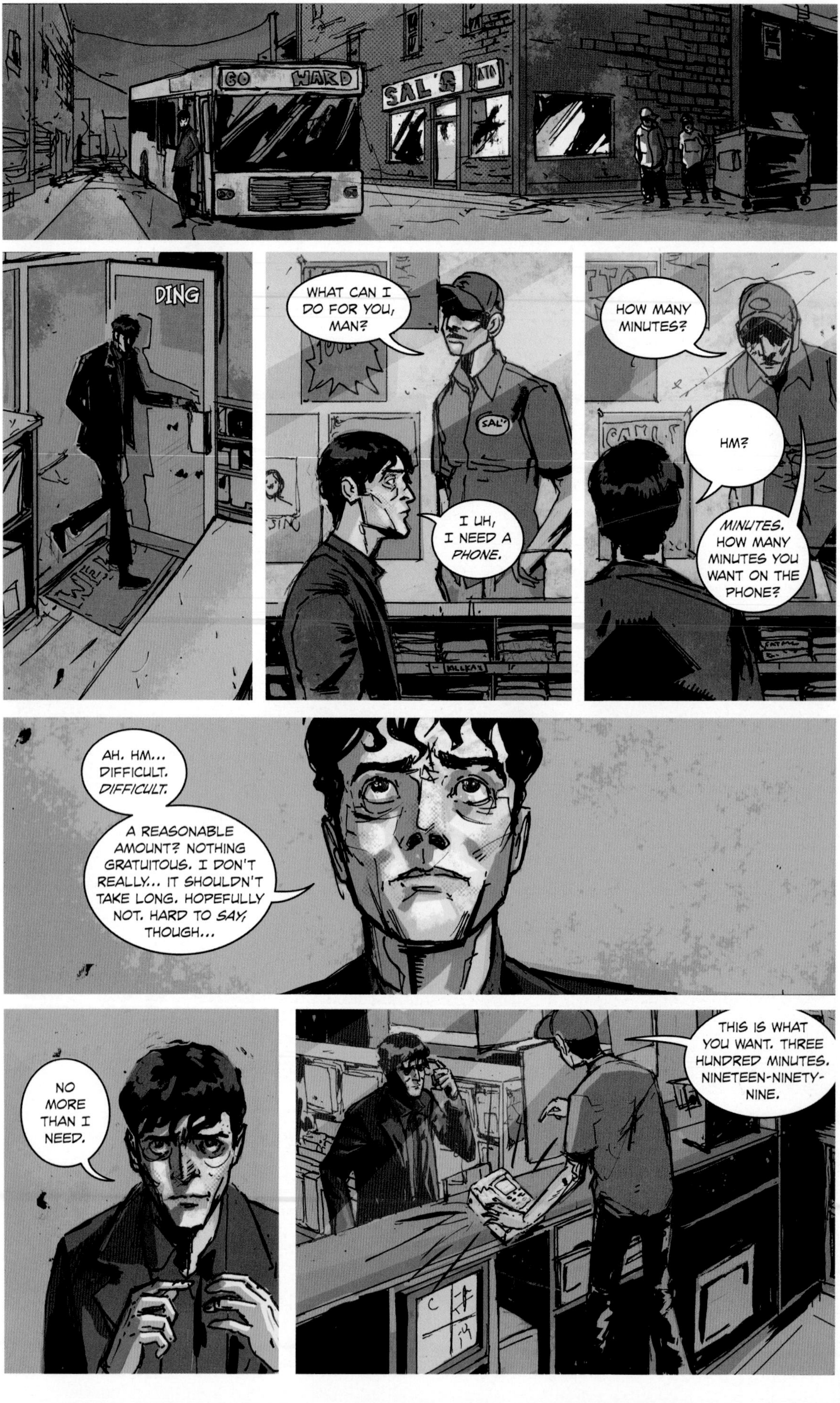
GO WARD
SAL'S
DING
WHAT CAN I DO FOR YOU, MAN?
I UH, I NEED A *PHONE*.
HOW MANY MINUTES?
HM?
MINUTES. HOW MANY MINUTES YOU WANT ON THE PHONE?
AH. HM... DIFFICULT. *DIFFICULT*.
A REASONABLE AMOUNT? NOTHING GRATUITOUS. I DON'T REALLY... IT SHOULDN'T TAKE LONG. HOPEFULLY NOT. HARD TO *SAY*, THOUGH...
NO MORE THAN I NEED.
THIS IS WHAT YOU WANT. THREE HUNDRED MINUTES. NINETEEN-NINETY-NINE.

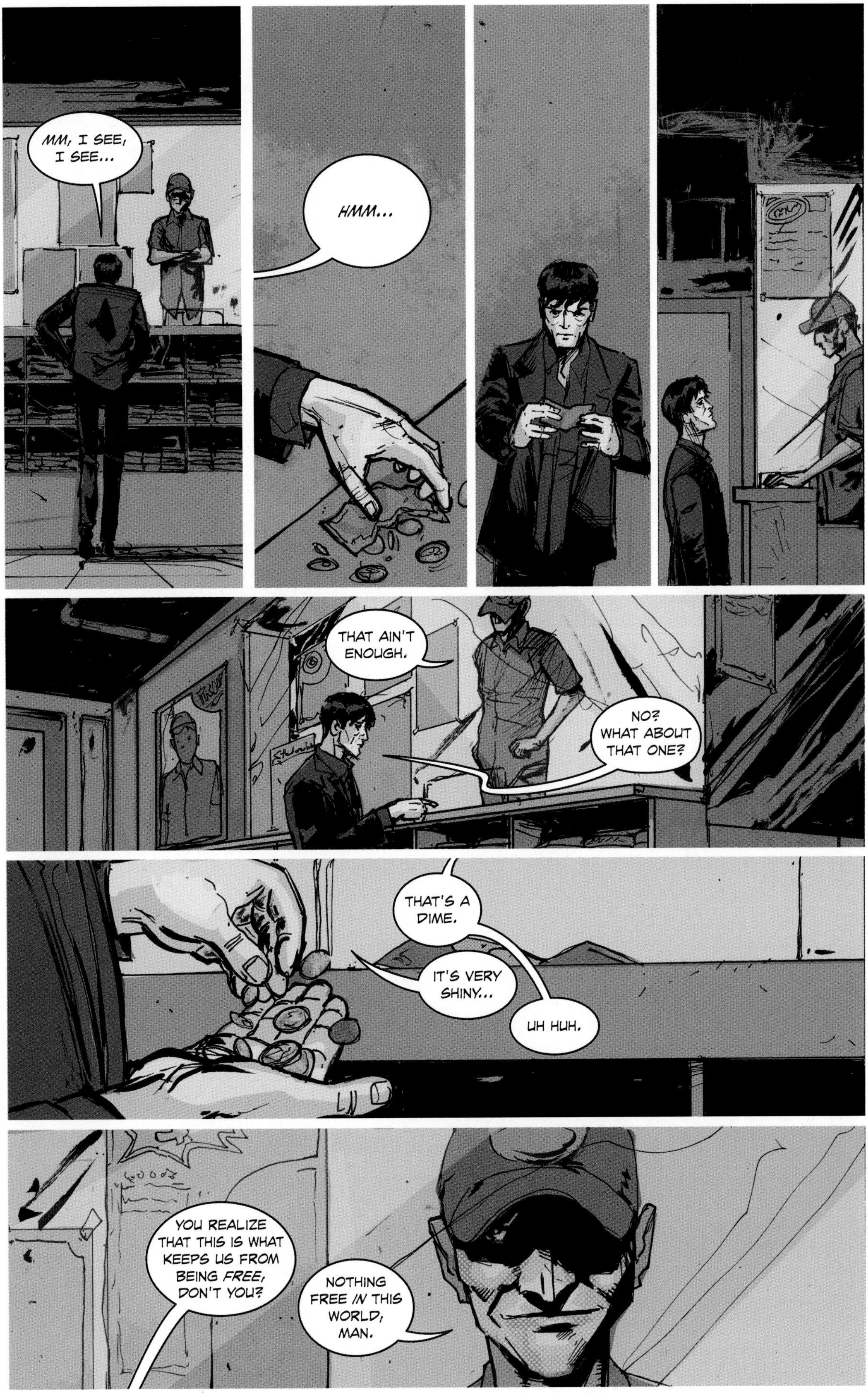
MM, I SEE, I SEE...
HMM...
THAT AIN'T ENOUGH.
NO? WHAT ABOUT THAT ONE?
THAT'S A DIME.
IT'S VERY SHINY...
UH HUH.
YOU REALIZE THAT THIS IS WHAT KEEPS US FROM BEING *FREE*, DON'T YOU?
NOTHING FREE *IN* THIS WORLD, MAN.

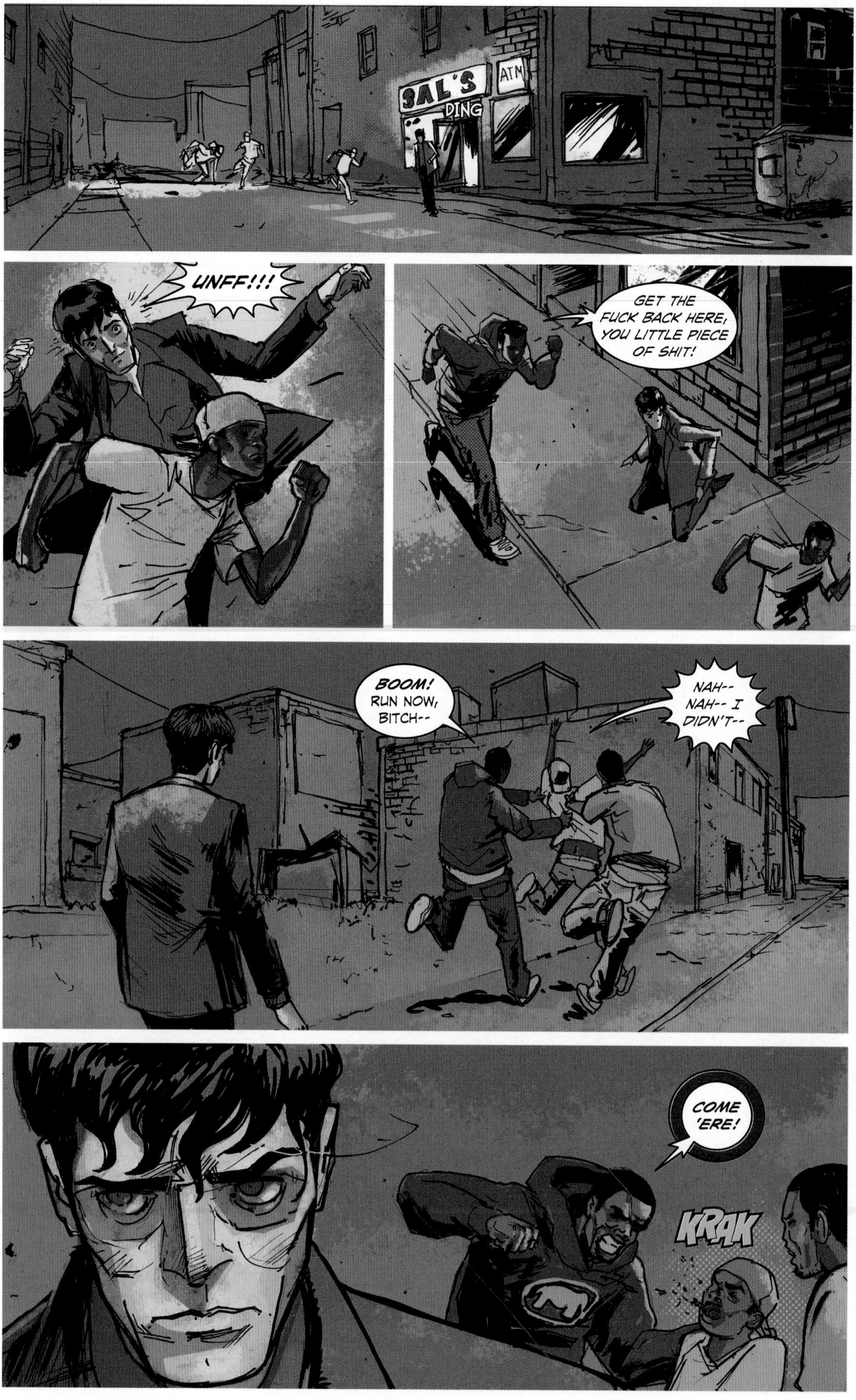
SAL'S
ATM
DING
UNFF!!!
GET THE FUCK BACK HERE, YOU LITTLE PIECE OF SHIT!
BOOM! RUN NOW, BITCH--
NAH-- NAH-- I DIDN'T--
COME 'ERE!
KRAK

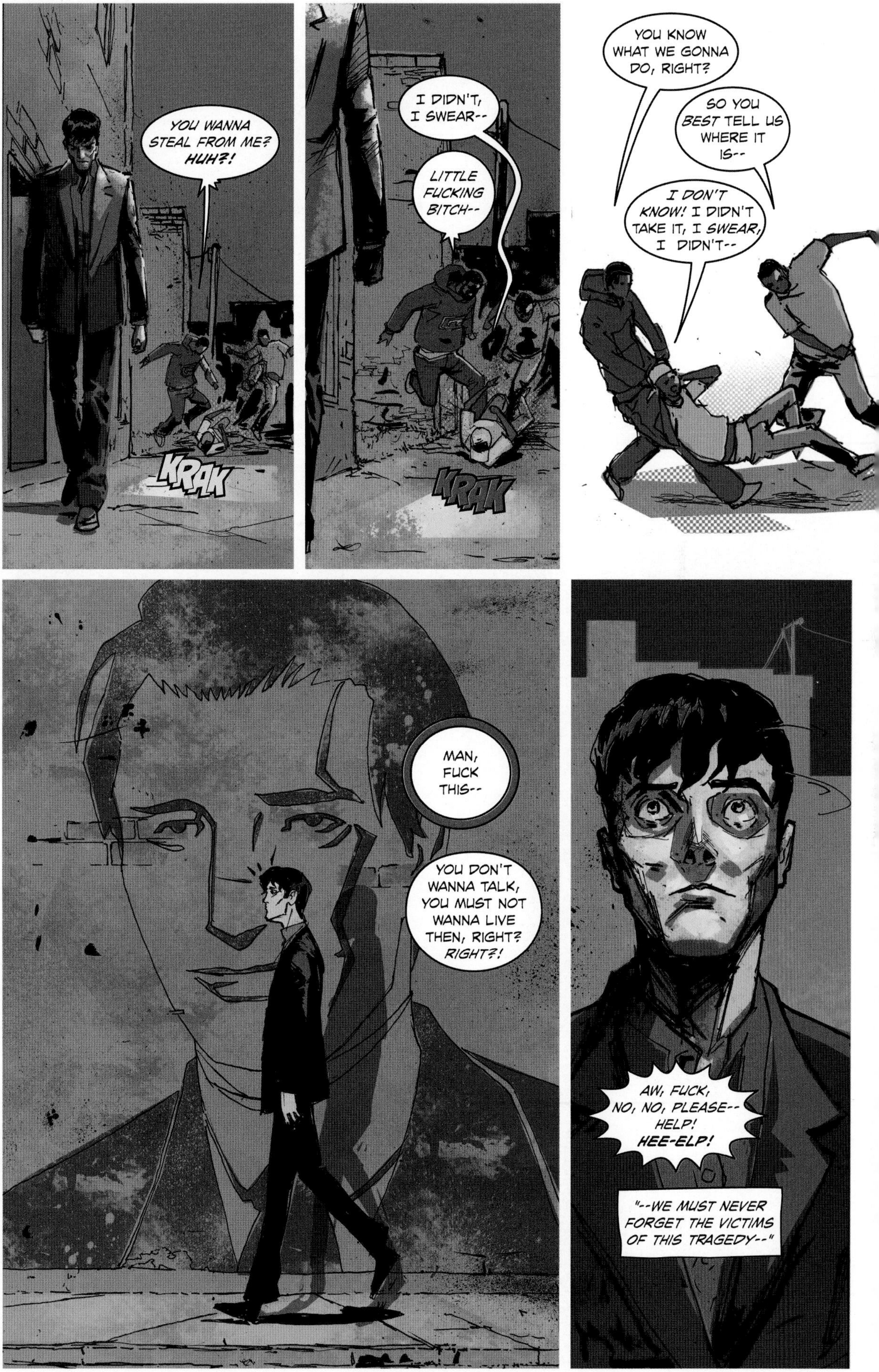
YOU WANNA STEAL FROM ME? HUH?!
KRAK
I DIDN'T, I SWEAR--
LITTLE FUCKING BITCH--
KRAK
YOU KNOW WHAT WE GONNA DO, RIGHT?
SO YOU BEST TELL US WHERE IT IS--
I DON'T KNOW! I DIDN'T TAKE IT, I SWEAR, I DIDN'T--
MAN, FUCK THIS--
YOU DON'T WANNA TALK, YOU MUST NOT WANNA LIVE THEN, RIGHT? RIGHT?!
AW, FUCK, NO, NO, PLEASE-- HELP! HEE-ELP!
"--WE MUST NEVER FORGET THE VICTIMS OF THIS TRAGEDY--"

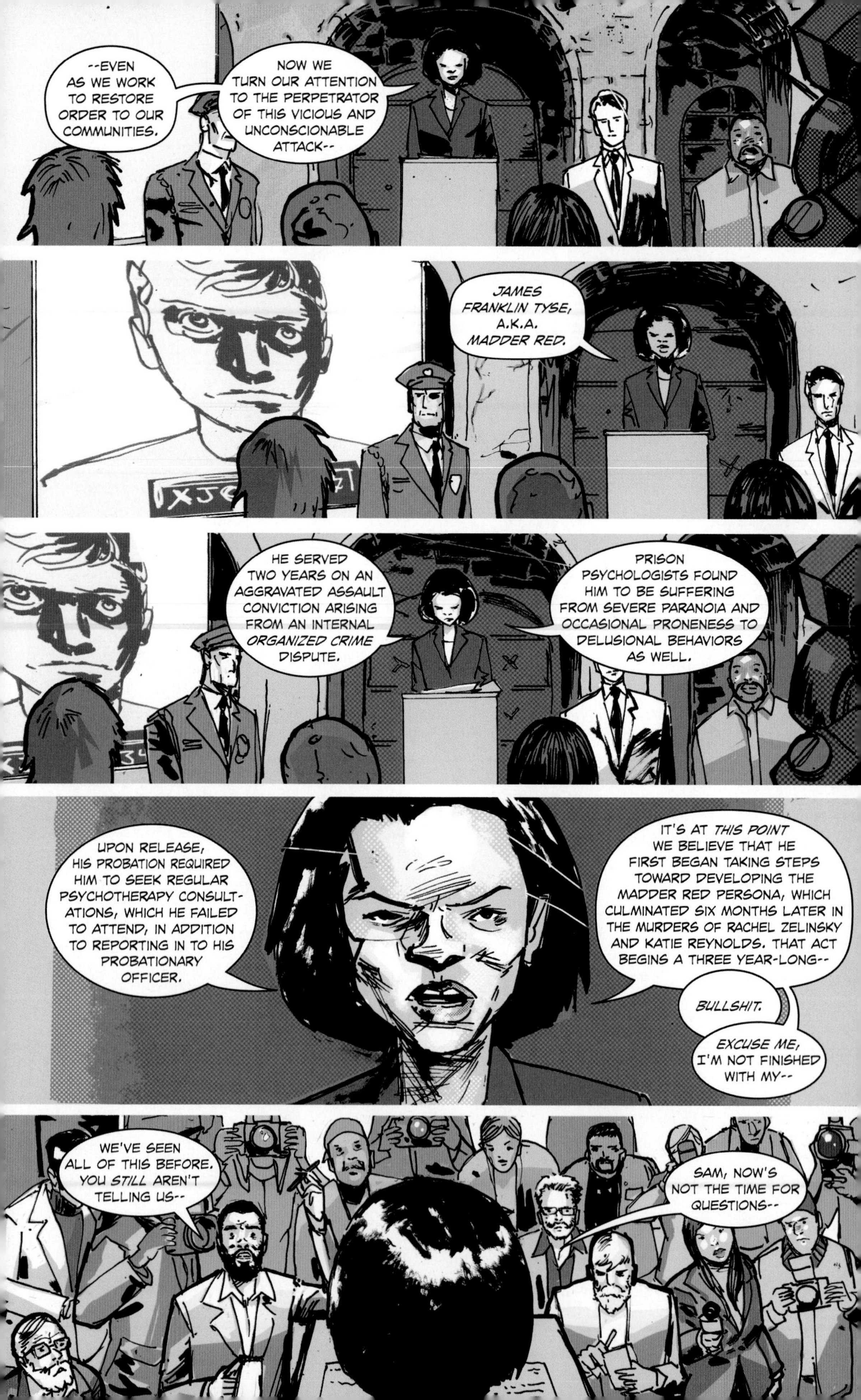
--EVEN AS WE WORK TO RESTORE ORDER TO OUR COMMUNITIES.
NOW WE TURN OUR ATTENTION TO THE PERPETRATOR OF THIS VICIOUS AND UNCONSCIONABLE ATTACK--
JAMES FRANKLIN TYSE, A.K.A. MADDER RED.
HE SERVED TWO YEARS ON AN AGGRAVATED ASSAULT CONVICTION ARISING FROM AN INTERNAL ORGANIZED CRIME DISPUTE.
PRISON PSYCHOLOGISTS FOUND HIM TO BE SUFFERING FROM SEVERE PARANOIA AND OCCASIONAL PRONENESS TO DELUSIONAL BEHAVIORS AS WELL.
UPON RELEASE, HIS PROBATION REQUIRED HIM TO SEEK REGULAR PSYCHOTHERAPY CONSULT-ATIONS, WHICH HE FAILED TO ATTEND, IN ADDITION TO REPORTING IN TO HIS PROBATIONARY OFFICER.
IT'S AT THIS POINT WE BELIEVE THAT HE FIRST BEGAN TAKING STEPS TOWARD DEVELOPING THE MADDER RED PERSONA, WHICH CULMINATED SIX MONTHS LATER IN THE MURDERS OF RACHEL ZELINSKY AND KATIE REYNOLDS. THAT ACT BEGINS A THREE YEAR-LONG--
BULLSHIT.
EXCUSE ME, I'M NOT FINISHED WITH MY--
WE'VE SEEN ALL OF THIS BEFORE. YOU STILL AREN'T TELLING US--
SAM, NOW'S NOT THE TIME FOR QUESTIONS--

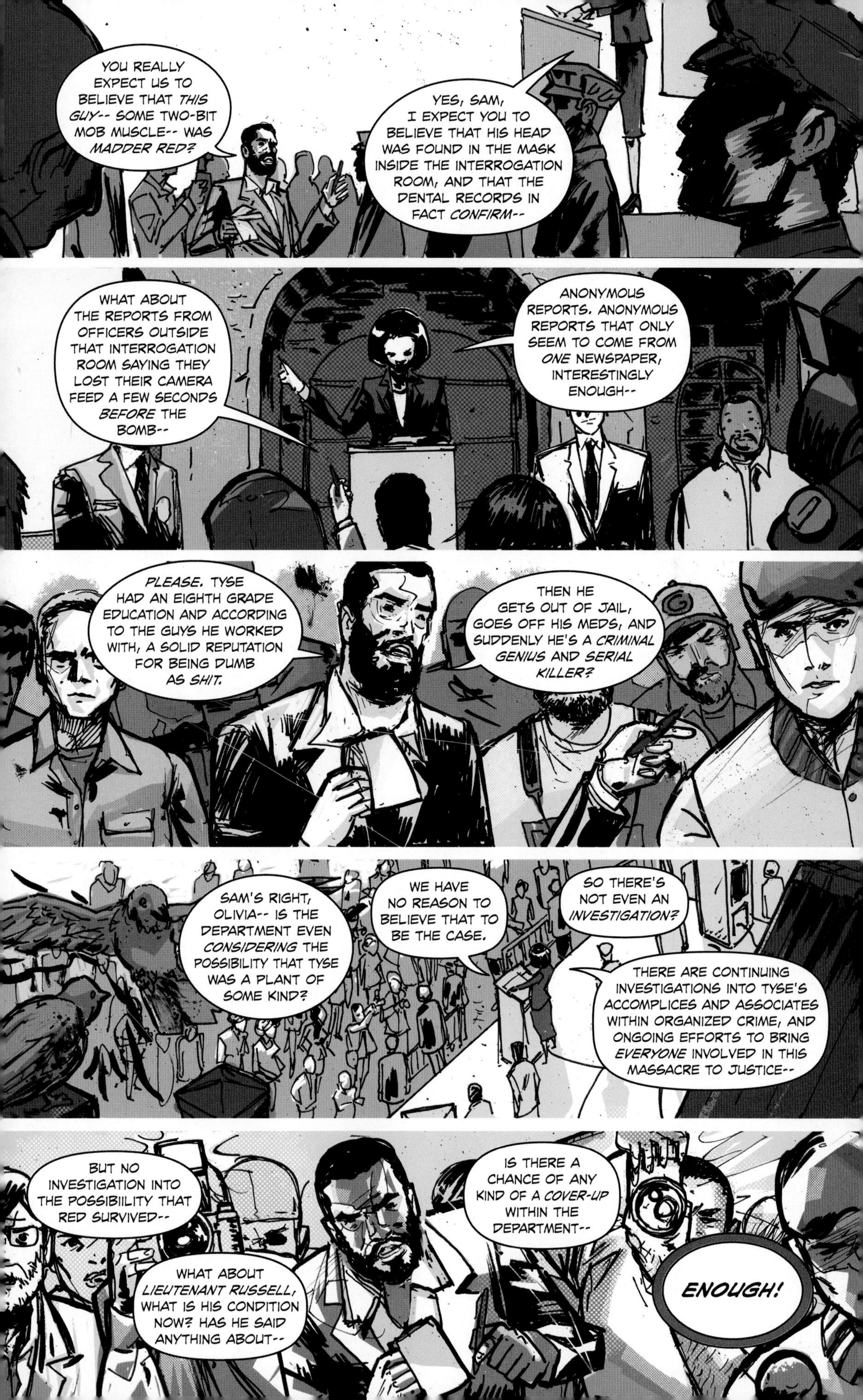
YOU REALLY EXPECT US TO BELIEVE THAT *THIS GUY*-- SOME TWO-BIT MOB MUSCLE-- WAS *MADDER RED?*
YES, SAM, I EXPECT YOU TO BELIEVE THAT HIS HEAD WAS FOUND IN THE MASK INSIDE THE INTERROGATION ROOM, AND THAT THE DENTAL RECORDS IN FACT *CONFIRM*--
WHAT ABOUT THE REPORTS FROM OFFICERS OUTSIDE THAT INTERROGATION ROOM SAYING THEY LOST THEIR CAMERA FEED A FEW SECONDS *BEFORE* THE BOMB--
ANONYMOUS REPORTS. ANONYMOUS REPORTS THAT ONLY SEEM TO COME FROM *ONE* NEWSPAPER, INTERESTINGLY ENOUGH--
PLEASE. TYSE HAD AN EIGHTH GRADE EDUCATION AND ACCORDING TO THE GUYS HE WORKED WITH, A SOLID REPUTATION FOR BEING DUMB AS *SHIT.*
THEN HE GETS OUT OF JAIL, GOES OFF HIS MEDS, AND SUDDENLY HE'S A *CRIMINAL GENIUS* AND *SERIAL KILLER?*
SAM'S RIGHT, OLIVIA-- IS THE DEPARTMENT EVEN *CONSIDERING* THE POSSIBILITY THAT TYSE WAS A PLANT OF SOME KIND?
WE HAVE NO REASON TO BELIEVE THAT TO BE THE CASE.
SO THERE'S NOT EVEN AN *INVESTIGATION?*
THERE ARE CONTINUING INVESTIGATIONS INTO TYSE'S ACCOMPLICES AND ASSOCIATES WITHIN ORGANIZED CRIME, AND ONGOING EFFORTS TO BRING *EVERYONE* INVOLVED IN THIS MASSACRE TO JUSTICE--
BUT NO INVESTIGATION INTO THE POSSIBIILITY THAT RED SURVIVED--
WHAT ABOUT *LIEUTENANT RUSSELL,* WHAT IS HIS CONDITION NOW? HAS HE SAID ANYTHING ABOUT--
IS THERE A CHANCE OF ANY KIND OF A *COVER-UP* WITHIN THE DEPARTMENT--
ENOUGH!

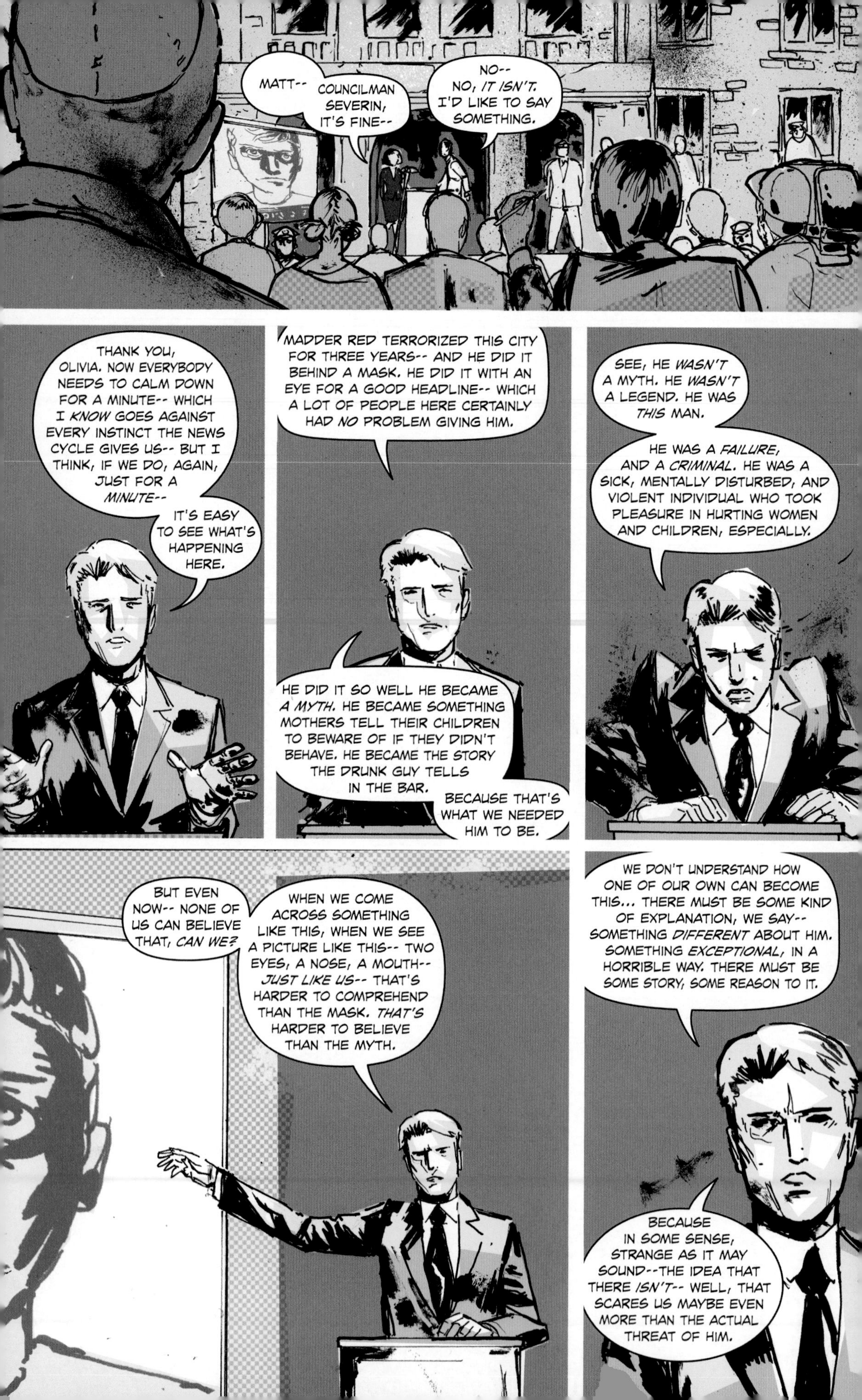
MATT--
COUNCILMAN SEVERIN, IT'S FINE--
NO-- NO, *IT ISN'T.* I'D LIKE TO SAY SOMETHING.
THANK YOU, OLIVIA. NOW EVERYBODY NEEDS TO CALM DOWN FOR A MINUTE-- WHICH I *KNOW* GOES AGAINST EVERY INSTINCT THE NEWS CYCLE GIVES US-- BUT I THINK, IF WE DO, AGAIN, JUST FOR A *MINUTE*--
IT'S EASY TO SEE WHAT'S HAPPENING HERE.
MADDER RED TERRORIZED THIS CITY FOR THREE YEARS-- AND HE DID IT BEHIND A MASK. HE DID IT WITH AN EYE FOR A GOOD HEADLINE-- WHICH A LOT OF PEOPLE HERE CERTAINLY HAD *NO* PROBLEM GIVING HIM.
HE DID IT SO WELL HE BECAME *A MYTH.* HE BECAME SOMETHING MOTHERS TELL THEIR CHILDREN TO BEWARE OF IF THEY DIDN'T BEHAVE. HE BECAME THE STORY THE DRUNK GUY TELLS IN THE BAR.
BECAUSE THAT'S WHAT WE NEEDED HIM TO BE.
SEE, HE *WASN'T* A MYTH. HE *WASN'T* A LEGEND. HE WAS *THIS* MAN.
HE WAS A *FAILURE,* AND A *CRIMINAL*. HE WAS A SICK, MENTALLY DISTURBED, AND VIOLENT INDIVIDUAL WHO TOOK PLEASURE IN HURTING WOMEN AND CHILDREN, ESPECIALLY.
BUT EVEN NOW-- NONE OF US CAN BELIEVE THAT, *CAN WE?*
WHEN WE COME ACROSS SOMETHING LIKE THIS, WHEN WE SEE A PICTURE LIKE THIS-- TWO EYES, A NOSE, A MOUTH-- *JUST LIKE US*-- THAT'S HARDER TO COMPREHEND THAN THE MASK. *THAT'S* HARDER TO BELIEVE THAN THE MYTH.
WE DON'T UNDERSTAND HOW ONE OF OUR OWN CAN BECOME THIS... THERE MUST BE SOME KIND OF EXPLANATION, WE SAY-- SOMETHING *DIFFERENT* ABOUT HIM. SOMETHING *EXCEPTIONAL,* IN A HORRIBLE WAY. THERE MUST BE SOME STORY, SOME REASON TO IT.
BECAUSE IN SOME SENSE, STRANGE AS IT MAY SOUND--THE IDEA THAT THERE *ISN'T*-- WELL, THAT SCARES US MAYBE EVEN MORE THAN THE ACTUAL THREAT OF HIM.

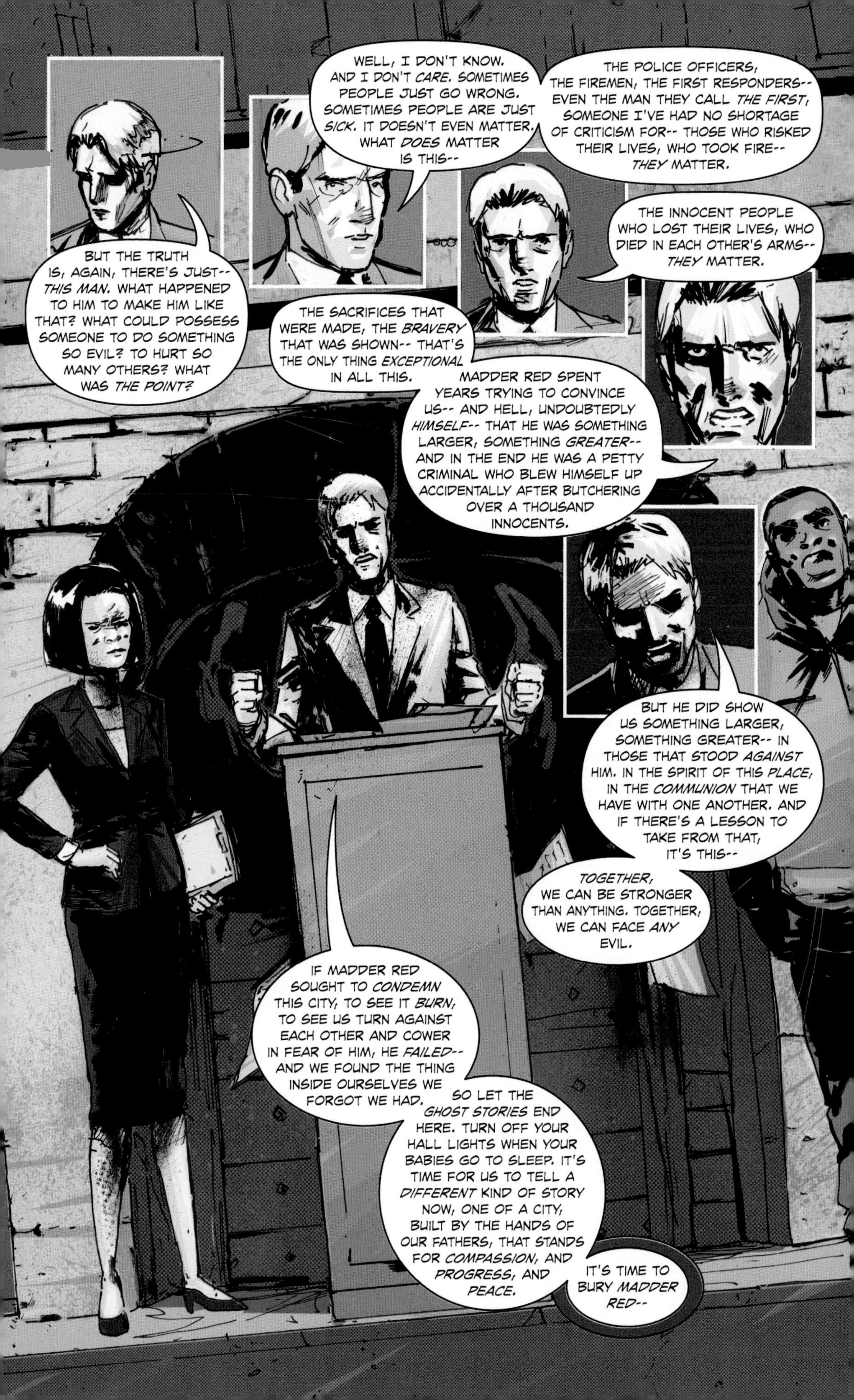
BUT THE TRUTH IS, AGAIN, THERE'S JUST-- *THIS MAN.* WHAT HAPPENED TO HIM TO MAKE HIM LIKE THAT? WHAT COULD POSSESS SOMEONE TO DO SOMETHING SO EVIL? TO HURT SO MANY OTHERS? WHAT WAS *THE POINT?*
WELL, I DON'T KNOW. AND I DON'T *CARE.* SOMETIMES PEOPLE JUST GO WRONG. SOMETIMES PEOPLE ARE JUST *SICK.* IT DOESN'T EVEN MATTER. WHAT *DOES* MATTER IS THIS--
THE SACRIFICES THAT WERE MADE, THE *BRAVERY* THAT WAS SHOWN-- THAT'S THE ONLY THING *EXCEPTIONAL* IN ALL THIS.
THE POLICE OFFICERS, THE FIREMEN, THE FIRST RESPONDERS-- EVEN THE MAN THEY CALL *THE FIRST,* SOMEONE I'VE HAD NO SHORTAGE OF CRITICISM FOR-- THOSE WHO RISKED THEIR LIVES, WHO TOOK FIRE-- *THEY* MATTER.
THE INNOCENT PEOPLE WHO LOST THEIR LIVES, WHO DIED IN EACH OTHER'S ARMS-- *THEY* MATTER.
MADDER RED SPENT YEARS TRYING TO CONVINCE US-- AND HELL, UNDOUBTEDLY *HIMSELF*-- THAT HE WAS SOMETHING LARGER, SOMETHING *GREATER*-- AND IN THE END HE WAS A PETTY CRIMINAL WHO BLEW HIMSELF UP ACCIDENTALLY AFTER BUTCHERING OVER A THOUSAND INNOCENTS.
BUT HE DID SHOW US SOMETHING LARGER, SOMETHING GREATER-- IN THOSE THAT STOOD *AGAINST* HIM. IN THE SPIRIT OF THIS *PLACE,* IN THE *COMMUNION* THAT WE HAVE WITH ONE ANOTHER. AND IF THERE'S A LESSON TO TAKE FROM THAT, IT'S THIS--
TOGETHER, WE CAN BE STRONGER THAN ANYTHING. TOGETHER, WE CAN FACE *ANY* EVIL.
IF MADDER RED SOUGHT TO *CONDEMN* THIS CITY, TO SEE IT *BURN,* TO SEE US TURN AGAINST EACH OTHER AND COWER IN FEAR OF HIM, HE *FAILED*-- AND WE FOUND THE THING INSIDE OURSELVES WE FORGOT WE HAD.
SO LET THE *GHOST STORIES* END HERE. TURN OFF YOUR HALL LIGHTS WHEN YOUR BABIES GO TO SLEEP. IT'S TIME FOR US TO TELL A *DIFFERENT* KIND OF STORY NOW, ONE OF A CITY, BUILT BY THE HANDS OF OUR FATHERS, THAT STANDS FOR *COMPASSION,* AND *PROGRESS,* AND *PEACE.*
IT'S TIME TO BURY *MADDER RED*--

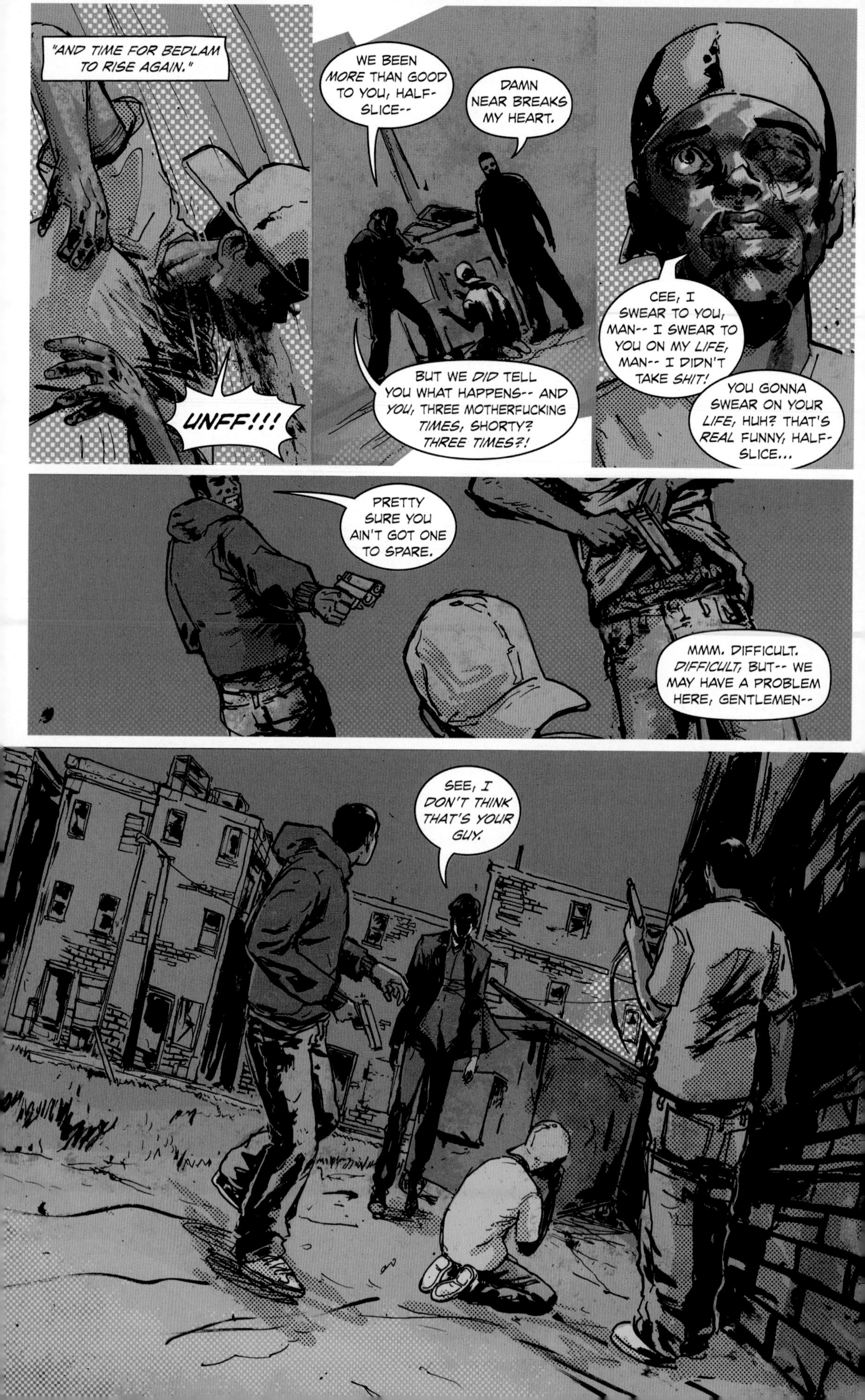
"AND TIME FOR BEDLAM TO RISE AGAIN."
UNFF!!!
WE BEEN MORE THAN GOOD TO YOU, HALF-SLICE--
DAMN NEAR BREAKS MY HEART.
BUT WE DID TELL YOU WHAT HAPPENS-- AND YOU, THREE MOTHERFUCKING TIMES, SHORTY? THREE TIMES?!
CEE, I SWEAR TO YOU, MAN-- I SWEAR TO YOU ON MY LIFE, MAN-- I DIDN'T TAKE SHIT!
YOU GONNA SWEAR ON YOUR LIFE, HUH? THAT'S REAL FUNNY, HALF-SLICE...
PRETTY SURE YOU AIN'T GOT ONE TO SPARE.
MMM. DIFFICULT. DIFFICULT, BUT-- WE MAY HAVE A PROBLEM HERE, GENTLEMEN--
SEE, I DON'T THINK THAT'S YOUR GUY.

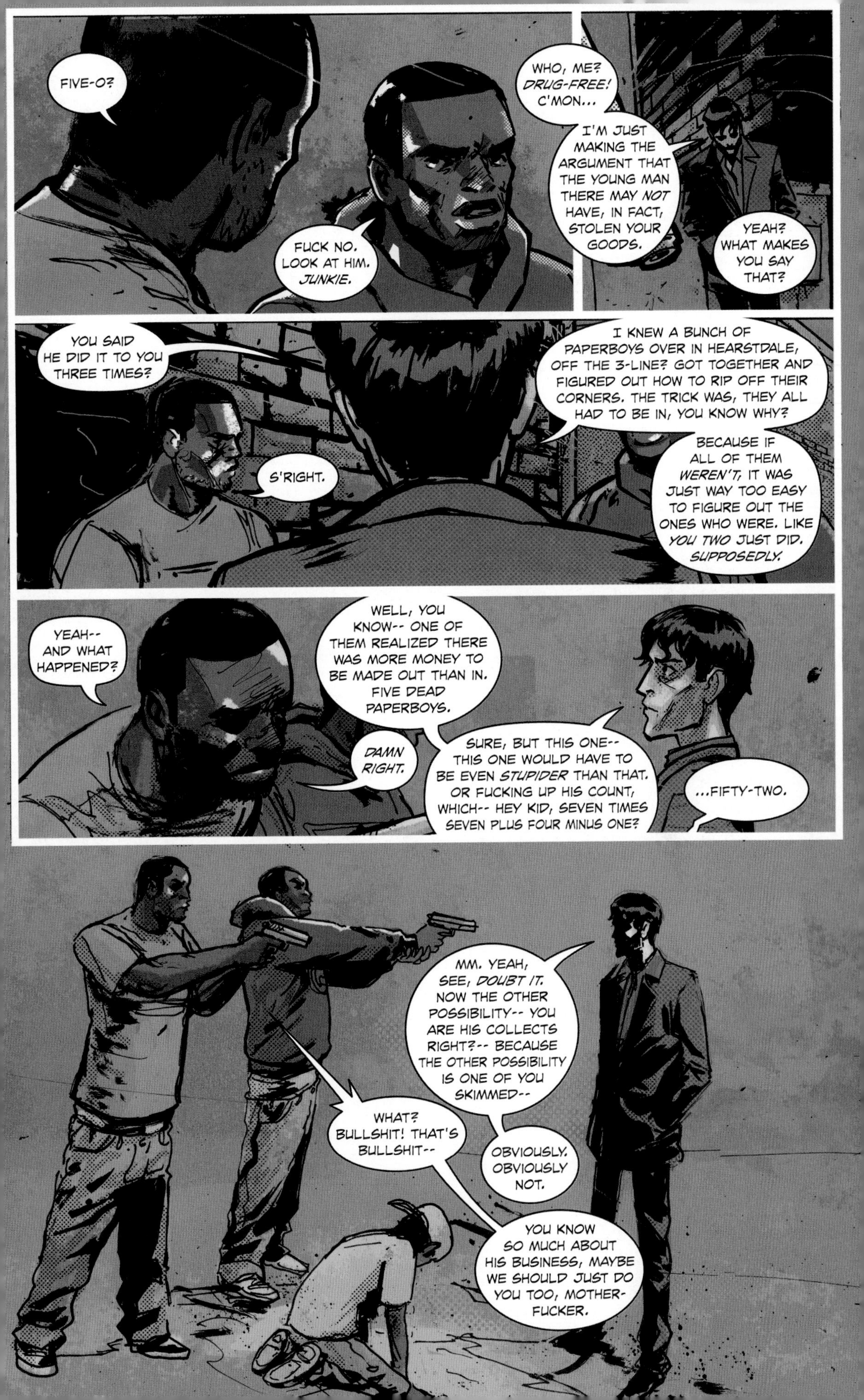
FIVE-O?
FUCK NO. LOOK AT HIM. *JUNKIE.*
WHO, ME? *DRUG-FREE!* C'MON...
I'M JUST MAKING THE ARGUMENT THAT THE YOUNG MAN THERE MAY *NOT* HAVE, IN FACT, STOLEN YOUR GOODS.
YEAH? WHAT MAKES YOU SAY THAT?
YOU SAID HE DID IT TO YOU THREE TIMES?
S'RIGHT.
I KNEW A BUNCH OF PAPERBOYS OVER IN HEARSTDALE, OFF THE 3-LINE? GOT TOGETHER AND FIGURED OUT HOW TO RIP OFF THEIR CORNERS. THE TRICK WAS, THEY ALL HAD TO BE IN, YOU KNOW WHY?
BECAUSE IF ALL OF THEM *WEREN'T,* IT WAS JUST WAY TOO EASY TO FIGURE OUT THE ONES WHO WERE. LIKE *YOU TWO* JUST DID. *SUPPOSEDLY.*
YEAH-- AND WHAT HAPPENED?
WELL, YOU KNOW-- ONE OF THEM REALIZED THERE WAS MORE MONEY TO BE MADE OUT THAN IN. FIVE DEAD PAPERBOYS.
DAMN RIGHT.
SURE, BUT THIS ONE-- THIS ONE WOULD HAVE TO BE EVEN *STUPIDER* THAN THAT. OR FUCKING UP HIS COUNT, WHICH-- HEY KID, SEVEN TIMES SEVEN PLUS FOUR MINUS ONE?
...FIFTY-TWO.
MM. YEAH, SEE, *DOUBT IT.* NOW THE OTHER POSSIBILITY-- YOU ARE HIS COLLECTS RIGHT?-- BECAUSE THE OTHER POSSIBILITY IS ONE OF YOU SKIMMED--
WHAT? BULLSHIT! THAT'S BULLSHIT--
OBVIOUSLY. OBVIOUSLY NOT.
YOU KNOW SO MUCH ABOUT HIS BUSINESS, MAYBE WE SHOULD JUST DO YOU TOO, MOTHER-FUCKER.

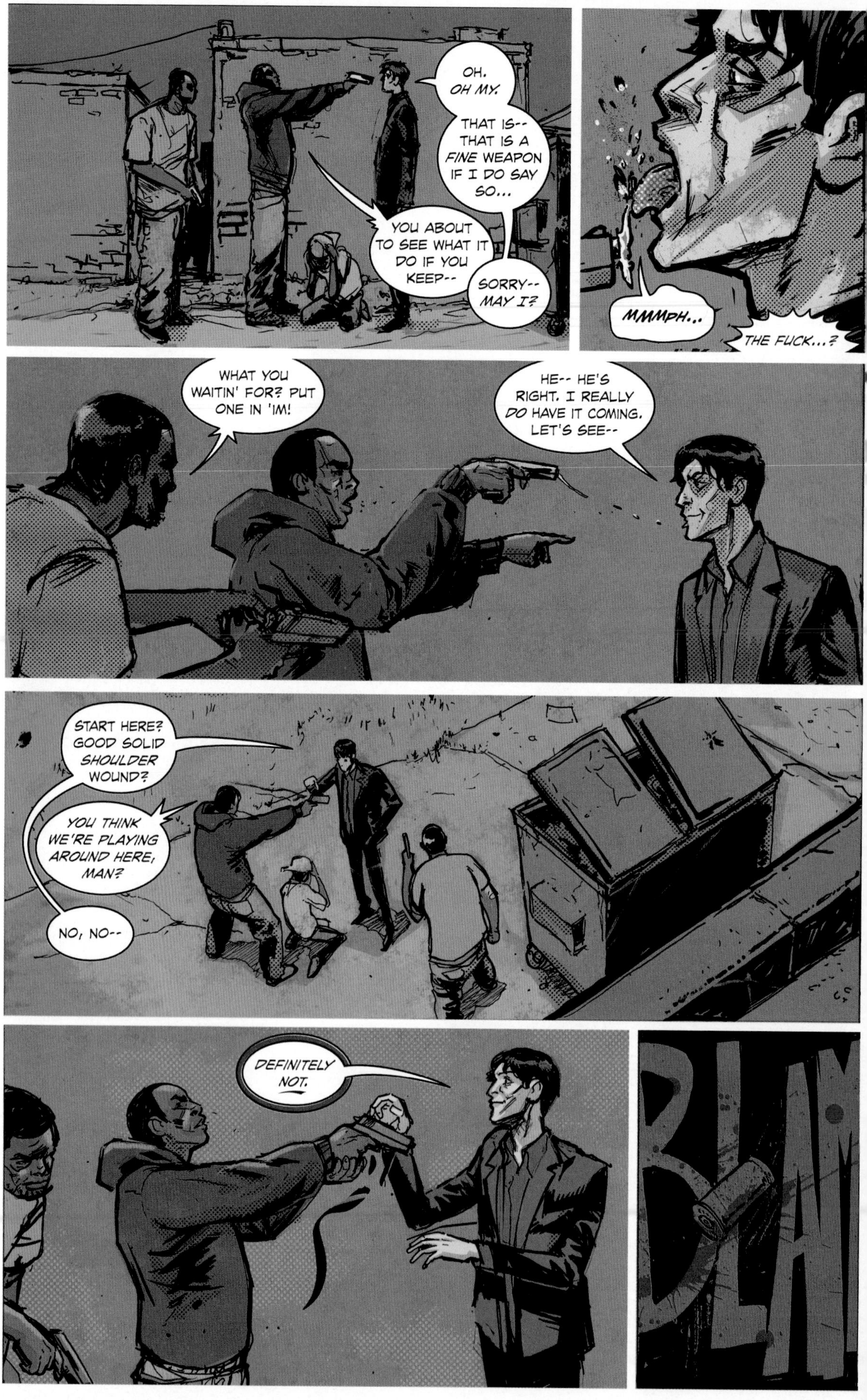
OH. OH MY.
THAT IS-- THAT IS A FINE WEAPON IF I DO SAY SO...
YOU ABOUT TO SEE WHAT IT DO IF YOU KEEP--
SORRY-- MAY I?
MMMPH...
THE FUCK...?
WHAT YOU WAITIN' FOR? PUT ONE IN 'IM!
HE-- HE'S RIGHT. I REALLY DO HAVE IT COMING. LET'S SEE--
START HERE? GOOD SOLID SHOULDER WOUND?
YOU THINK WE'RE PLAYING AROUND HERE, MAN?
NO, NO--
DEFINITELY NOT.
BLAM

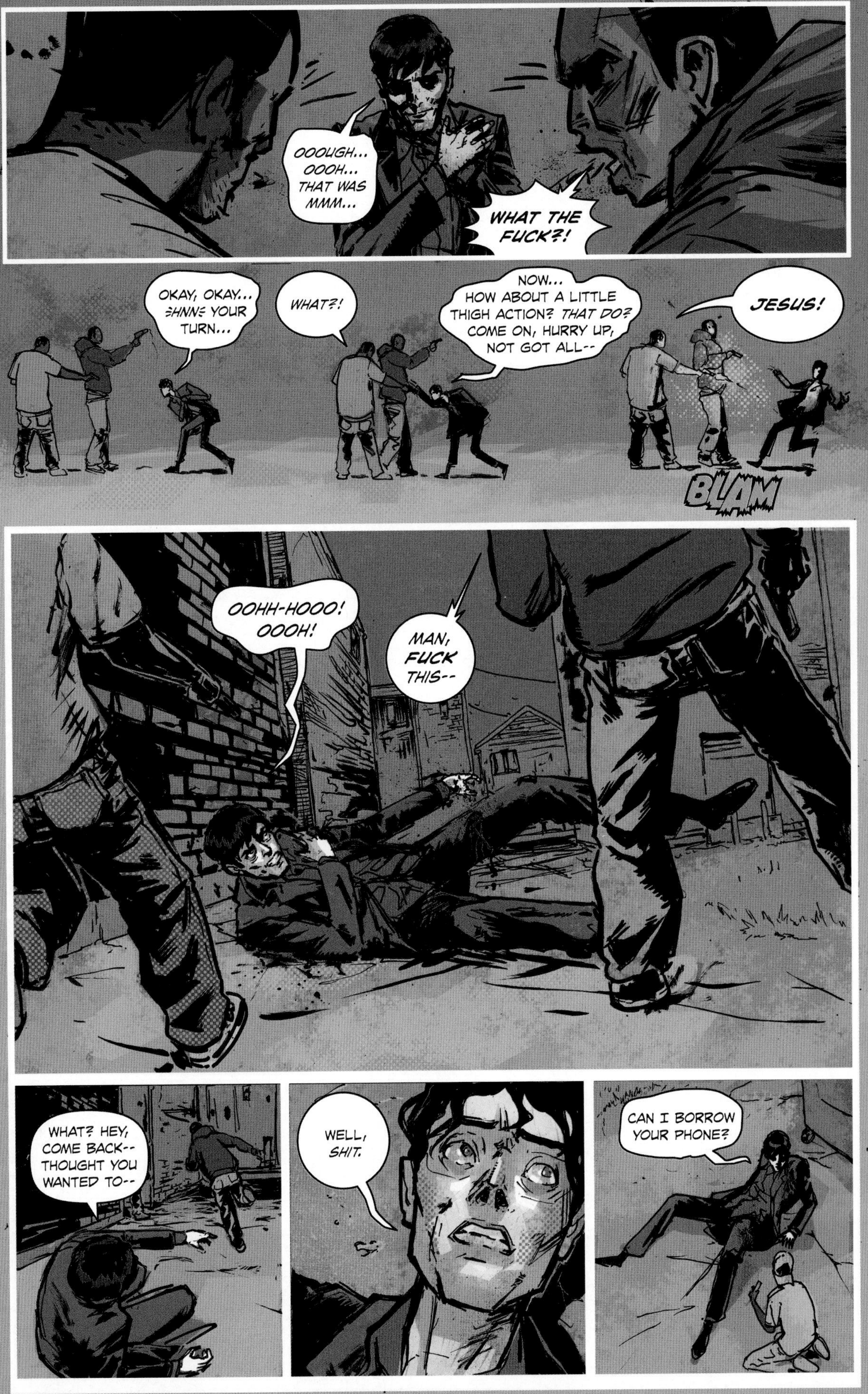
OOOUGH... OOOH... THAT WAS MMM...
WHAT THE FUCK?!
OKAY, OKAY... SHNN YOUR TURN...
WHAT?!
NOW... HOW ABOUT A LITTLE THIGH ACTION? THAT DO? COME ON, HURRY UP, NOT GOT ALL--
JESUS!
BLAM
OOHH-HOOO! OOOH!
MAN, FUCK THIS--
WHAT? HEY, COME BACK-- THOUGHT YOU WANTED TO--
WELL, SHIT.
CAN I BORROW YOUR PHONE?

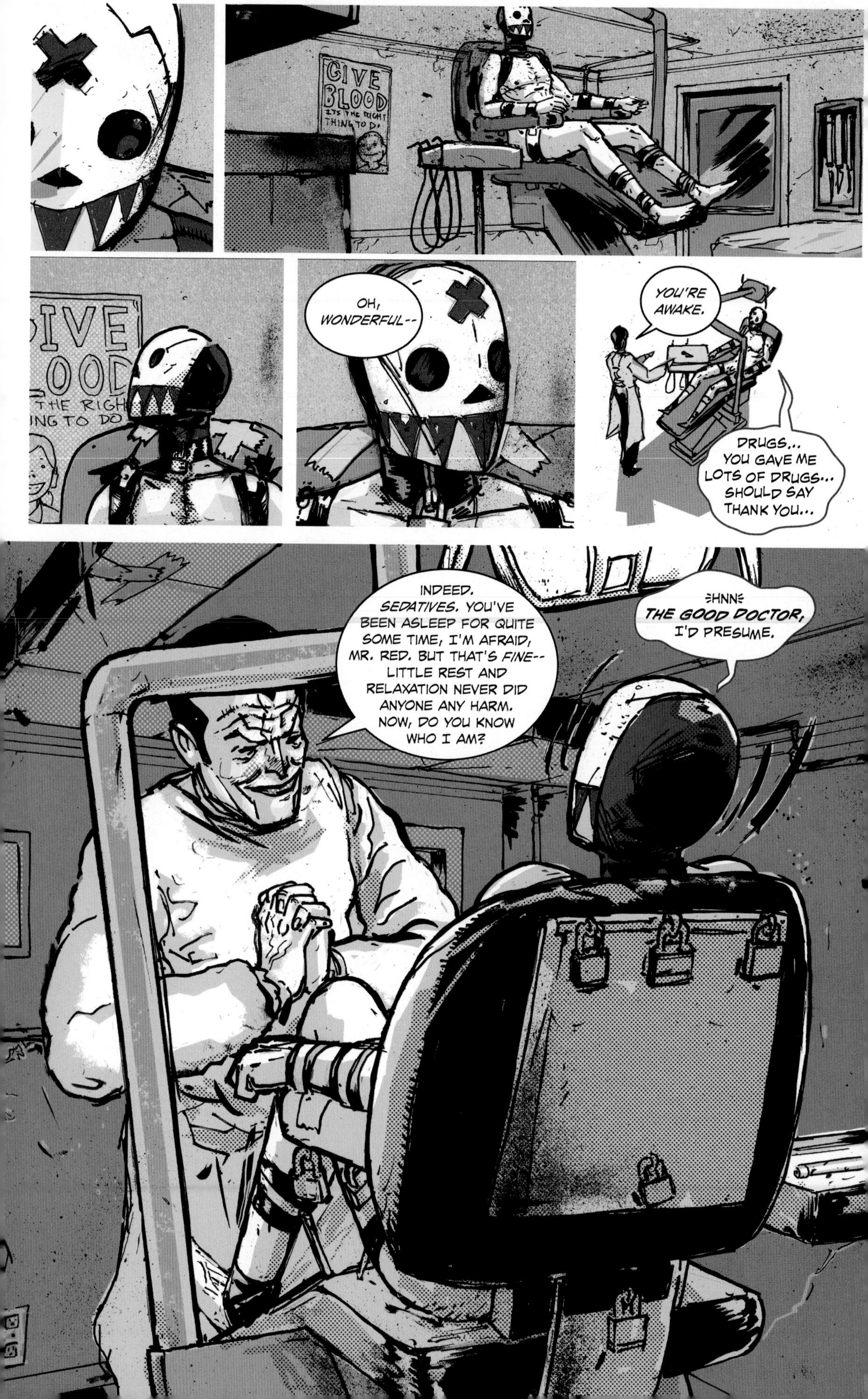
GIVE BLOOD
ITS THE RIGHT THING TO DO
OH, WONDERFUL--
YOU'RE AWAKE.
DRUGS... YOU GAVE ME LOTS OF DRUGS... SHOULD SAY THANK YOU...
INDEED. SEDATIVES. YOU'VE BEEN ASLEEP FOR QUITE SOME TIME, I'M AFRAID, MR. RED. BUT THAT'S FINE-- LITTLE REST AND RELAXATION NEVER DID ANYONE ANY HARM. NOW, DO YOU KNOW WHO I AM?
HNN THE GOOD DOCTOR, I'D PRESUME.

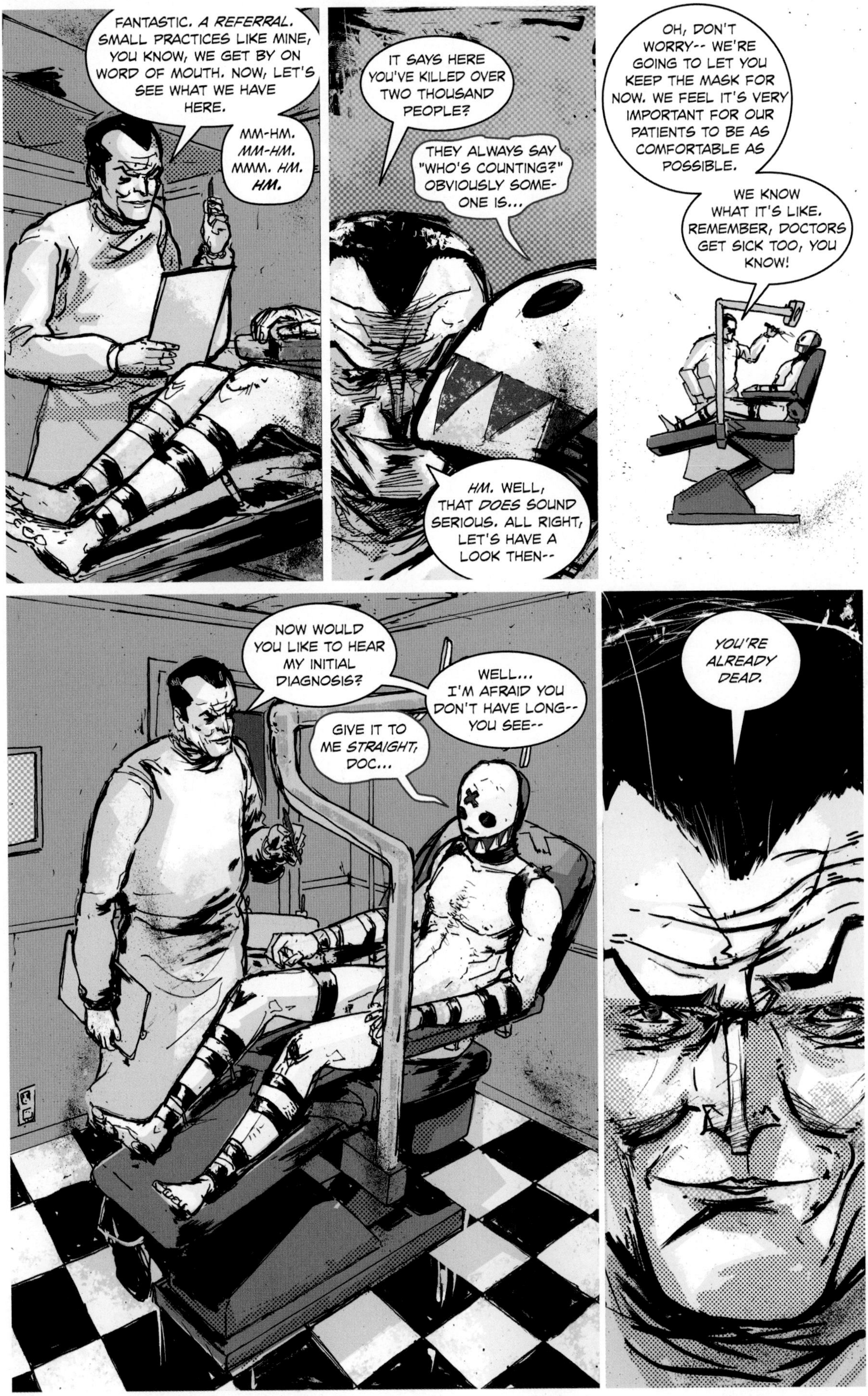
FANTASTIC. A *REFERRAL.* SMALL PRACTICES LIKE MINE, YOU KNOW, WE GET BY ON WORD OF MOUTH. NOW, LET'S SEE WHAT WE HAVE HERE.
MM-HM. *MM-HM.* MMM. HM. ***HM.***
IT SAYS HERE YOU'VE KILLED OVER TWO THOUSAND PEOPLE?
THEY ALWAYS SAY "WHO'S COUNTING?" OBVIOUSLY SOME-ONE IS...
HM. WELL, THAT *DOES* SOUND SERIOUS. ALL RIGHT, LET'S HAVE A LOOK THEN--
OH, DON'T WORRY-- WE'RE GOING TO LET YOU KEEP THE MASK FOR NOW. WE FEEL IT'S VERY IMPORTANT FOR OUR PATIENTS TO BE AS COMFORTABLE AS POSSIBLE.
WE KNOW WHAT IT'S LIKE. REMEMBER, DOCTORS GET SICK TOO, YOU KNOW!
NOW WOULD YOU LIKE TO HEAR MY INITIAL DIAGNOSIS?
GIVE IT TO ME *STRAIGHT,* DOC...
WELL... I'M AFRAID YOU DON'T HAVE LONG-- YOU SEE--
YOU'RE ALREADY DEAD.

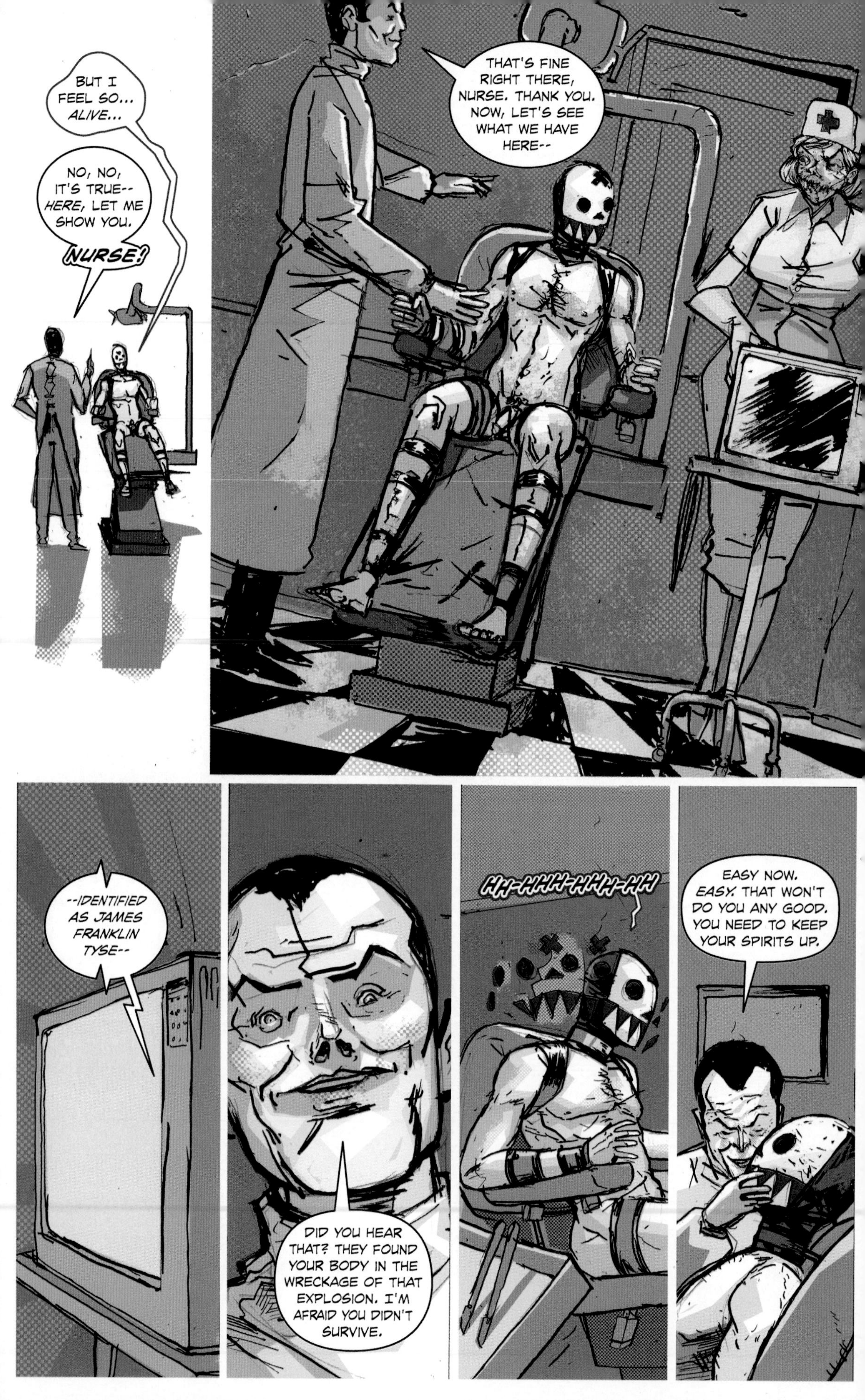
BUT I FEEL SO... ALIVE...
NO, NO, IT'S TRUE-- HERE, LET ME SHOW YOU.
NURSE!
THAT'S FINE RIGHT THERE, NURSE. THANK YOU. NOW, LET'S SEE WHAT WE HAVE HERE--
--IDENTIFIED AS JAMES FRANKLIN TYSE--
DID YOU HEAR THAT? THEY FOUND YOUR BODY IN THE WRECKAGE OF THAT EXPLOSION. I'M AFRAID YOU DIDN'T SURVIVE.
HH-HHHH-HHH-HH
EASY NOW. EASY. THAT WON'T DO YOU ANY GOOD. YOU NEED TO KEEP YOUR SPIRITS UP.

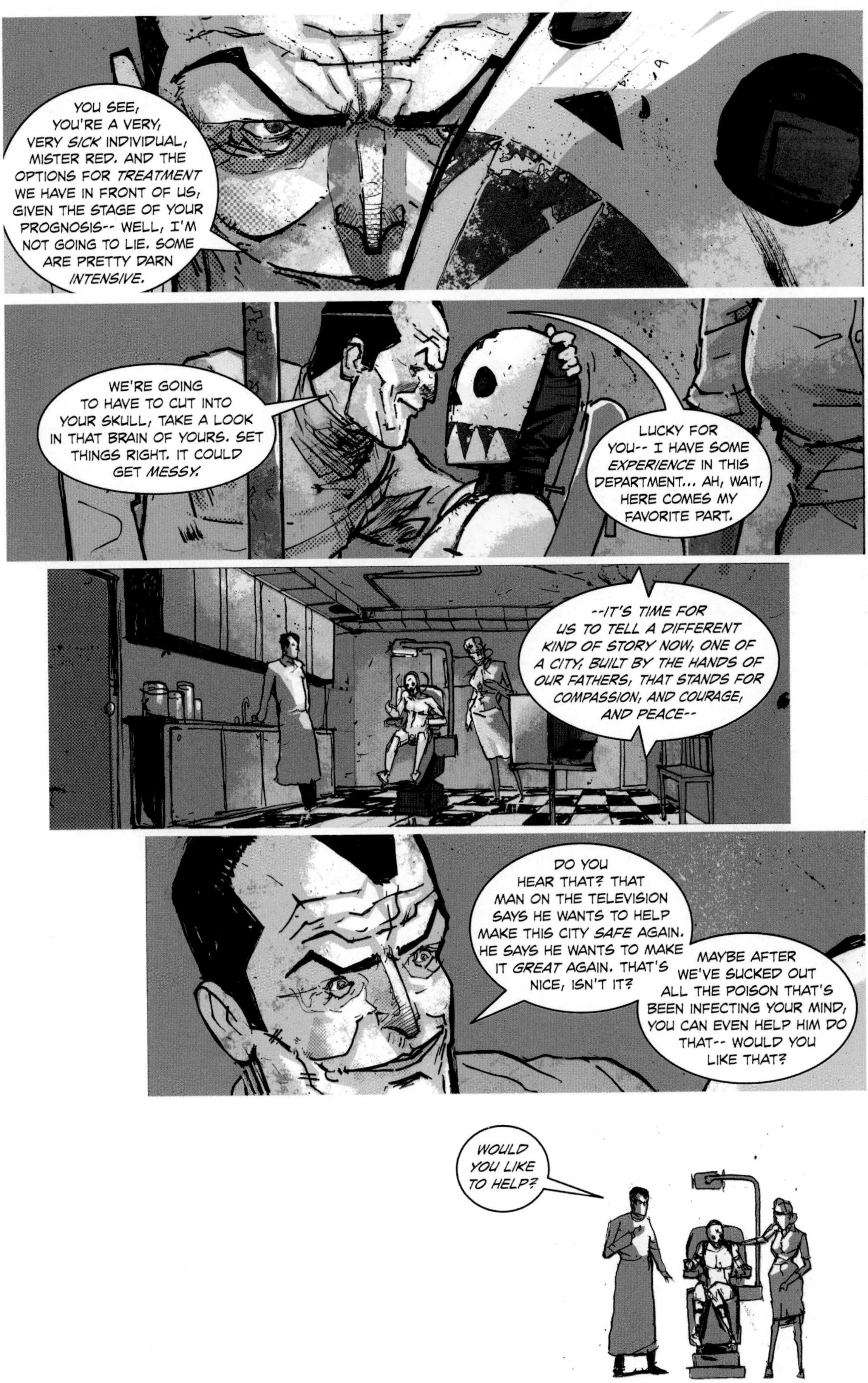
YOU SEE, YOU'RE A VERY, VERY SICK INDIVIDUAL, MISTER RED. AND THE OPTIONS FOR TREATMENT WE HAVE IN FRONT OF US, GIVEN THE STAGE OF YOUR PROGNOSIS-- WELL, I'M NOT GOING TO LIE. SOME ARE PRETTY DARN INTENSIVE.
WE'RE GOING TO HAVE TO CUT INTO YOUR SKULL, TAKE A LOOK IN THAT BRAIN OF YOURS. SET THINGS RIGHT. IT COULD GET MESSY.
LUCKY FOR YOU-- I HAVE SOME EXPERIENCE IN THIS DEPARTMENT... AH, WAIT, HERE COMES MY FAVORITE PART.
--IT'S TIME FOR US TO TELL A DIFFERENT KIND OF STORY NOW, ONE OF A CITY, BUILT BY THE HANDS OF OUR FATHERS, THAT STANDS FOR COMPASSION, AND COURAGE, AND PEACE--
DO YOU HEAR THAT? THAT MAN ON THE TELEVISION SAYS HE WANTS TO HELP MAKE THIS CITY SAFE AGAIN. HE SAYS HE WANTS TO MAKE IT GREAT AGAIN. THAT'S NICE, ISN'T IT?
MAYBE AFTER WE'VE SUCKED OUT ALL THE POISON THAT'S BEEN INFECTING YOUR MIND, YOU CAN EVEN HELP HIM DO THAT-- WOULD YOU LIKE THAT?
WOULD YOU LIKE TO HELP?

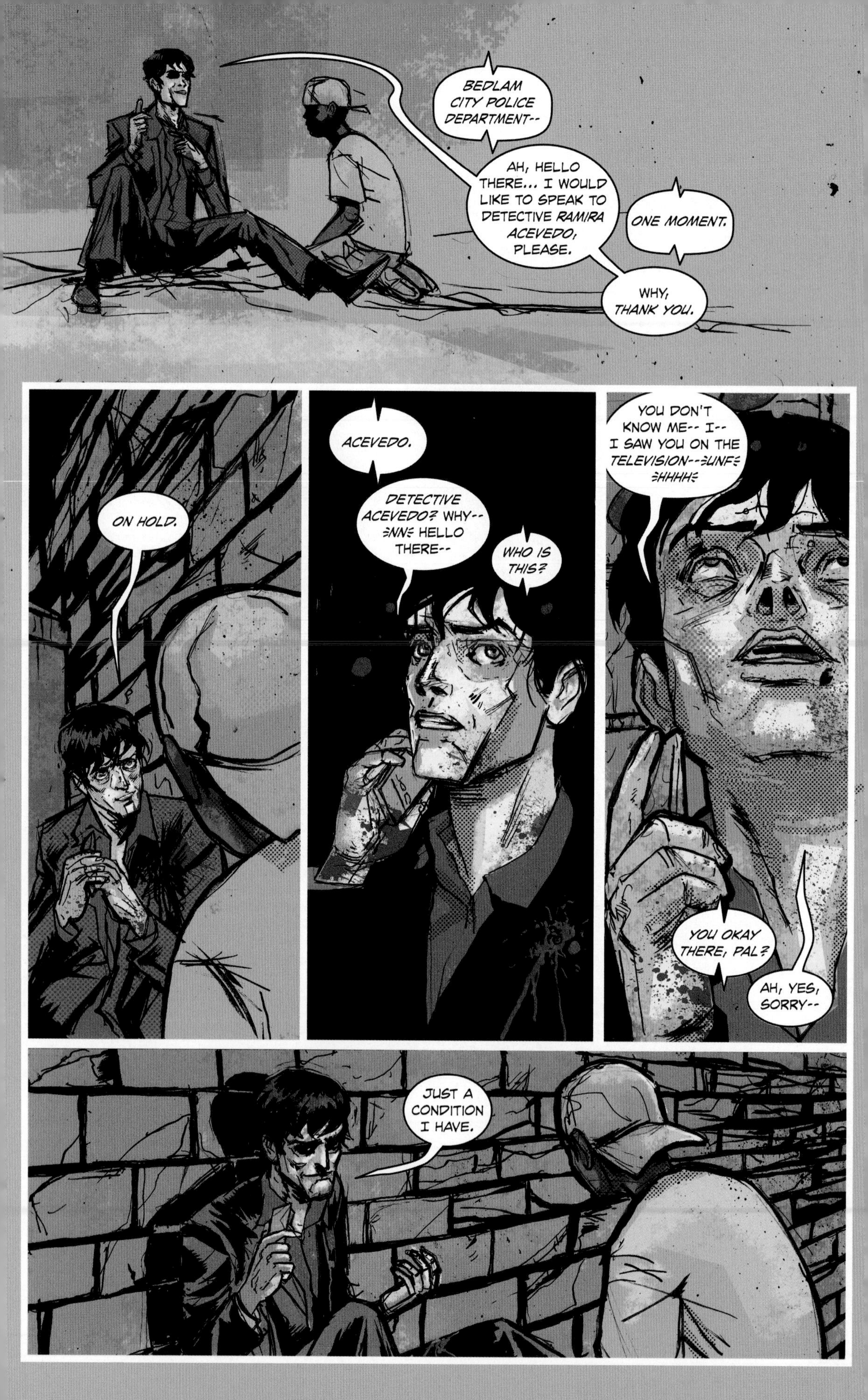
BEDLAM CITY POLICE DEPARTMENT--
AH, HELLO THERE... I WOULD LIKE TO SPEAK TO DETECTIVE RAMIRA ACEVEDO, PLEASE.
ONE MOMENT.
WHY, THANK YOU.
ON HOLD.
ACEVEDO.
DETECTIVE ACEVEDO? WHY-- =NN= HELLO THERE--
WHO IS THIS?
YOU DON'T KNOW ME-- I-- I SAW YOU ON THE TELEVISION--=UNF= =HHHH=
YOU OKAY THERE, PAL?
AH, YES, SORRY--
JUST A CONDITION I HAVE.

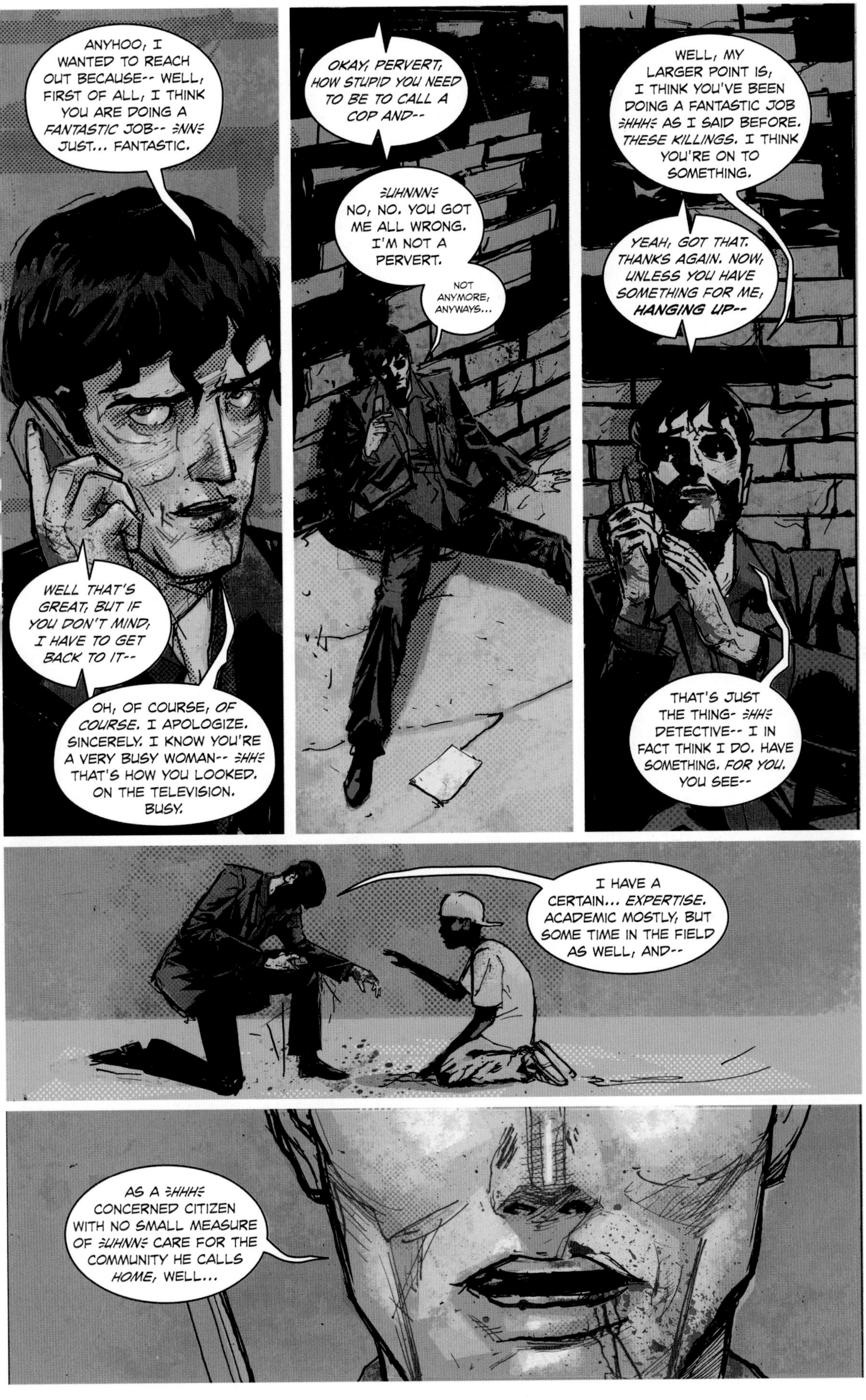
ANYHOO, I WANTED TO REACH OUT BECAUSE-- WELL, FIRST OF ALL, I THINK YOU ARE DOING A *FANTASTIC* JOB-- =NN= JUST... FANTASTIC.
WELL THAT'S GREAT, BUT IF YOU DON'T MIND, I HAVE TO GET BACK TO IT--
OH, OF COURSE, *OF COURSE*. I APOLOGIZE. SINCERELY. I KNOW YOU'RE A VERY BUSY WOMAN-- =HH= THAT'S HOW YOU LOOKED. ON THE TELEVISION. BUSY.
OKAY, PERVERT, HOW STUPID YOU NEED TO BE TO CALL A COP AND--
=UHNNN= NO, NO. YOU GOT ME ALL WRONG. I'M NOT A PERVERT.
NOT ANYMORE, ANYWAYS...
WELL, MY LARGER POINT IS, I THINK YOU'VE BEEN DOING A FANTASTIC JOB *=HHH=* AS I SAID BEFORE. *THESE KILLINGS*. I THINK YOU'RE ON TO SOMETHING.
YEAH, GOT THAT. THANKS AGAIN. NOW, UNLESS YOU HAVE SOMETHING FOR ME, ***HANGING UP--***
THAT'S JUST THE THING- *=HH=* DETECTIVE-- I IN FACT THINK I DO. HAVE SOMETHING. *FOR YOU*. YOU SEE--
I HAVE A CERTAIN... *EXPERTISE*. ACADEMIC MOSTLY, BUT SOME TIME IN THE FIELD AS WELL, AND--
AS A *=HHH=* CONCERNED CITIZEN WITH NO SMALL MEASURE OF *=UHNN=* CARE FOR THE COMMUNITY HE CALLS *HOME*, WELL...

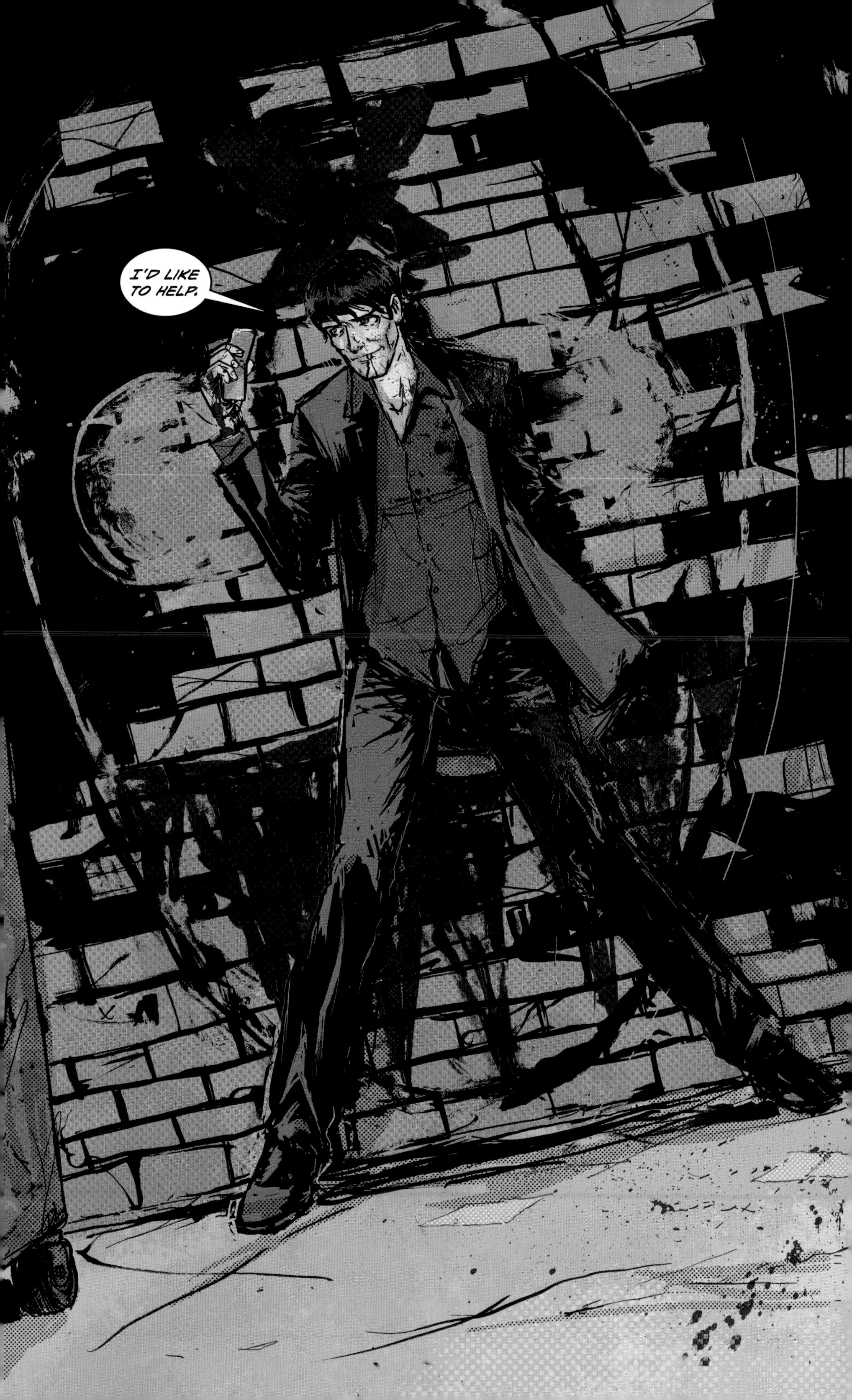
I'D LIKE TO HELP.

CHAPTER

2

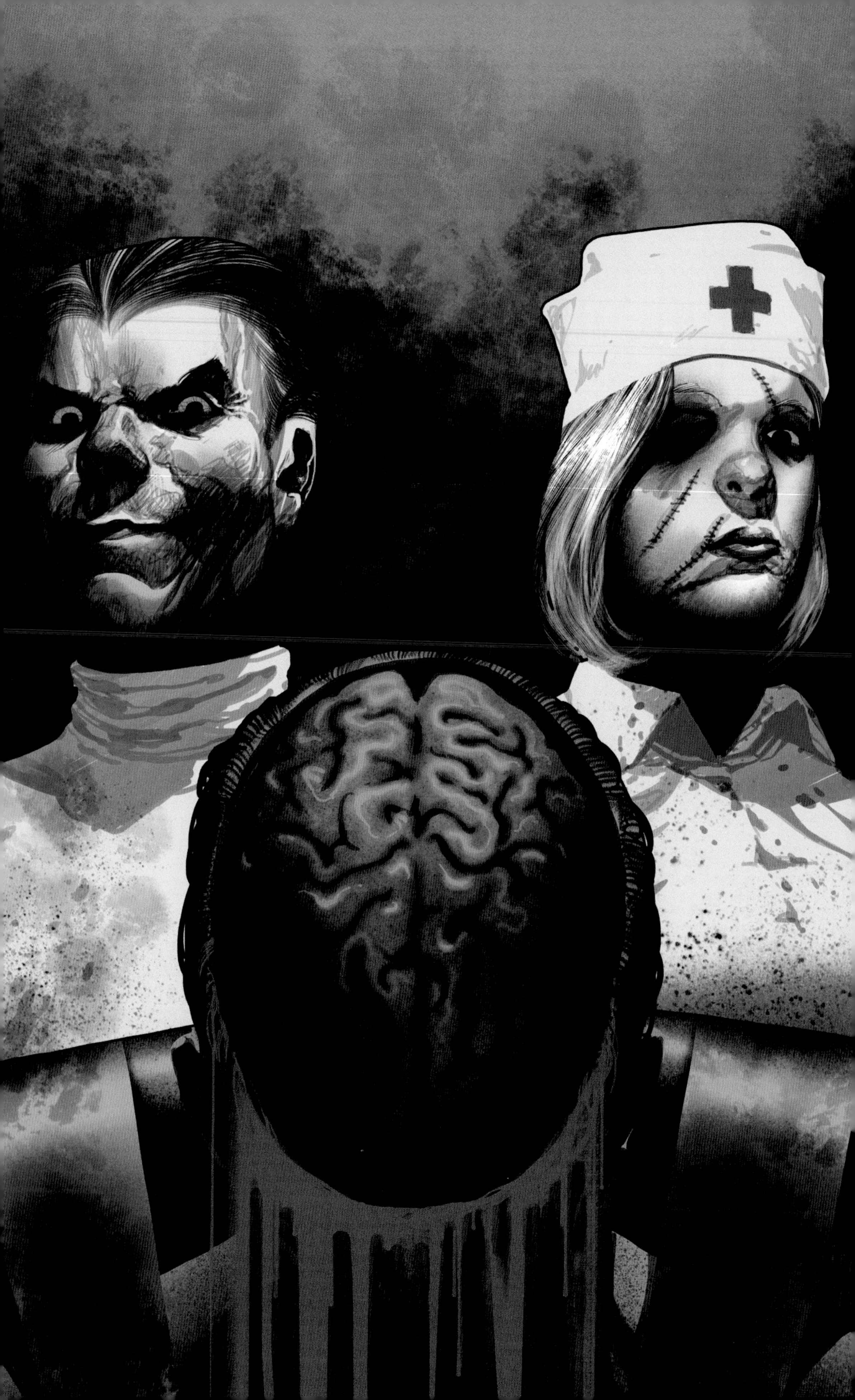

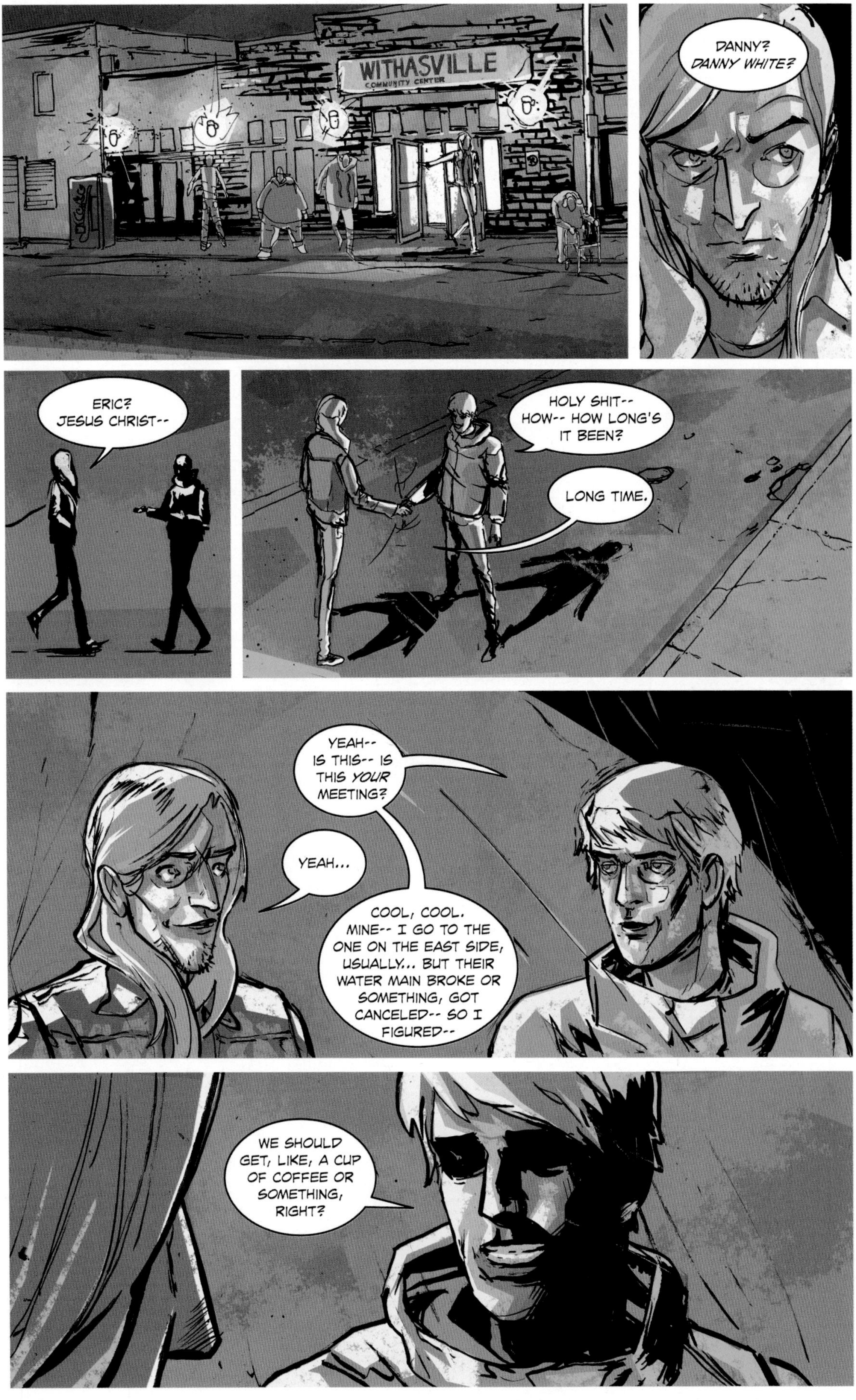
WITHASVILLE
COMMUNITY CENTER
DANNY? DANNY WHITE?
ERIC? JESUS CHRIST--
HOLY SHIT-- HOW-- HOW LONG'S IT BEEN?
LONG TIME.
YEAH-- IS THIS-- IS THIS *YOUR* MEETING?
YEAH...
COOL, COOL. MINE-- I GO TO THE ONE ON THE EAST SIDE, USUALLY... BUT THEIR WATER MAIN BROKE OR SOMETHING, GOT CANCELED-- SO I FIGURED--
WE SHOULD GET, LIKE, A CUP OF COFFEE OR SOMETHING, RIGHT?

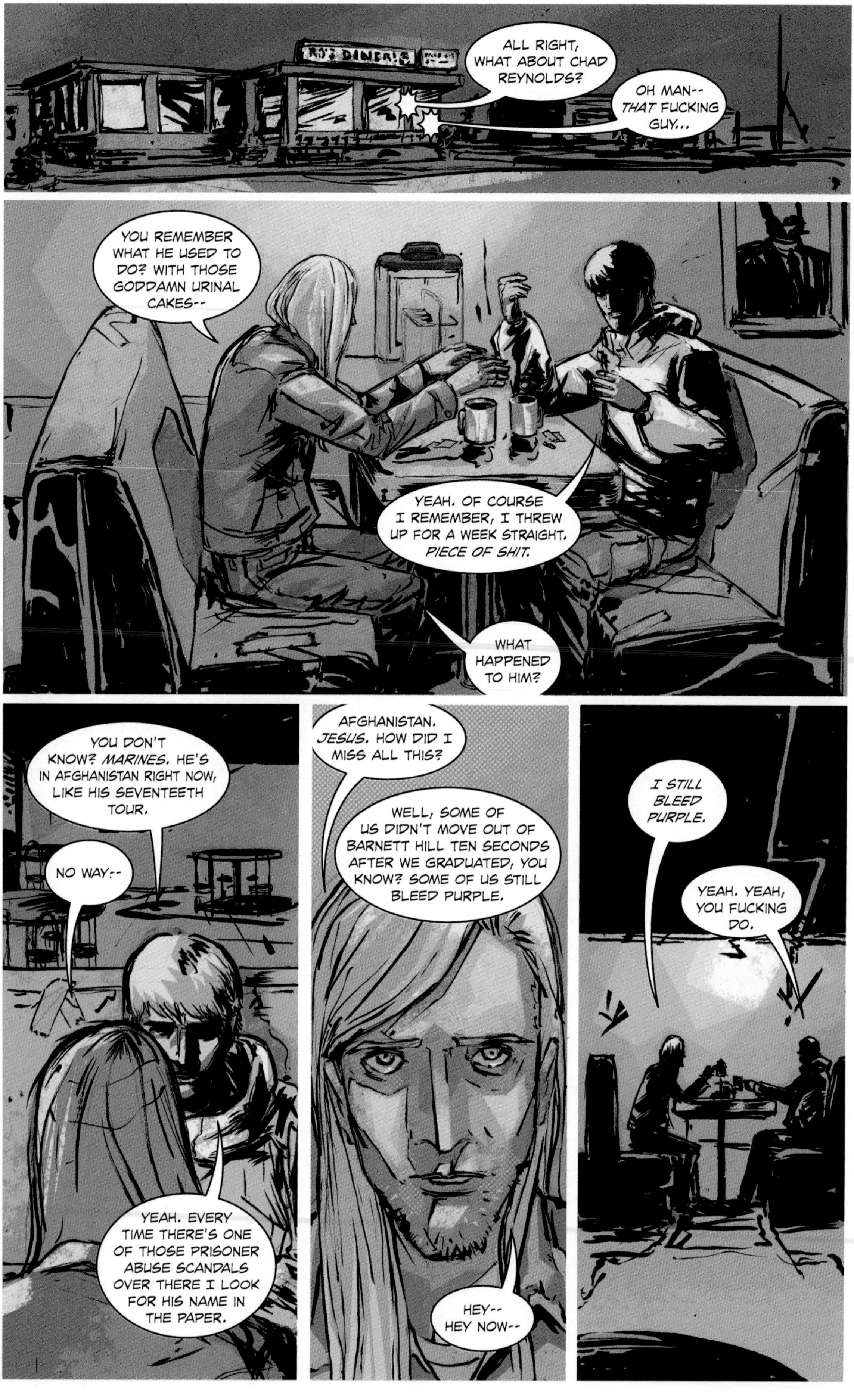
RAY'S DINER
ALL RIGHT, WHAT ABOUT CHAD REYNOLDS?
OH MAN-- *THAT* FUCKING GUY...
YOU REMEMBER WHAT HE USED TO DO? WITH THOSE GODDAMN URINAL CAKES--
YEAH. OF COURSE I REMEMBER, I THREW UP FOR A WEEK STRAIGHT. *PIECE OF SHIT.*
WHAT HAPPENED TO HIM?
YOU DON'T KNOW? *MARINES.* HE'S IN AFGHANISTAN RIGHT NOW, LIKE HIS SEVENTEETH TOUR.
NO WAY--
YEAH. EVERY TIME THERE'S ONE OF THOSE PRISONER ABUSE SCANDALS OVER THERE I LOOK FOR HIS NAME IN THE PAPER.
AFGHANISTAN. *JESUS.* HOW DID I MISS ALL THIS?
WELL, SOME OF US DIDN'T MOVE OUT OF BARNETT HILL TEN SECONDS AFTER WE GRADUATED, YOU KNOW? SOME OF US STILL BLEED PURPLE.
HEY-- HEY NOW--
I STILL BLEED PURPLE.
YEAH. YEAH, YOU FUCKING DO.

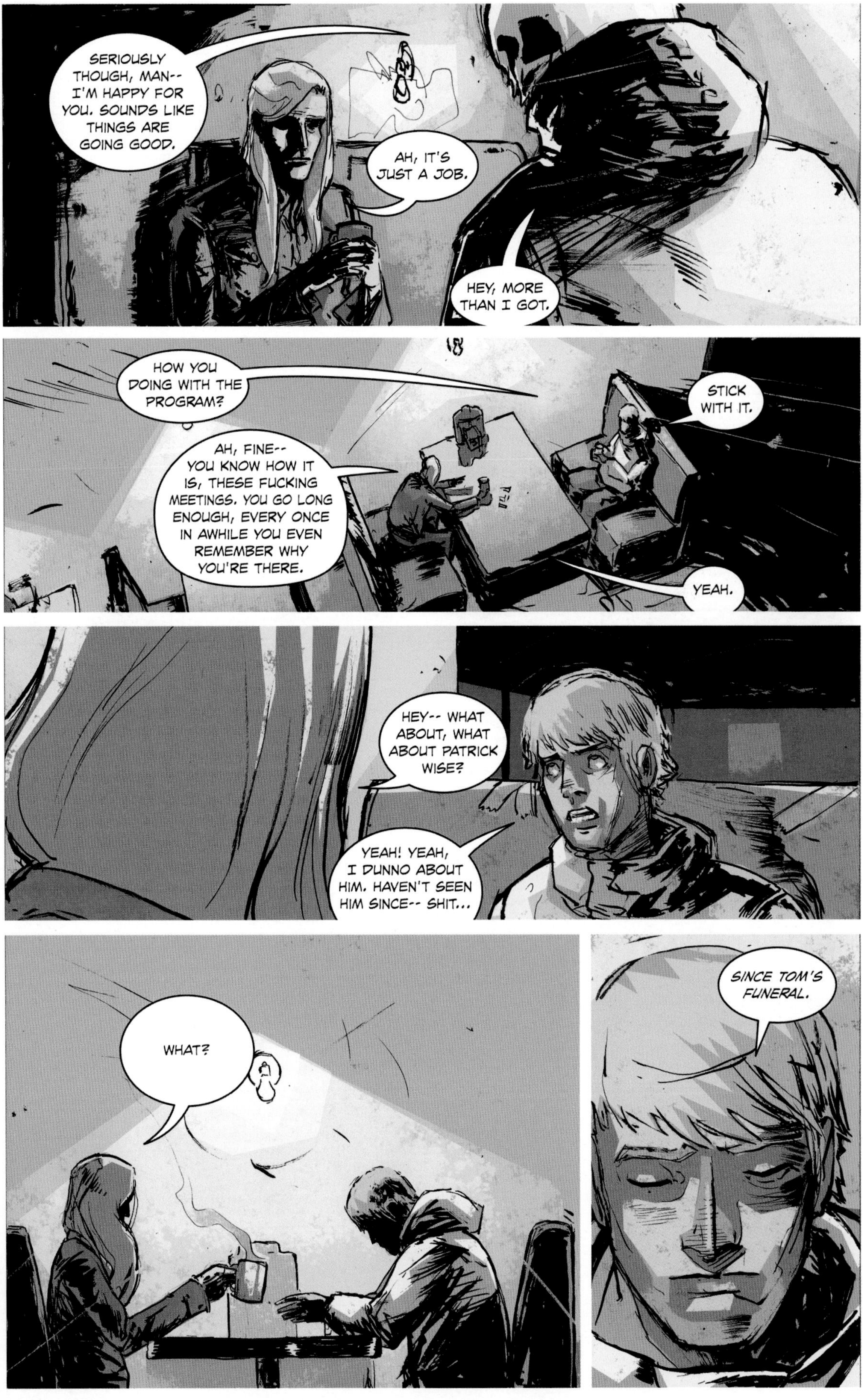
SERIOUSLY THOUGH, MAN-- I'M HAPPY FOR YOU. SOUNDS LIKE THINGS ARE GOING GOOD.
AH, IT'S JUST A JOB.
HEY, MORE THAN I GOT.
HOW YOU DOING WITH THE PROGRAM?
STICK WITH IT.
AH, FINE-- YOU KNOW HOW IT IS, THESE FUCKING MEETINGS. YOU GO LONG ENOUGH, EVERY ONCE IN AWHILE YOU EVEN REMEMBER WHY YOU'RE THERE.
YEAH.
HEY-- WHAT ABOUT, WHAT ABOUT PATRICK WISE?
YEAH! YEAH, I DUNNO ABOUT HIM. HAVEN'T SEEN HIM SINCE-- SHIT...
WHAT?
SINCE TOM'S FUNERAL.

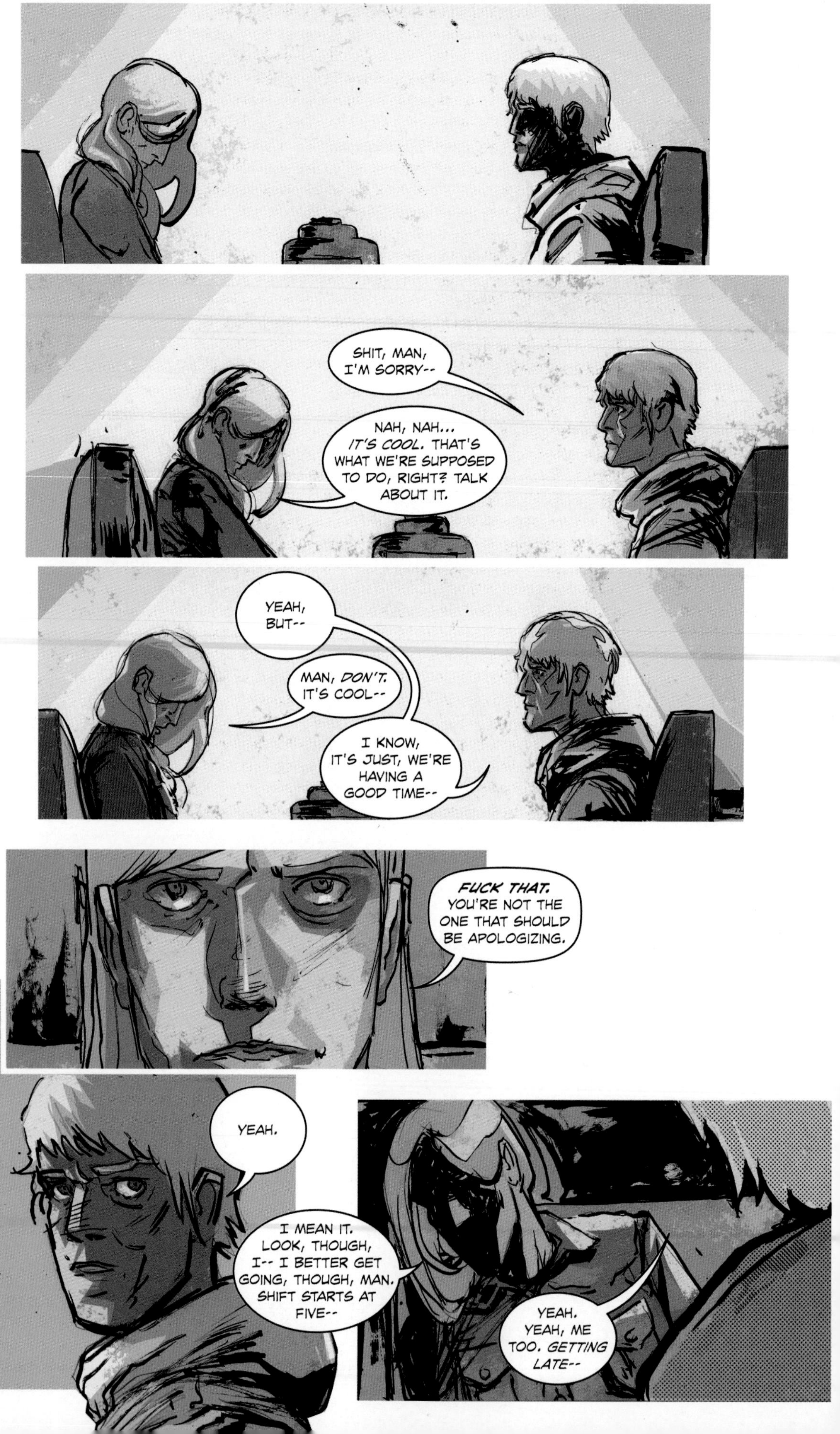
SHIT, MAN, I'M SORRY--
NAH, NAH... IT'S COOL. THAT'S WHAT WE'RE SUPPOSED TO DO, RIGHT? TALK ABOUT IT.
YEAH, BUT--
MAN, DON'T. IT'S COOL--
I KNOW, IT'S JUST, WE'RE HAVING A GOOD TIME--
FUCK THAT. YOU'RE NOT THE ONE THAT SHOULD BE APOLOGIZING.
YEAH.
I MEAN IT. LOOK, THOUGH, I-- I BETTER GET GOING, THOUGH, MAN. SHIFT STARTS AT FIVE--
YEAH. YEAH, ME TOO. GETTING LATE--

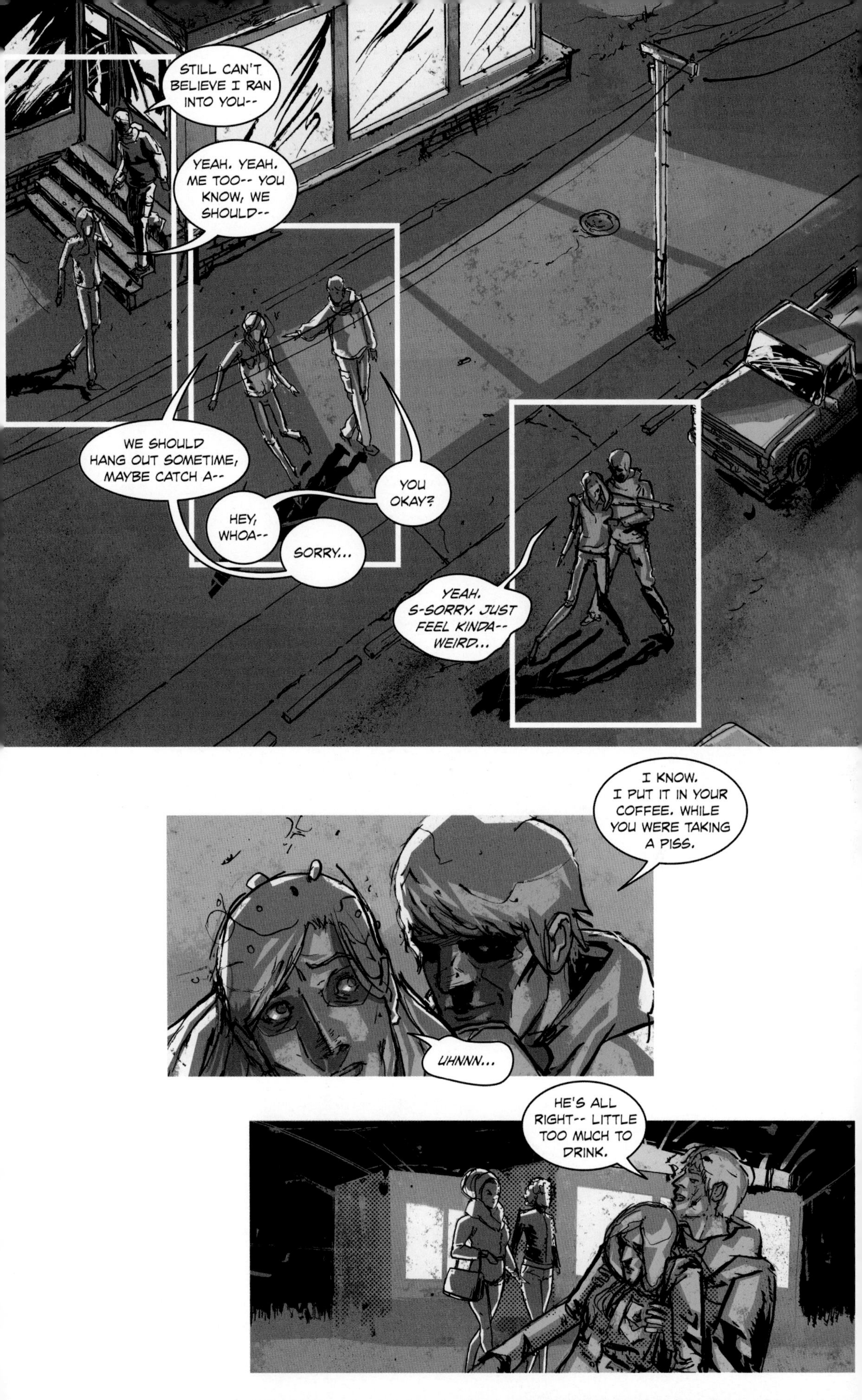
STILL CAN'T BELIEVE I RAN INTO YOU--
YEAH. YEAH. ME TOO-- YOU KNOW, WE SHOULD--
WE SHOULD HANG OUT SOMETIME, MAYBE CATCH A--
SORRY...
HEY, WHOA--
YOU OKAY?
YEAH. S-SORRY. JUST FEEL KINDA-- WEIRD...
I KNOW. I PUT IT IN YOUR COFFEE. WHILE YOU WERE TAKING A PISS.
UHNNN...
HE'S ALL RIGHT-- LITTLE TOO MUCH TO DRINK.

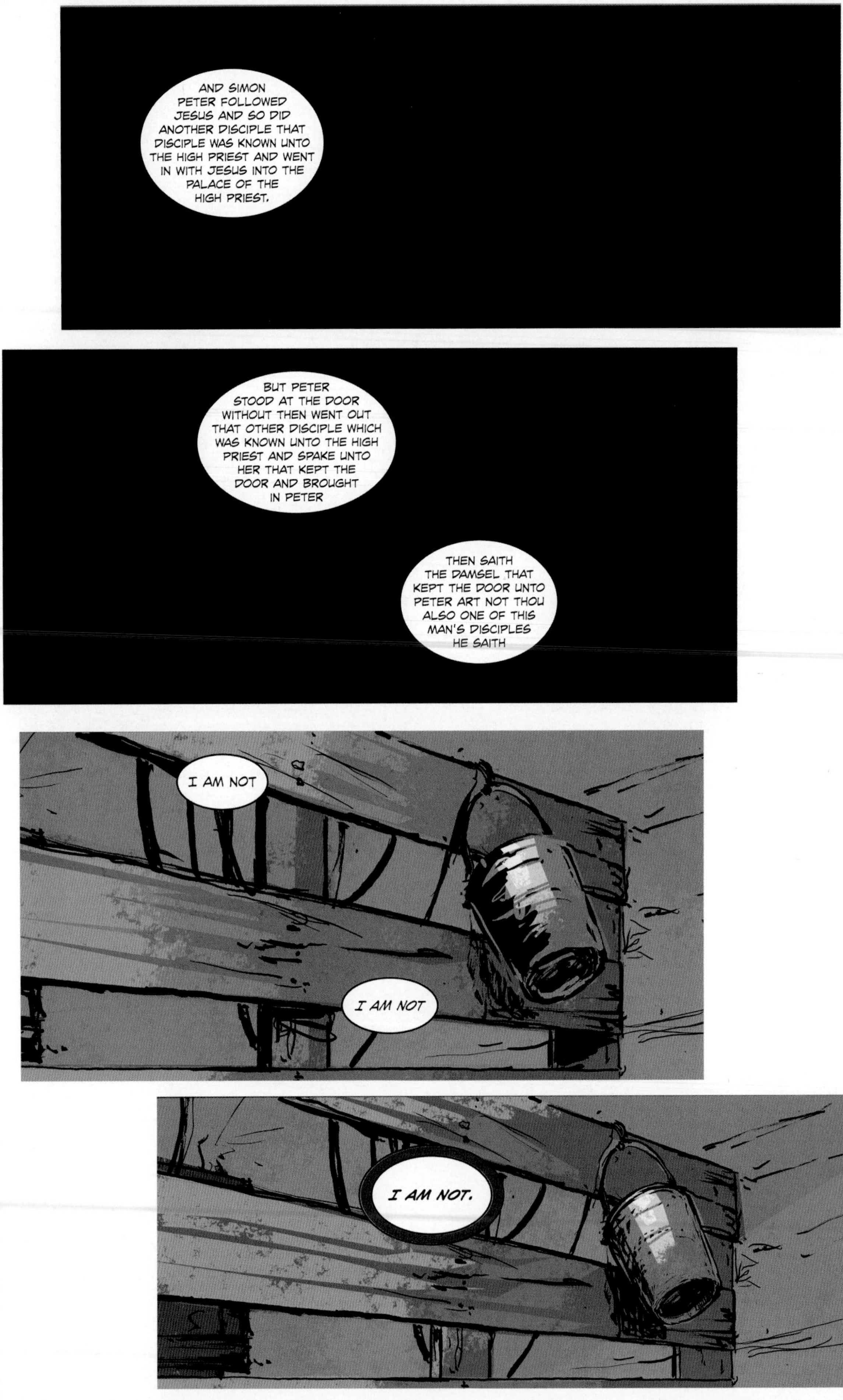
AND SIMON PETER FOLLOWED JESUS AND SO DID ANOTHER DISCIPLE THAT DISCIPLE WAS KNOWN UNTO THE HIGH PRIEST AND WENT IN WITH JESUS INTO THE PALACE OF THE HIGH PRIEST.
BUT PETER STOOD AT THE DOOR WITHOUT THEN WENT OUT THAT OTHER DISCIPLE WHICH WAS KNOWN UNTO THE HIGH PRIEST AND SPAKE UNTO HER THAT KEPT THE DOOR AND BROUGHT IN PETER
THEN SAITH THE DAMSEL THAT KEPT THE DOOR UNTO PETER ART NOT THOU ALSO ONE OF THIS MAN'S DISCIPLES HE SAITH
I AM NOT
I AM NOT
I AM NOT.

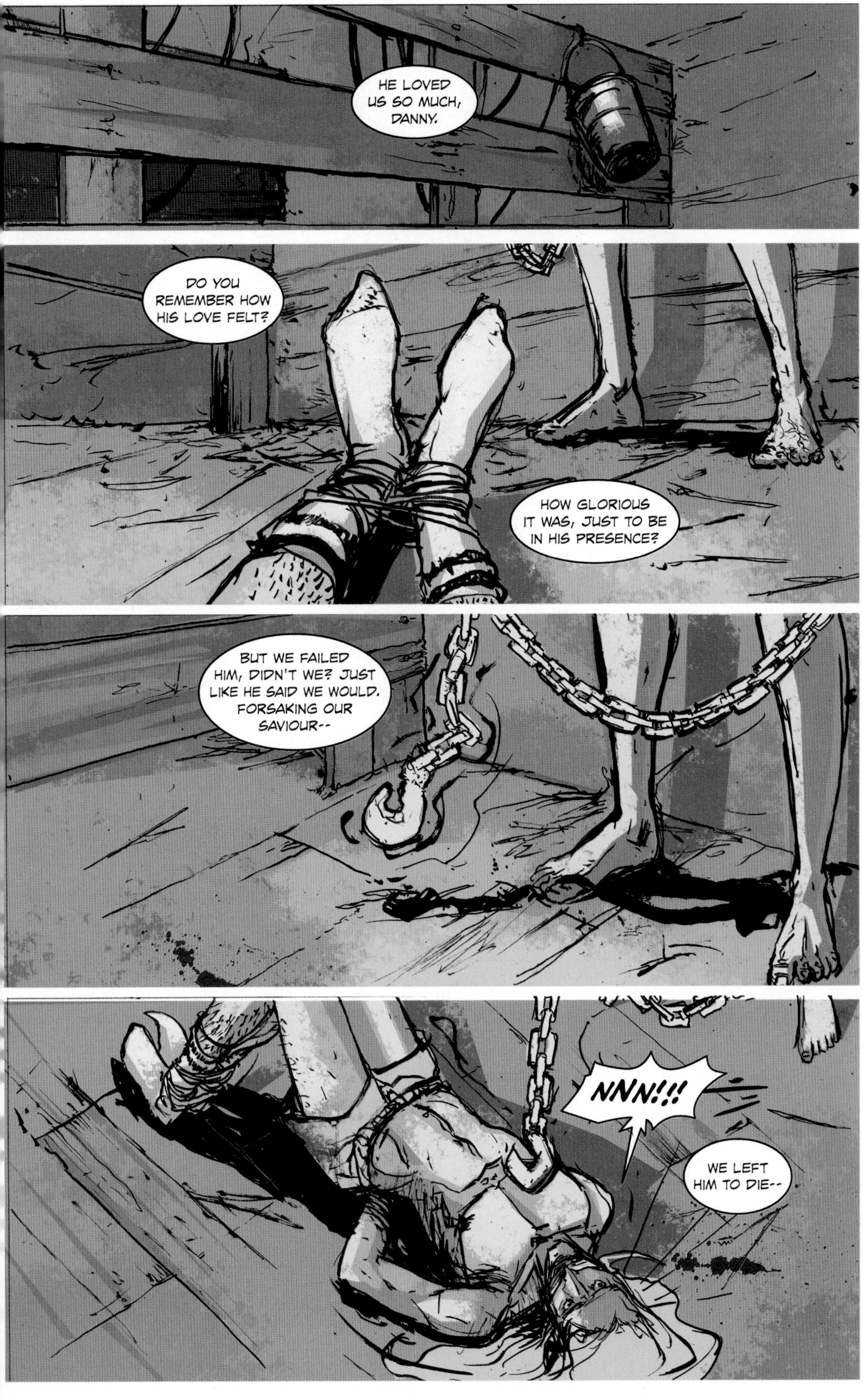
HE LOVED US SO MUCH, DANNY.
DO YOU REMEMBER HOW HIS LOVE FELT?
HOW GLORIOUS IT WAS, JUST TO BE IN HIS PRESENCE?
BUT WE FAILED HIM, DIDN'T WE? JUST LIKE HE SAID WE WOULD. FORSAKING OUR SAVIOUR--
NNN!!!
WE LEFT HIM TO DIE--

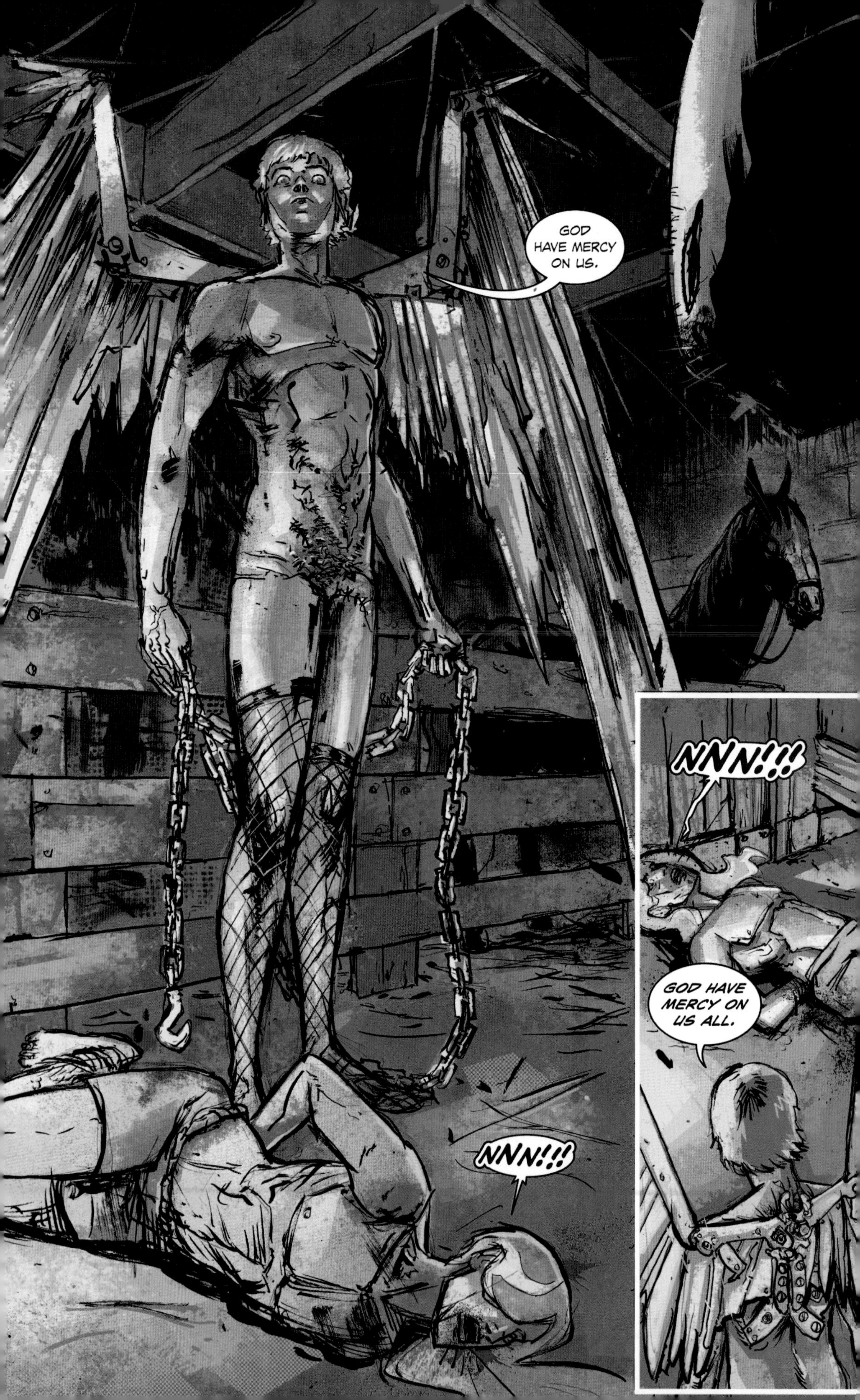
GOD HAVE MERCY ON US.
NNN!!!
NNN!!!
GOD HAVE MERCY ON US ALL.

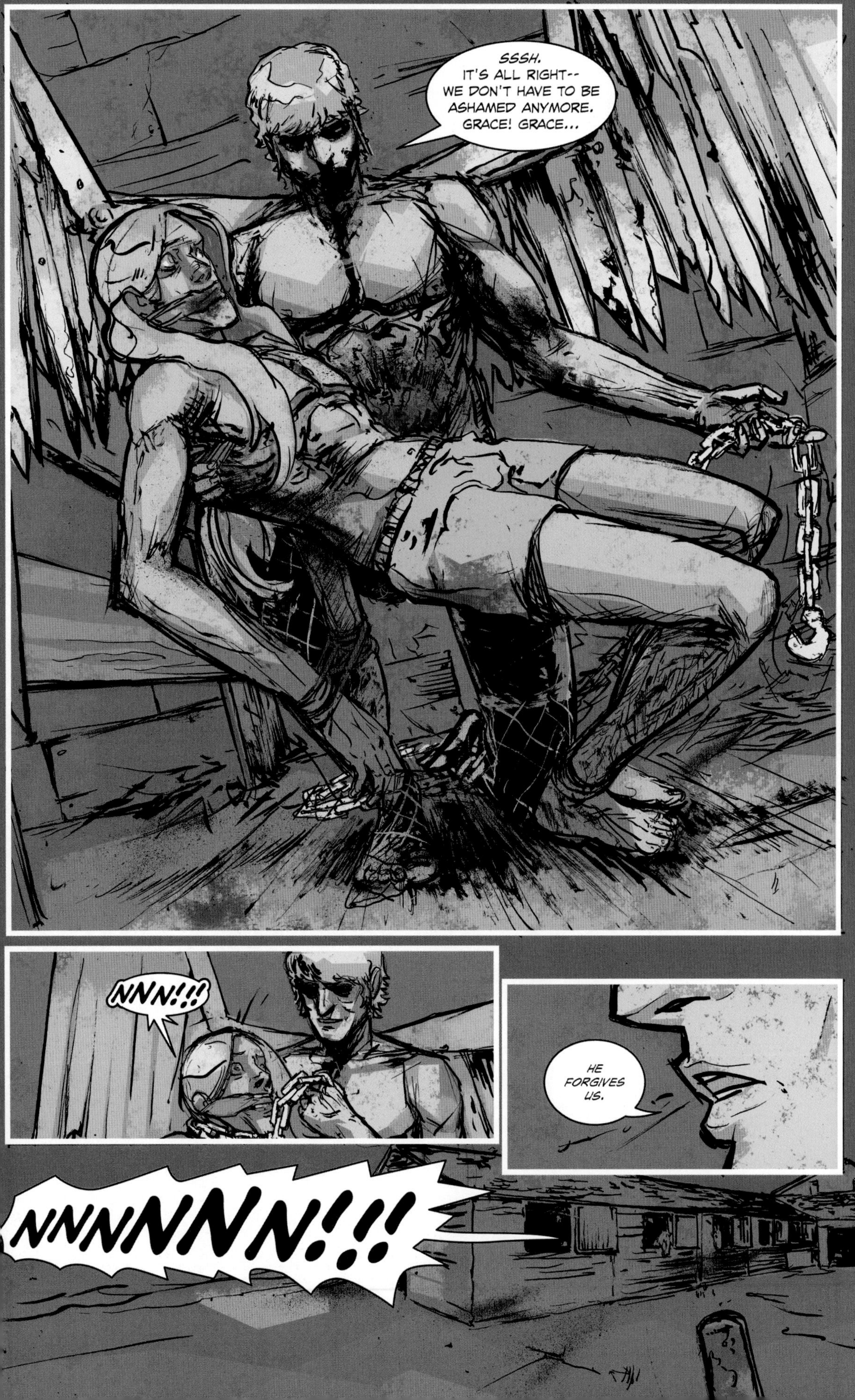
SSSH. IT'S ALL RIGHT-- WE DON'T HAVE TO BE ASHAMED ANYMORE. GRACE! GRACE...
NNN!!!
HE FORGIVES US.
NNNNNN!!!

CHAPTER TWO
EVERYBODY WINS

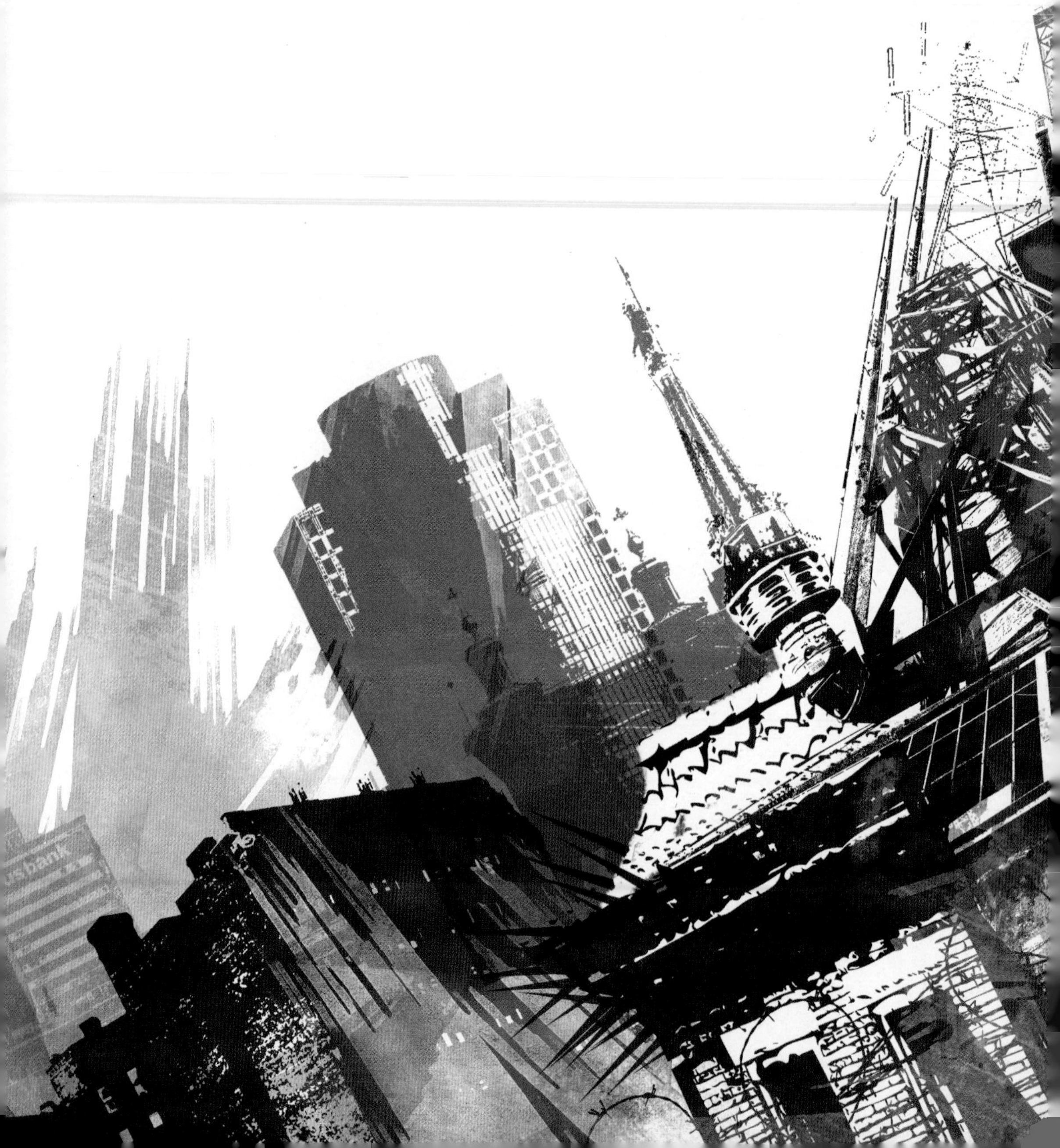
usbank

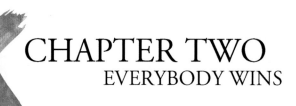

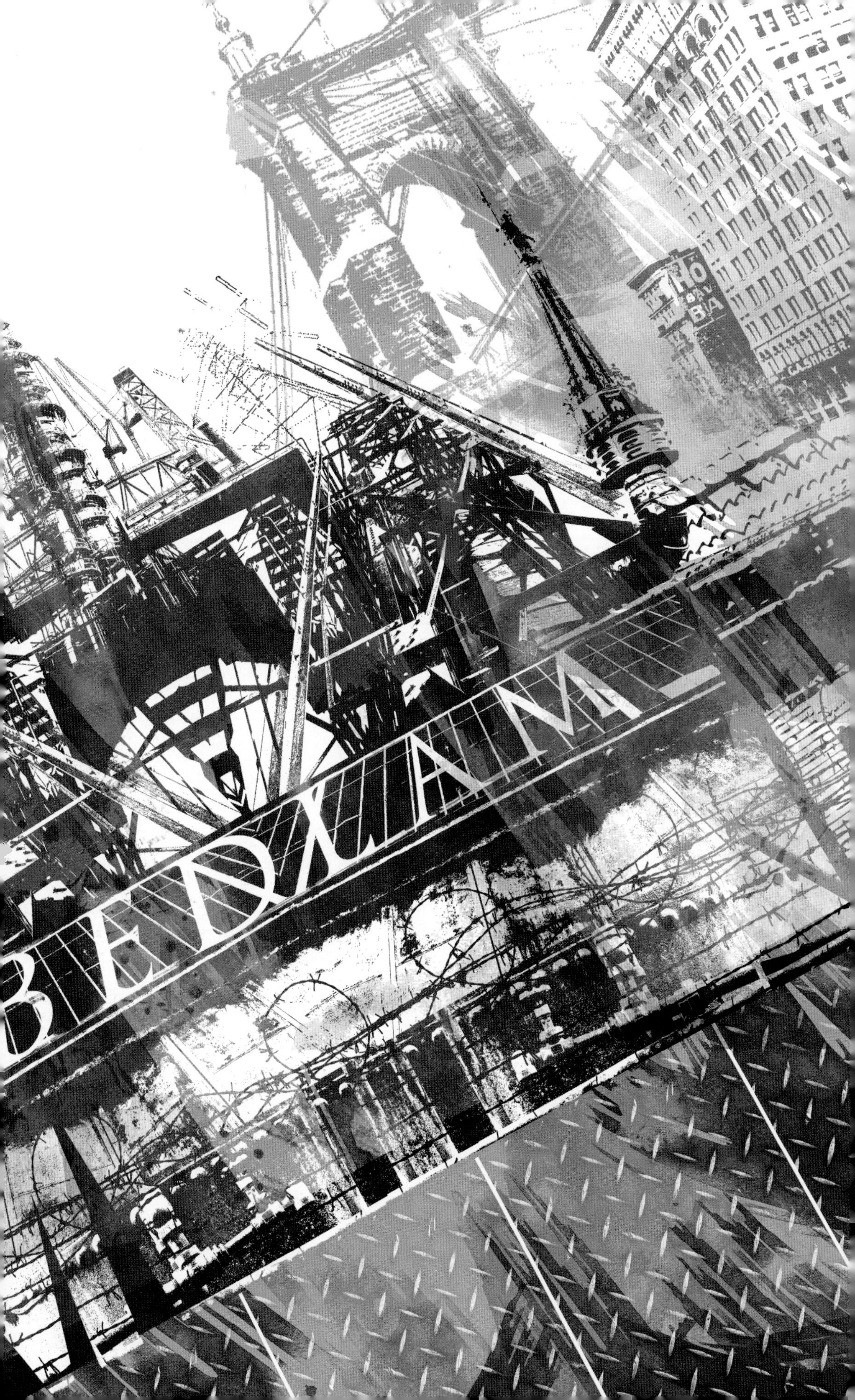
BEDLAM

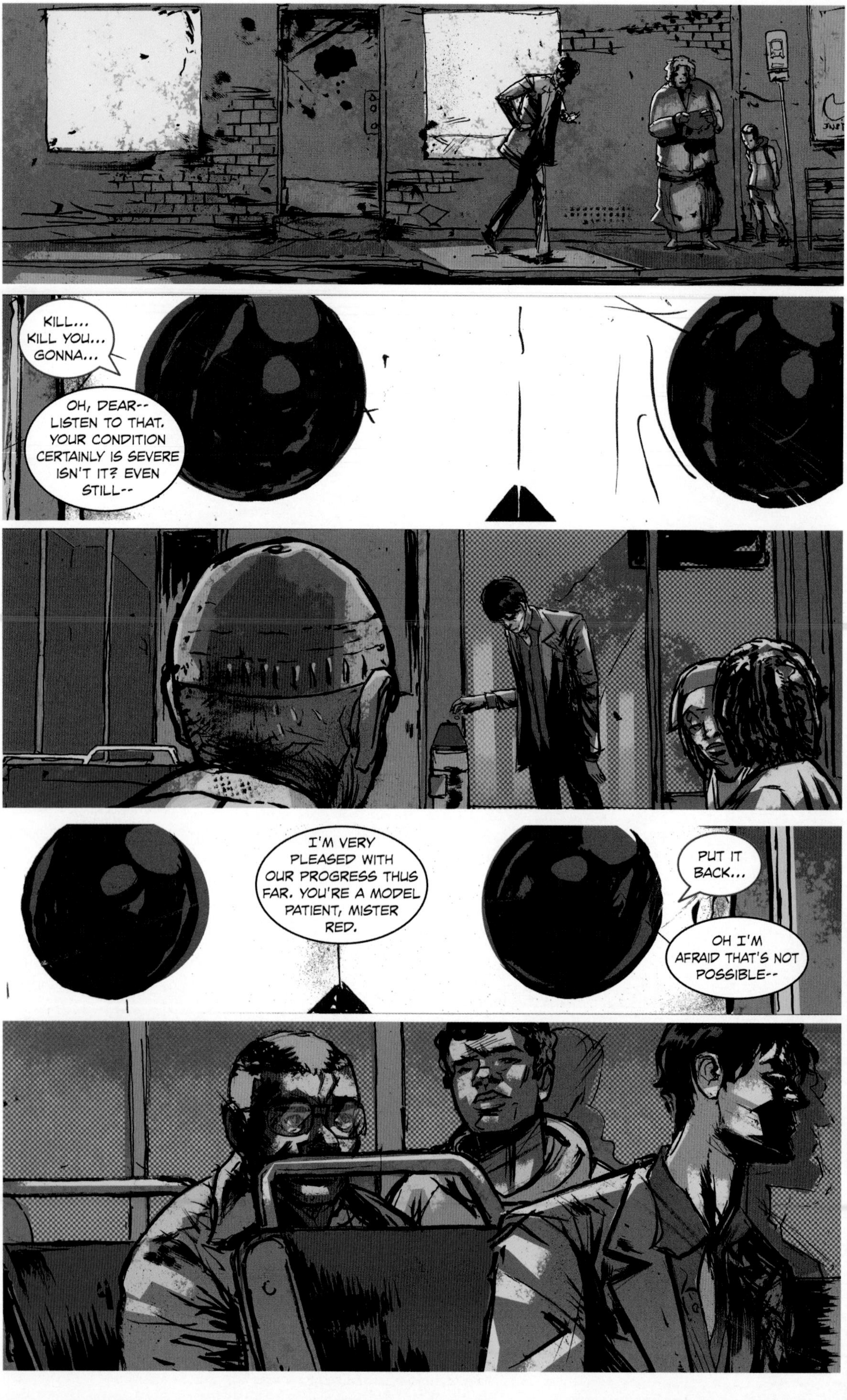
KILL... KILL YOU... GONNA...
OH, DEAR-- LISTEN TO THAT. YOUR CONDITION CERTAINLY IS SEVERE ISN'T IT? EVEN STILL--
I'M VERY PLEASED WITH OUR PROGRESS THUS FAR. YOU'RE A MODEL PATIENT, MISTER RED.
PUT IT BACK...
OH I'M AFRAID THAT'S NOT POSSIBLE--

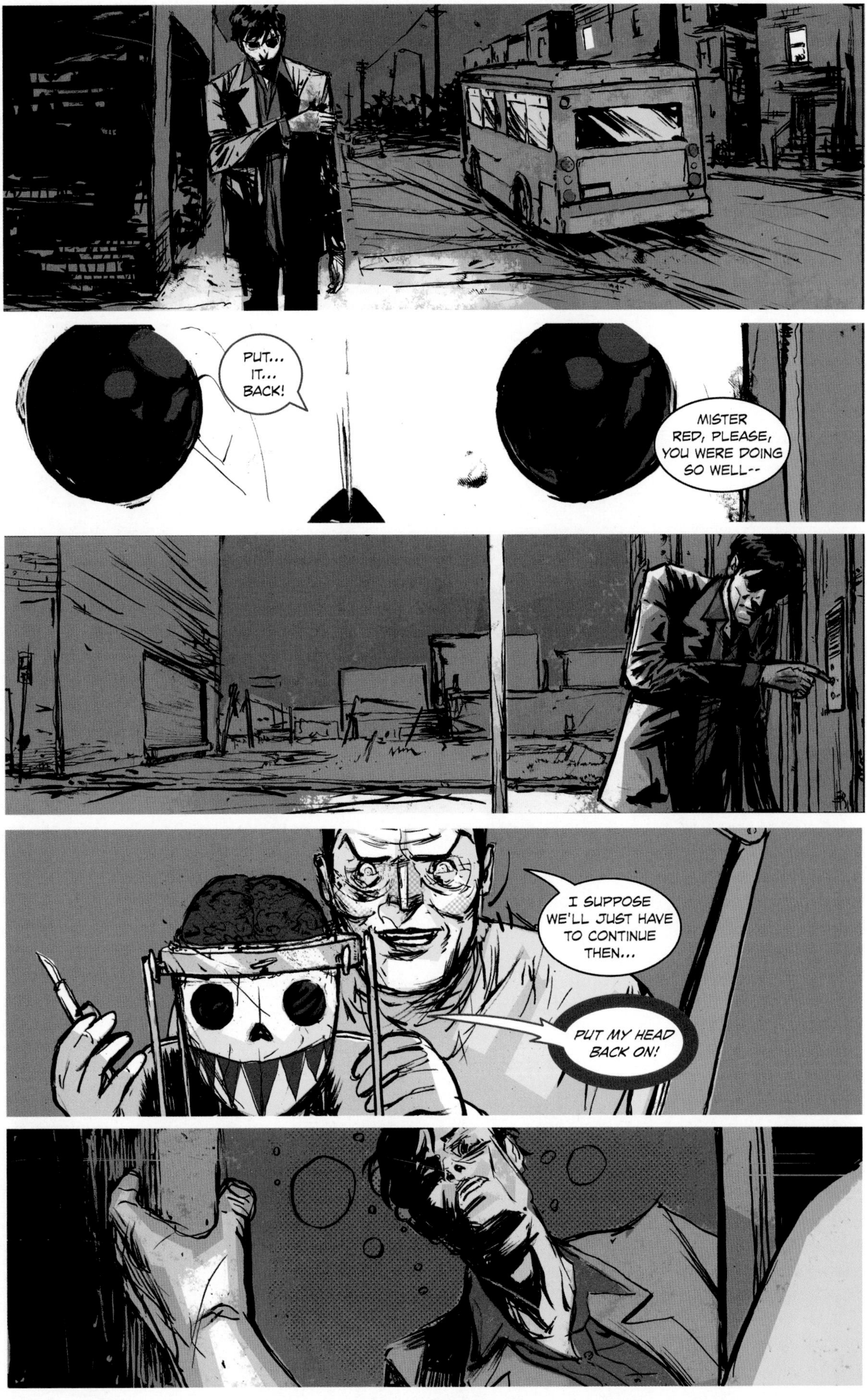
PUT... IT... BACK!
MISTER RED, PLEASE, YOU WERE DOING SO WELL--
I SUPPOSE WE'LL JUST HAVE TO CONTINUE THEN...
PUT MY HEAD BACK ON!

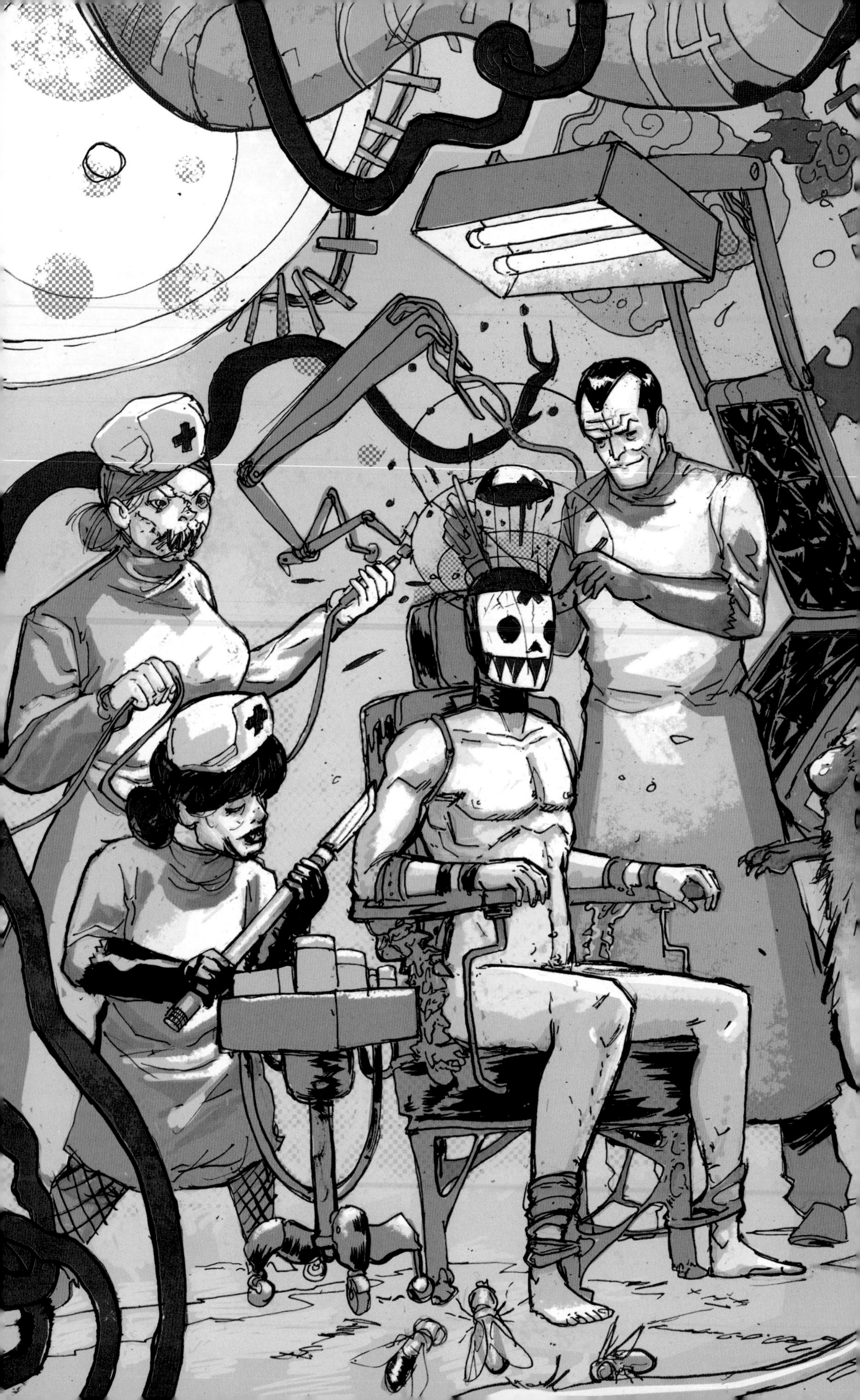

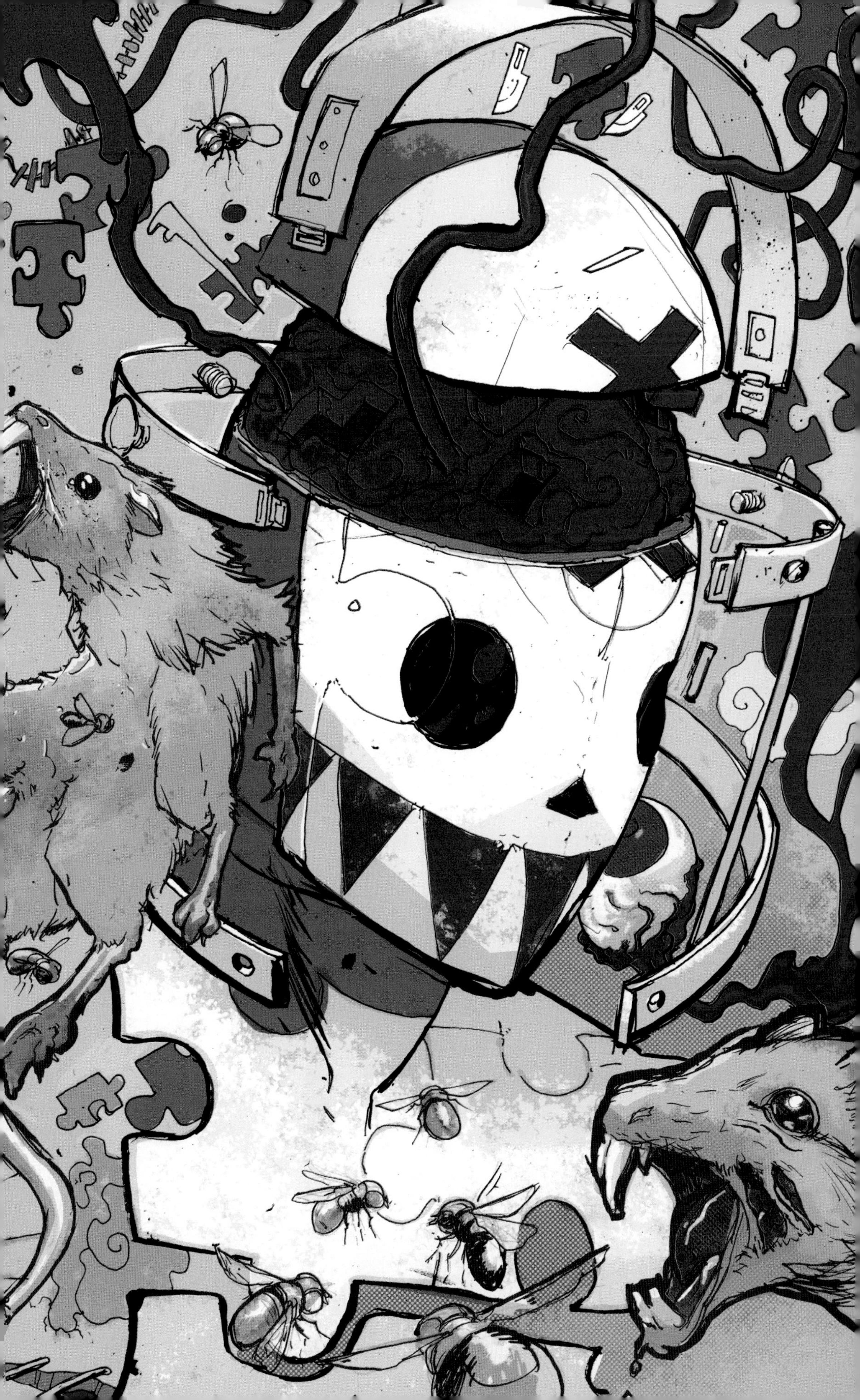

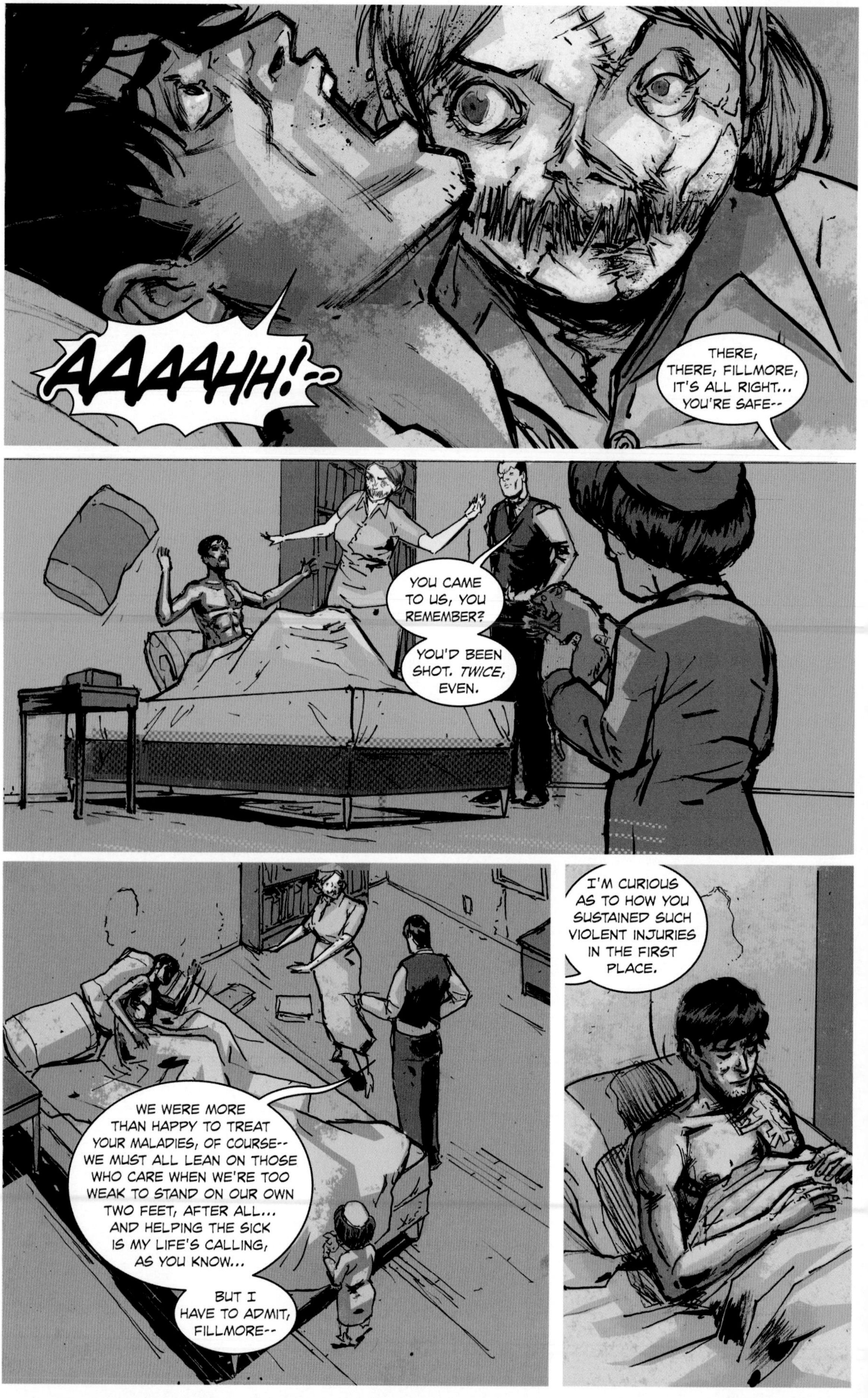
AAAAHH!--
THERE, THERE, FILLMORE, IT'S ALL RIGHT... YOU'RE SAFE--
YOU CAME TO US, YOU REMEMBER?
YOU'D BEEN SHOT. *TWICE,* EVEN.
WE WERE MORE THAN HAPPY TO TREAT YOUR MALADIES, OF COURSE-- WE MUST ALL LEAN ON THOSE WHO CARE WHEN WE'RE TOO WEAK TO STAND ON OUR OWN TWO FEET, AFTER ALL... AND HELPING THE SICK IS MY LIFE'S CALLING, AS YOU KNOW...
BUT I HAVE TO ADMIT, FILLMORE--
I'M CURIOUS AS TO HOW YOU SUSTAINED SUCH VIOLENT INJURIES IN THE FIRST PLACE.

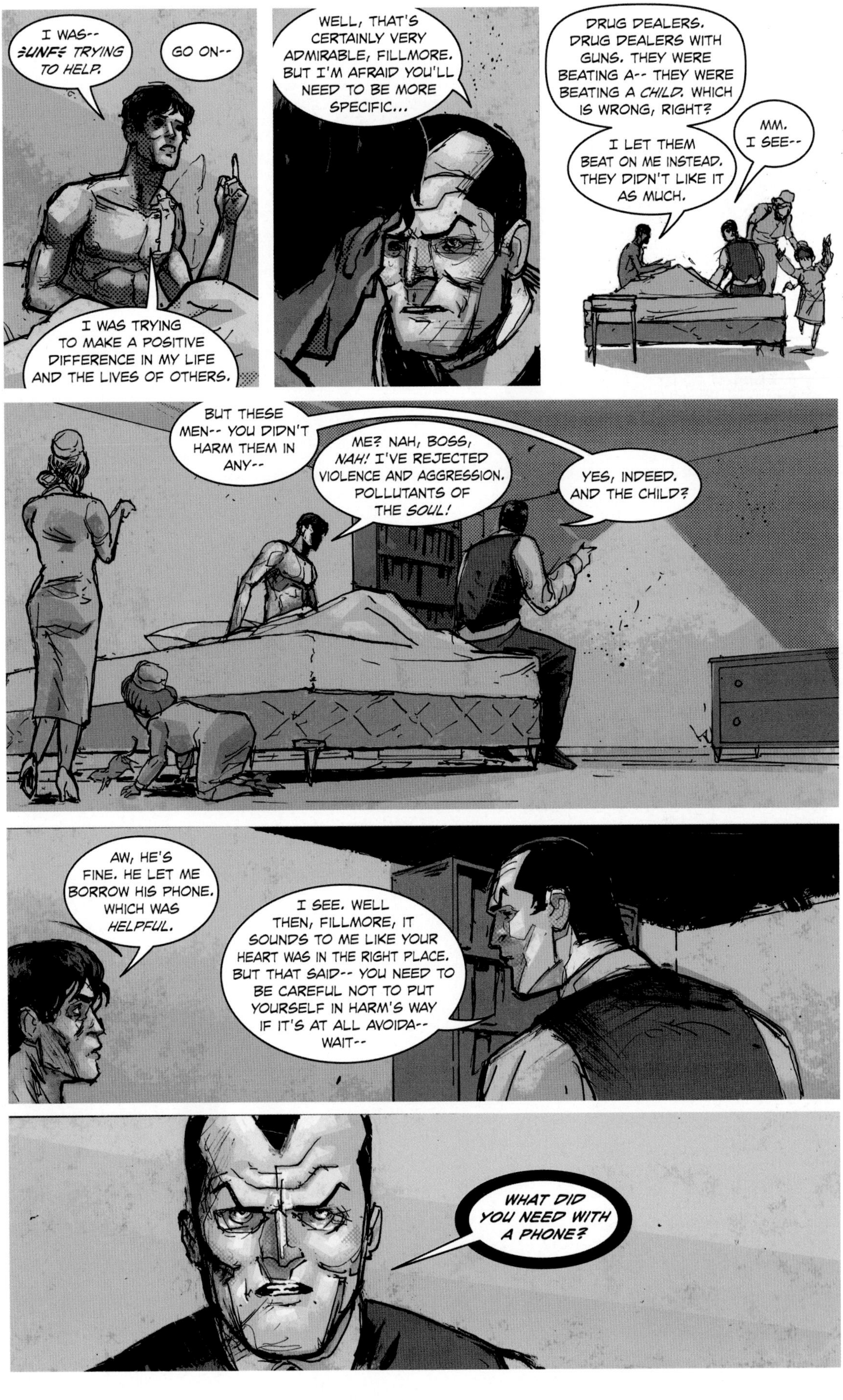

I WAS-- ≈UNF≈ TRYING TO HELP.
GO ON--
I WAS TRYING TO MAKE A POSITIVE DIFFERENCE IN MY LIFE AND THE LIVES OF OTHERS.
WELL, THAT'S CERTAINLY VERY ADMIRABLE, FILLMORE. BUT I'M AFRAID YOU'LL NEED TO BE MORE SPECIFIC...
DRUG DEALERS. DRUG DEALERS WITH GUNS. THEY WERE BEATING A-- THEY WERE BEATING A CHILD. WHICH IS WRONG, RIGHT?
I LET THEM BEAT ON ME INSTEAD. THEY DIDN'T LIKE IT AS MUCH.
MM. I SEE--
BUT THESE MEN-- YOU DIDN'T HARM THEM IN ANY--
ME? NAH, BOSS, NAH! I'VE REJECTED VIOLENCE AND AGGRESSION. POLLUTANTS OF THE SOUL!
YES, INDEED. AND THE CHILD?
AW, HE'S FINE. HE LET ME BORROW HIS PHONE. WHICH WAS HELPFUL.
I SEE. WELL THEN, FILLMORE, IT SOUNDS TO ME LIKE YOUR HEART WAS IN THE RIGHT PLACE. BUT THAT SAID-- YOU NEED TO BE CAREFUL NOT TO PUT YOURSELF IN HARM'S WAY IF IT'S AT ALL AVOIDA-- WAIT--
WHAT DID YOU NEED WITH A PHONE?

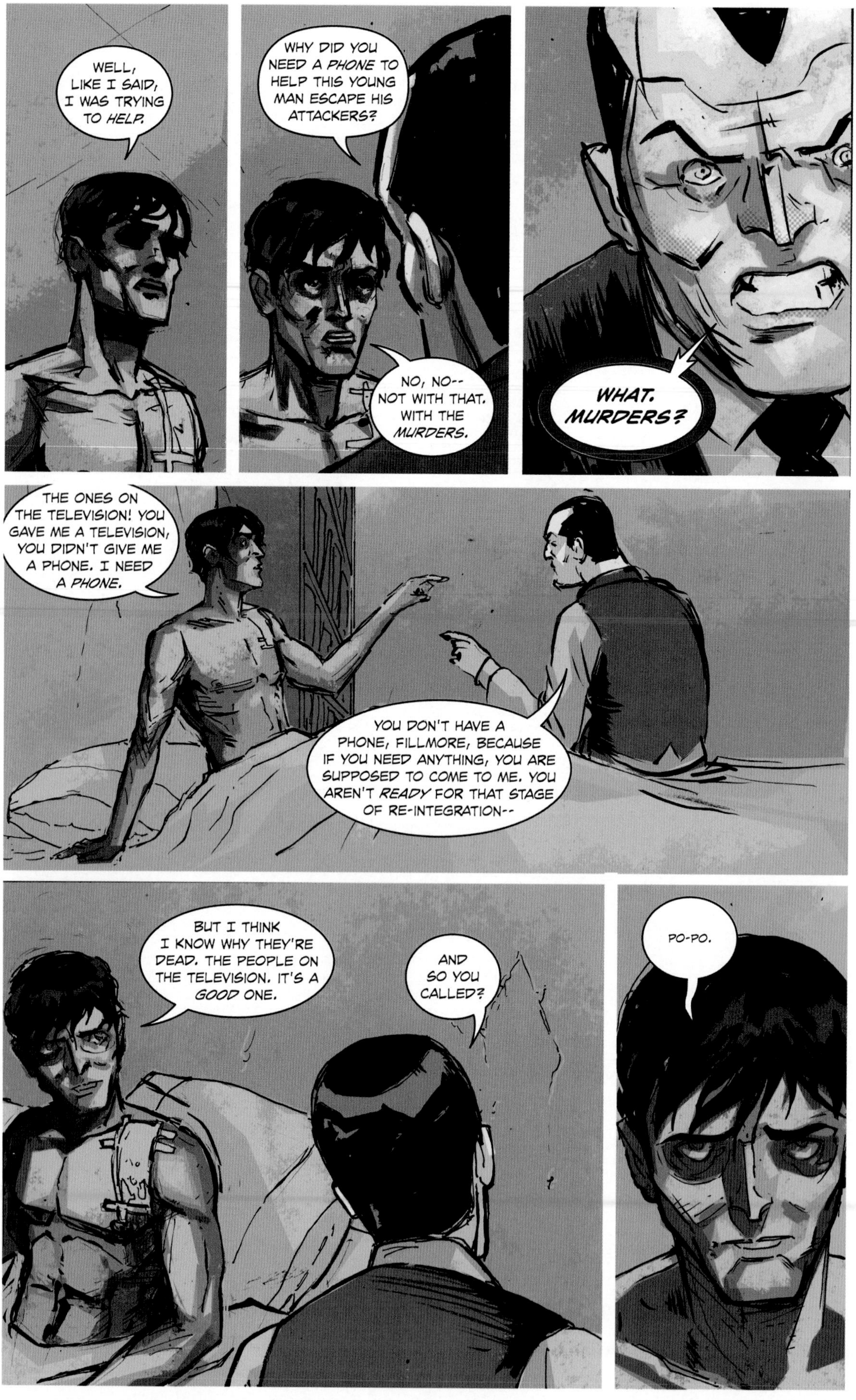
WELL, LIKE I SAID, I WAS TRYING TO *HELP.*
WHY DID YOU NEED A *PHONE* TO HELP THIS YOUNG MAN ESCAPE HIS ATTACKERS?
NO, NO-- NOT WITH THAT. WITH THE *MURDERS.*
WHAT. MURDERS?
THE ONES ON THE TELEVISION! YOU GAVE ME A TELEVISION, YOU DIDN'T GIVE ME A PHONE. I NEED A *PHONE.*
YOU DON'T HAVE A PHONE, FILLMORE, BECAUSE IF YOU NEED ANYTHING, YOU ARE SUPPOSED TO COME TO ME. YOU AREN'T *READY* FOR THAT STAGE OF RE-INTEGRATION--
BUT I THINK I KNOW WHY THEY'RE DEAD. THE PEOPLE ON THE TELEVISION. IT'S A *GOOD* ONE.
AND SO YOU CALLED?
PO-PO.

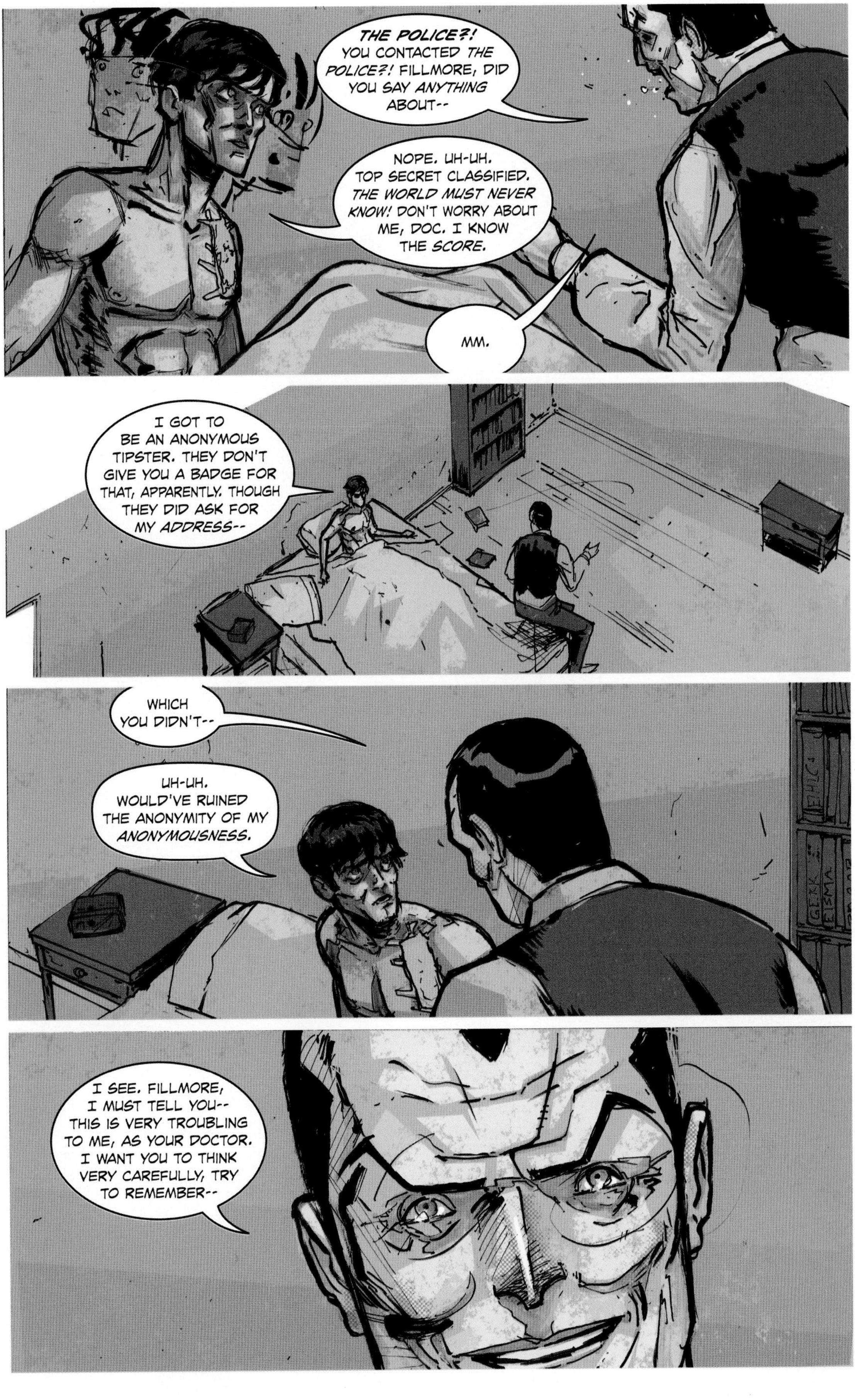
THE POLICE?! YOU CONTACTED *THE POLICE?!* FILLMORE, DID YOU SAY *ANYTHING* ABOUT--
NOPE. UH-UH. TOP SECRET CLASSIFIED. *THE WORLD MUST NEVER KNOW!* DON'T WORRY ABOUT ME, DOC. I KNOW THE *SCORE.*
MM.
I GOT TO BE AN ANONYMOUS TIPSTER. THEY DON'T GIVE YOU A BADGE FOR THAT, APPARENTLY. THOUGH THEY DID ASK FOR MY *ADDRESS*--
WHICH YOU DIDN'T--
UH-UH. WOULD'VE RUINED THE ANONYMITY OF MY *ANONYMOUSNESS.*
I SEE. FILLMORE, I MUST TELL YOU-- THIS IS VERY TROUBLING TO ME, AS YOUR DOCTOR. I WANT YOU TO THINK VERY CAREFULLY, TRY TO REMEMBER--

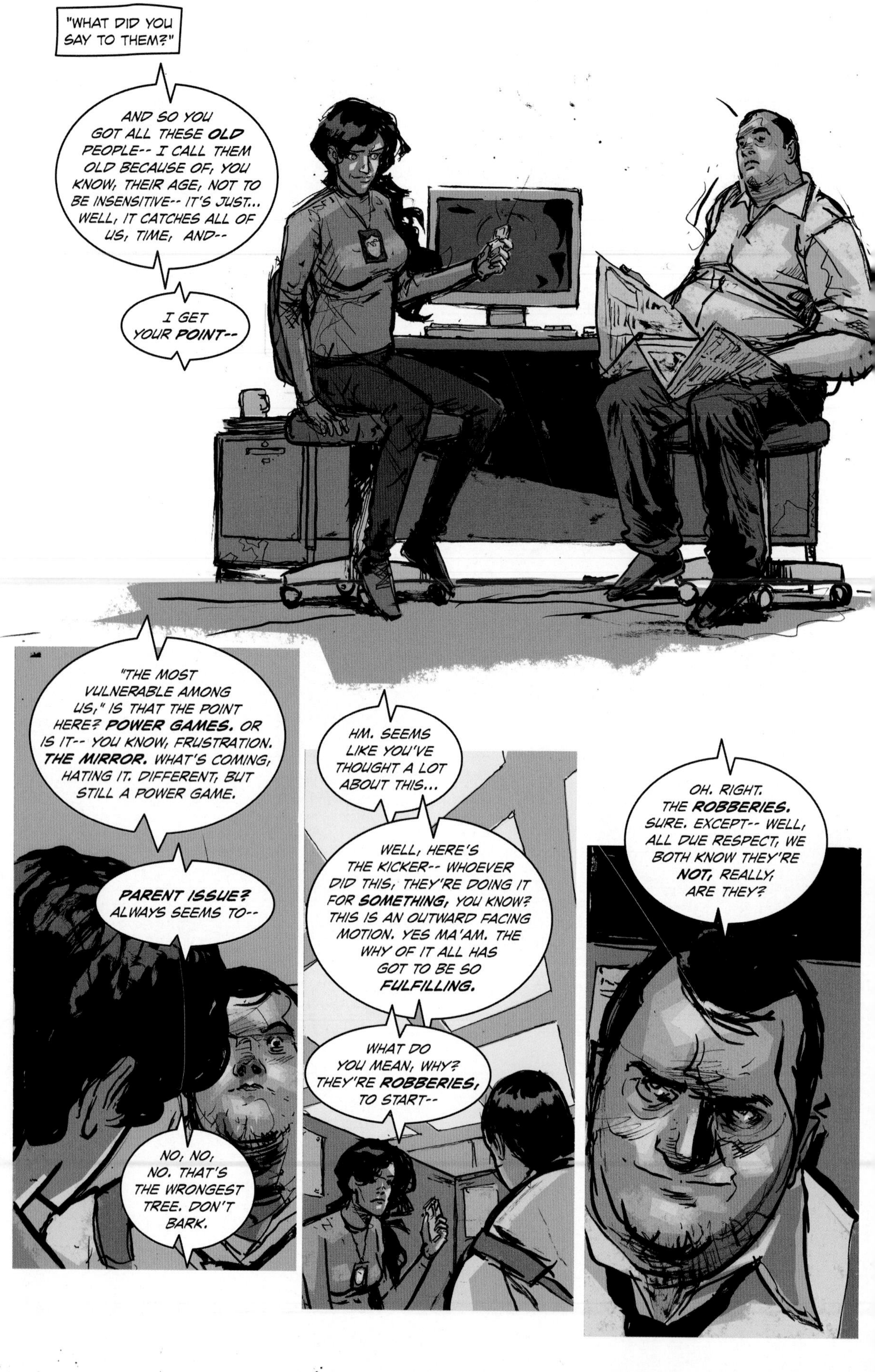
"WHAT DID YOU SAY TO THEM?"
AND SO YOU GOT ALL THESE OLD PEOPLE-- I CALL THEM OLD BECAUSE OF, YOU KNOW, THEIR AGE, NOT TO BE INSENSITIVE-- IT'S JUST... WELL, IT CATCHES ALL OF US, TIME, AND--
I GET YOUR POINT--
"THE MOST VULNERABLE AMONG US," IS THAT THE POINT HERE? POWER GAMES. OR IS IT-- YOU KNOW, FRUSTRATION. THE MIRROR. WHAT'S COMING, HATING IT. DIFFERENT, BUT STILL A POWER GAME.
PARENT ISSUE? ALWAYS SEEMS TO--
NO, NO, NO. THAT'S THE WRONGEST TREE. DON'T BARK.
HM. SEEMS LIKE YOU'VE THOUGHT A LOT ABOUT THIS...
WELL, HERE'S THE KICKER-- WHOEVER DID THIS, THEY'RE DOING IT FOR SOMETHING, YOU KNOW? THIS IS AN OUTWARD FACING MOTION. YES MA'AM. THE WHY OF IT ALL HAS GOT TO BE SO FULFILLING.
WHAT DO YOU MEAN, WHY? THEY'RE ROBBERIES, TO START--
OH. RIGHT. THE ROBBERIES. SURE. EXCEPT-- WELL, ALL DUE RESPECT, WE BOTH KNOW THEY'RE NOT, REALLY, ARE THEY?

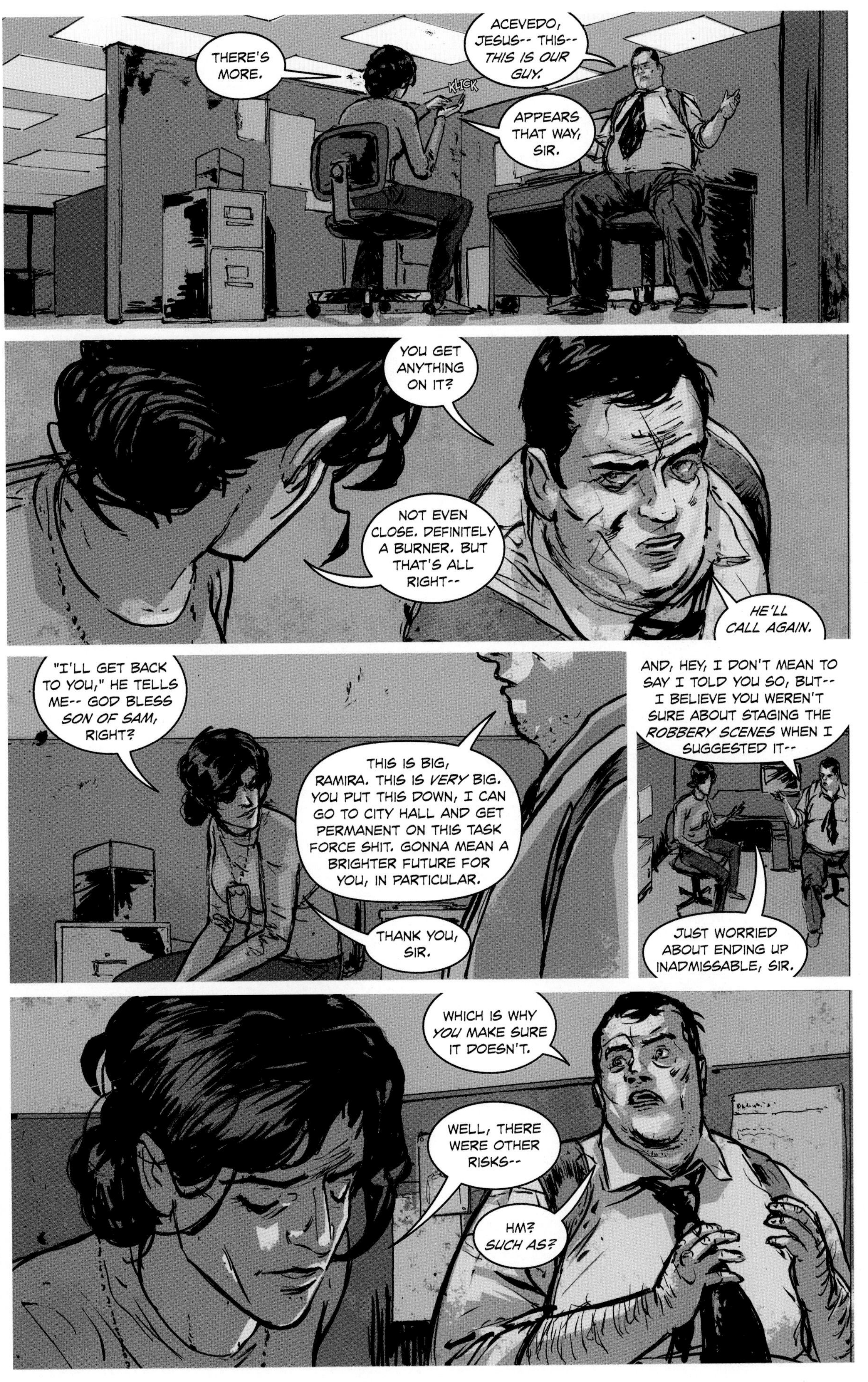
THERE'S MORE.
ACEVEDO, JESUS-- THIS-- THIS IS OUR GUY.
KLICK
APPEARS THAT WAY, SIR.
YOU GET ANYTHING ON IT?
NOT EVEN CLOSE. DEFINITELY A BURNER. BUT THAT'S ALL RIGHT--
HE'LL CALL AGAIN.
"I'LL GET BACK TO YOU," HE TELLS ME-- GOD BLESS SON OF SAM, RIGHT?
THIS IS BIG, RAMIRA. THIS IS VERY BIG. YOU PUT THIS DOWN, I CAN GO TO CITY HALL AND GET PERMANENT ON THIS TASK FORCE SHIT. GONNA MEAN A BRIGHTER FUTURE FOR YOU, IN PARTICULAR.
THANK YOU, SIR.
AND, HEY, I DON'T MEAN TO SAY I TOLD YOU SO, BUT-- I BELIEVE YOU WEREN'T SURE ABOUT STAGING THE ROBBERY SCENES WHEN I SUGGESTED IT--
JUST WORRIED ABOUT ENDING UP INADMISSABLE, SIR.
WHICH IS WHY YOU MAKE SURE IT DOESN'T.
WELL, THERE WERE OTHER RISKS--
HM? SUCH AS?

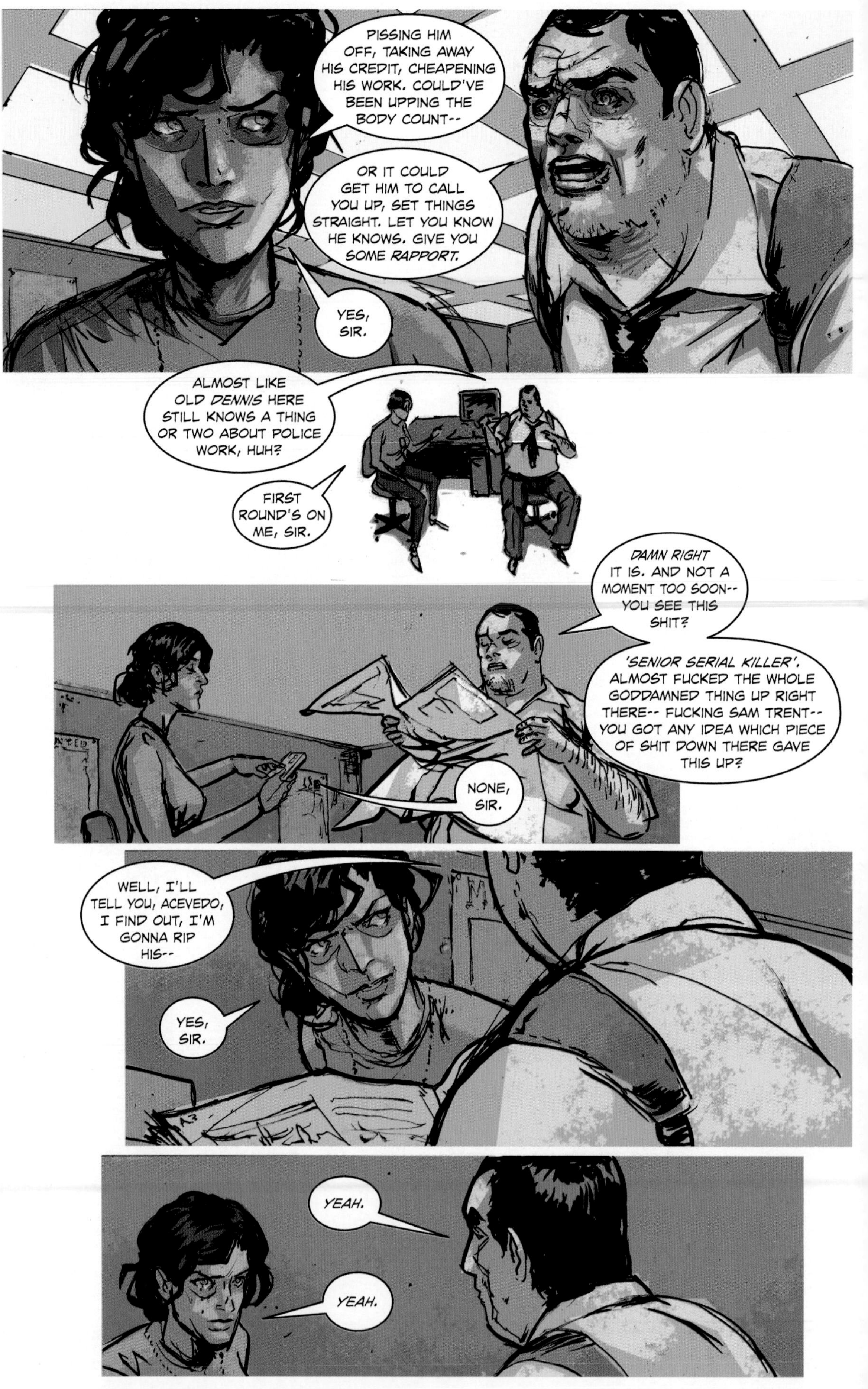
PISSING HIM OFF, TAKING AWAY HIS CREDIT, CHEAPENING HIS WORK. COULD'VE BEEN UPPING THE BODY COUNT--
OR IT COULD GET HIM TO CALL YOU UP, SET THINGS STRAIGHT. LET YOU KNOW HE KNOWS. GIVE YOU SOME *RAPPORT.*
YES, SIR.
ALMOST LIKE OLD *DENNIS* HERE STILL KNOWS A THING OR TWO ABOUT POLICE WORK, HUH?
FIRST ROUND'S ON ME, SIR.
DAMN RIGHT IT IS. AND NOT A MOMENT TOO SOON-- YOU SEE THIS SHIT?
'SENIOR SERIAL KILLER'. ALMOST FUCKED THE WHOLE GODDAMNED THING UP RIGHT THERE-- FUCKING SAM TRENT-- YOU GOT ANY IDEA WHICH PIECE OF SHIT DOWN THERE GAVE THIS UP?
NONE, SIR.
WELL, I'LL TELL YOU, ACEVEDO, I FIND OUT, I'M GONNA RIP HIS--
YES, SIR.
YEAH.
YEAH.

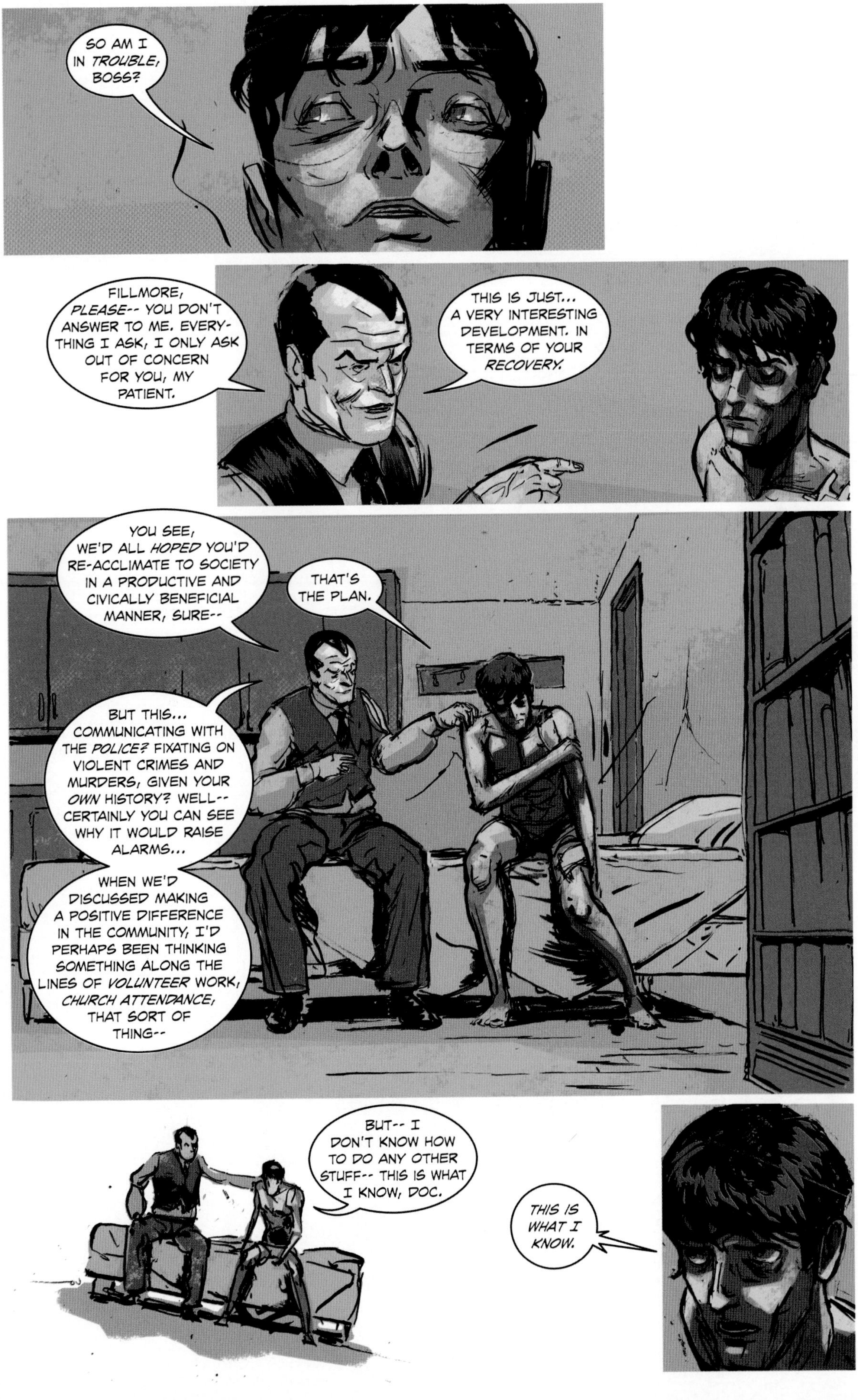
SO AM I IN TROUBLE, BOSS?
FILLMORE, PLEASE-- YOU DON'T ANSWER TO ME. EVERYTHING I ASK, I ONLY ASK OUT OF CONCERN FOR YOU, MY PATIENT.
THIS IS JUST... A VERY INTERESTING DEVELOPMENT. IN TERMS OF YOUR RECOVERY.
YOU SEE, WE'D ALL HOPED YOU'D RE-ACCLIMATE TO SOCIETY IN A PRODUCTIVE AND CIVICALLY BENEFICIAL MANNER, SURE--
THAT'S THE PLAN.
BUT THIS... COMMUNICATING WITH THE POLICE? FIXATING ON VIOLENT CRIMES AND MURDERS, GIVEN YOUR OWN HISTORY? WELL-- CERTAINLY YOU CAN SEE WHY IT WOULD RAISE ALARMS...
WHEN WE'D DISCUSSED MAKING A POSITIVE DIFFERENCE IN THE COMMUNITY, I'D PERHAPS BEEN THINKING SOMETHING ALONG THE LINES OF VOLUNTEER WORK, CHURCH ATTENDANCE, THAT SORT OF THING--
BUT-- I DON'T KNOW HOW TO DO ANY OTHER STUFF-- THIS IS WHAT I KNOW, DOC.
THIS IS WHAT I KNOW.

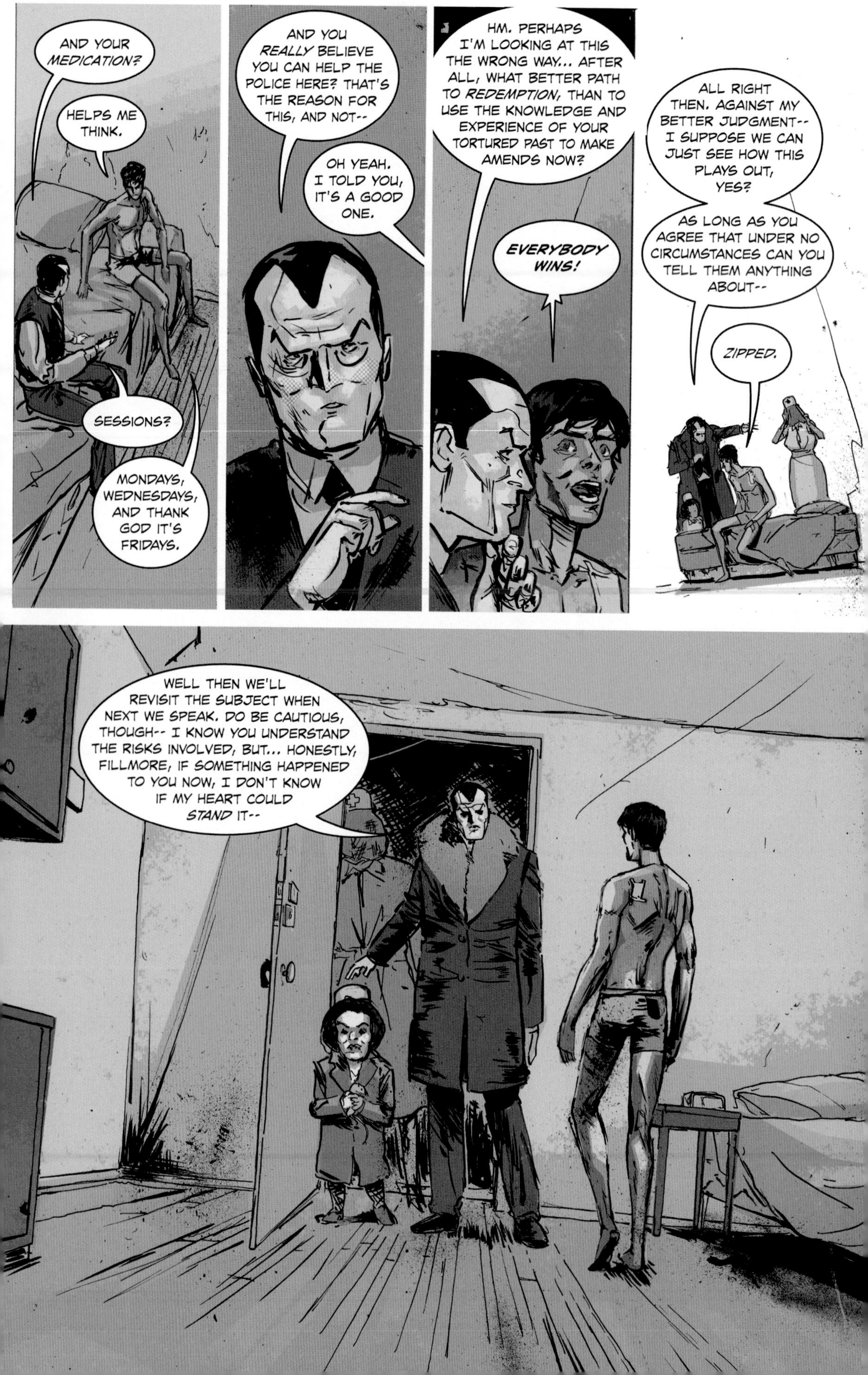

AND YOUR MEDICATION?
HELPS ME THINK.
SESSIONS?
MONDAYS, WEDNESDAYS, AND THANK GOD IT'S FRIDAYS.
AND YOU REALLY BELIEVE YOU CAN HELP THE POLICE HERE? THAT'S THE REASON FOR THIS, AND NOT--
OH YEAH. I TOLD YOU, IT'S A GOOD ONE.
HM. PERHAPS I'M LOOKING AT THIS THE WRONG WAY... AFTER ALL, WHAT BETTER PATH TO REDEMPTION, THAN TO USE THE KNOWLEDGE AND EXPERIENCE OF YOUR TORTURED PAST TO MAKE AMENDS NOW?
EVERYBODY WINS!
ALL RIGHT THEN. AGAINST MY BETTER JUDGMENT-- I SUPPOSE WE CAN JUST SEE HOW THIS PLAYS OUT, YES?
AS LONG AS YOU AGREE THAT UNDER NO CIRCUMSTANCES CAN YOU TELL THEM ANYTHING ABOUT--
ZIPPED.
WELL THEN WE'LL REVISIT THE SUBJECT WHEN NEXT WE SPEAK. DO BE CAUTIOUS, THOUGH-- I KNOW YOU UNDERSTAND THE RISKS INVOLVED, BUT... HONESTLY, FILLMORE, IF SOMETHING HAPPENED TO YOU NOW, I DON'T KNOW IF MY HEART COULD STAND IT--

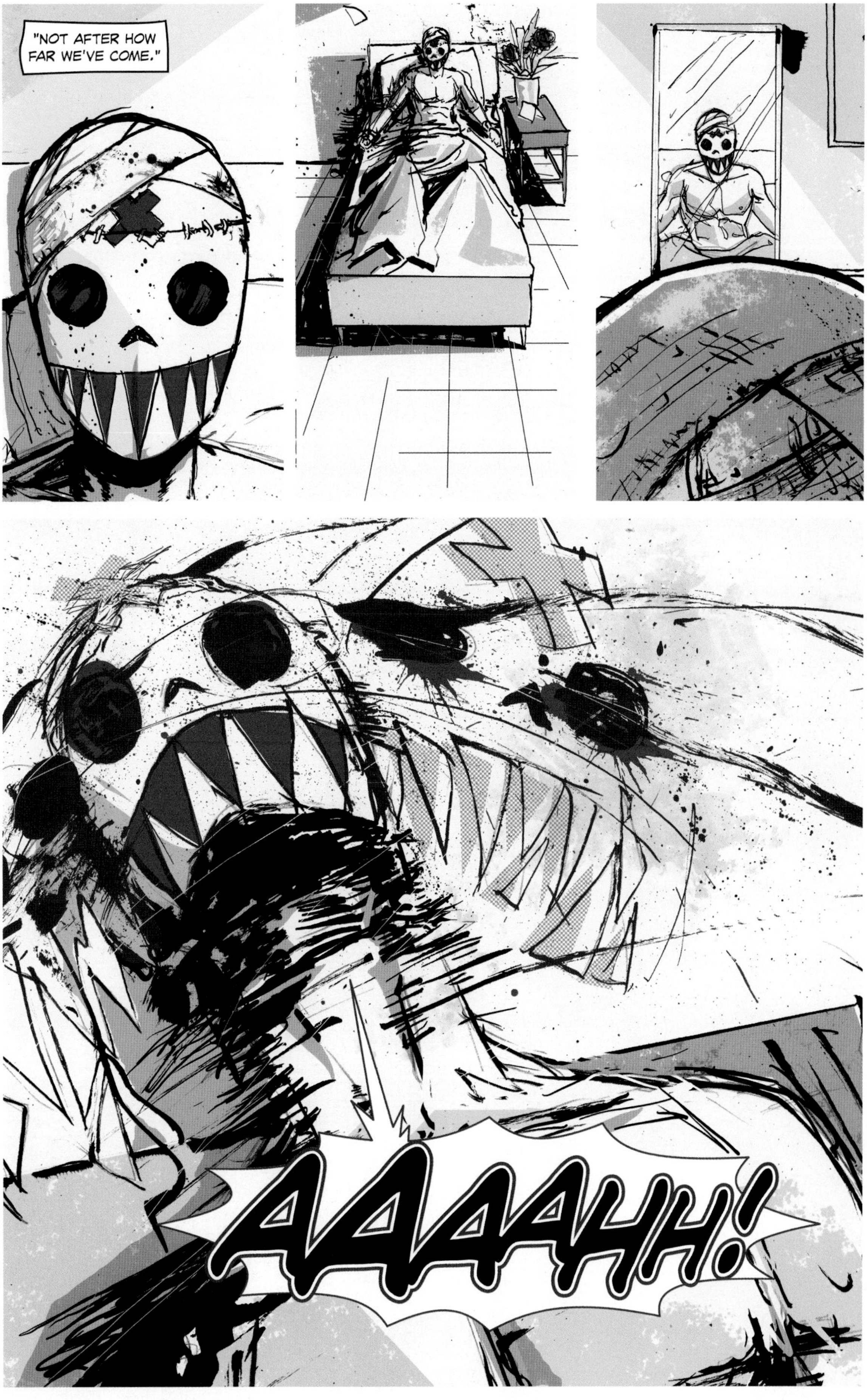
"NOT AFTER HOW FAR WE'VE COME."
AAAAHH!

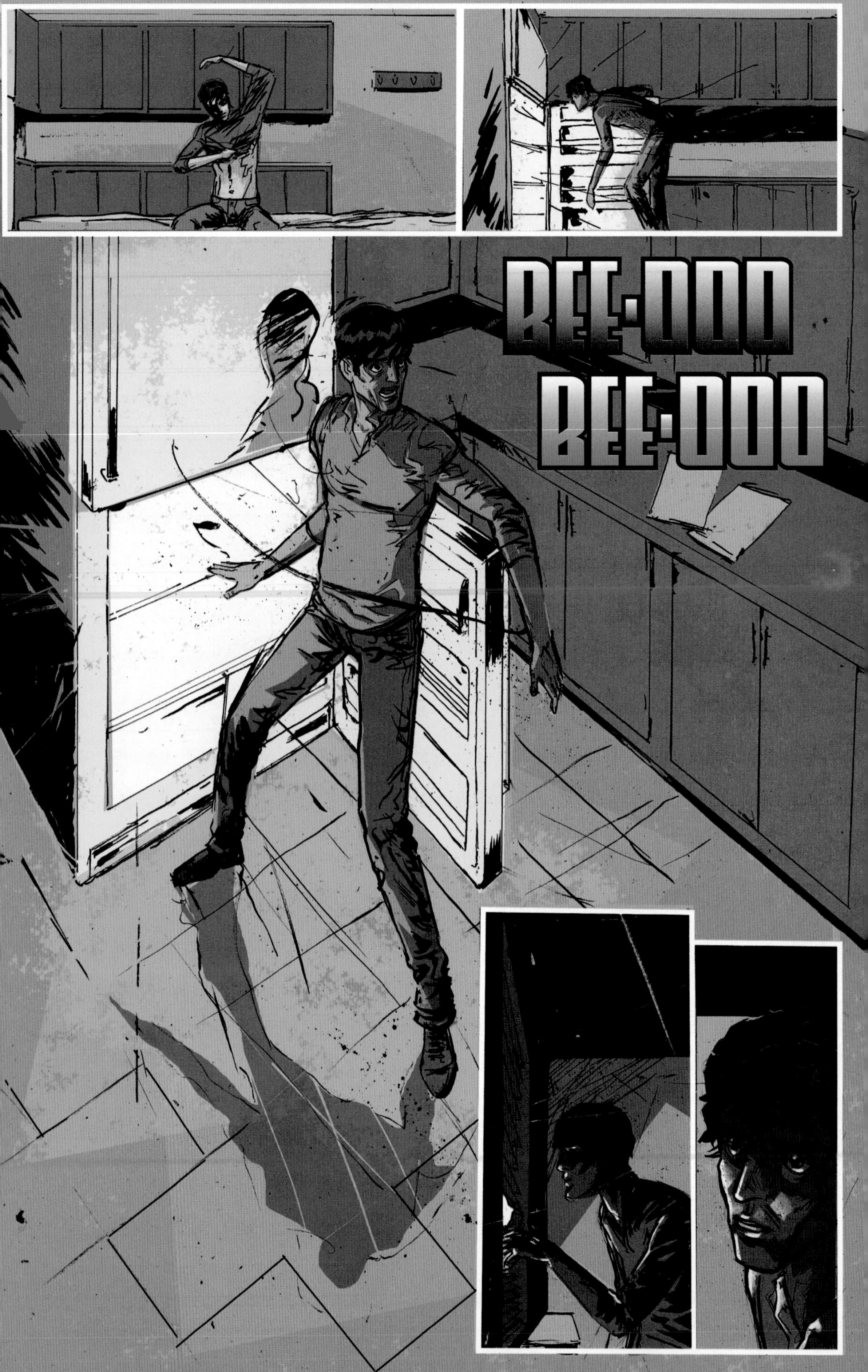
BEE-DOO
BEE-DOO

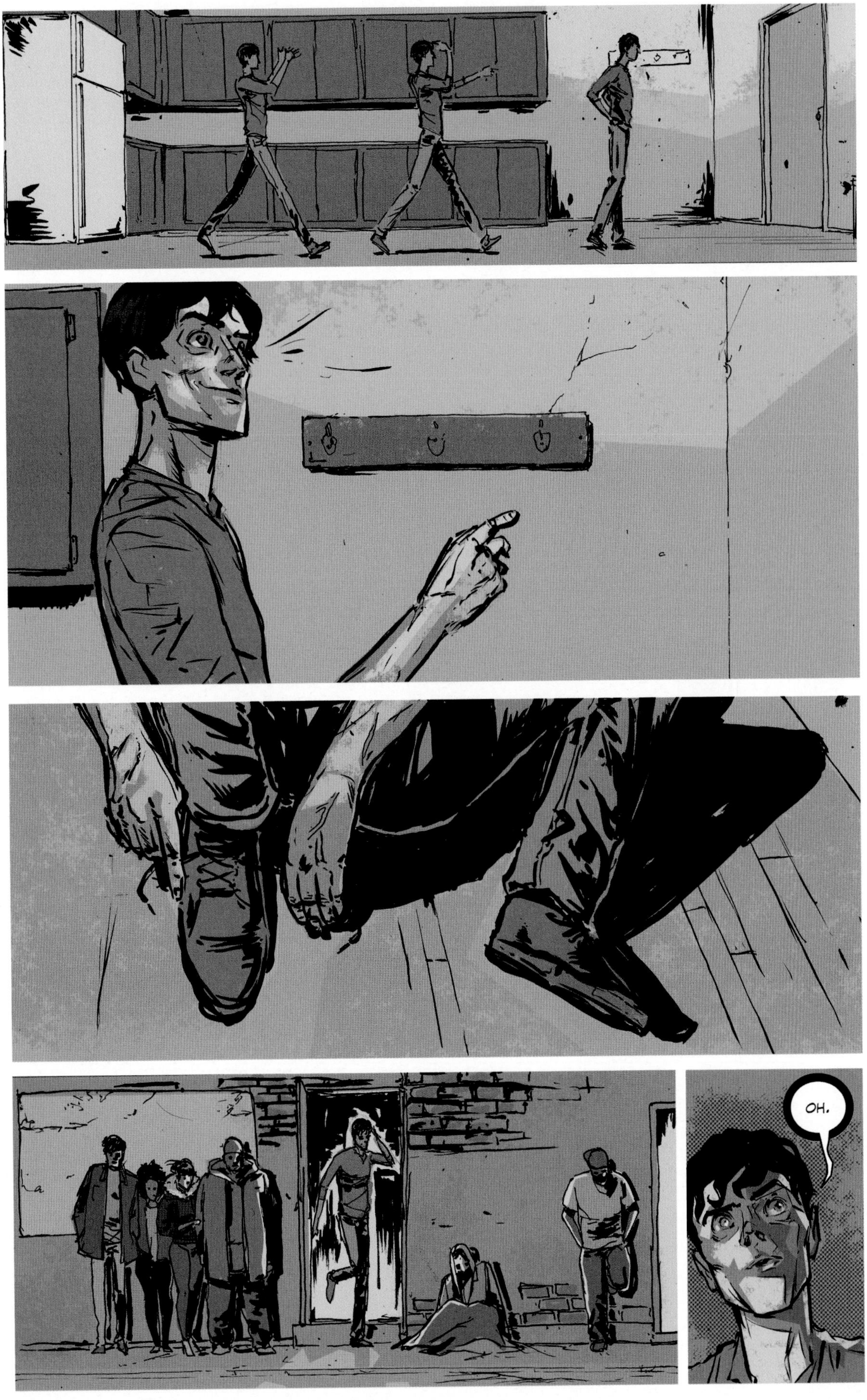
OH.

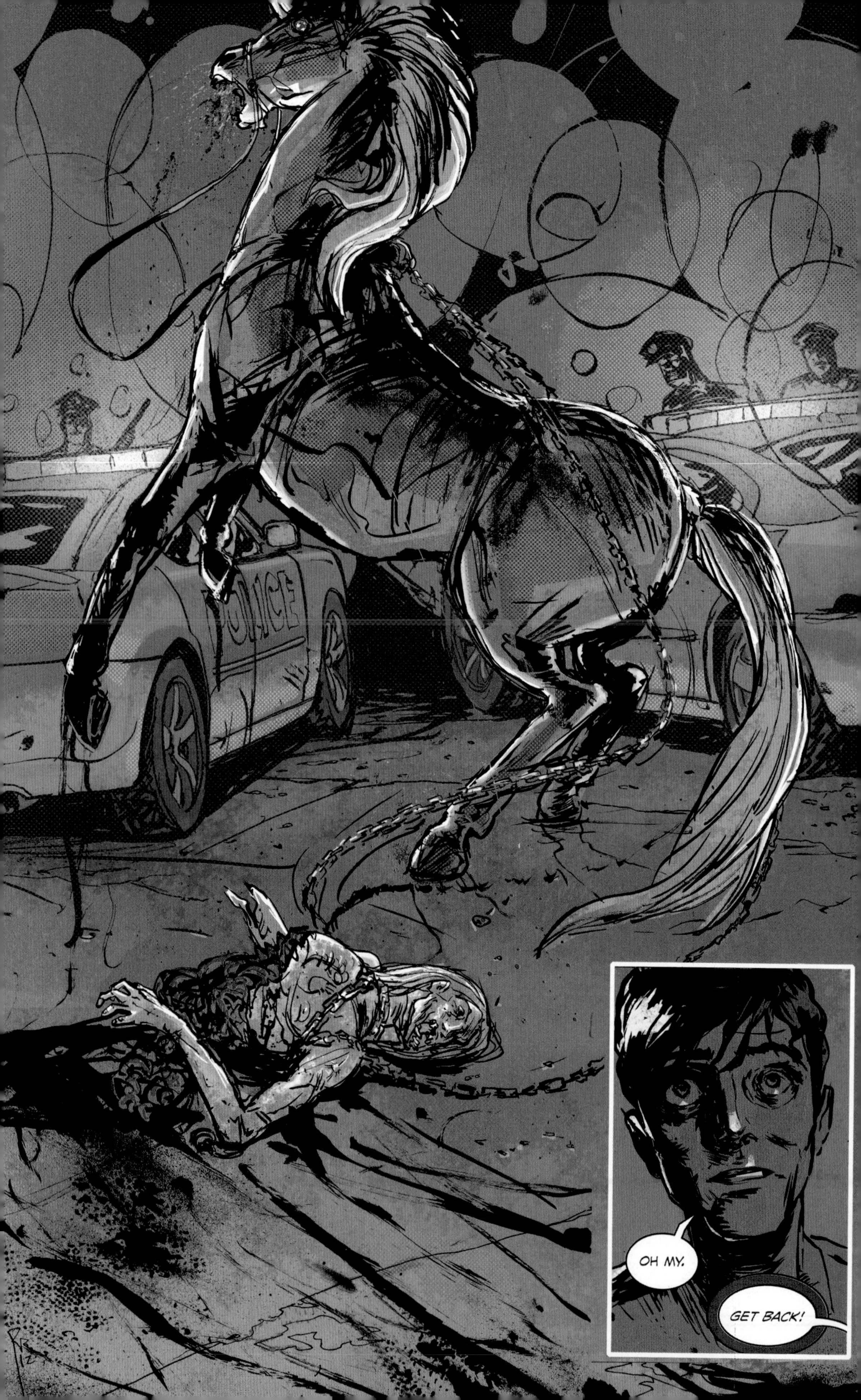
OH MY.
GET BACK!

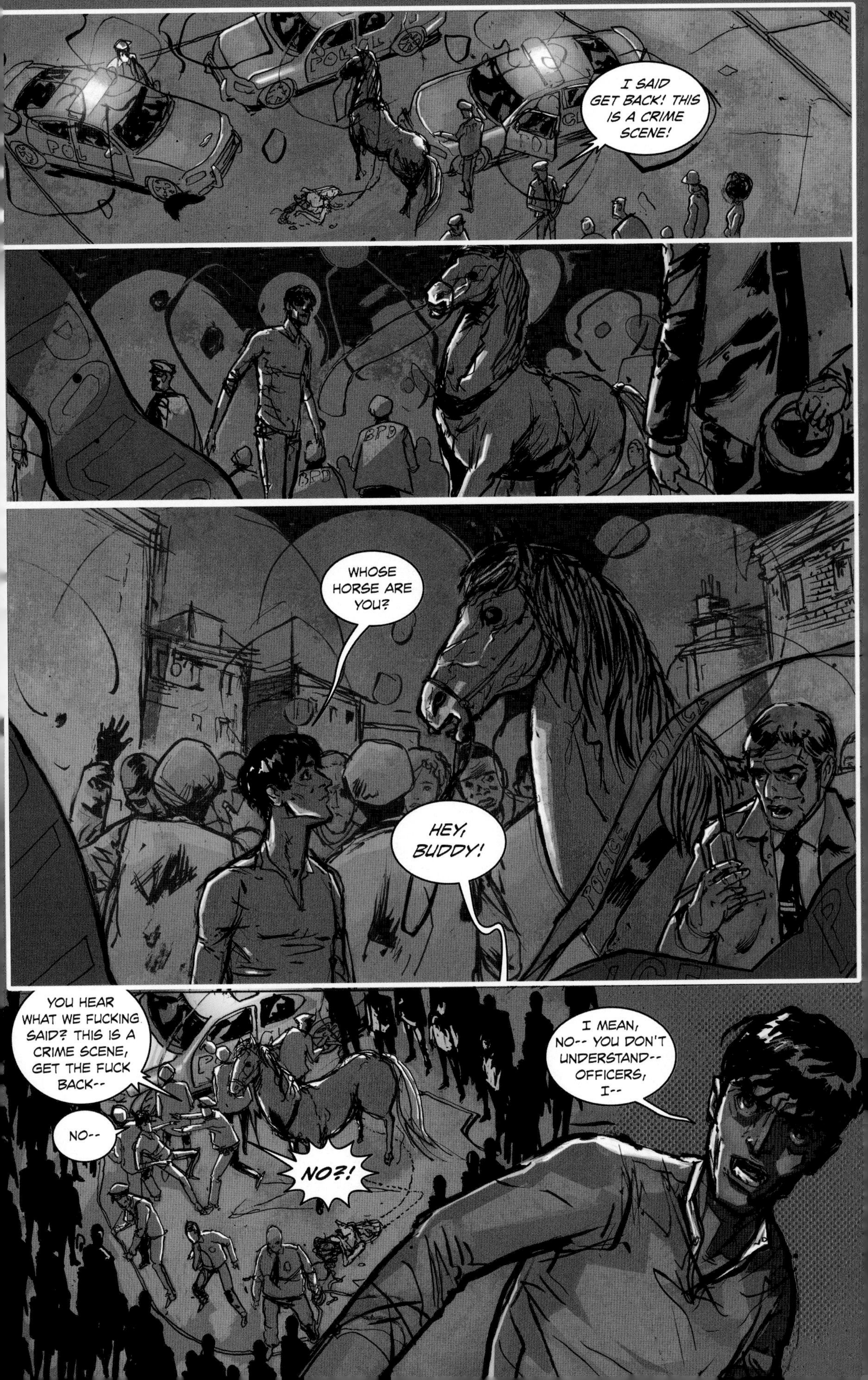
I SAID GET BACK! THIS IS A CRIME SCENE!
WHOSE HORSE ARE YOU?
HEY, BUDDY!
YOU HEAR WHAT WE FUCKING SAID? THIS IS A CRIME SCENE, GET THE FUCK BACK--
NO--
NO?!
I MEAN, NO-- YOU DON'T UNDERSTAND-- OFFICERS, I--

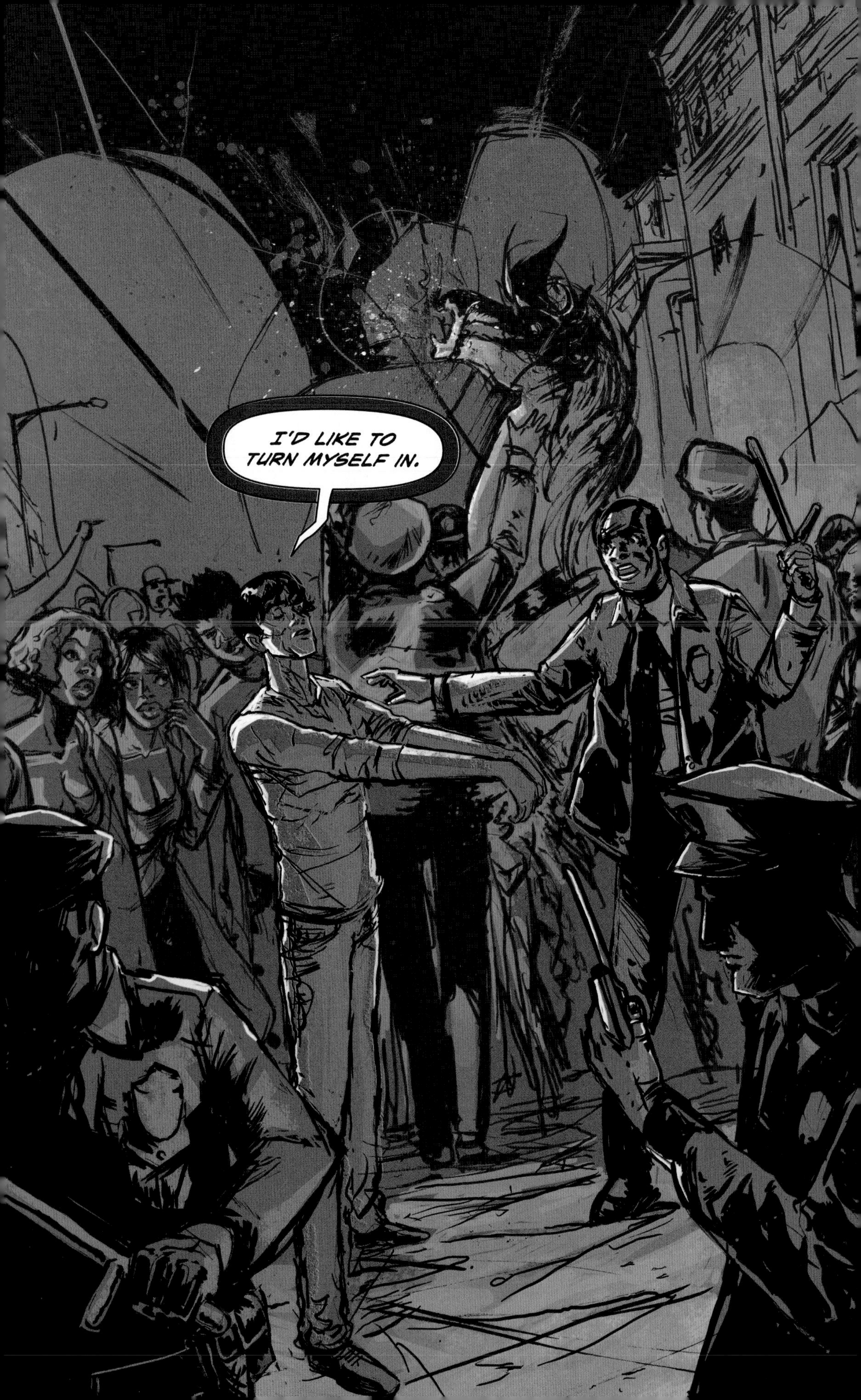
I'D LIKE TO TURN MYSELF IN.

3
CHAPTER

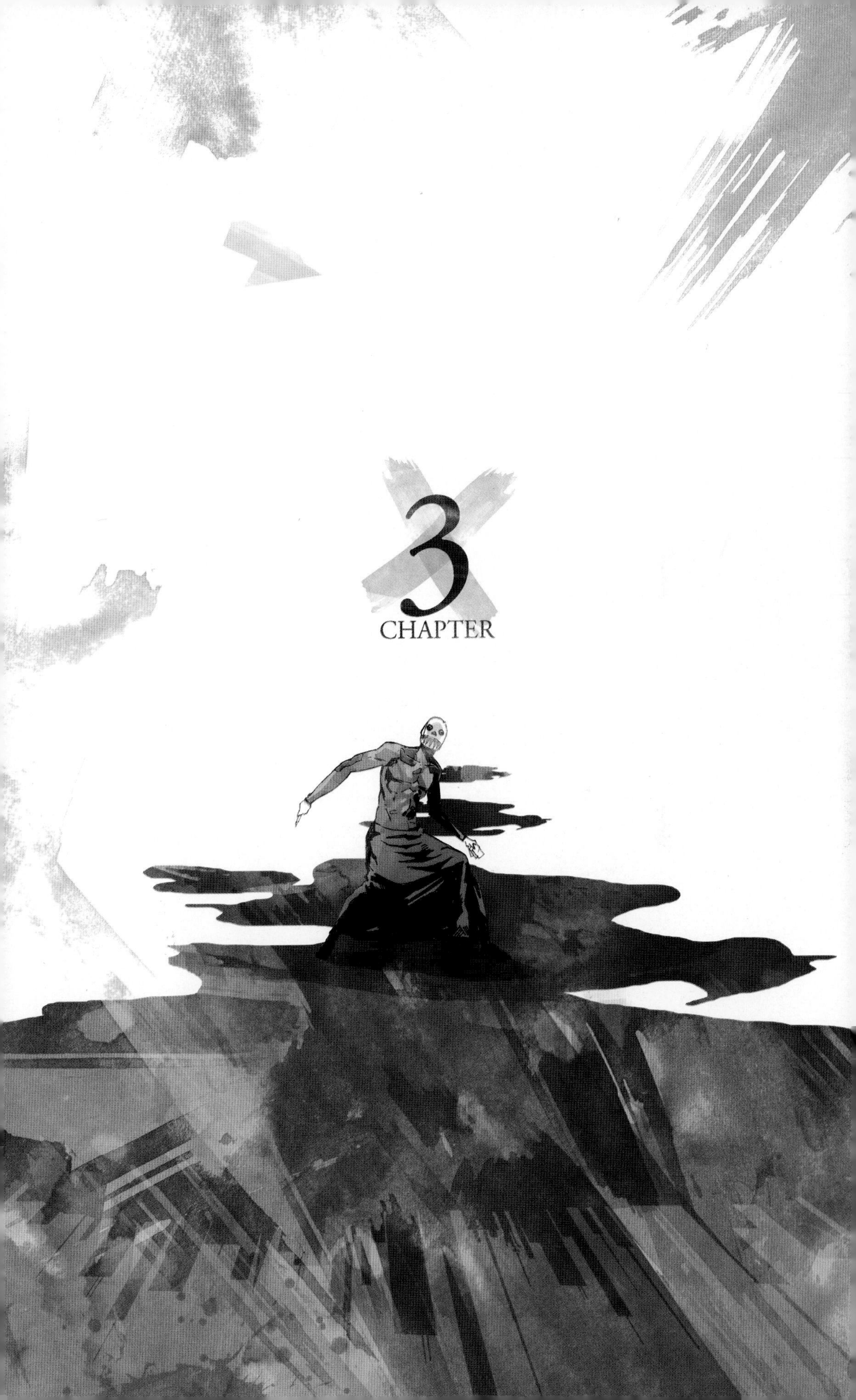

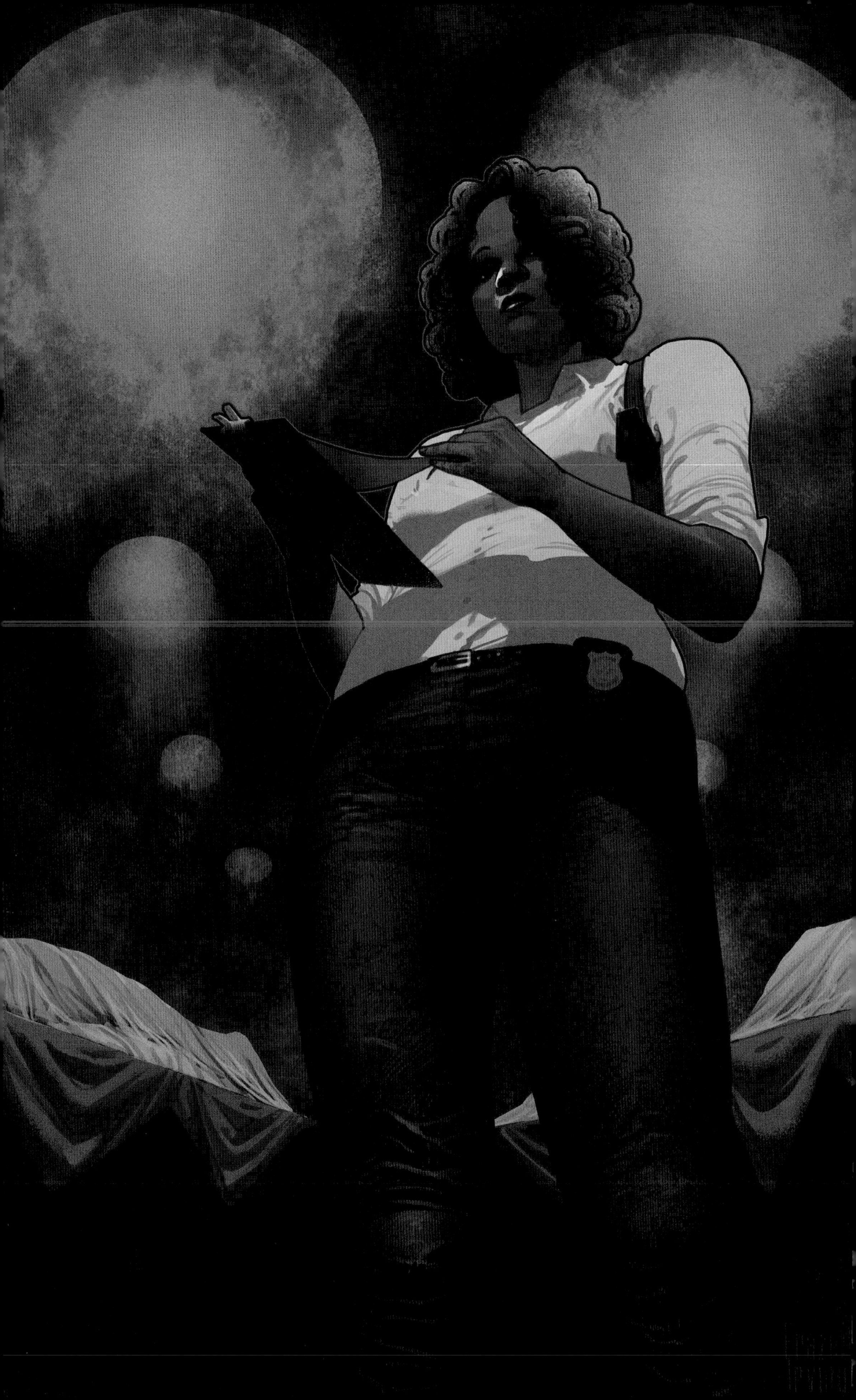

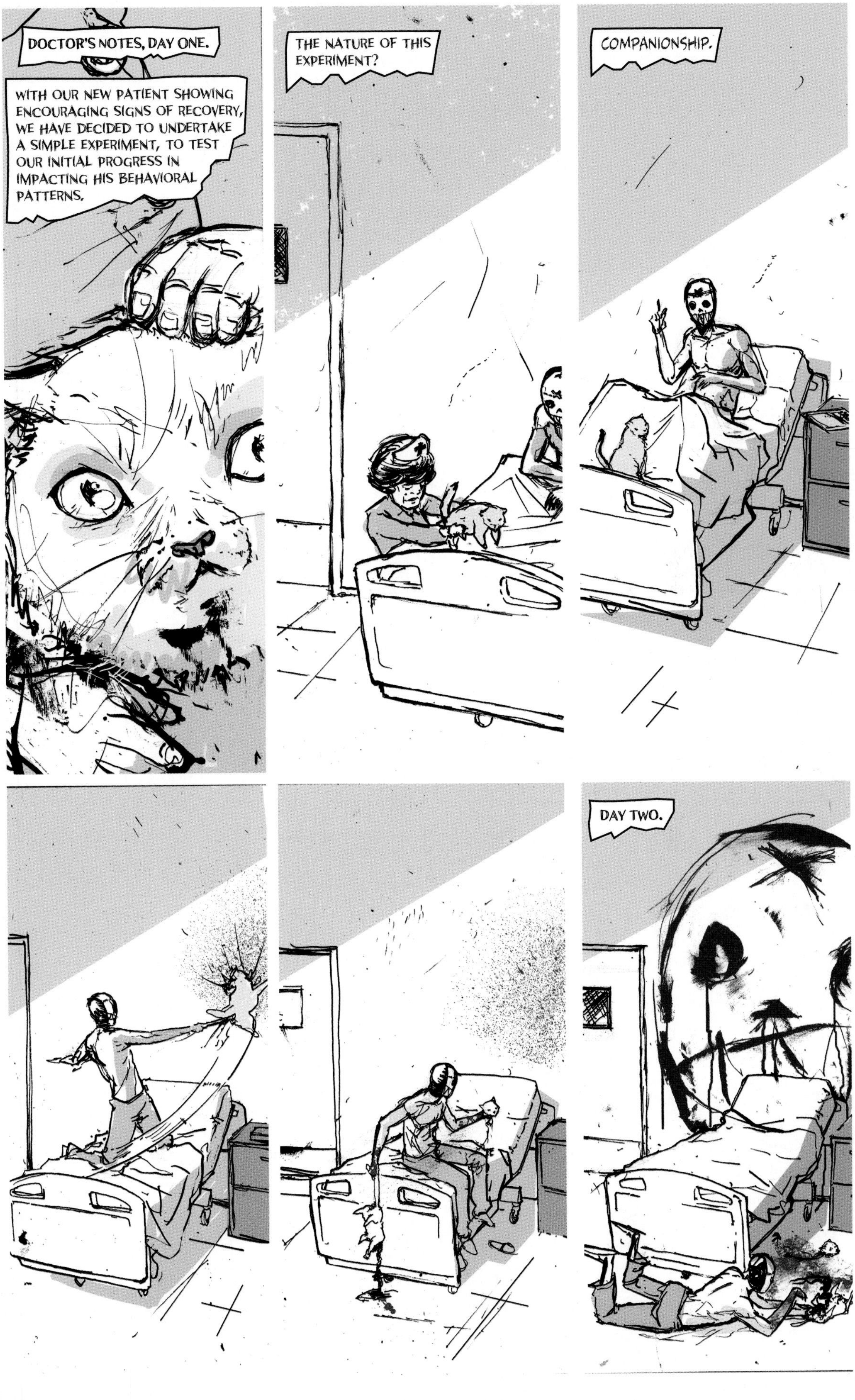
DOCTOR'S NOTES, DAY ONE.
WITH OUR NEW PATIENT SHOWING ENCOURAGING SIGNS OF RECOVERY, WE HAVE DECIDED TO UNDERTAKE A SIMPLE EXPERIMENT, TO TEST OUR INITIAL PROGRESS IN IMPACTING HIS BEHAVIORAL PATTERNS.
THE NATURE OF THIS EXPERIMENT?
COMPANIONSHIP.
DAY TWO.

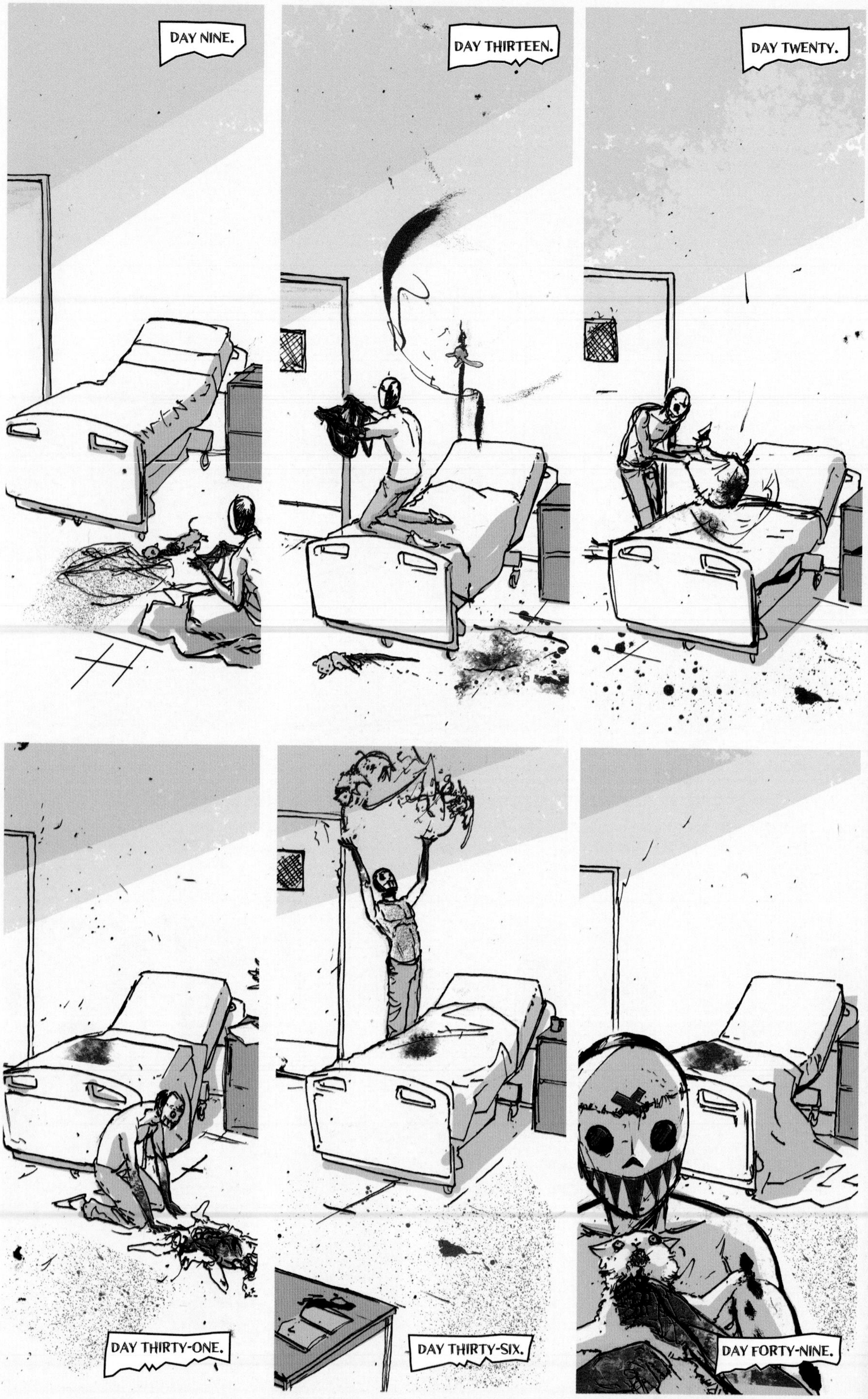
DAY NINE.
DAY THIRTEEN.
DAY TWENTY.
DAY THIRTY-ONE.
DAY THIRTY-SIX.
DAY FORTY-NINE.

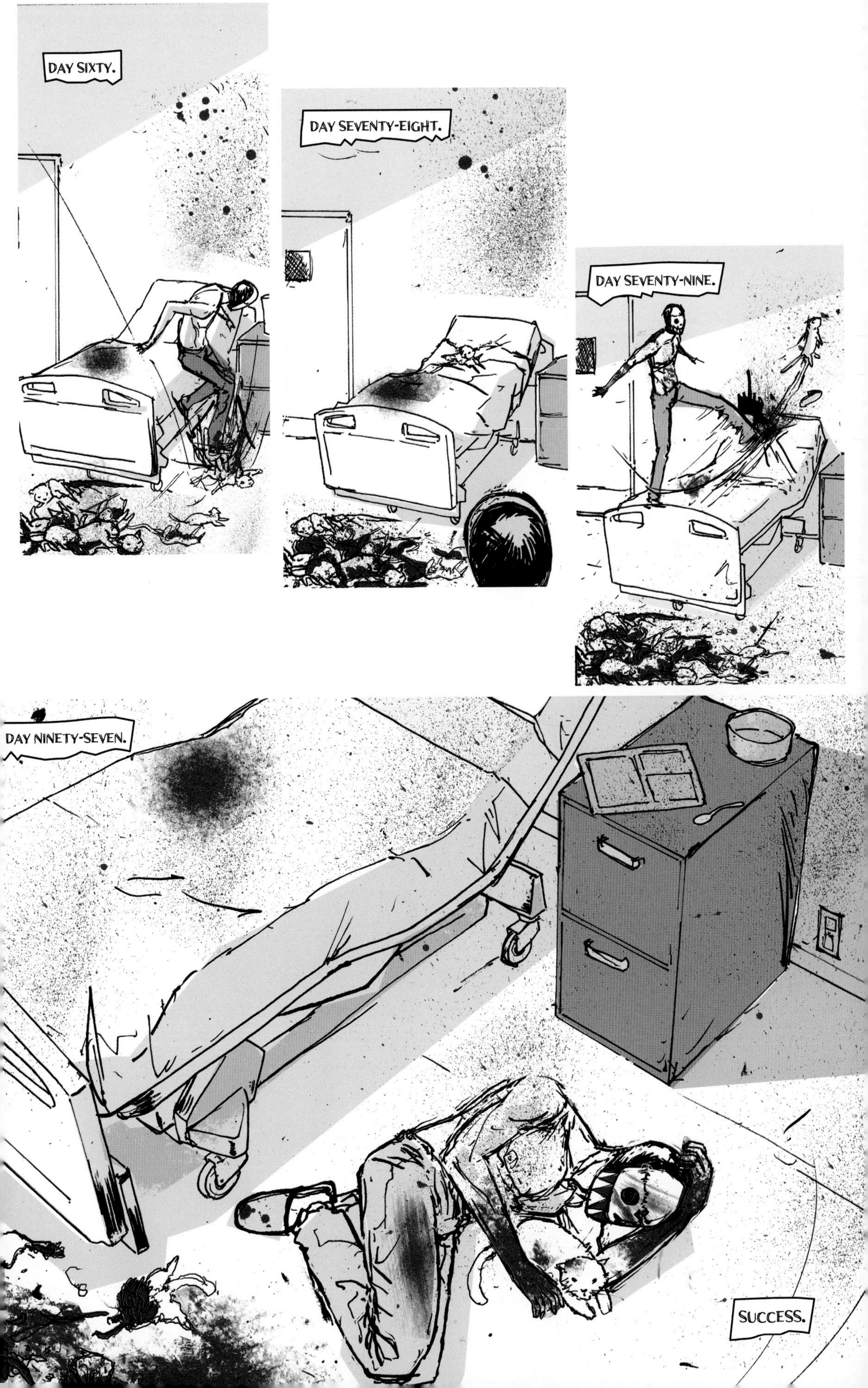
DAY SIXTY.
DAY SEVENTY-EIGHT.
DAY SEVENTY-NINE.
DAY NINETY-SEVEN.
SUCCESS.

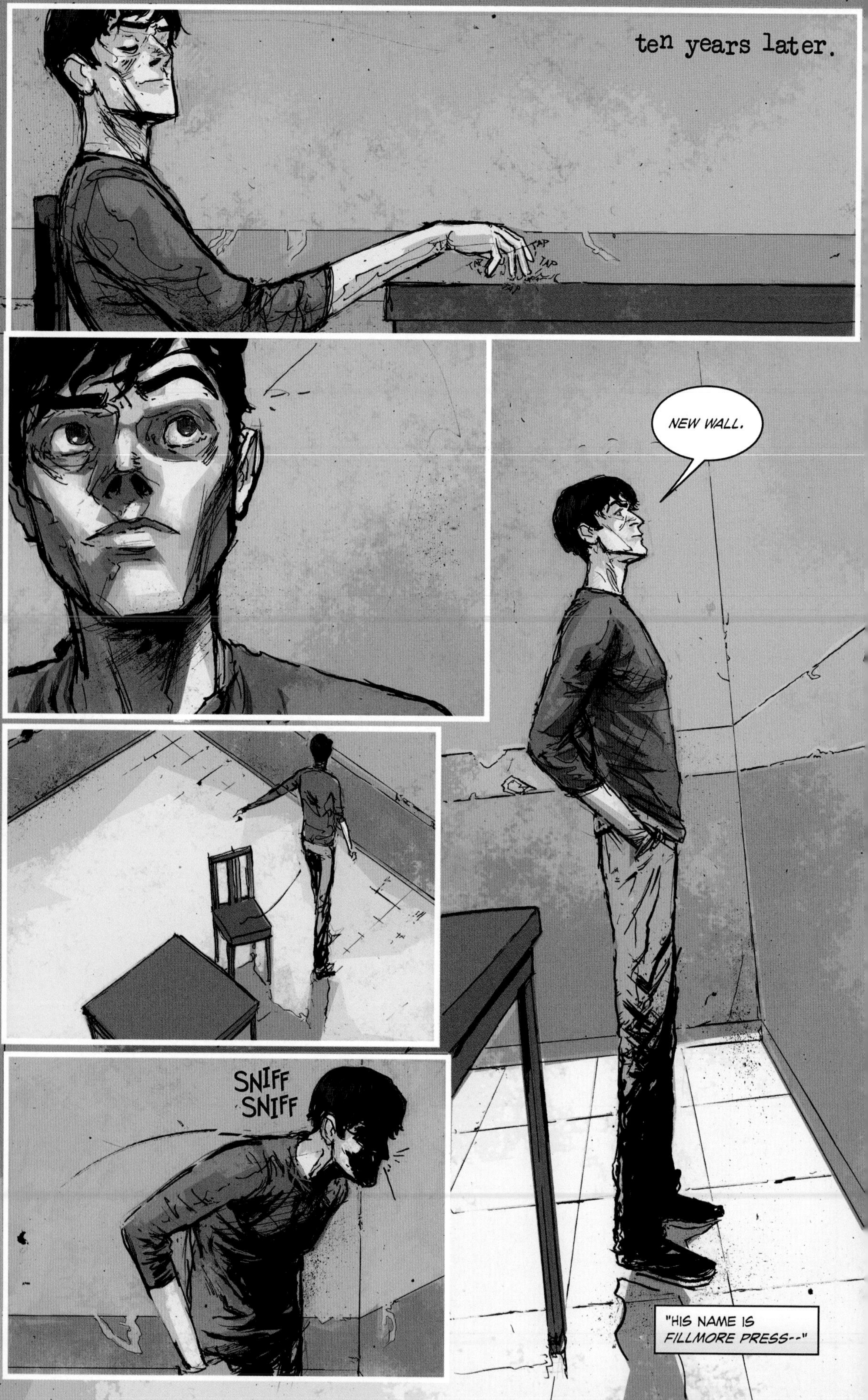
ten years later.
TAP TAP TAP TAP
NEW WALL.
SNIFF SNIFF
"HIS NAME IS FILLMORE PRESS--"

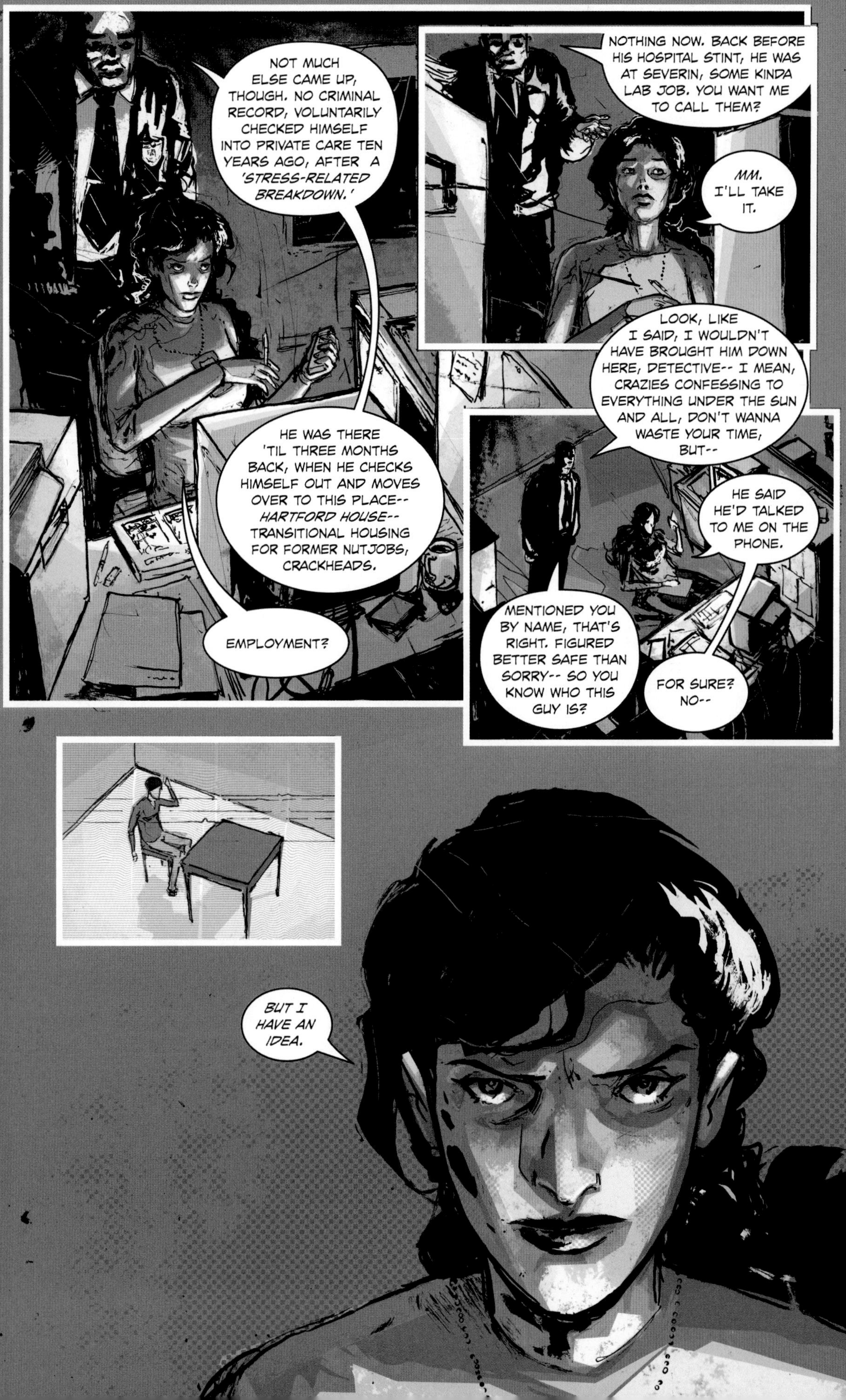
NOT MUCH ELSE CAME UP, THOUGH. NO CRIMINAL RECORD, VOLUNTARILY CHECKED HIMSELF INTO PRIVATE CARE TEN YEARS AGO, AFTER A 'STRESS-RELATED BREAKDOWN.'
HE WAS THERE 'TIL THREE MONTHS BACK, WHEN HE CHECKS HIMSELF OUT AND MOVES OVER TO THIS PLACE-- HARTFORD HOUSE-- TRANSITIONAL HOUSING FOR FORMER NUTJOBS, CRACKHEADS.
EMPLOYMENT?
NOTHING NOW. BACK BEFORE HIS HOSPITAL STINT, HE WAS AT SEVERIN, SOME KINDA LAB JOB. YOU WANT ME TO CALL THEM?
MM. I'LL TAKE IT.
LOOK, LIKE I SAID, I WOULDN'T HAVE BROUGHT HIM DOWN HERE, DETECTIVE-- I MEAN, CRAZIES CONFESSING TO EVERYTHING UNDER THE SUN AND ALL, DON'T WANNA WASTE YOUR TIME, BUT--
HE SAID HE'D TALKED TO ME ON THE PHONE.
MENTIONED YOU BY NAME, THAT'S RIGHT. FIGURED BETTER SAFE THAN SORRY-- SO YOU KNOW WHO THIS GUY IS?
FOR SURE? NO--
BUT I HAVE AN IDEA.

CHAPTER THREE
LET HIM HAVE HIS FUN

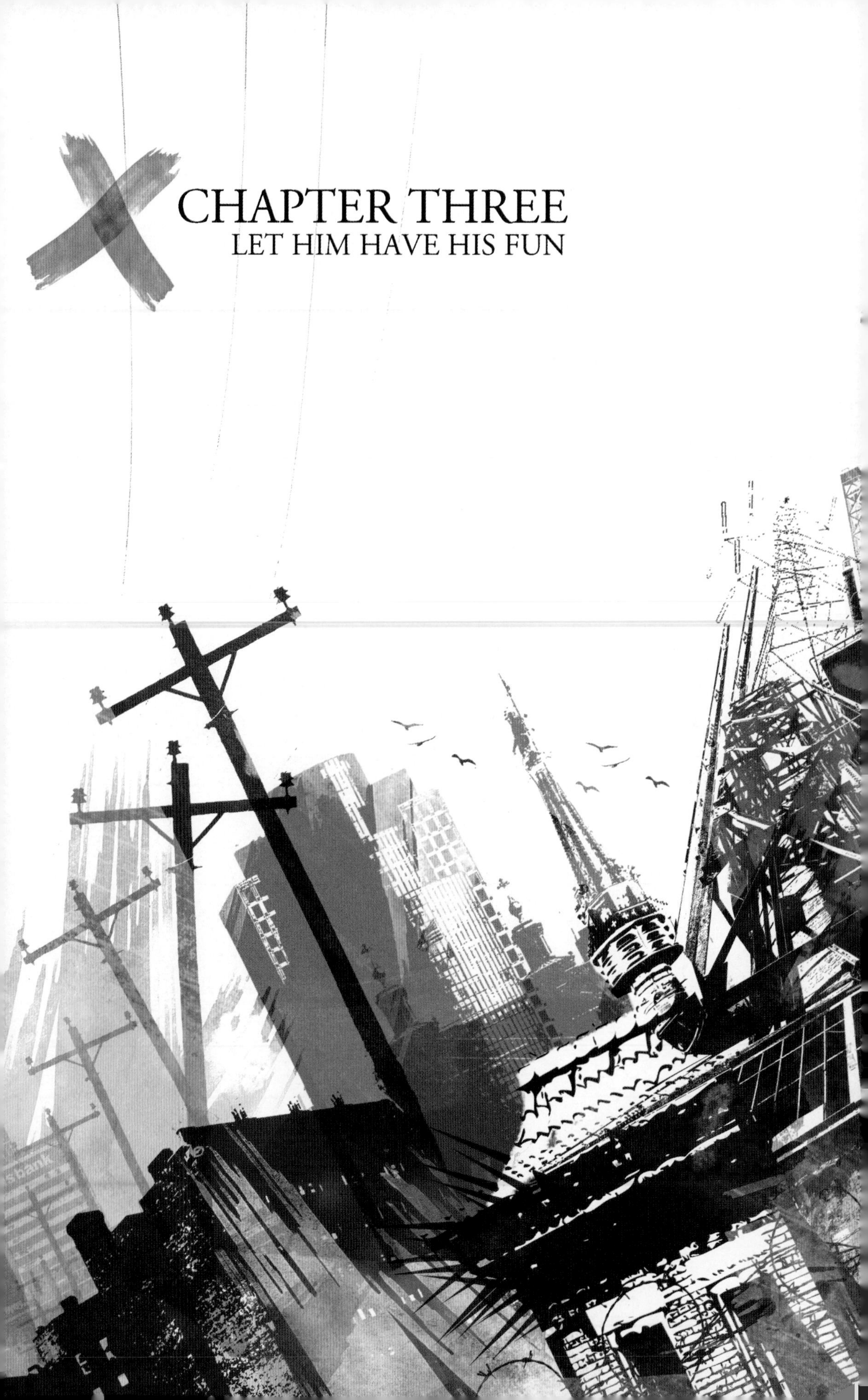

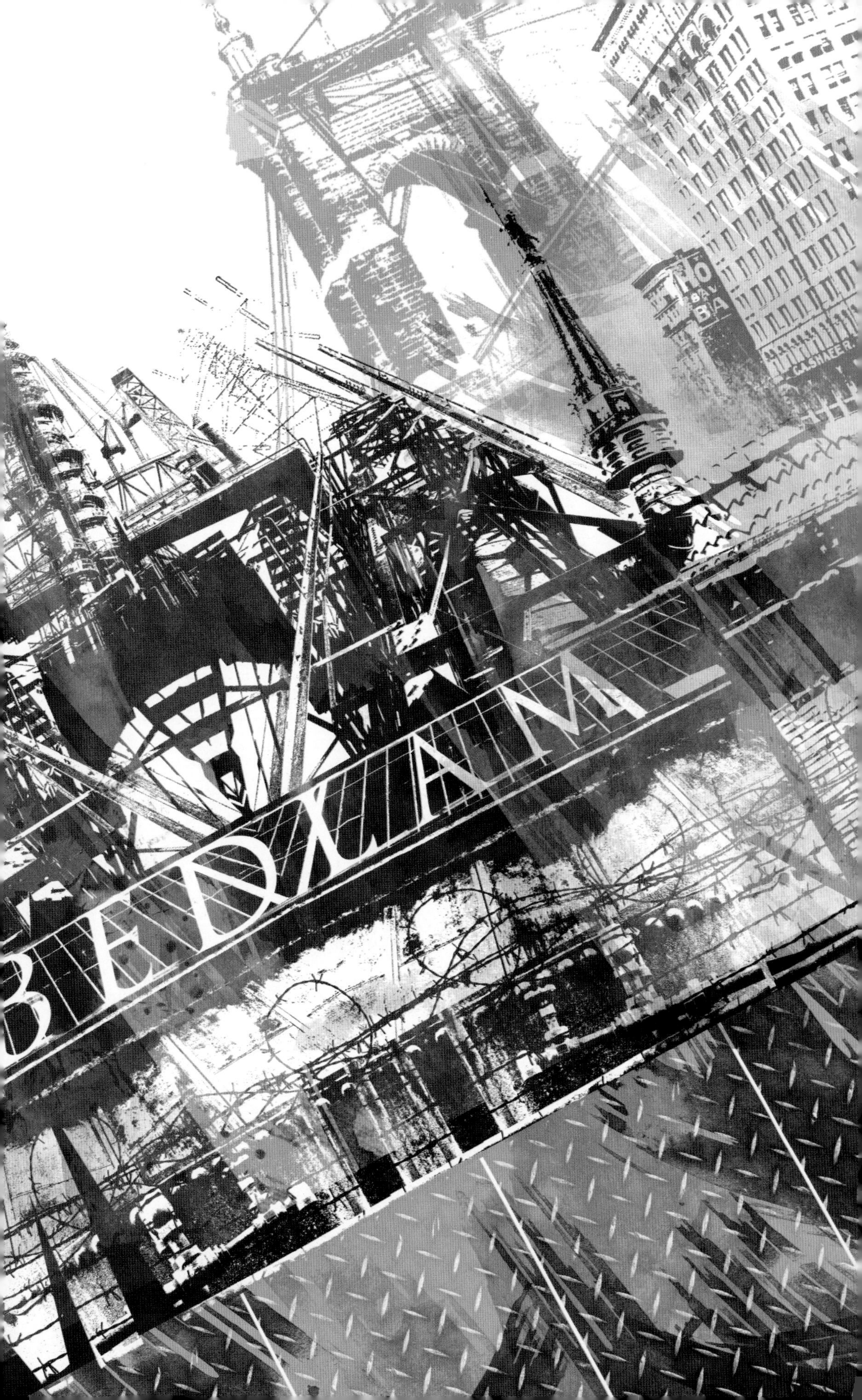
BEDLAM

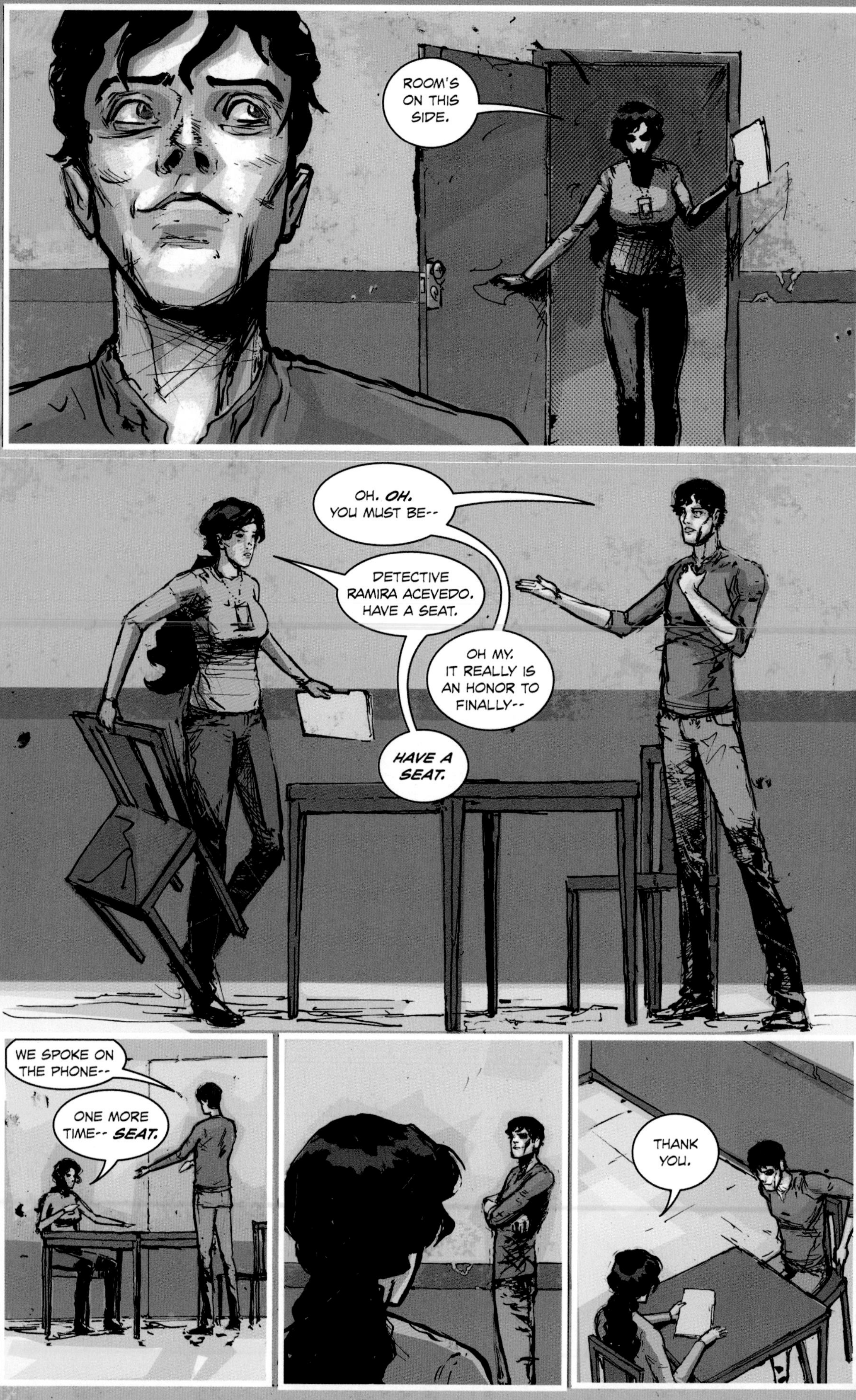
ROOM'S ON THIS SIDE.
OH. OH. YOU MUST BE--
DETECTIVE RAMIRA ACEVEDO. HAVE A SEAT.
OH MY. IT REALLY IS AN HONOR TO FINALLY--
HAVE A SEAT.
WE SPOKE ON THE PHONE--
ONE MORE TIME-- SEAT.
THANK YOU.

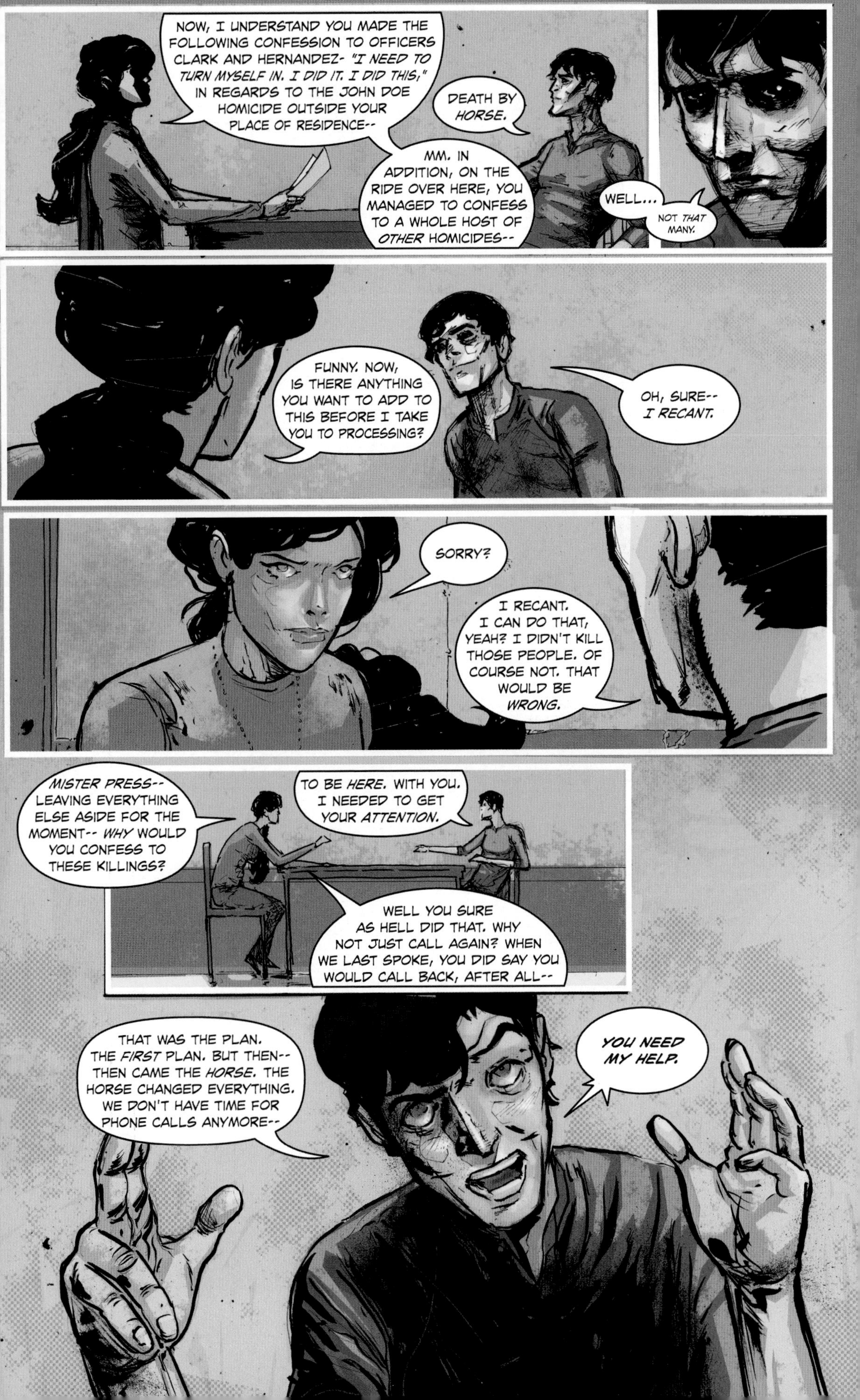
NOW, I UNDERSTAND YOU MADE THE FOLLOWING CONFESSION TO OFFICERS CLARK AND HERNANDEZ- *"I NEED TO TURN MYSELF IN. I DID IT. I DID THIS,"* IN REGARDS TO THE JOHN DOE HOMICIDE OUTSIDE YOUR PLACE OF RESIDENCE--
DEATH BY *HORSE.*
MM. IN ADDITION, ON THE RIDE OVER HERE, YOU MANAGED TO CONFESS TO A WHOLE HOST OF *OTHER* HOMICIDES--
WELL...
NOT *THAT* MANY.
FUNNY. NOW, IS THERE ANYTHING YOU WANT TO ADD TO THIS BEFORE I TAKE YOU TO PROCESSING?
OH, SURE-- *I RECANT.*
SORRY?
I RECANT. I CAN DO THAT, YEAH? I DIDN'T KILL THOSE PEOPLE. OF COURSE NOT. THAT WOULD BE *WRONG.*
MISTER PRESS-- LEAVING EVERYTHING ELSE ASIDE FOR THE MOMENT-- *WHY* WOULD YOU CONFESS TO THESE KILLINGS?
TO BE *HERE*. WITH YOU. I NEEDED TO GET YOUR *ATTENTION.*
WELL YOU SURE AS HELL DID THAT. WHY NOT JUST CALL AGAIN? WHEN WE LAST SPOKE, YOU DID SAY YOU WOULD CALL BACK, AFTER ALL--
THAT WAS THE PLAN. THE *FIRST* PLAN. BUT THEN-- THEN CAME THE *HORSE*. THE HORSE CHANGED EVERYTHING. WE DON'T HAVE TIME FOR PHONE CALLS ANYMORE--
YOU NEED MY HELP.

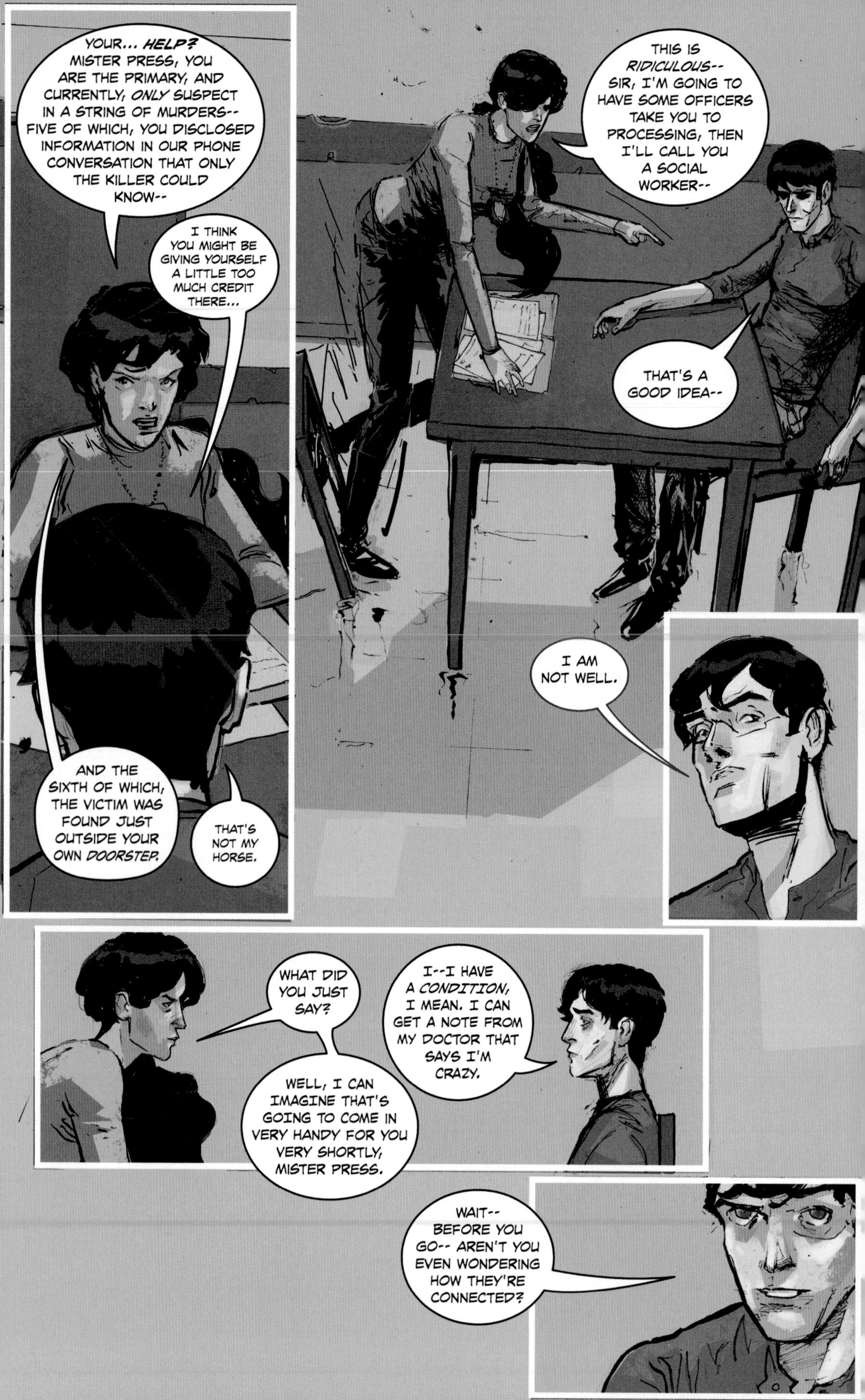
YOUR... *HELP?* MISTER PRESS, YOU ARE THE PRIMARY, AND CURRENTLY, *ONLY* SUSPECT IN A STRING OF MURDERS-- FIVE OF WHICH, YOU DISCLOSED INFORMATION IN OUR PHONE CONVERSATION THAT ONLY THE KILLER COULD KNOW--
I THINK YOU MIGHT BE GIVING YOURSELF A LITTLE TOO MUCH CREDIT THERE...
AND THE SIXTH OF WHICH, THE VICTIM WAS FOUND JUST OUTSIDE YOUR OWN *DOORSTEP.*
THAT'S NOT MY HORSE.
THIS IS *RIDICULOUS*-- SIR, I'M GOING TO HAVE SOME OFFICERS TAKE YOU TO PROCESSING, THEN I'LL CALL YOU A SOCIAL WORKER--
THAT'S A GOOD IDEA--
I AM NOT WELL.
I--I HAVE A *CONDITION,* I MEAN. I CAN GET A NOTE FROM MY DOCTOR THAT SAYS I'M CRAZY.
WHAT DID YOU JUST SAY?
WELL, I CAN IMAGINE THAT'S GOING TO COME IN VERY HANDY FOR YOU VERY SHORTLY, MISTER PRESS.
WAIT-- BEFORE YOU GO-- AREN'T YOU EVEN WONDERING HOW THEY'RE CONNECTED?

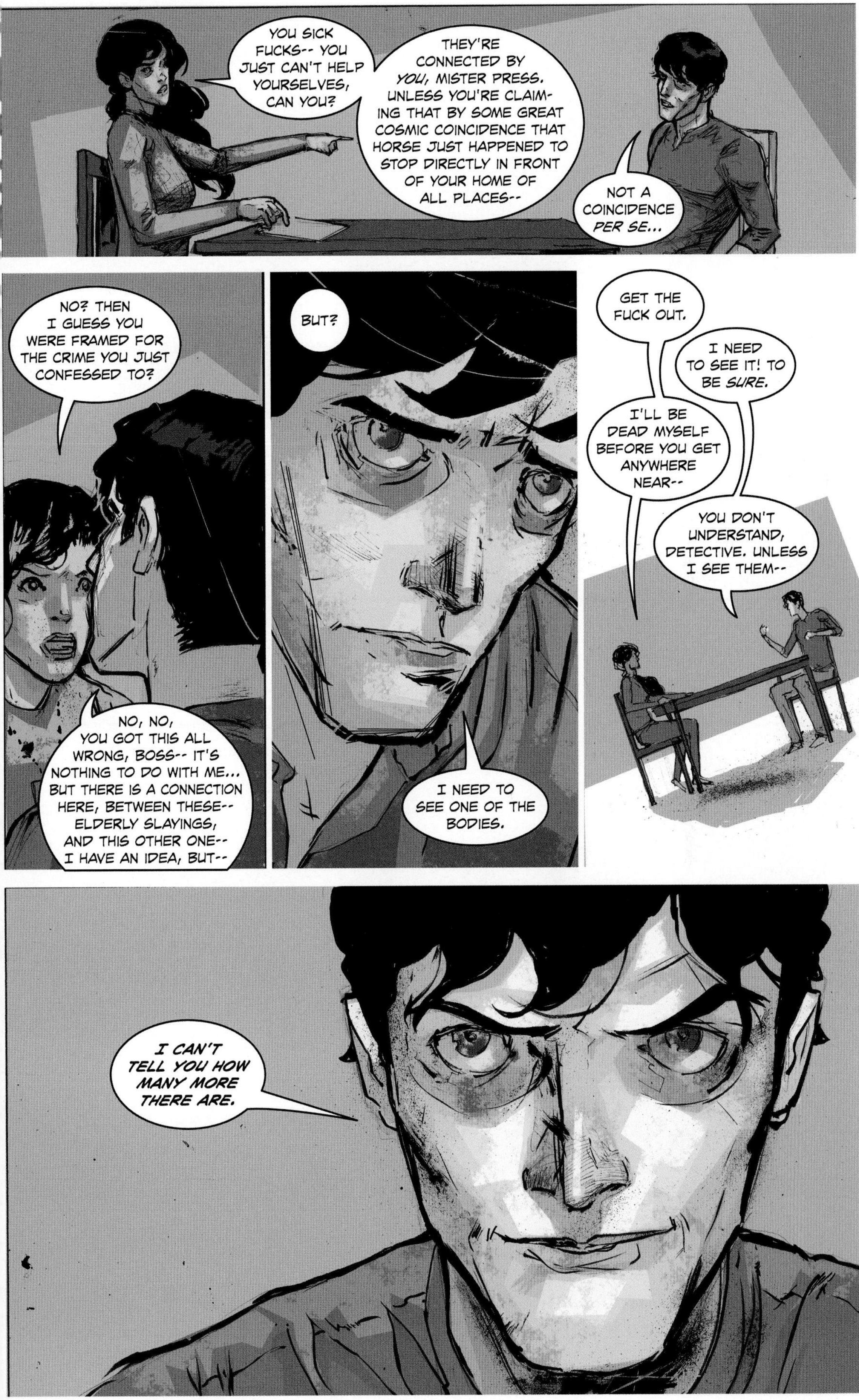
YOU SICK FUCKS-- YOU JUST CAN'T HELP YOURSELVES, CAN YOU?
THEY'RE CONNECTED BY *YOU*, MISTER PRESS. UNLESS YOU'RE CLAIMING THAT BY SOME GREAT COSMIC COINCIDENCE THAT HORSE JUST HAPPENED TO STOP DIRECTLY IN FRONT OF YOUR HOME OF ALL PLACES--
NOT A COINCIDENCE *PER SE*...
NO? THEN I GUESS YOU WERE FRAMED FOR THE CRIME YOU JUST CONFESSED TO?
NO, NO, YOU GOT THIS ALL WRONG, BOSS-- IT'S NOTHING TO DO WITH ME... BUT THERE IS A CONNECTION HERE, BETWEEN THESE-- ELDERLY SLAYINGS, AND THIS OTHER ONE-- I HAVE AN IDEA, BUT--
BUT?
I NEED TO SEE ONE OF THE BODIES.
GET THE FUCK OUT.
I NEED TO SEE IT! TO BE *SURE*.
I'LL BE DEAD MYSELF BEFORE YOU GET ANYWHERE NEAR--
YOU DON'T UNDERSTAND, DETECTIVE. UNLESS I SEE THEM--
I CAN'T TELL YOU HOW MANY MORE THERE ARE.

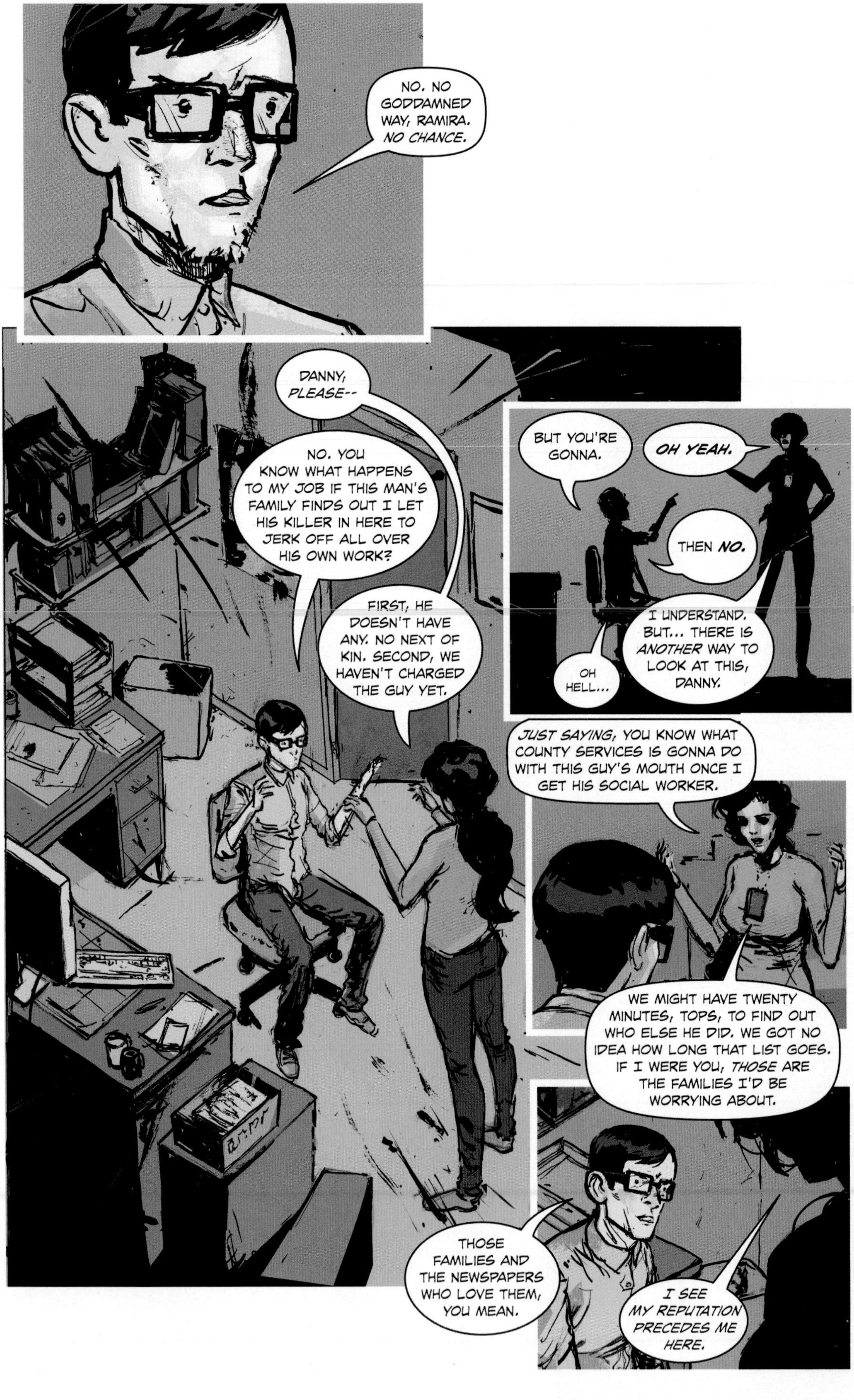
NO. NO GODDAMNED WAY, RAMIRA. *NO CHANCE.*
DANNY, *PLEASE--*
NO. YOU KNOW WHAT HAPPENS TO MY JOB IF THIS MAN'S FAMILY FINDS OUT I LET HIS KILLER IN HERE TO JERK OFF ALL OVER HIS OWN WORK?
FIRST, HE DOESN'T HAVE ANY. NO NEXT OF KIN. SECOND, WE HAVEN'T CHARGED THE GUY YET.
BUT YOU'RE GONNA.
OH YEAH.
THEN *NO.*
OH HELL...
I UNDERSTAND. BUT... THERE IS *ANOTHER* WAY TO LOOK AT THIS, DANNY.
JUST SAYING, YOU KNOW WHAT COUNTY SERVICES IS GONNA DO WITH THIS GUY'S MOUTH ONCE I GET HIS SOCIAL WORKER.
WE MIGHT HAVE TWENTY MINUTES, TOPS, TO FIND OUT WHO ELSE HE DID. WE GOT NO IDEA HOW LONG THAT LIST GOES. IF I WERE YOU, *THOSE* ARE THE FAMILIES I'D BE WORRYING ABOUT.
THOSE FAMILIES AND THE NEWSPAPERS WHO LOVE THEM, YOU MEAN.
I SEE MY REPUTATION PRECEDES ME HERE.

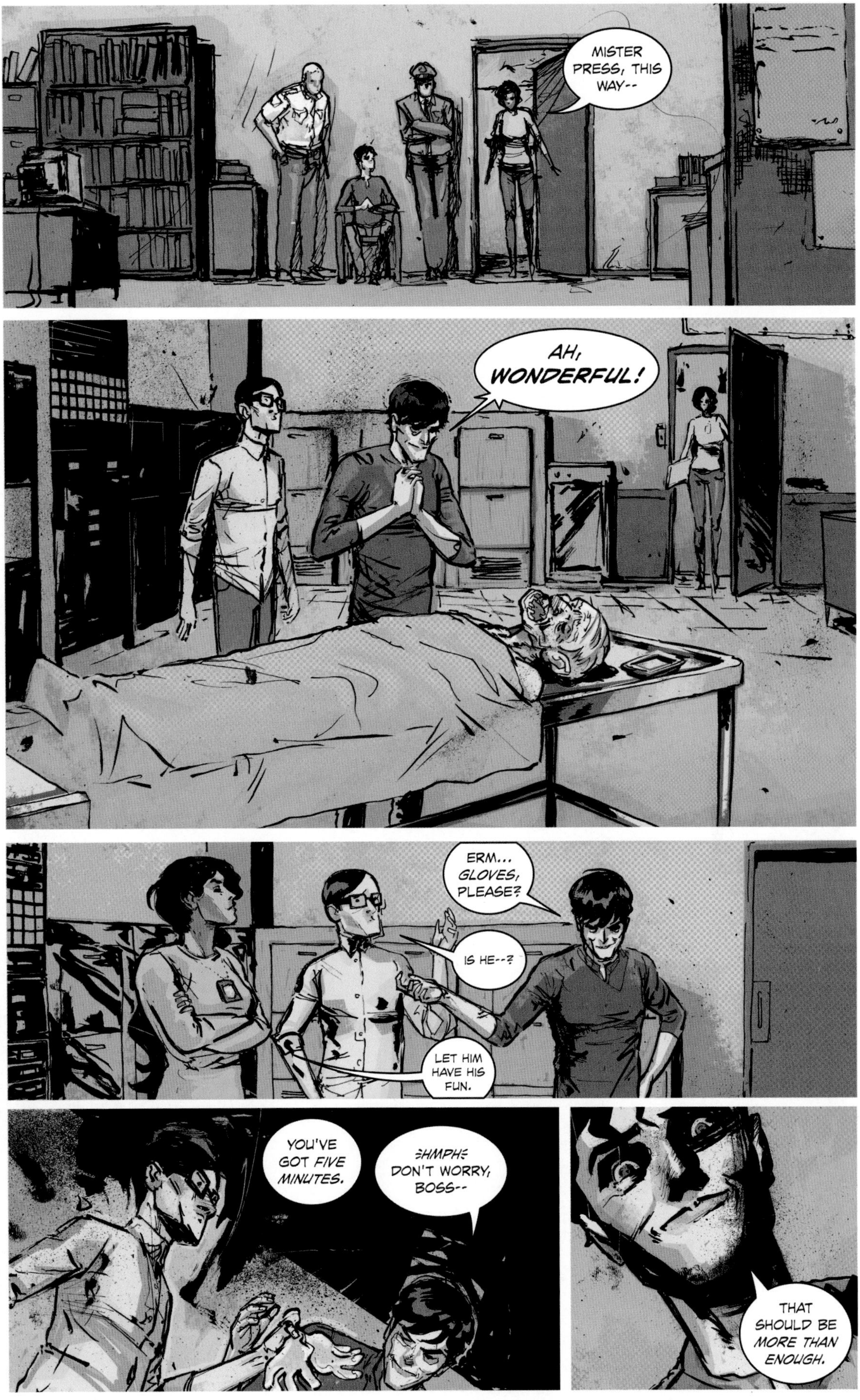
MISTER PRESS, THIS WAY--
AH, WONDERFUL!
ERM... GLOVES, PLEASE?
IS HE--?
LET HIM HAVE HIS FUN.
YOU'VE GOT FIVE MINUTES.
=HMPH= DON'T WORRY, BOSS--
THAT SHOULD BE MORE THAN ENOUGH.

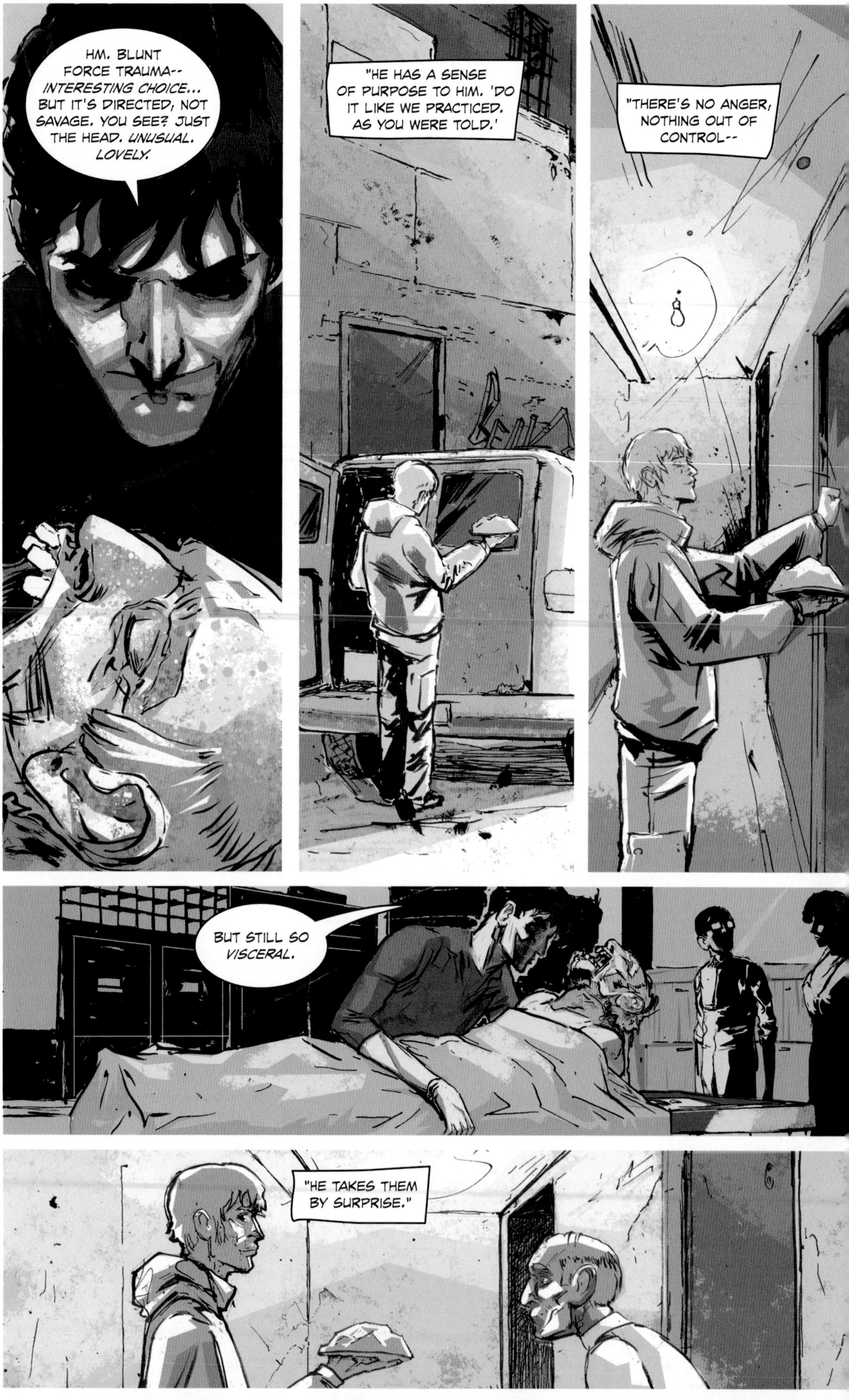
HM. BLUNT FORCE TRAUMA-- INTERESTING CHOICE... BUT IT'S DIRECTED, NOT SAVAGE. YOU SEE? JUST THE HEAD. UNUSUAL. LOVELY.
"HE HAS A SENSE OF PURPOSE TO HIM. 'DO IT LIKE WE PRACTICED. AS YOU WERE TOLD.'
"THERE'S NO ANGER, NOTHING OUT OF CONTROL--
BUT STILL SO VISCERAL.
"HE TAKES THEM BY SURPRISE."

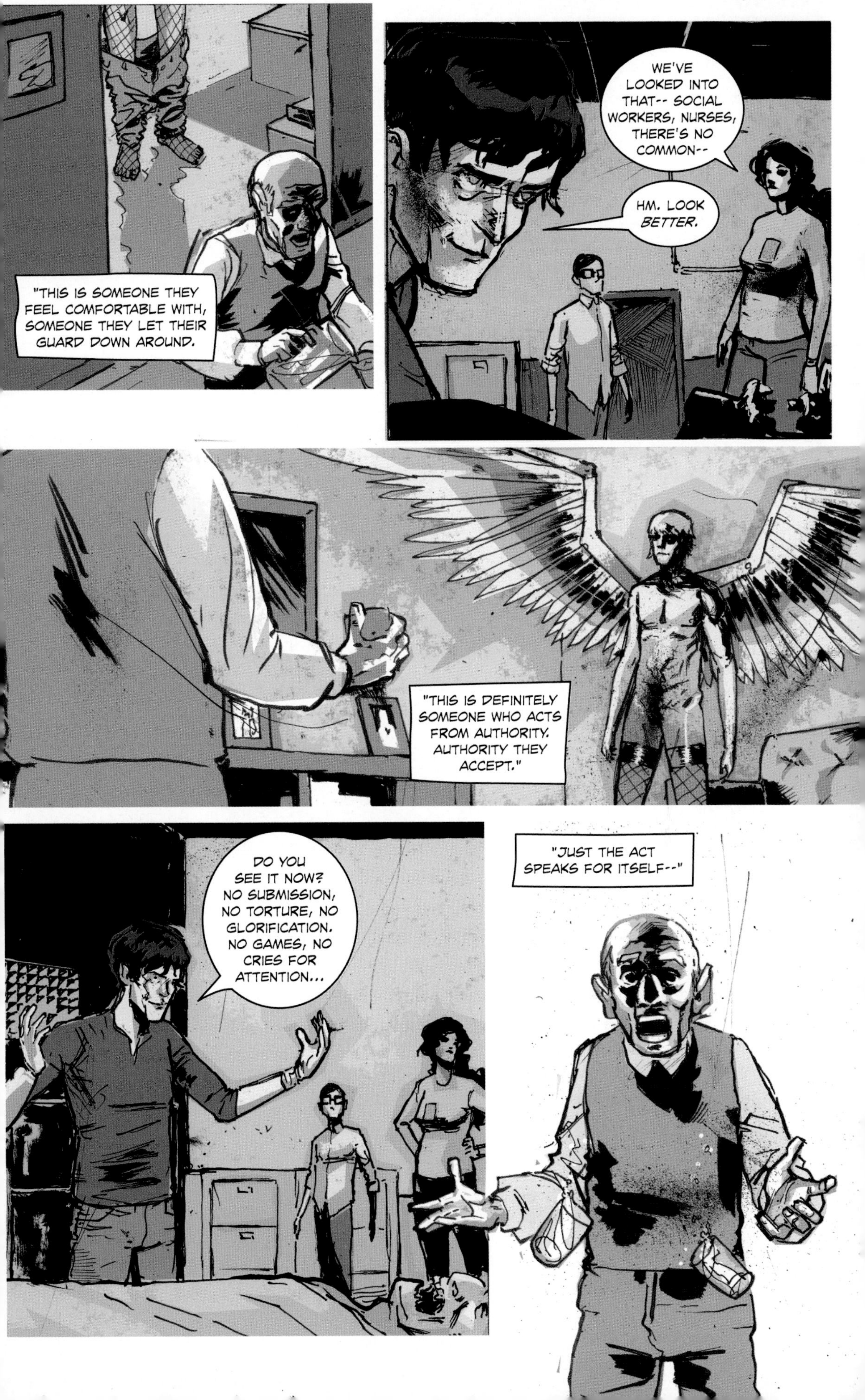
"THIS IS SOMEONE THEY FEEL COMFORTABLE WITH, SOMEONE THEY LET THEIR GUARD DOWN AROUND.
WE'VE LOOKED INTO THAT-- SOCIAL WORKERS, NURSES, THERE'S NO COMMON--
HM. LOOK BETTER.
"THIS IS DEFINITELY SOMEONE WHO ACTS FROM AUTHORITY. AUTHORITY THEY ACCEPT."
DO YOU SEE IT NOW? NO SUBMISSION, NO TORTURE, NO GLORIFICATION. NO GAMES, NO CRIES FOR ATTENTION...
"JUST THE ACT SPEAKS FOR ITSELF--"

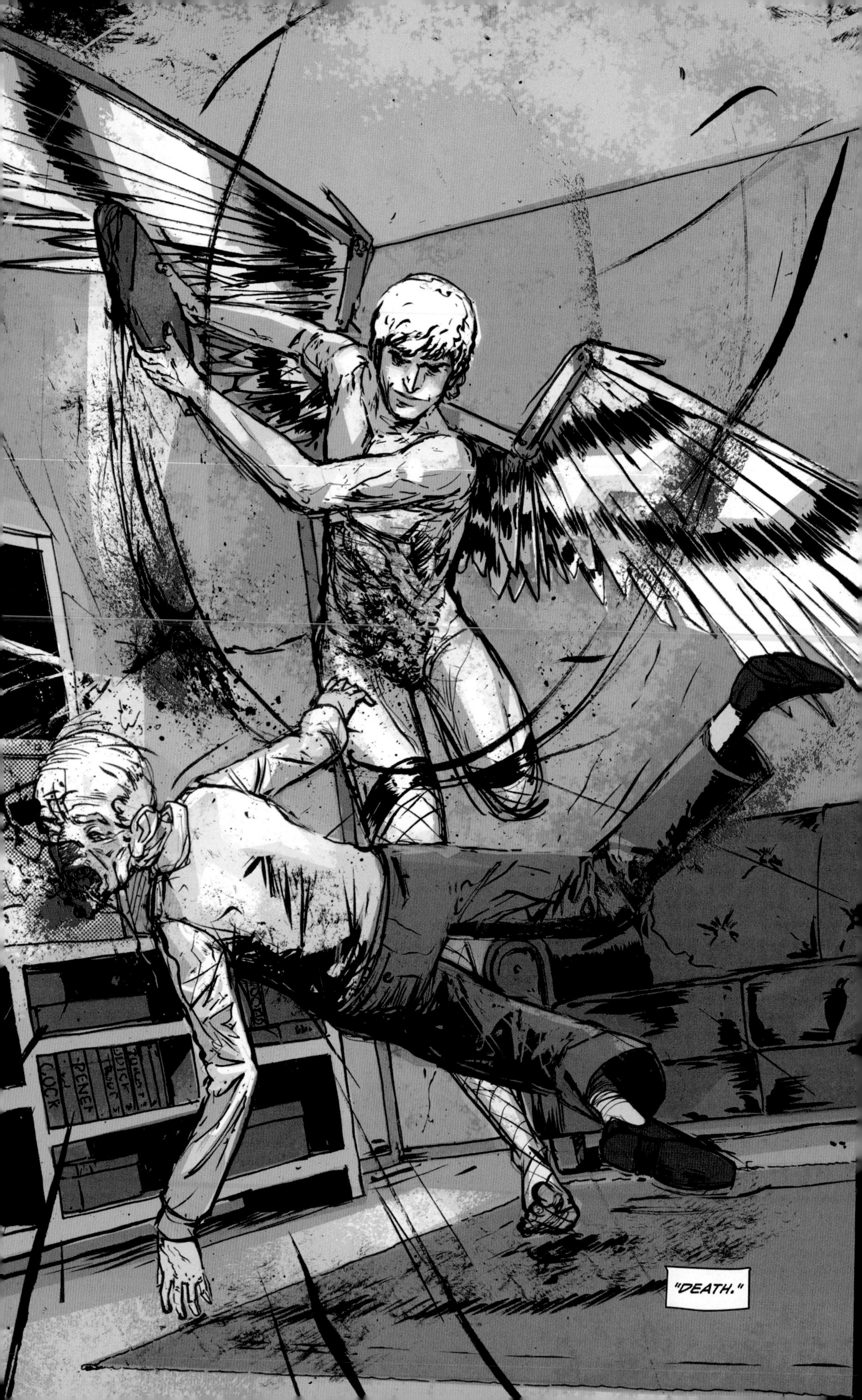
"DEATH."

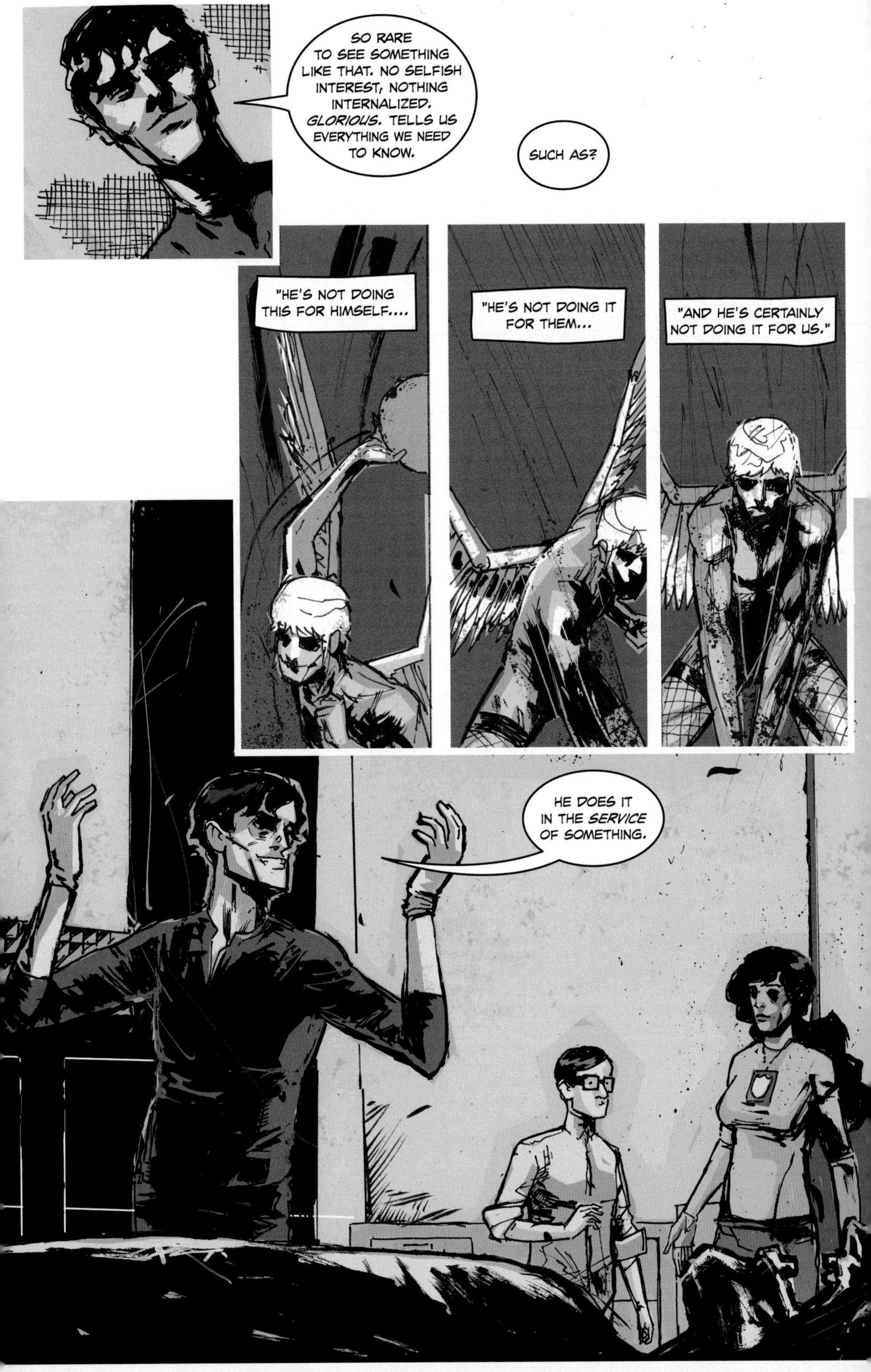
SO RARE TO SEE SOMETHING LIKE THAT. NO SELFISH INTEREST, NOTHING INTERNALIZED. *GLORIOUS*. TELLS US EVERYTHING WE NEED TO KNOW.
SUCH AS?
"HE'S NOT DOING THIS FOR HIMSELF....
"HE'S NOT DOING IT FOR THEM...
"AND HE'S CERTAINLY NOT DOING IT FOR US."
HE DOES IT IN THE *SERVICE* OF SOMETHING.

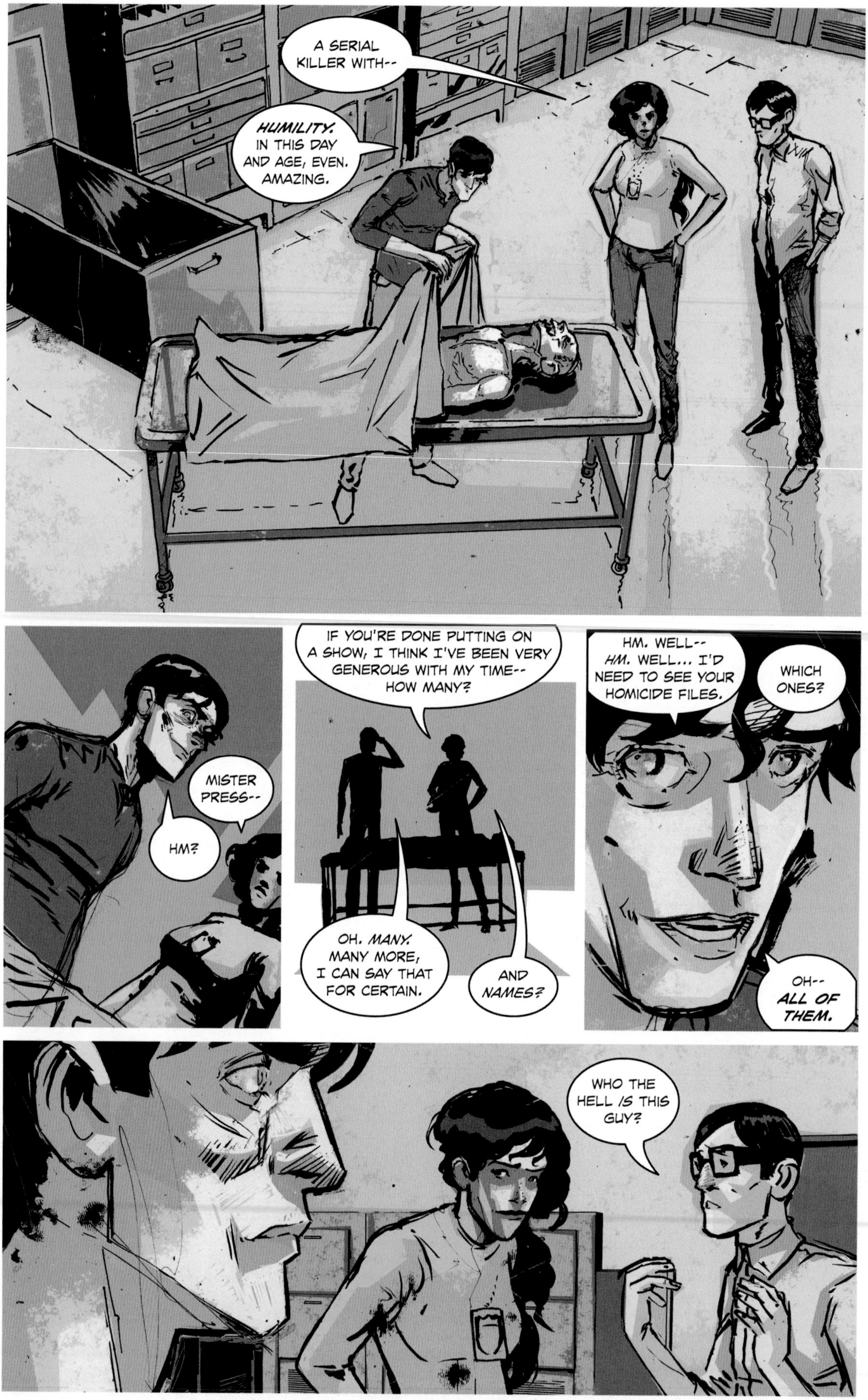
A SERIAL KILLER WITH--
HUMILITY. IN THIS DAY AND AGE, EVEN. AMAZING.
MISTER PRESS--
HM?
IF YOU'RE DONE PUTTING ON A SHOW, I THINK I'VE BEEN VERY GENEROUS WITH MY TIME-- HOW MANY?
OH. *MANY.* MANY MORE, I CAN SAY THAT FOR CERTAIN.
AND *NAMES?*
HM. WELL-- *HM.* WELL... I'D NEED TO SEE YOUR HOMICIDE FILES.
WHICH ONES?
OH-- ***ALL OF THEM.***
WHO THE HELL *IS* THIS GUY?

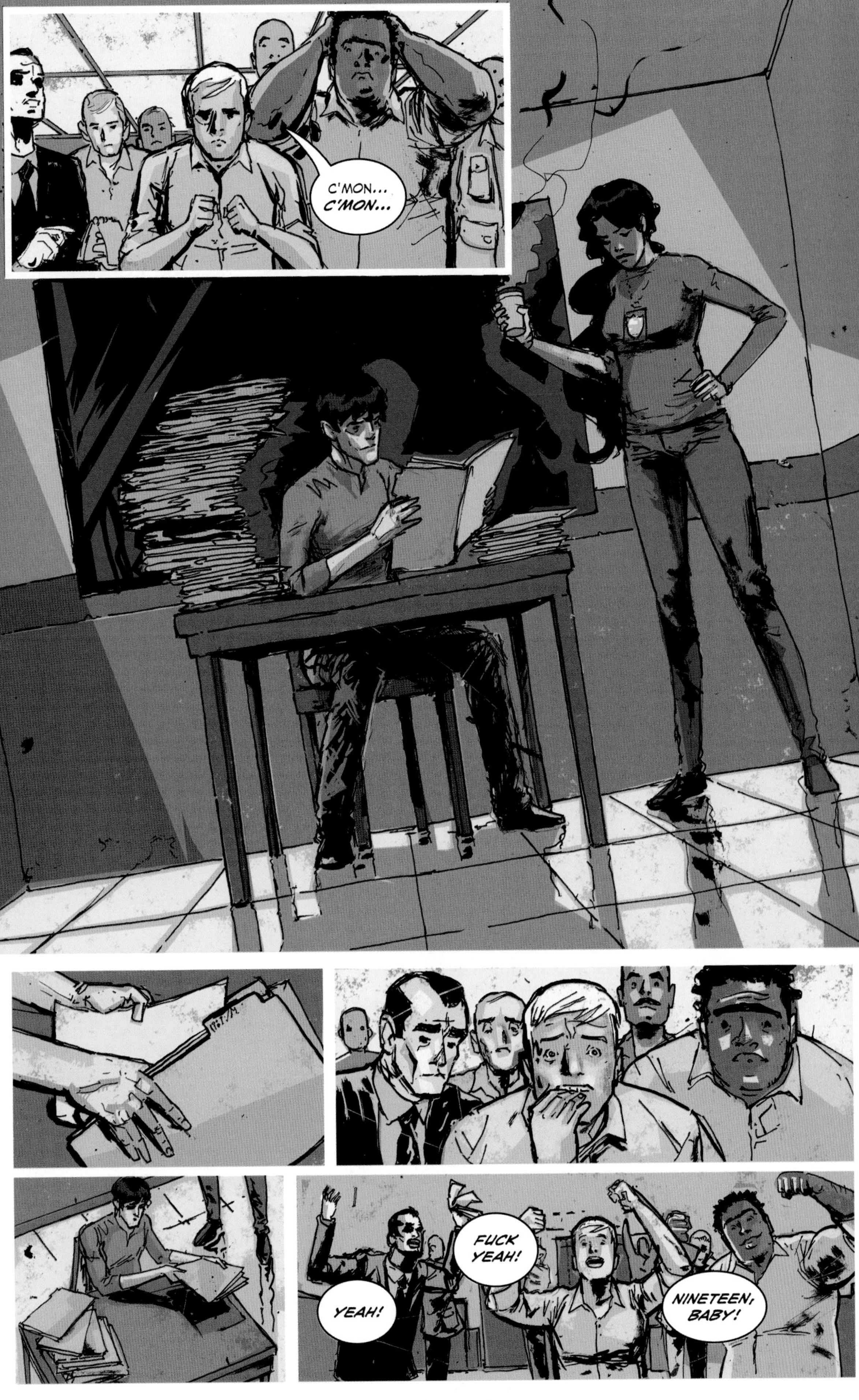
C'MON...
C'MON...
FUCK YEAH!
YEAH!
NINETEEN, BABY!

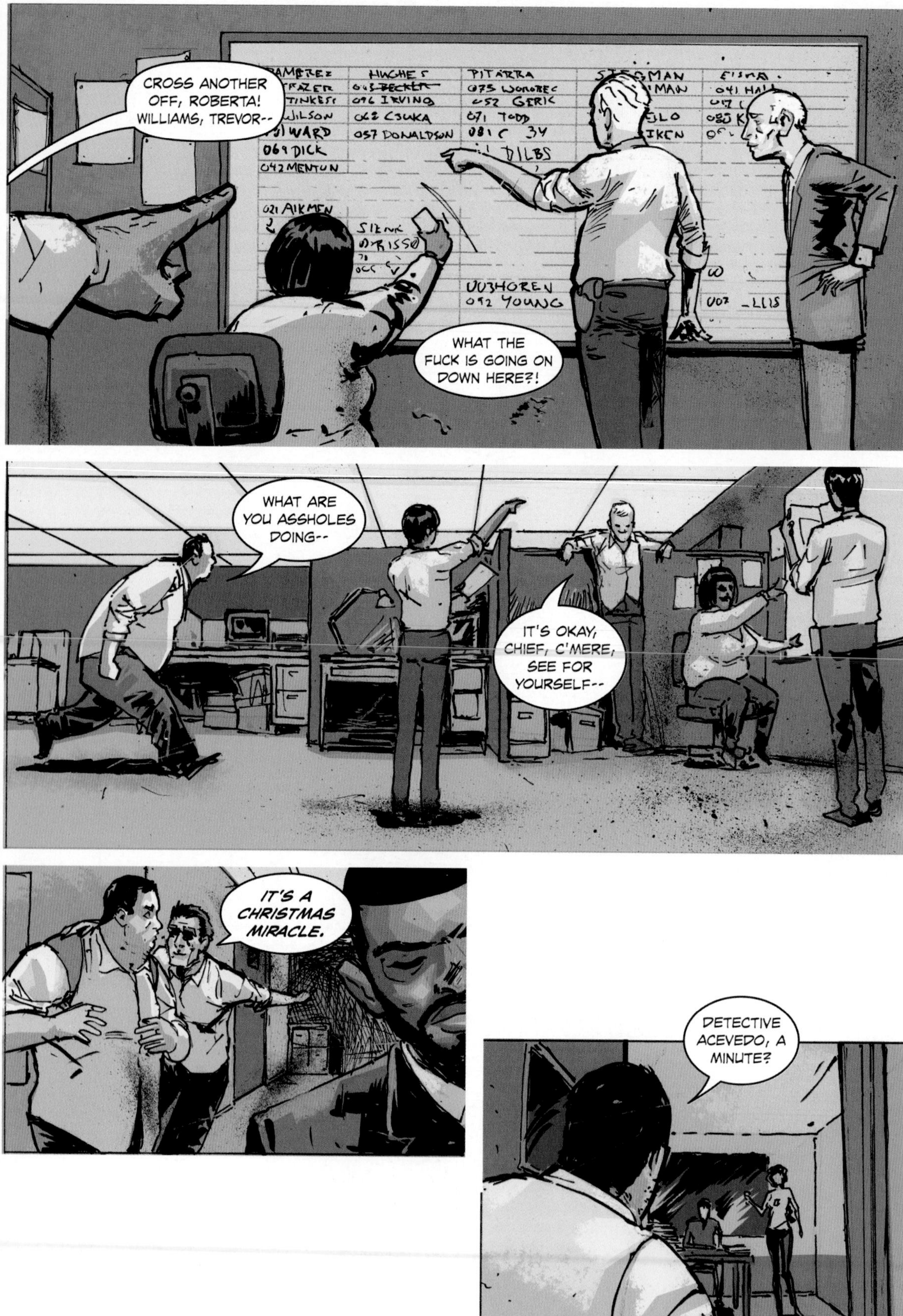

CROSS ANOTHER OFF, ROBERTA! WILLIAMS, TREVOR--
WHAT THE FUCK IS GOING ON DOWN HERE?!
WHAT ARE YOU ASSHOLES DOING--
IT'S OKAY, CHIEF, C'MERE, SEE FOR YOURSELF--
IT'S A CHRISTMAS MIRACLE.
DETECTIVE ACEVEDO, A MINUTE?

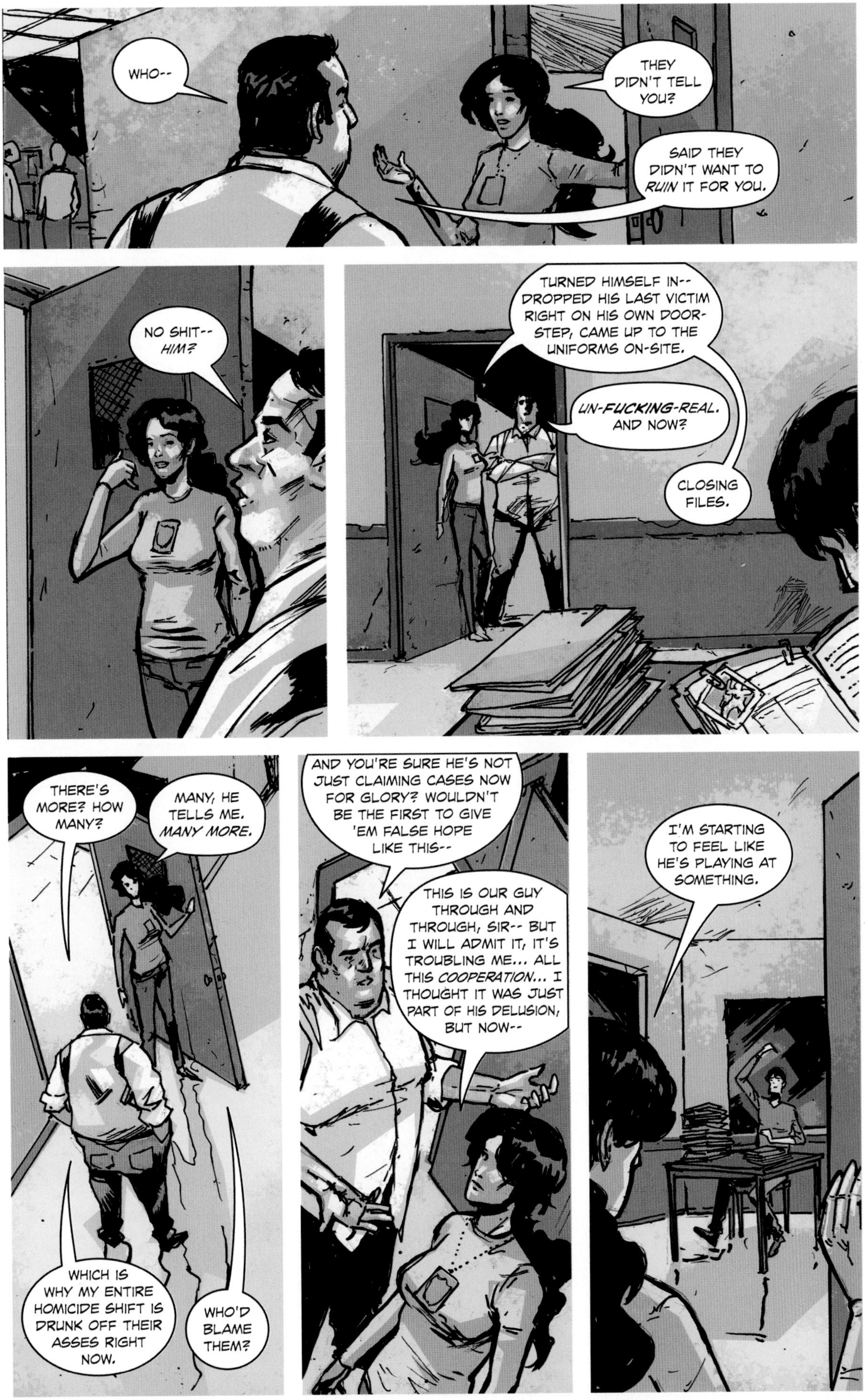
WHO--
THEY DIDN'T TELL YOU?
SAID THEY DIDN'T WANT TO *RUIN* IT FOR YOU.
NO SHIT-- *HIM?*
TURNED HIMSELF IN-- DROPPED HIS LAST VICTIM RIGHT ON HIS OWN DOOR-STEP, CAME UP TO THE UNIFORMS ON-SITE.
UN-FUCKING-REAL. AND NOW?
CLOSING FILES.
THERE'S MORE? HOW MANY?
MANY, HE TELLS ME. *MANY MORE.*
WHICH IS WHY MY ENTIRE HOMICIDE SHIFT IS DRUNK OFF THEIR ASSES RIGHT NOW.
WHO'D BLAME THEM?
AND YOU'RE SURE HE'S NOT JUST CLAIMING CASES NOW FOR GLORY? WOULDN'T BE THE FIRST TO GIVE 'EM FALSE HOPE LIKE THIS--
THIS IS OUR GUY THROUGH AND THROUGH, SIR-- BUT I WILL ADMIT IT, IT'S TROUBLING ME... ALL THIS *COOPERATION*... I THOUGHT IT WAS JUST PART OF HIS DELUSION, BUT NOW--
I'M STARTING TO FEEL LIKE HE'S PLAYING AT SOMETHING.

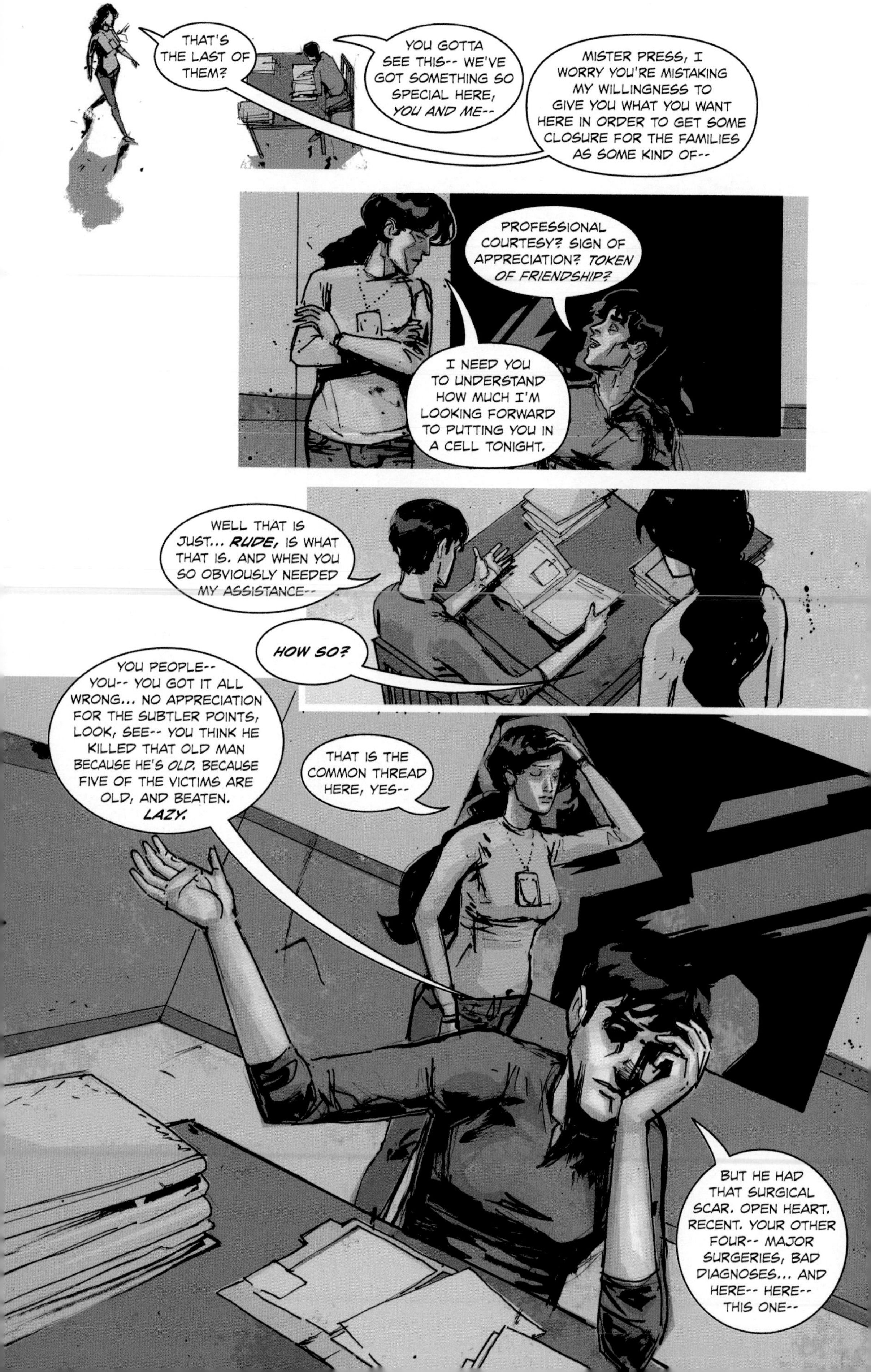
THAT'S THE LAST OF THEM?
YOU GOTTA SEE THIS-- WE'VE GOT SOMETHING SO SPECIAL HERE, *YOU AND ME*--
MISTER PRESS, I WORRY YOU'RE MISTAKING MY WILLINGNESS TO GIVE YOU WHAT YOU WANT HERE IN ORDER TO GET SOME CLOSURE FOR THE FAMILIES AS SOME KIND OF--
PROFESSIONAL COURTESY? SIGN OF APPRECIATION? *TOKEN OF FRIENDSHIP?*
I NEED YOU TO UNDERSTAND HOW MUCH I'M LOOKING FORWARD TO PUTTING YOU IN A CELL TONIGHT.
WELL THAT IS JUST... ***RUDE,*** IS WHAT THAT IS. AND WHEN YOU SO OBVIOUSLY NEEDED MY ASSISTANCE--
HOW SO?
YOU PEOPLE-- YOU-- YOU GOT IT ALL WRONG... NO APPRECIATION FOR THE SUBTLER POINTS. LOOK, SEE-- YOU THINK HE KILLED THAT OLD MAN BECAUSE HE'S *OLD.* BECAUSE FIVE OF THE VICTIMS ARE OLD, AND BEATEN. ***LAZY.***
THAT IS THE COMMON THREAD HERE, YES--
BUT HE HAD THAT SURGICAL SCAR. OPEN HEART. RECENT. YOUR OTHER FOUR-- MAJOR SURGERIES, BAD DIAGNOSES... AND HERE-- HERE-- THIS ONE--

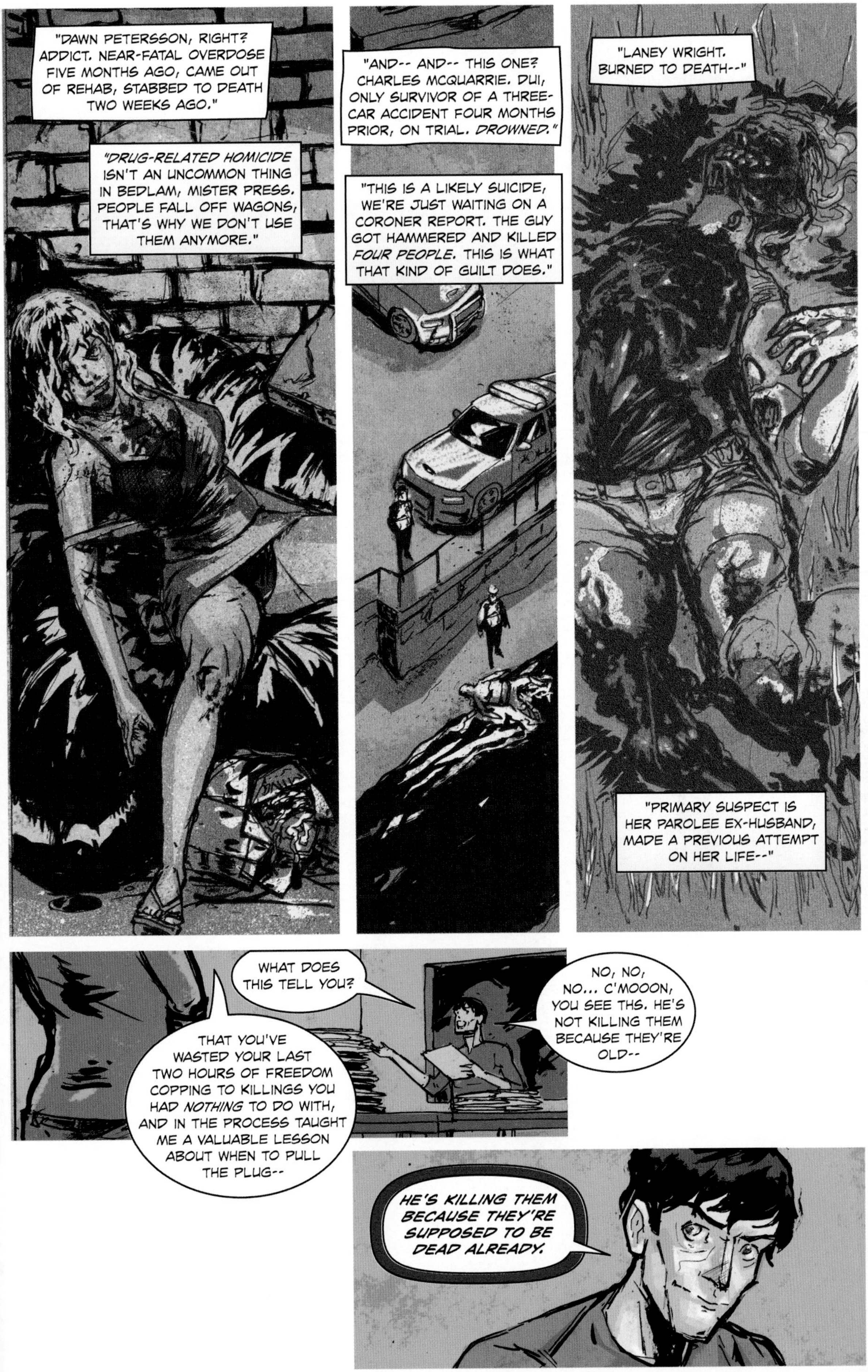
"DAWN PETERSSON, RIGHT? ADDICT. NEAR-FATAL OVERDOSE FIVE MONTHS AGO, CAME OUT OF REHAB, STABBED TO DEATH TWO WEEKS AGO."
"*DRUG-RELATED HOMICIDE* ISN'T AN UNCOMMON THING IN BEDLAM, MISTER PRESS. PEOPLE FALL OFF WAGONS, THAT'S WHY WE DON'T USE THEM ANYMORE."
"AND-- AND-- THIS ONE? CHARLES MCQUARRIE. DUI, ONLY SURVIVOR OF A THREE-CAR ACCIDENT FOUR MONTHS PRIOR, ON TRIAL. *DROWNED.*"
"THIS IS A LIKELY SUICIDE, WE'RE JUST WAITING ON A CORONER REPORT. THE GUY GOT HAMMERED AND KILLED *FOUR PEOPLE*. THIS IS WHAT THAT KIND OF GUILT DOES."
"LANEY WRIGHT. BURNED TO DEATH--"
"PRIMARY SUSPECT IS HER PAROLEE EX-HUSBAND, MADE A PREVIOUS ATTEMPT ON HER LIFE--"
WHAT DOES THIS TELL YOU?
THAT YOU'VE WASTED YOUR LAST TWO HOURS OF FREEDOM COPPING TO KILLINGS YOU HAD *NOTHING* TO DO WITH, AND IN THE PROCESS TAUGHT ME A VALUABLE LESSON ABOUT WHEN TO PULL THE PLUG--
NO, NO, NO... C'MOOON, YOU SEE THS. HE'S NOT KILLING THEM BECAUSE THEY'RE OLD--
HE'S KILLING THEM BECAUSE THEY'RE SUPPOSED TO BE DEAD ALREADY.

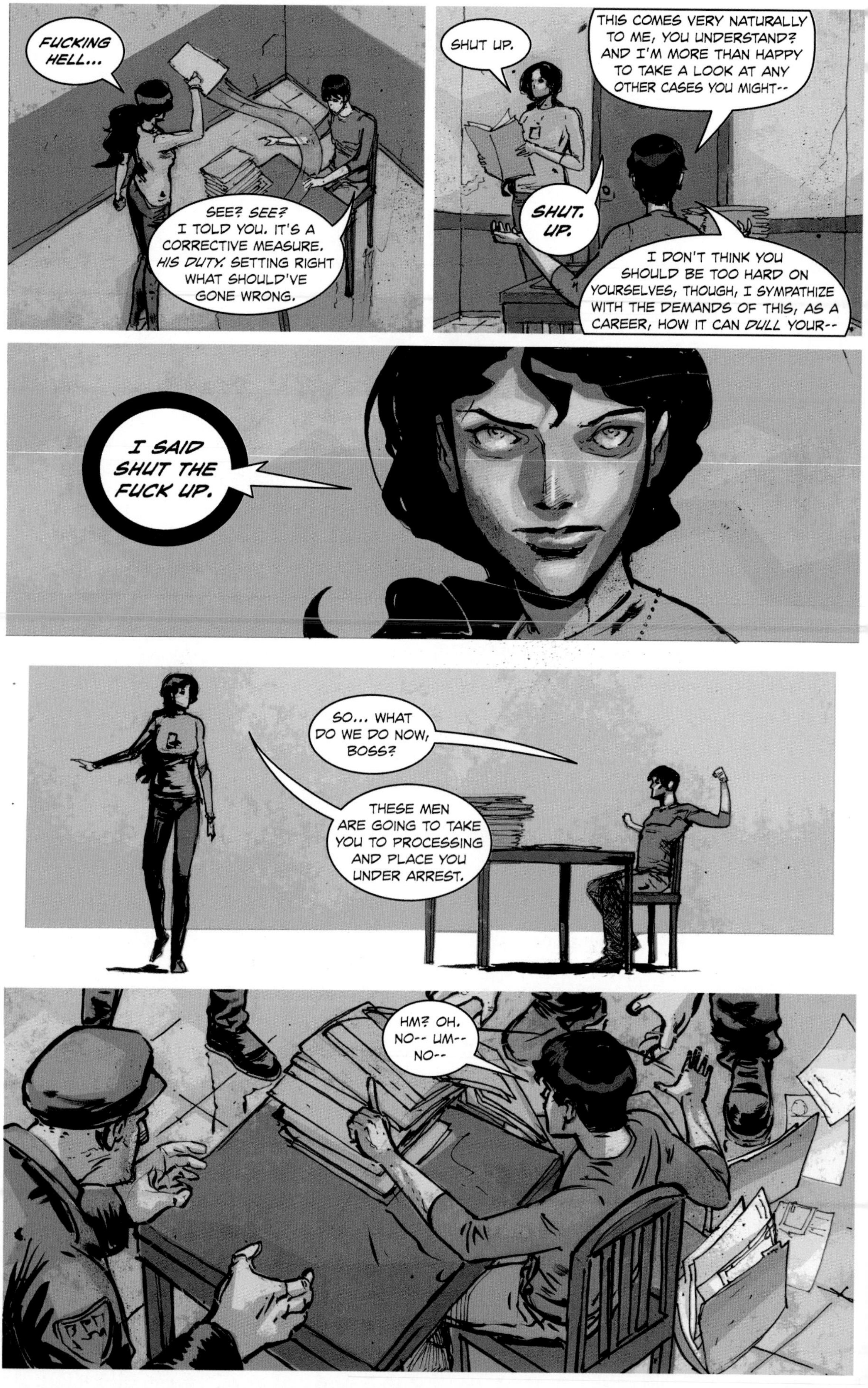
FUCKING HELL...
SEE? SEE? I TOLD YOU. IT'S A CORRECTIVE MEASURE. HIS DUTY. SETTING RIGHT WHAT SHOULD'VE GONE WRONG.
SHUT UP.
THIS COMES VERY NATURALLY TO ME, YOU UNDERSTAND? AND I'M MORE THAN HAPPY TO TAKE A LOOK AT ANY OTHER CASES YOU MIGHT--
SHUT. UP.
I DON'T THINK YOU SHOULD BE TOO HARD ON YOURSELVES, THOUGH, I SYMPATHIZE WITH THE DEMANDS OF THIS, AS A CAREER, HOW IT CAN DULL YOUR--
I SAID SHUT THE FUCK UP.
SO... WHAT DO WE DO NOW, BOSS?
THESE MEN ARE GOING TO TAKE YOU TO PROCESSING AND PLACE YOU UNDER ARREST.
HM? OH. NO-- UM-- NO--

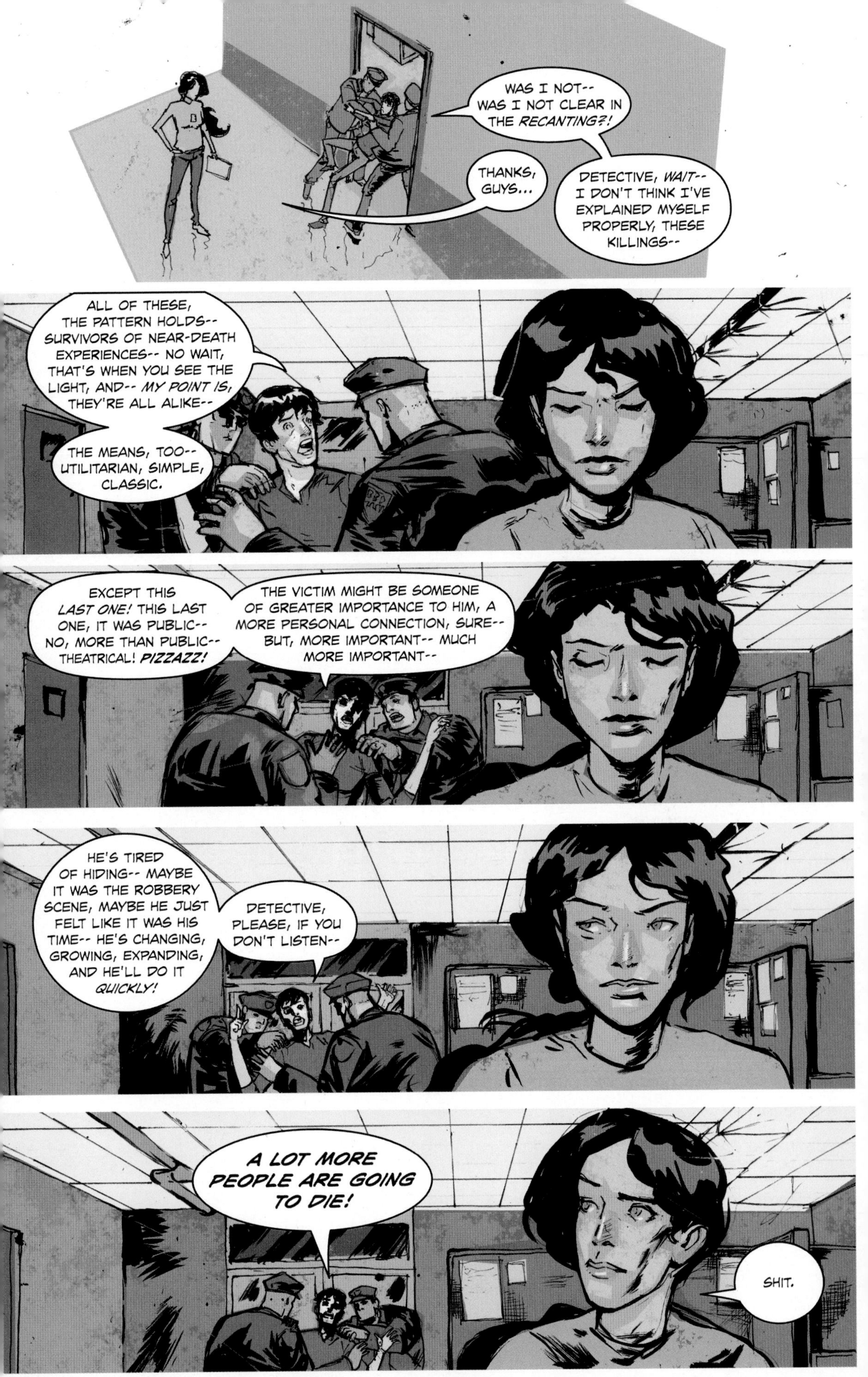
WAS I NOT-- WAS I NOT CLEAR IN THE RECANTING?!
THANKS, GUYS...
DETECTIVE, WAIT-- I DON'T THINK I'VE EXPLAINED MYSELF PROPERLY, THESE KILLINGS--
ALL OF THESE, THE PATTERN HOLDS-- SURVIVORS OF NEAR-DEATH EXPERIENCES-- NO WAIT, THAT'S WHEN YOU SEE THE LIGHT, AND-- MY POINT IS, THEY'RE ALL ALIKE--
THE MEANS, TOO-- UTILITARIAN, SIMPLE, CLASSIC.
EXCEPT THIS LAST ONE! THIS LAST ONE, IT WAS PUBLIC-- NO, MORE THAN PUBLIC-- THEATRICAL! PIZZAZZ!
THE VICTIM MIGHT BE SOMEONE OF GREATER IMPORTANCE TO HIM, A MORE PERSONAL CONNECTION, SURE-- BUT, MORE IMPORTANT-- MUCH MORE IMPORTANT--
HE'S TIRED OF HIDING-- MAYBE IT WAS THE ROBBERY SCENE, MAYBE HE JUST FELT LIKE IT WAS HIS TIME-- HE'S CHANGING, GROWING, EXPANDING, AND HE'LL DO IT QUICKLY!
DETECTIVE, PLEASE, IF YOU DON'T LISTEN--
A LOT MORE PEOPLE ARE GOING TO DIE!
SHIT.

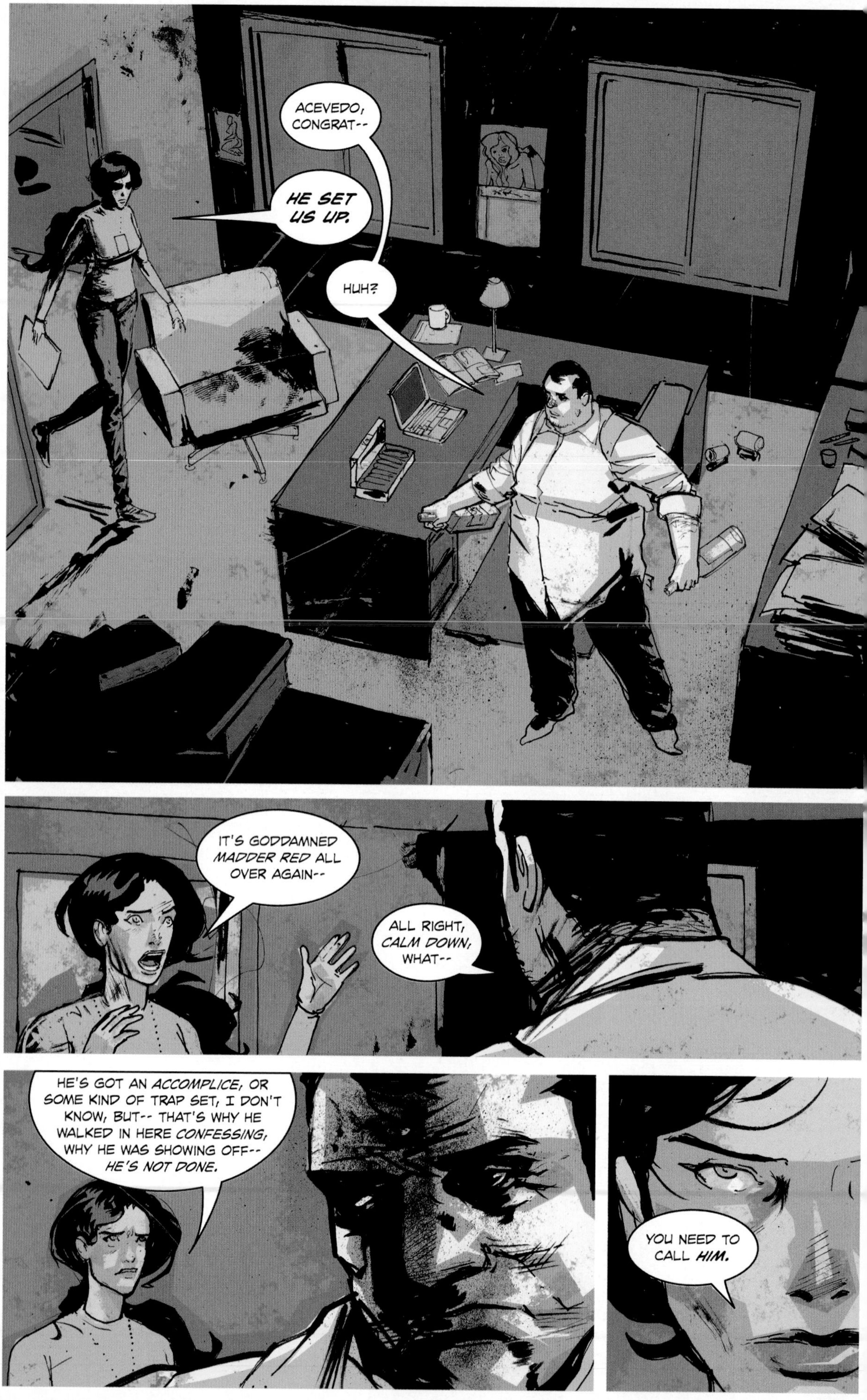
ACEVEDO, CONGRAT--
HE SET US UP.
HUH?
IT'S GODDAMNED *MADDER RED* ALL OVER AGAIN--
ALL RIGHT, *CALM DOWN,* WHAT--
HE'S GOT AN *ACCOMPLICE,* OR SOME KIND OF TRAP SET, I DON'T KNOW, BUT-- THAT'S WHY HE WALKED IN HERE *CONFESSING,* WHY HE WAS SHOWING OFF-- *HE'S NOT DONE.*
YOU NEED TO CALL *HIM.*

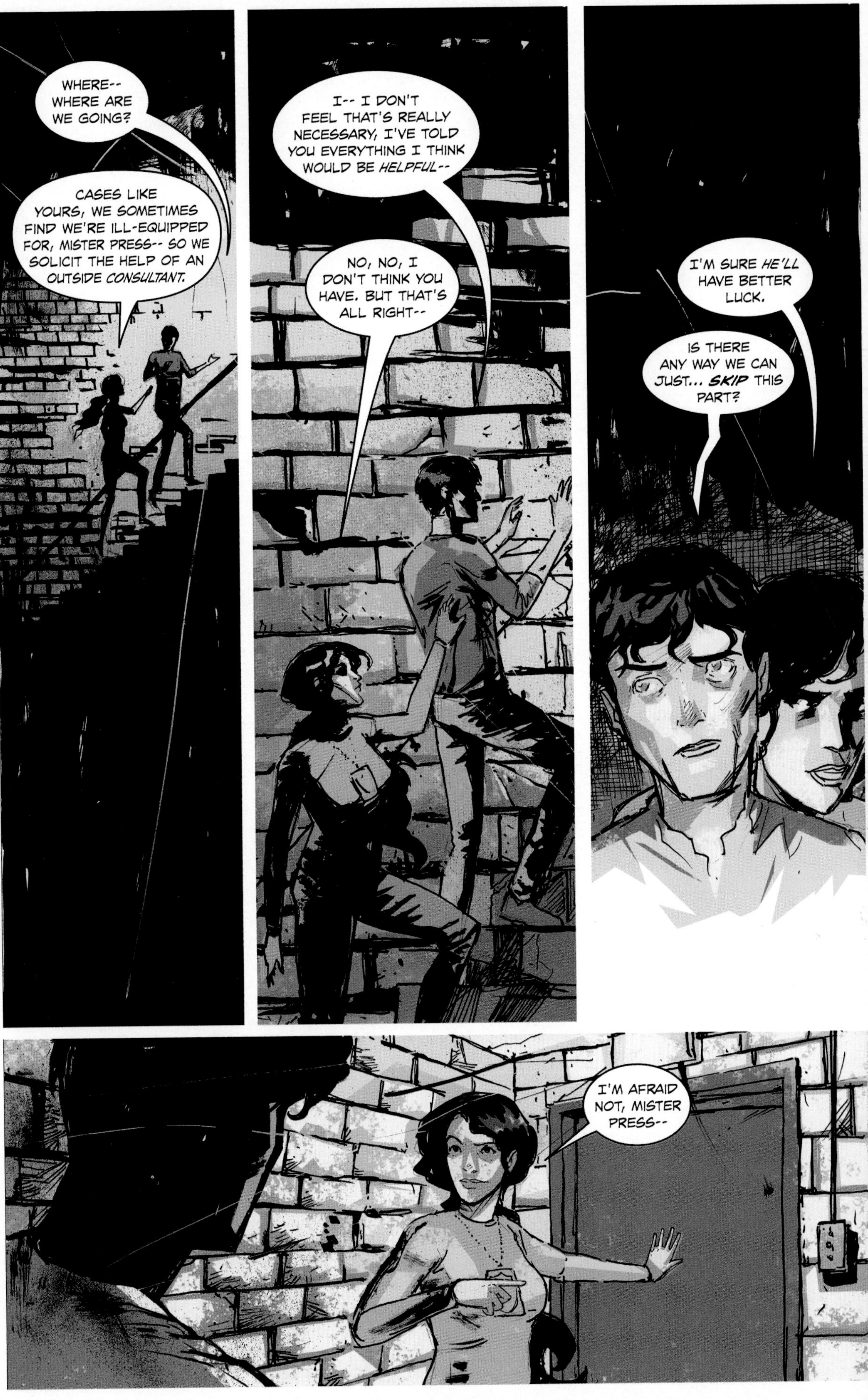
WHERE-- WHERE ARE WE GOING?
CASES LIKE YOURS, WE SOMETIMES FIND WE'RE ILL-EQUIPPED FOR, MISTER PRESS-- SO WE SOLICIT THE HELP OF AN OUTSIDE *CONSULTANT.*
I-- I DON'T FEEL THAT'S REALLY NECESSARY, I'VE TOLD YOU EVERYTHING I THINK WOULD BE *HELPFUL*--
NO, NO, I DON'T THINK YOU HAVE. BUT THAT'S ALL RIGHT--
I'M SURE *HE'LL* HAVE BETTER LUCK.
IS THERE ANY WAY WE CAN JUST... ***SKIP*** THIS PART?
I'M AFRAID NOT, MISTER PRESS--

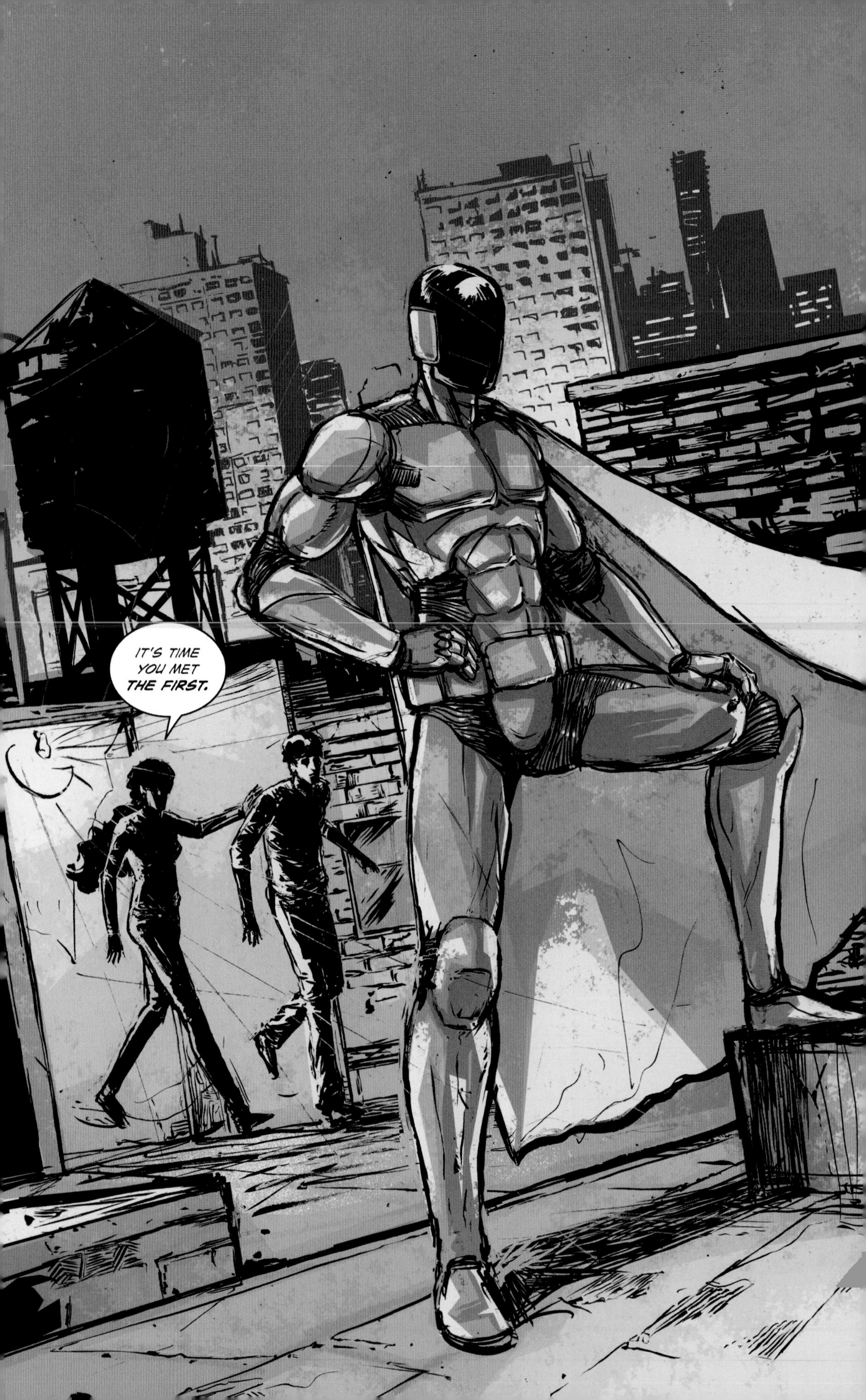
IT'S TIME YOU MET THE FIRST.

4
CHAPTER

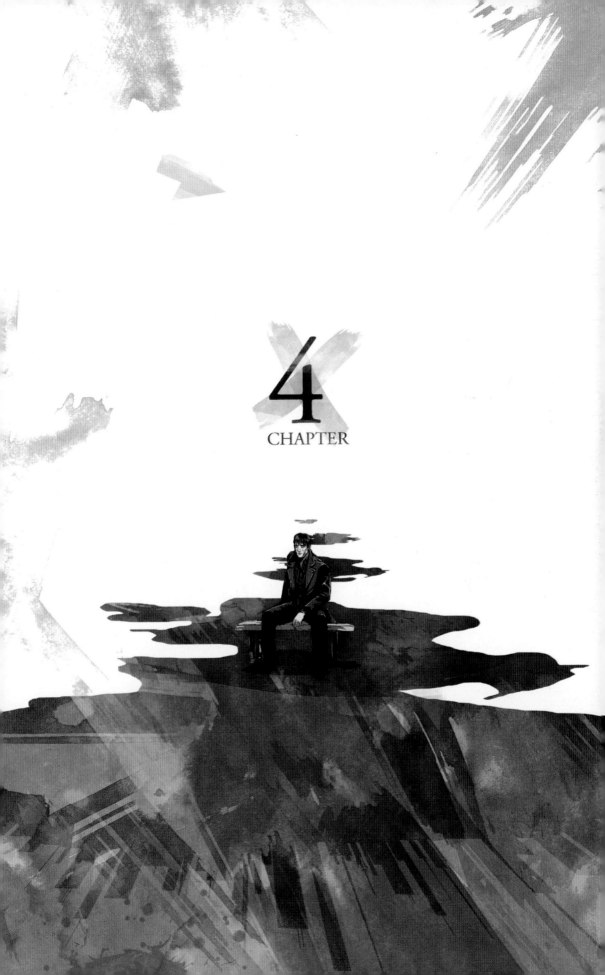

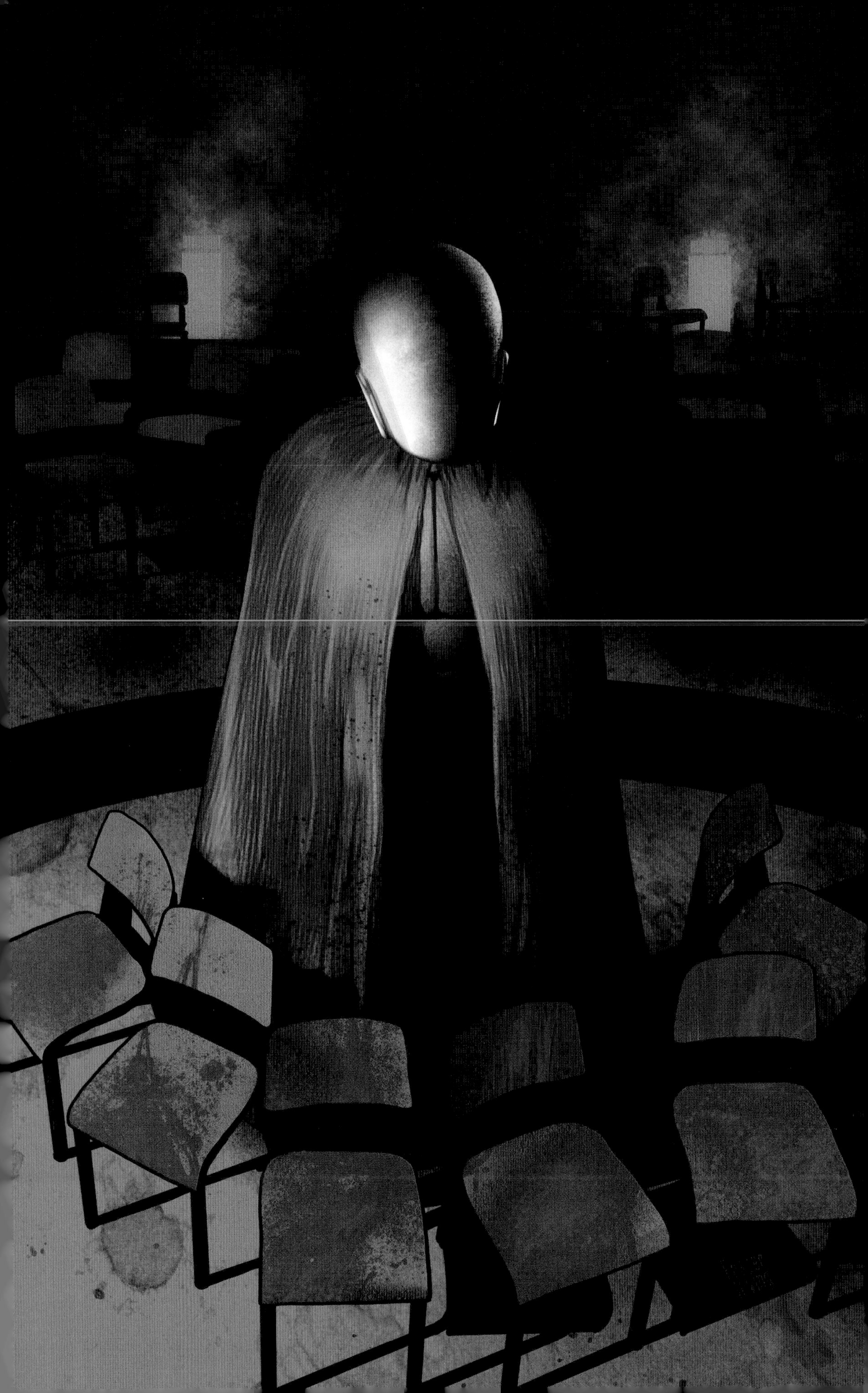

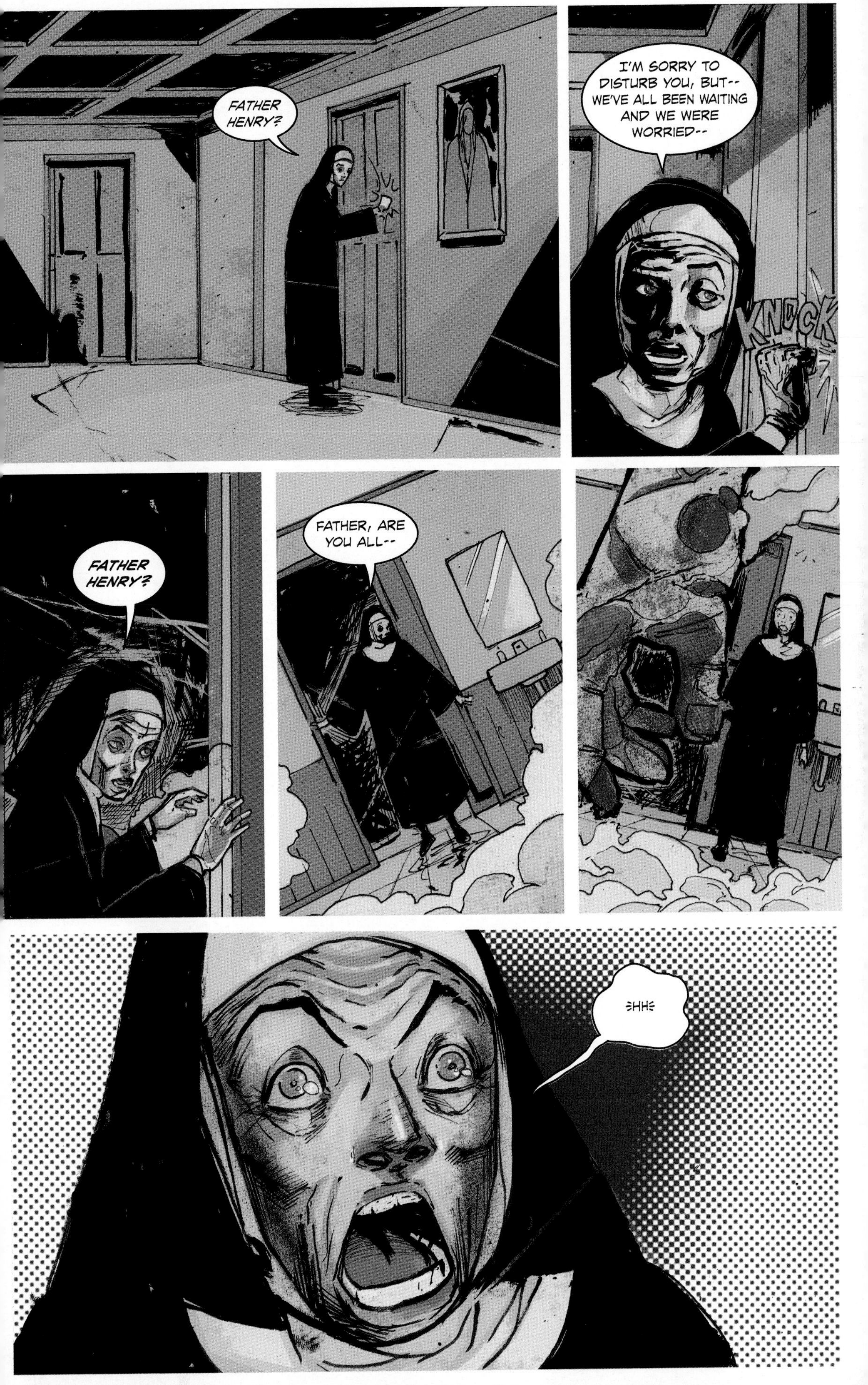
FATHER HENRY?
I'M SORRY TO DISTURB YOU, BUT-- WE'VE ALL BEEN WAITING AND WE WERE WORRIED--
KNOCK
FATHER HENRY?
FATHER, ARE YOU ALL--
=HH=

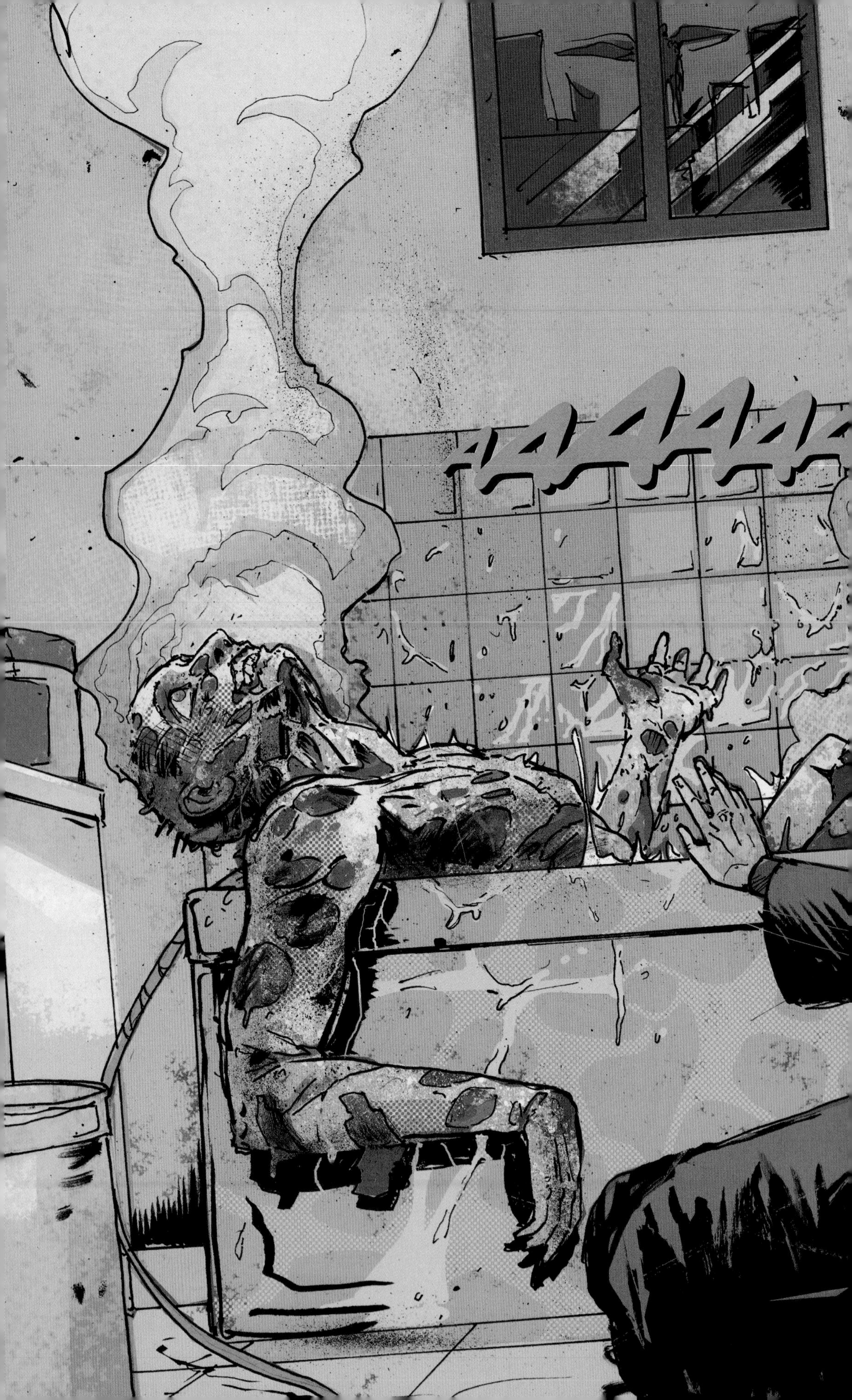
AAAAA

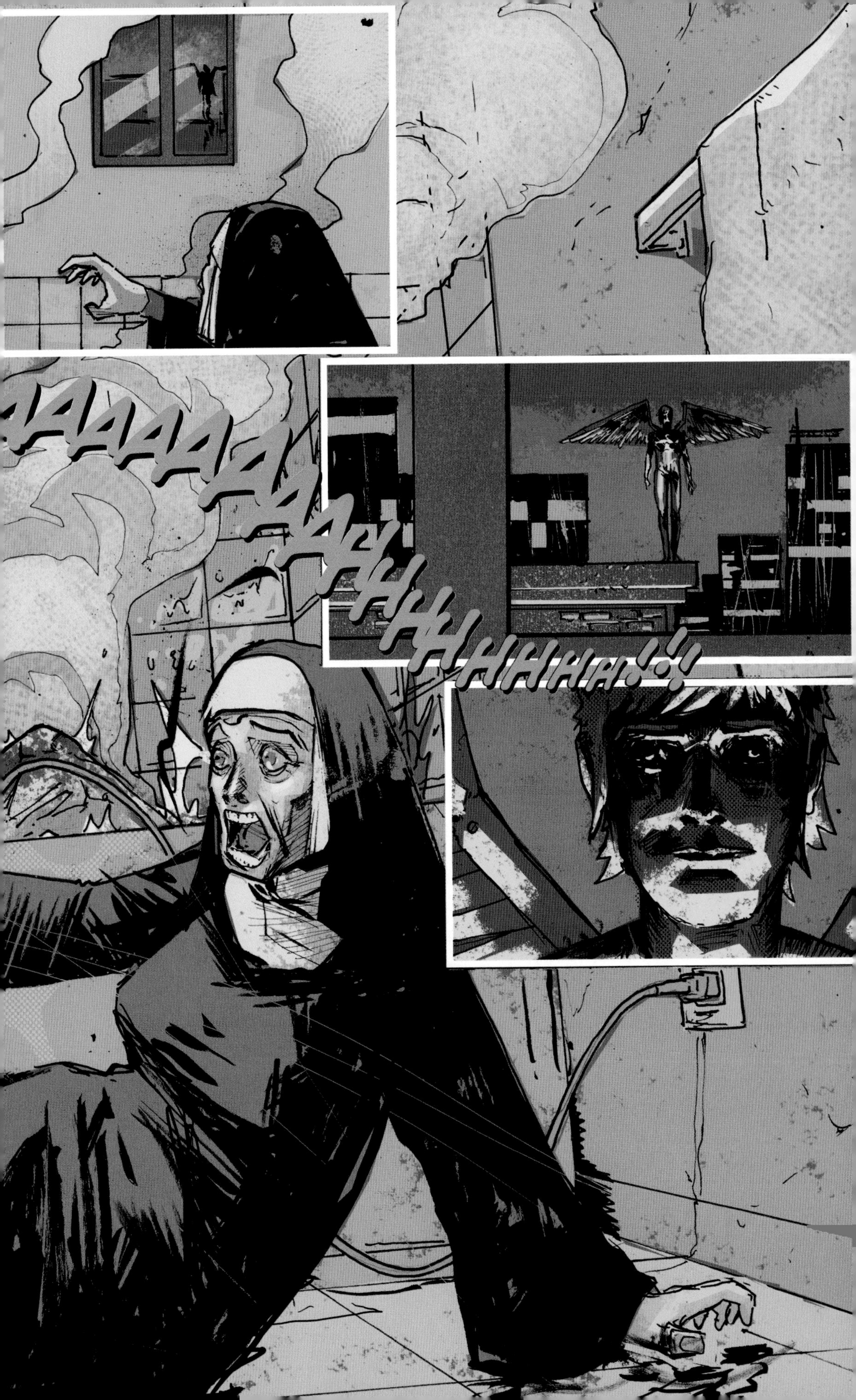
AAAAAAAAAHHHHHHHHHH!!!

CHAPTER FOUR
IF I STARTED TALKING ABOUT RELIGION

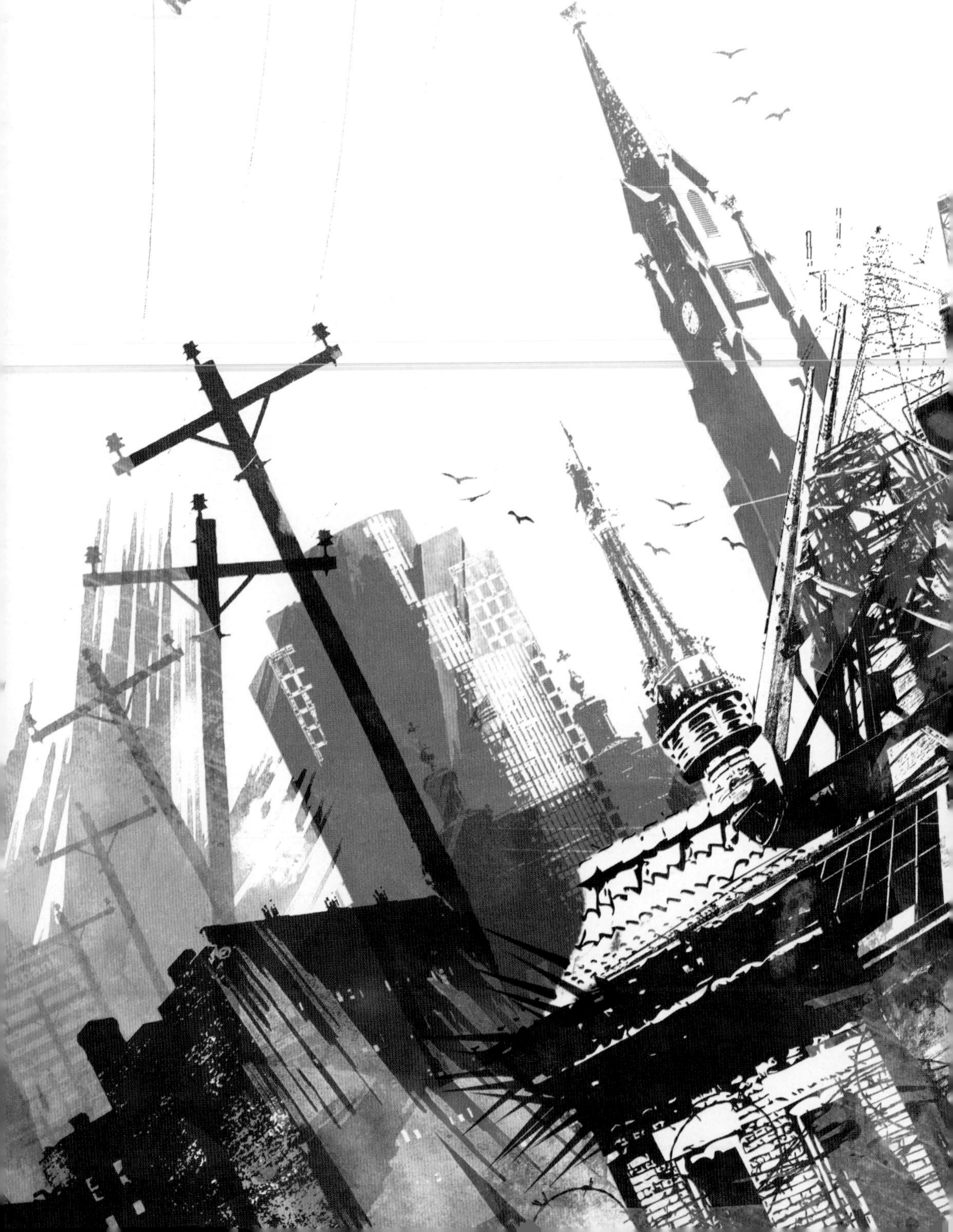

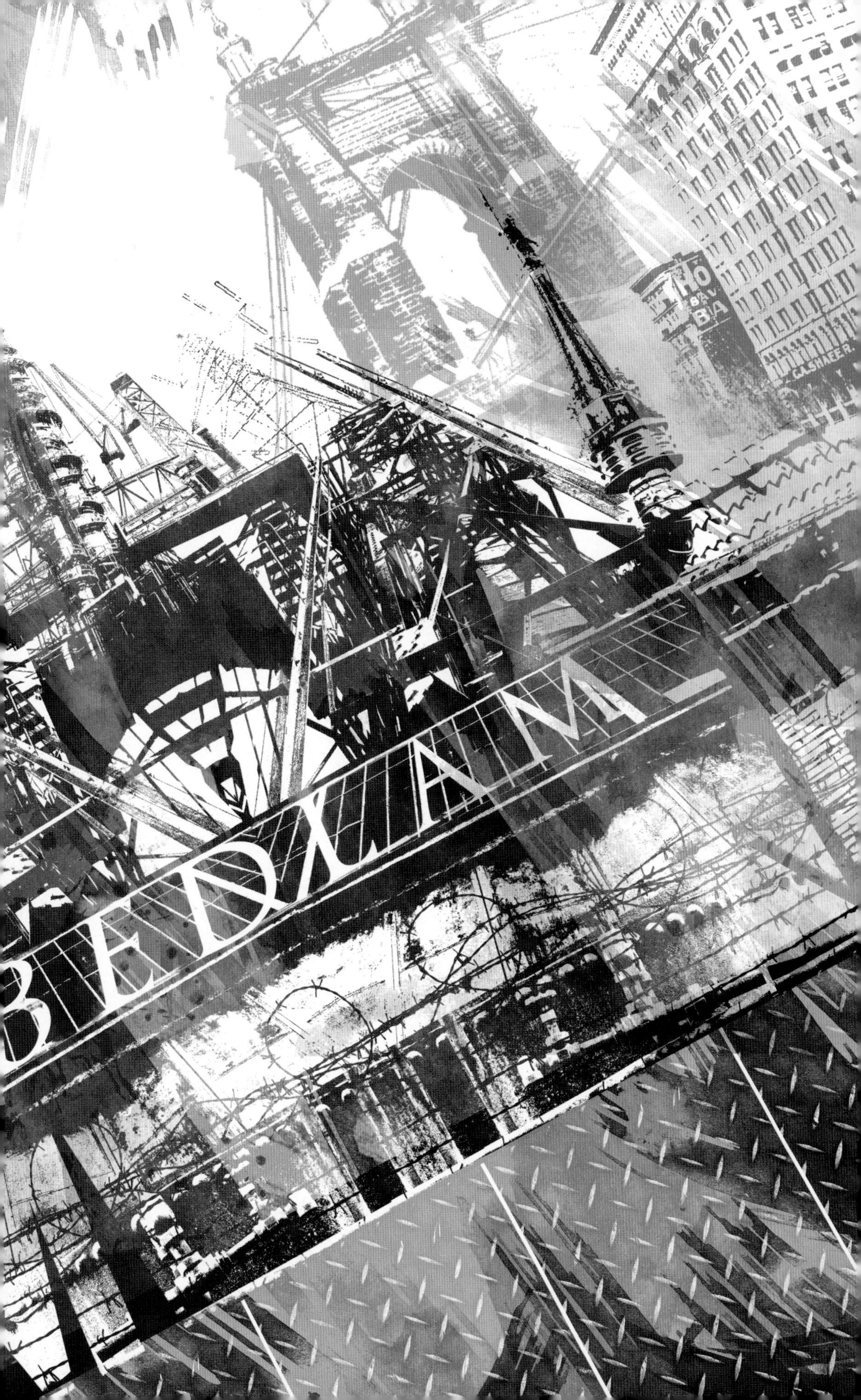
BEDLAM

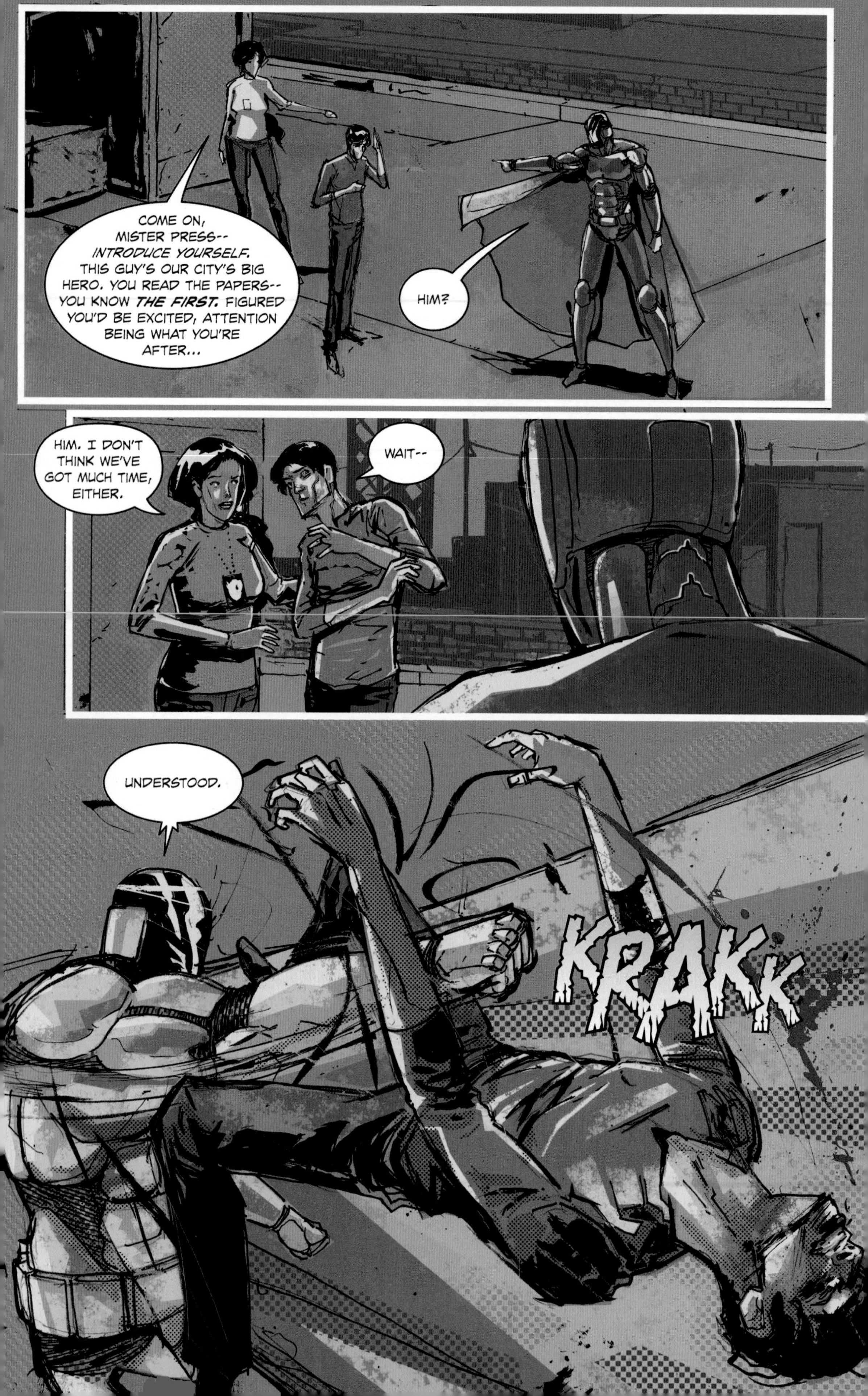
COME ON, MISTER PRESS-- *INTRODUCE YOURSELF.* THIS GUY'S OUR CITY'S BIG HERO. YOU READ THE PAPERS-- YOU KNOW ***THE FIRST.*** FIGURED YOU'D BE EXCITED, ATTENTION BEING WHAT YOU'RE AFTER...
HIM?
HIM. I DON'T THINK WE'VE GOT MUCH TIME, EITHER.
WAIT--
UNDERSTOOD.
KRAKK

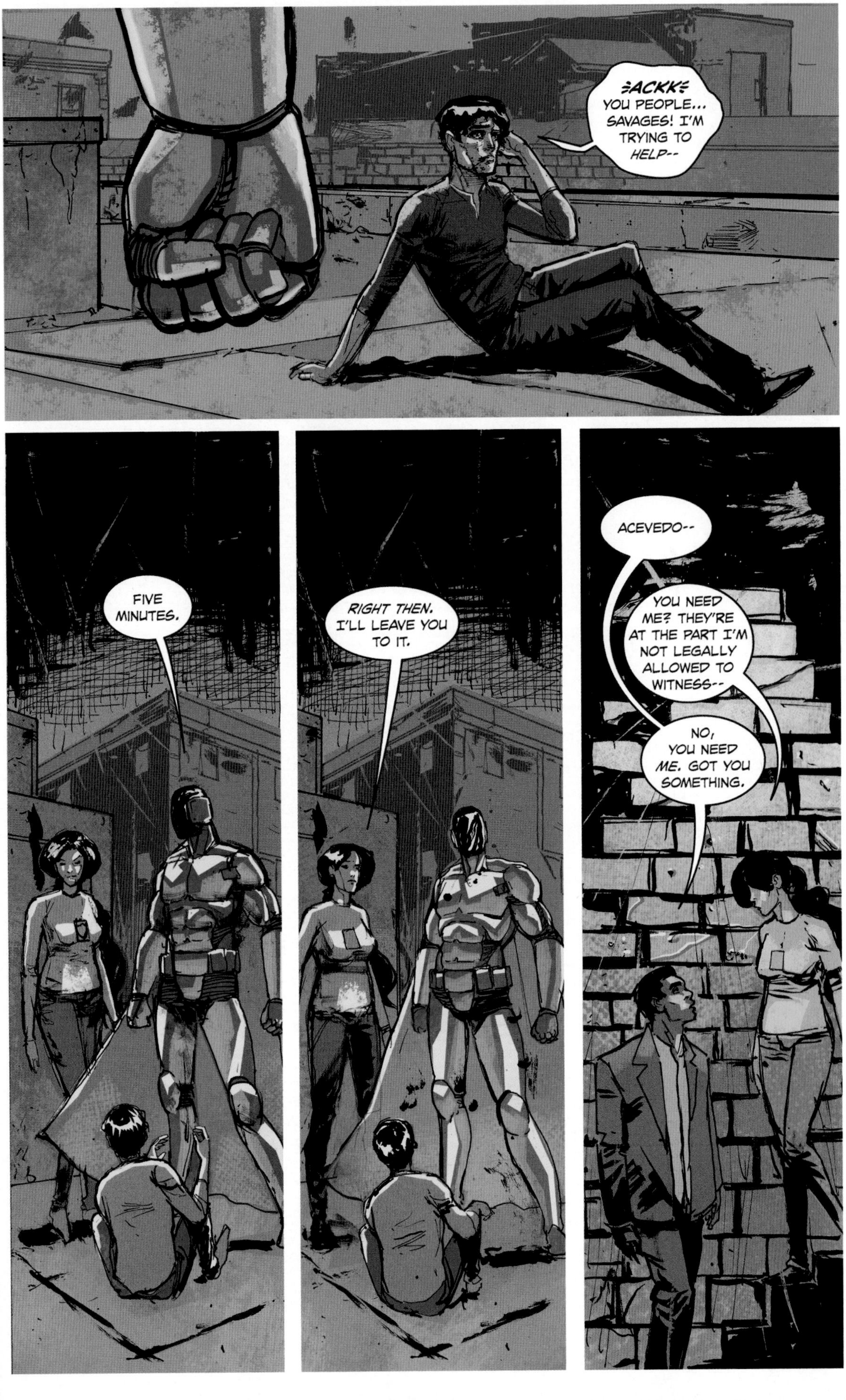
ACKK
YOU PEOPLE... SAVAGES! I'M TRYING TO *HELP*--
FIVE MINUTES.
RIGHT THEN. I'LL LEAVE YOU TO IT.
ACEVEDO--
YOU NEED ME? THEY'RE AT THE PART I'M NOT LEGALLY ALLOWED TO WITNESS--
NO, YOU NEED *ME*. GOT YOU SOMETHING.

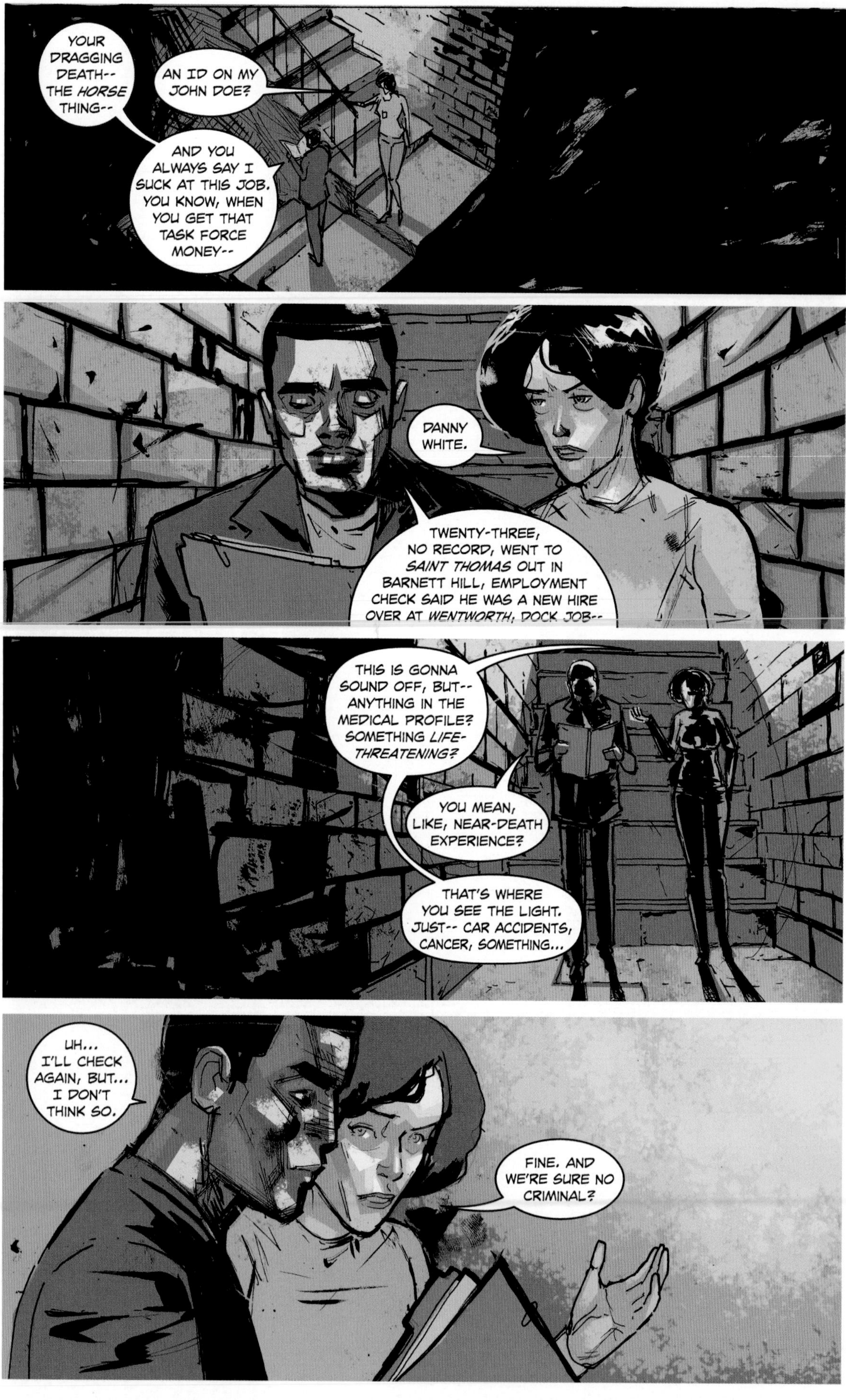
YOUR DRAGGING DEATH-- THE *HORSE* THING--
AN ID ON MY JOHN DOE?
AND YOU ALWAYS SAY I SUCK AT THIS JOB. YOU KNOW, WHEN YOU GET THAT TASK FORCE MONEY--
DANNY WHITE.
TWENTY-THREE, NO RECORD, WENT TO *SAINT THOMAS* OUT IN BARNETT HILL, EMPLOYMENT CHECK SAID HE WAS A NEW HIRE OVER AT *WENTWORTH*; DOCK JOB--
THIS IS GONNA SOUND OFF, BUT-- ANYTHING IN THE MEDICAL PROFILE? SOMETHING *LIFE-THREATENING?*
YOU MEAN, LIKE, NEAR-DEATH EXPERIENCE?
THAT'S WHERE YOU SEE THE LIGHT. JUST-- CAR ACCIDENTS, CANCER, SOMETHING...
UH... I'LL CHECK AGAIN, BUT... I DON'T THINK SO.
FINE. AND WE'RE SURE NO CRIMINAL?

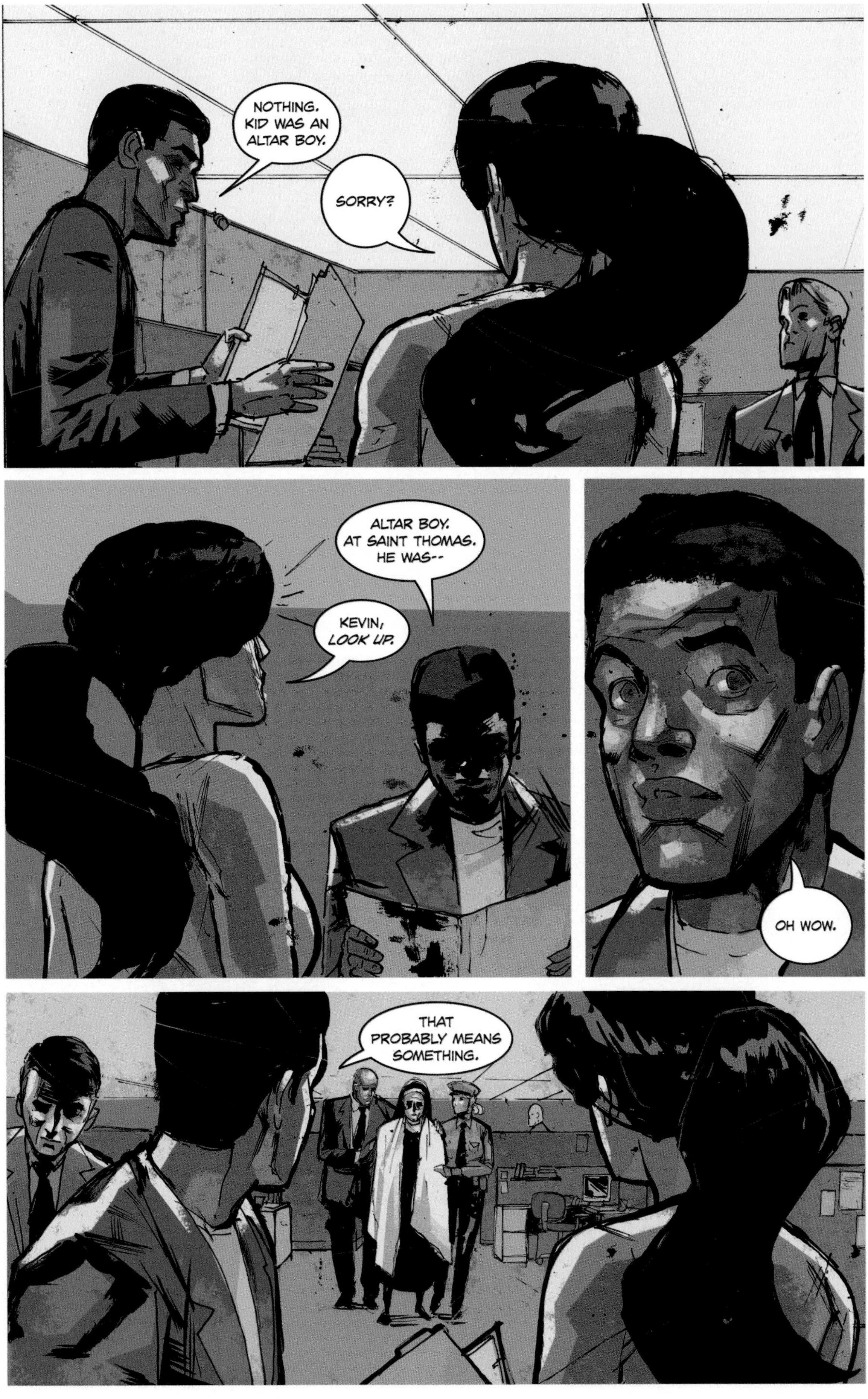
NOTHING. KID WAS AN ALTAR BOY.
SORRY?
ALTAR BOY. AT SAINT THOMAS. HE WAS--
KEVIN, LOOK UP.
OH WOW.
THAT PROBABLY MEANS SOMETHING.

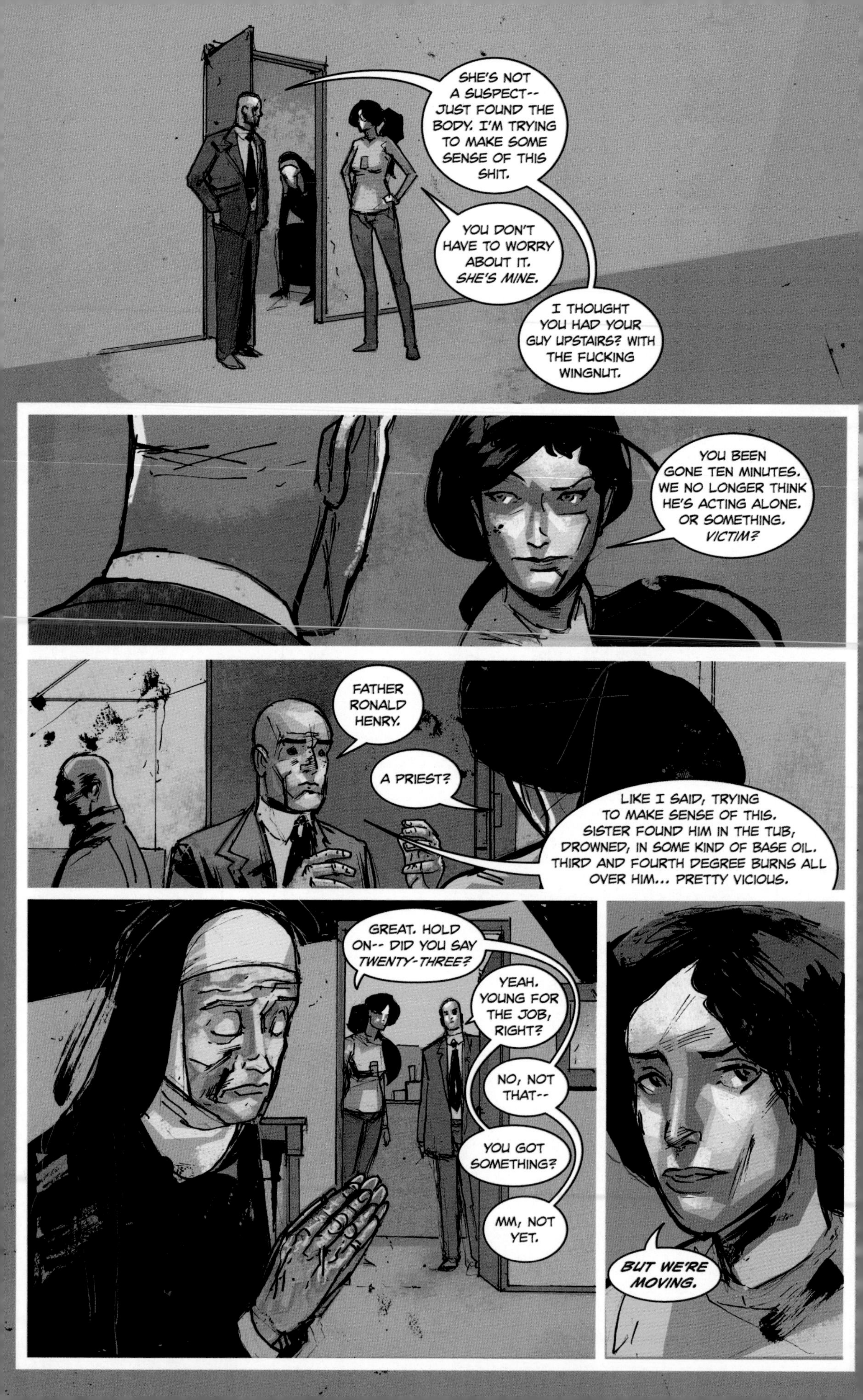
SHE'S NOT A SUSPECT-- JUST FOUND THE BODY. I'M TRYING TO MAKE SOME SENSE OF THIS SHIT.
YOU DON'T HAVE TO WORRY ABOUT IT. *SHE'S MINE.*
I THOUGHT YOU HAD YOUR GUY UPSTAIRS? WITH THE FUCKING WINGNUT.
YOU BEEN GONE TEN MINUTES. WE NO LONGER THINK HE'S ACTING ALONE. OR SOMETHING. *VICTIM?*
FATHER RONALD HENRY.
A PRIEST?
LIKE I SAID, TRYING TO MAKE SENSE OF THIS. SISTER FOUND HIM IN THE TUB, DROWNED, IN SOME KIND OF BASE OIL. THIRD AND FOURTH DEGREE BURNS ALL OVER HIM... PRETTY VICIOUS.
GREAT. HOLD ON-- DID YOU SAY *TWENTY-THREE?*
YEAH. YOUNG FOR THE JOB, RIGHT?
NO, NOT THAT--
YOU GOT SOMETHING?
MM, NOT YET.
BUT WE'RE MOVING.

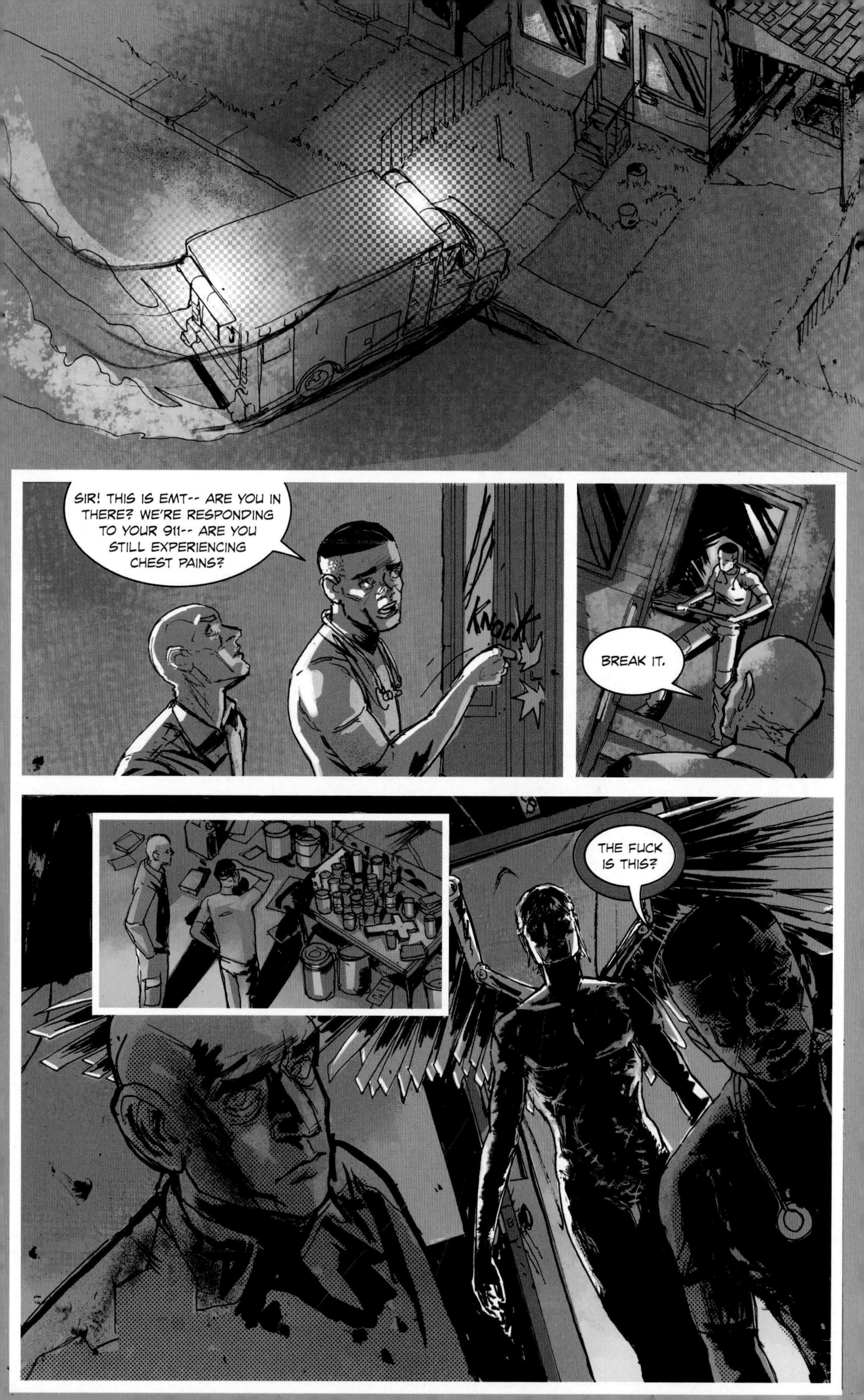
SIR! THIS IS EMT-- ARE YOU IN THERE? WE'RE RESPONDING TO YOUR 911-- ARE YOU STILL EXPERIENCING CHEST PAINS?
KNOCK
BREAK IT.
THE FUCK IS THIS?

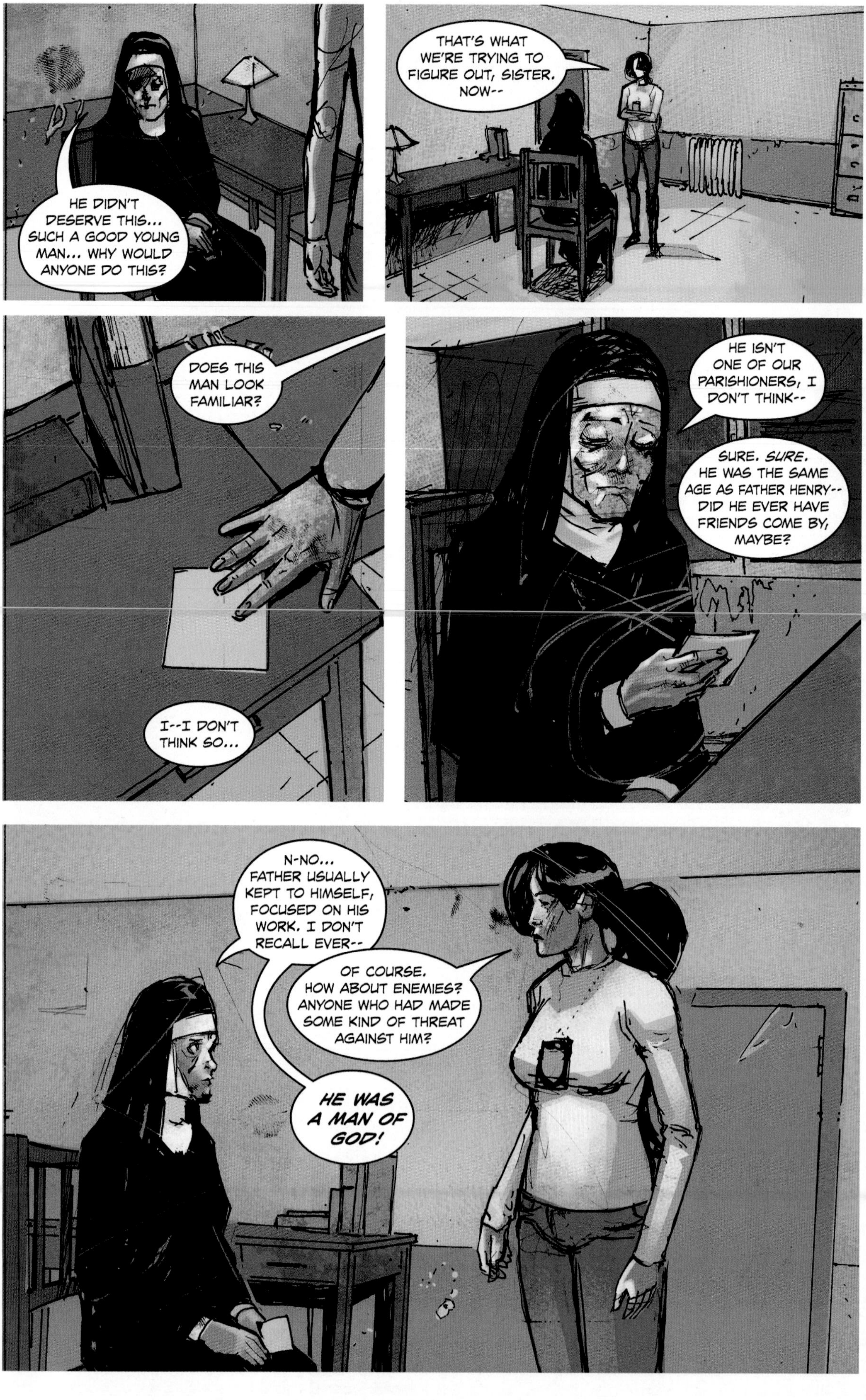
HE DIDN'T DESERVE THIS... SUCH A GOOD YOUNG MAN... WHY WOULD ANYONE DO THIS?
THAT'S WHAT WE'RE TRYING TO FIGURE OUT, SISTER. NOW--
DOES THIS MAN LOOK FAMILIAR?
I--I DON'T THINK SO...
HE ISN'T ONE OF OUR PARISHIONERS, I DON'T THINK--
SURE. *SURE.* HE WAS THE SAME AGE AS FATHER HENRY-- DID HE EVER HAVE FRIENDS COME BY, MAYBE?
N-NO... FATHER USUALLY KEPT TO HIMSELF, FOCUSED ON HIS WORK. I DON'T RECALL EVER--
OF COURSE. HOW ABOUT ENEMIES? ANYONE WHO HAD MADE SOME KIND OF THREAT AGAINST HIM?
HE WAS A MAN OF GOD!

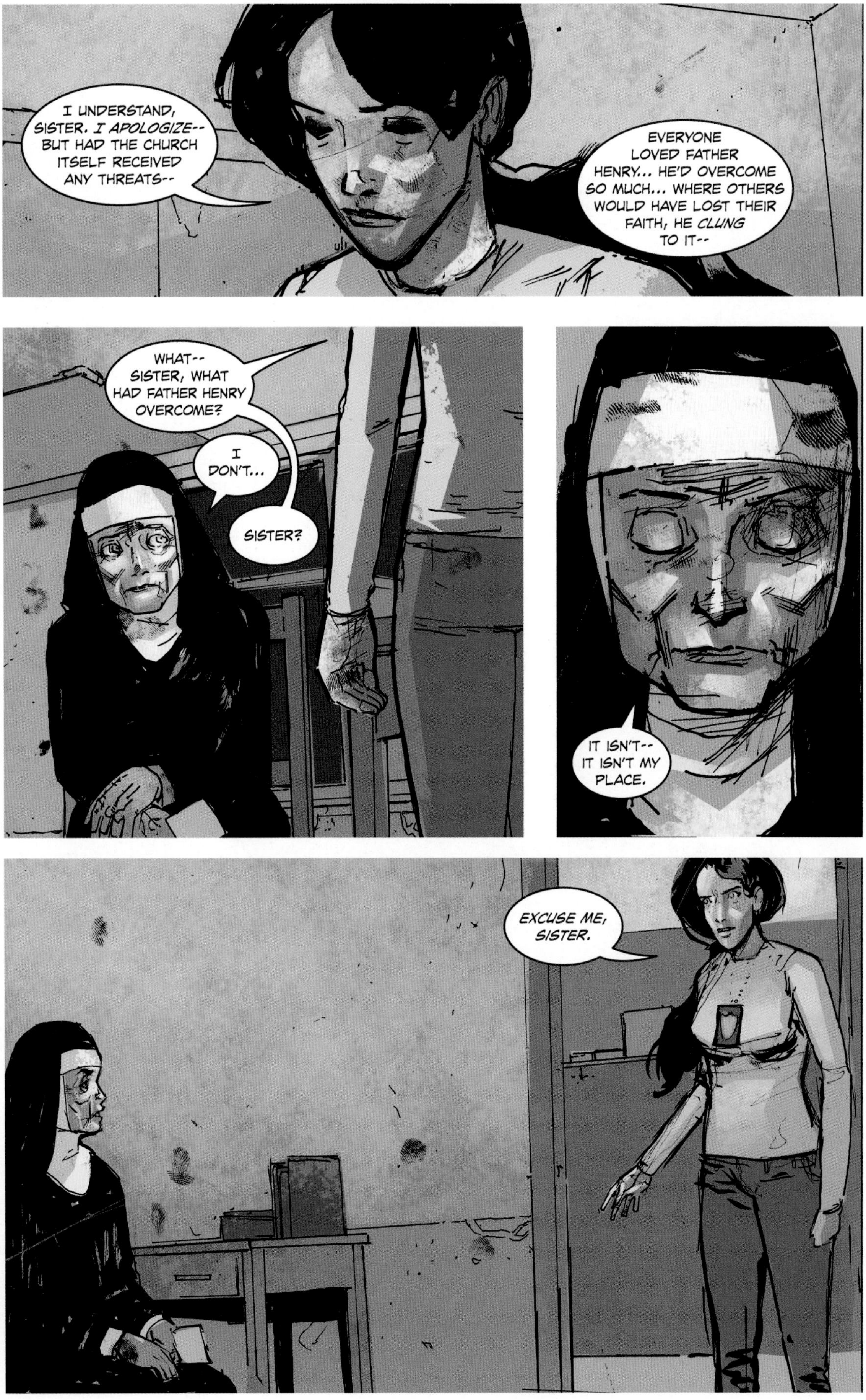
I UNDERSTAND, SISTER. I APOLOGIZE-- BUT HAD THE CHURCH ITSELF RECEIVED ANY THREATS--
EVERYONE LOVED FATHER HENRY... HE'D OVERCOME SO MUCH... WHERE OTHERS WOULD HAVE LOST THEIR FAITH, HE CLUNG TO IT--
WHAT-- SISTER, WHAT HAD FATHER HENRY OVERCOME?
I DON'T...
SISTER?
IT ISN'T-- IT ISN'T MY PLACE.
EXCUSE ME, SISTER.

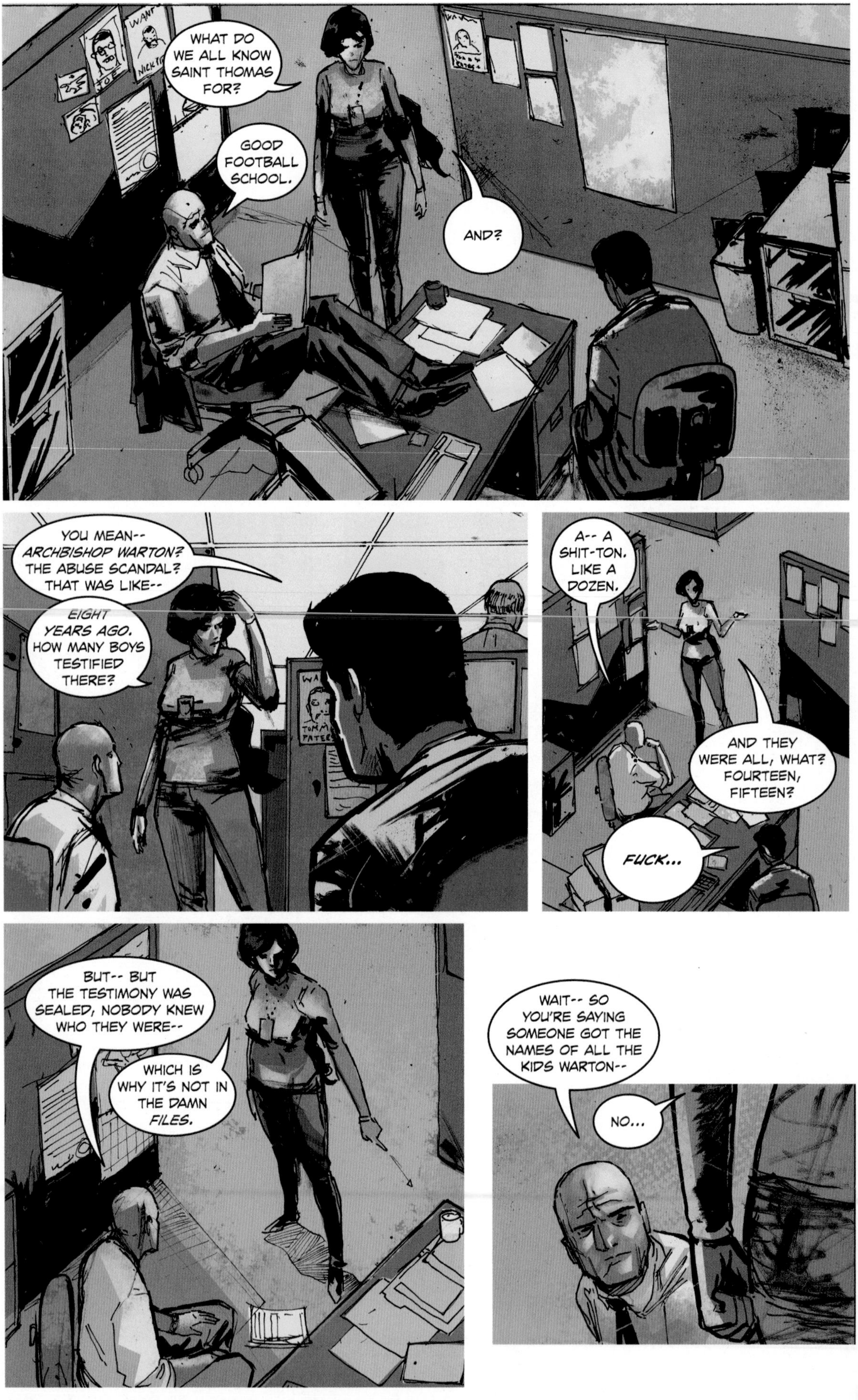
WHAT DO WE ALL KNOW SAINT THOMAS FOR?
GOOD FOOTBALL SCHOOL.
AND?
YOU MEAN-- *ARCHBISHOP WARTON?* THE ABUSE SCANDAL? THAT WAS LIKE--
EIGHT YEARS AGO. HOW MANY BOYS TESTIFIED THERE?
A-- A SHIT-TON. LIKE A DOZEN.
AND THEY WERE ALL, WHAT? FOURTEEN, FIFTEEN?
FUCK...
BUT-- BUT THE TESTIMONY WAS SEALED, NOBODY KNEW WHO THEY WERE--
WHICH IS WHY IT'S NOT IN THE DAMN *FILES.*
WAIT-- SO YOU'RE SAYING SOMEONE GOT THE NAMES OF ALL THE KIDS WARTON--
NO...

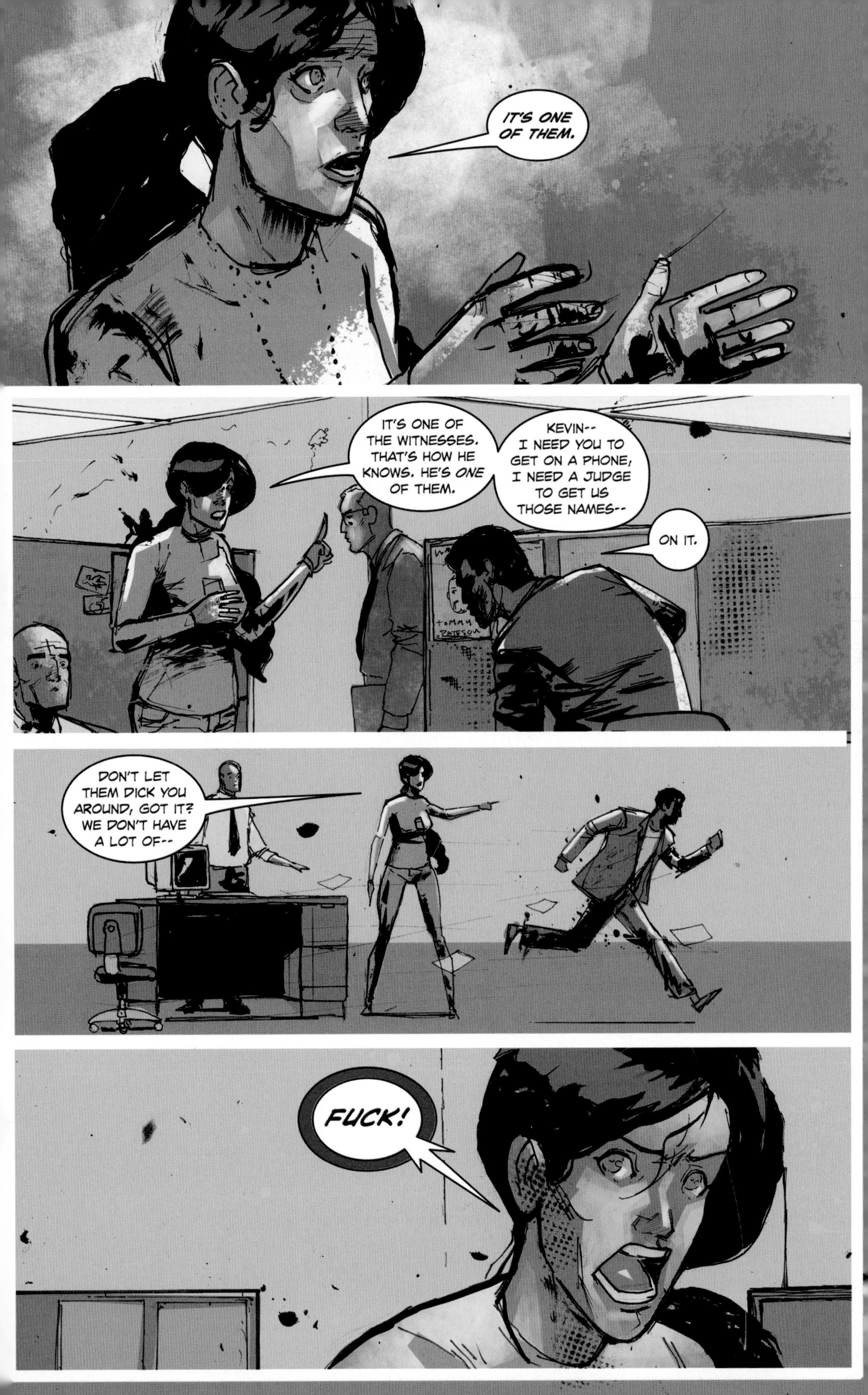
IT'S ONE OF THEM.
IT'S ONE OF THE WITNESSES. THAT'S HOW HE KNOWS. HE'S *ONE* OF THEM.
KEVIN-- I NEED YOU TO GET ON A PHONE, I NEED A JUDGE TO GET US THOSE NAMES--
ON IT.
DON'T LET THEM DICK YOU AROUND, GOT IT? WE DON'T HAVE A LOT OF--
FUCK!

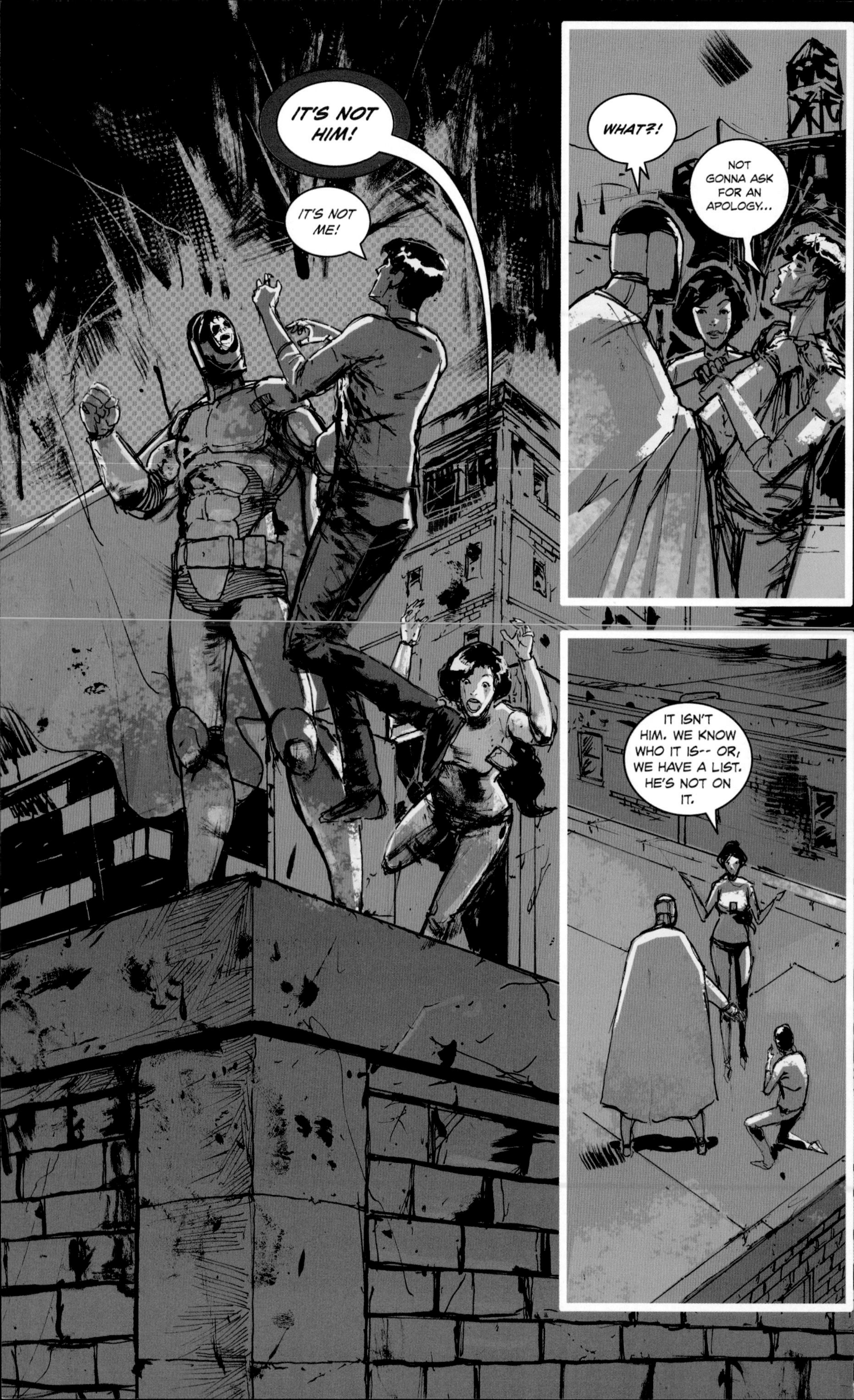
IT'S NOT HIM!
IT'S NOT ME!
WHAT?!
NOT GONNA ASK FOR AN APOLOGY...
IT ISN'T HIM. WE KNOW WHO IT IS-- OR, WE HAVE A LIST. HE'S NOT ON IT.

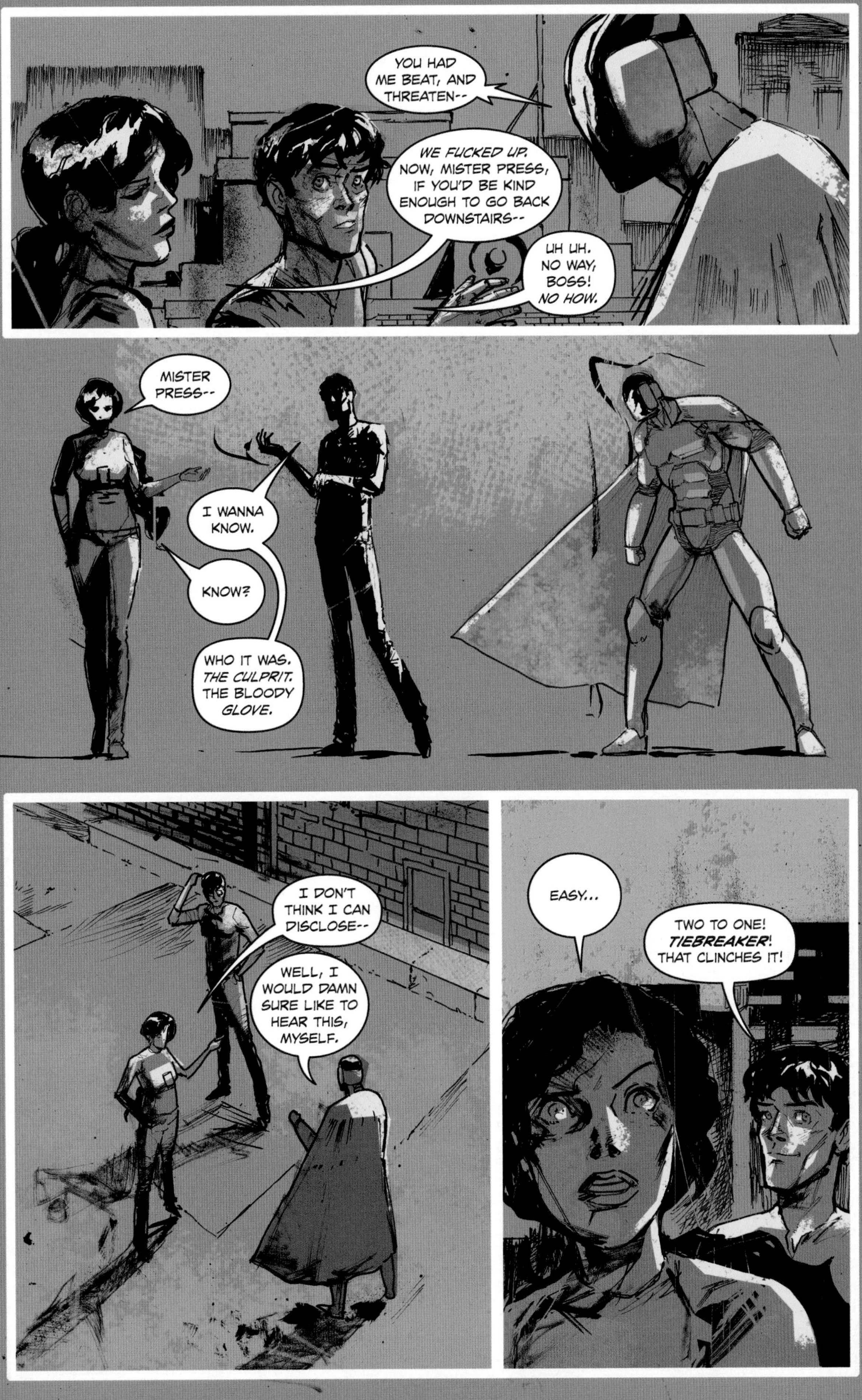

YOU HAD ME BEAT, AND THREATEN--
WE FUCKED UP. NOW, MISTER PRESS, IF YOU'D BE KIND ENOUGH TO GO BACK DOWNSTAIRS--
UH UH. NO WAY, BOSS! NO HOW.
MISTER PRESS--
I WANNA KNOW.
KNOW?
WHO IT WAS. THE CULPRIT. THE BLOODY GLOVE.
I DON'T THINK I CAN DISCLOSE--
WELL, I WOULD DAMN SURE LIKE TO HEAR THIS, MYSELF.
EASY...
TWO TO ONE! TIEBREAKER! THAT CLINCHES IT!

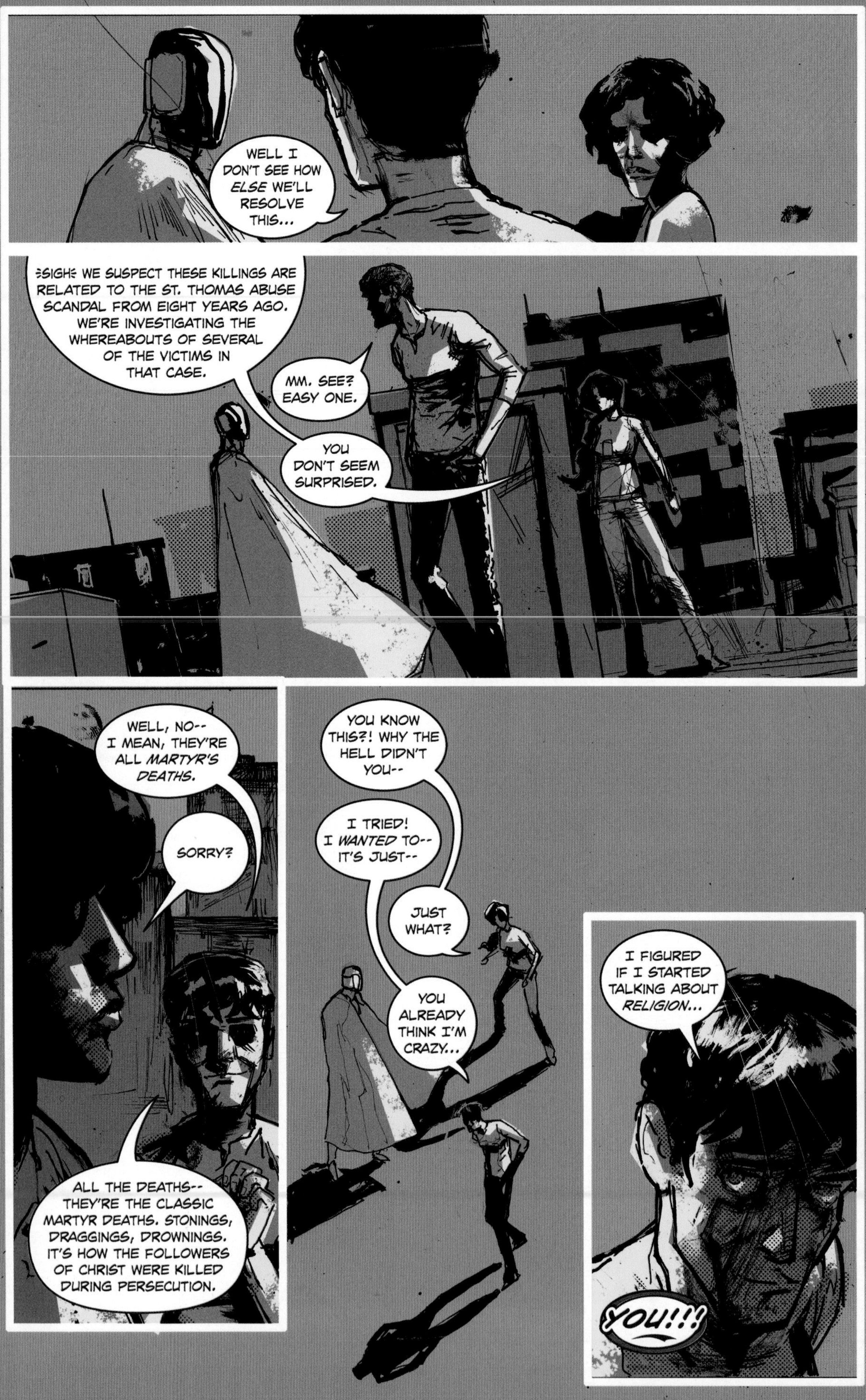
WELL I DON'T SEE HOW *ELSE* WE'LL RESOLVE THIS...
=SIGH= WE SUSPECT THESE KILLINGS ARE RELATED TO THE ST. THOMAS ABUSE SCANDAL FROM EIGHT YEARS AGO. WE'RE INVESTIGATING THE WHEREABOUTS OF SEVERAL OF THE VICTIMS IN THAT CASE.
MM. SEE? EASY ONE.
YOU DON'T SEEM SURPRISED.
WELL, NO-- I MEAN, THEY'RE ALL *MARTYR'S DEATHS.*
SORRY?
ALL THE DEATHS-- THEY'RE THE CLASSIC MARTYR DEATHS. STONINGS, DRAGGINGS, DROWNINGS. IT'S HOW THE FOLLOWERS OF CHRIST WERE KILLED DURING PERSECUTION.
YOU KNOW THIS?! WHY THE HELL DIDN'T YOU--
I TRIED! I *WANTED* TO-- IT'S JUST--
JUST WHAT?
YOU ALREADY THINK I'M CRAZY...
I FIGURED IF I STARTED TALKING ABOUT *RELIGION*...
YOU!!!

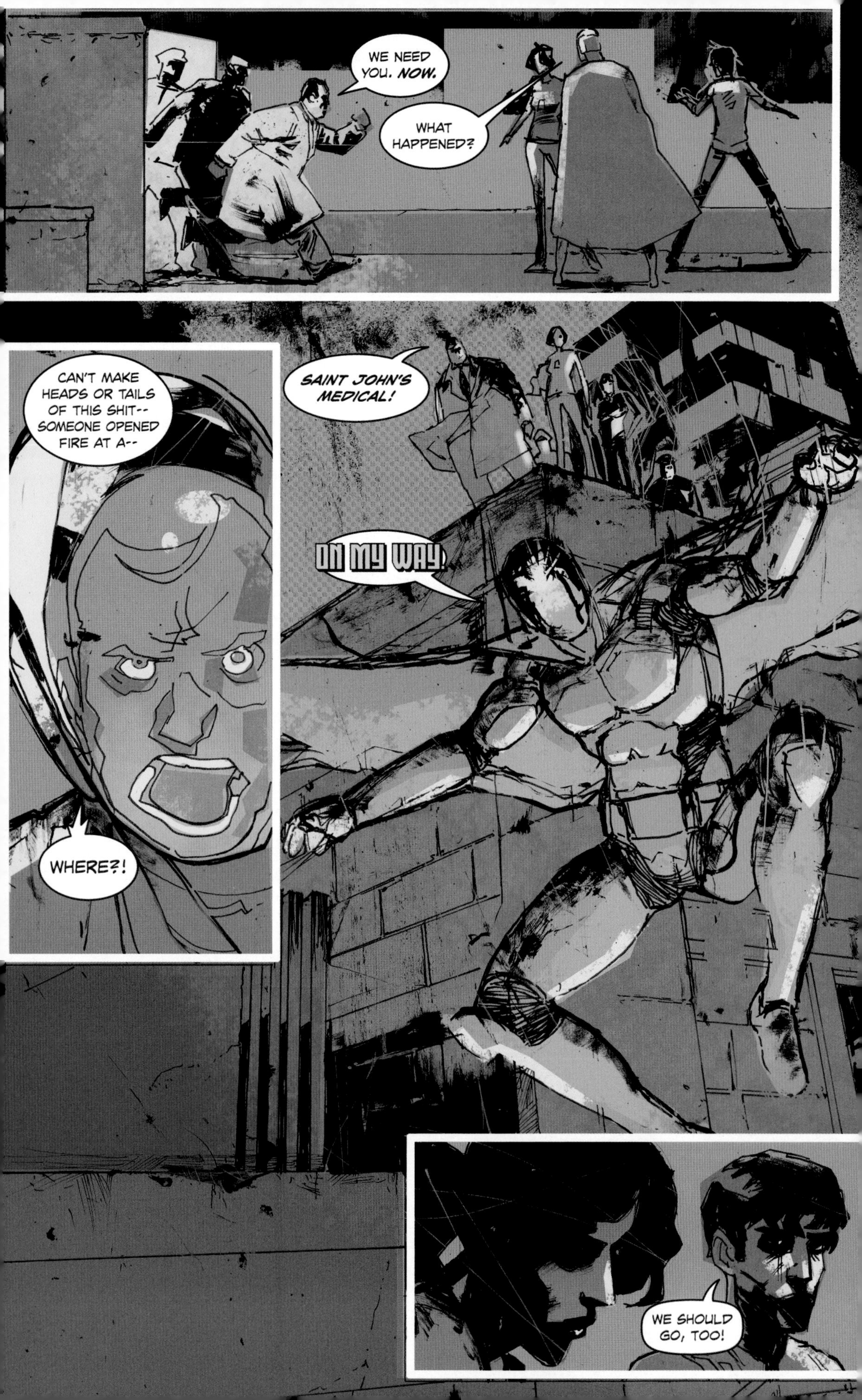

WE NEED YOU. NOW.
WHAT HAPPENED?
CAN'T MAKE HEADS OR TAILS OF THIS SHIT-- SOMEONE OPENED FIRE AT A--
WHERE?!
SAINT JOHN'S MEDICAL!
ON MY WAY!
WE SHOULD GO, TOO!

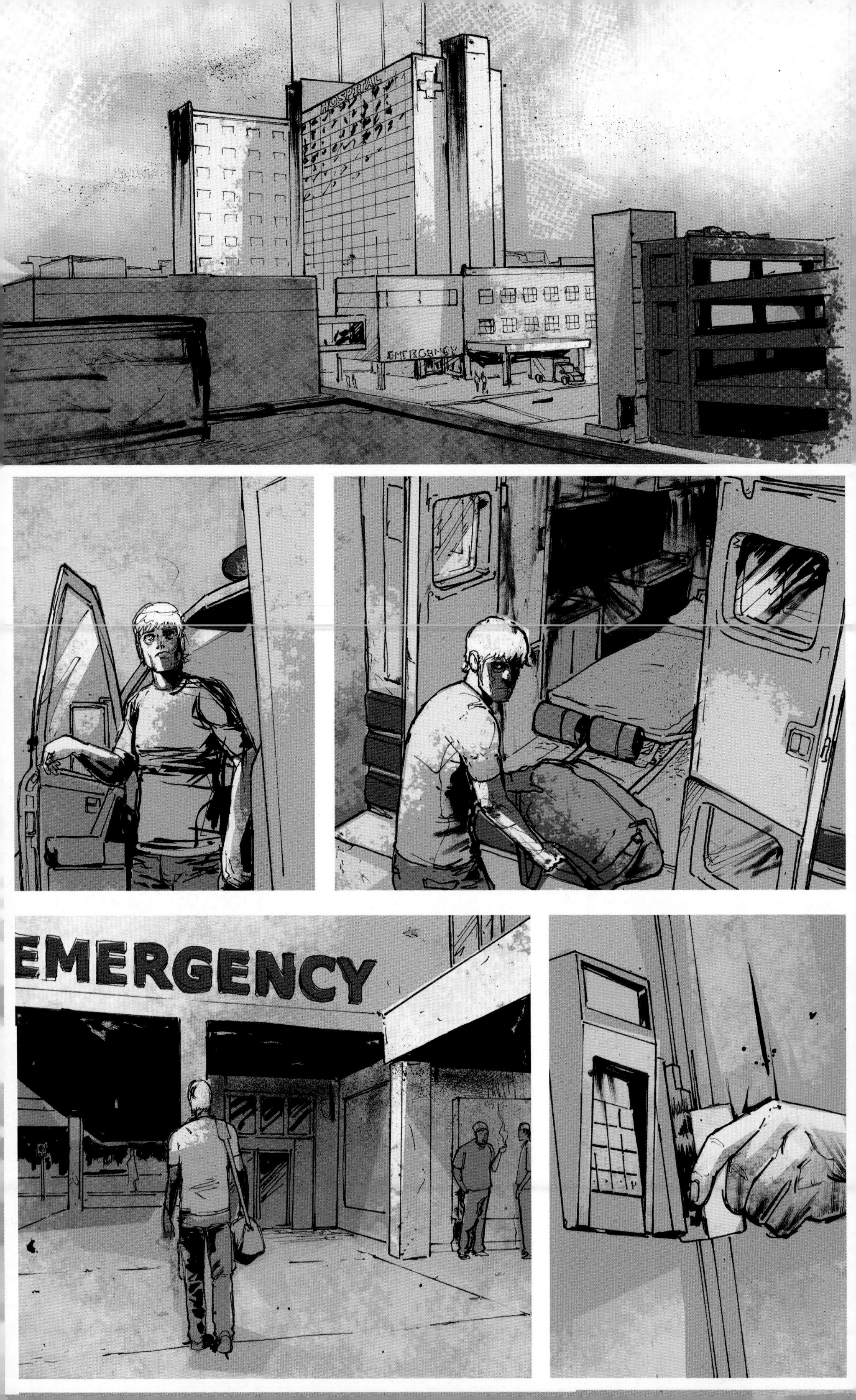
HOSPITAL
EMERGENCY

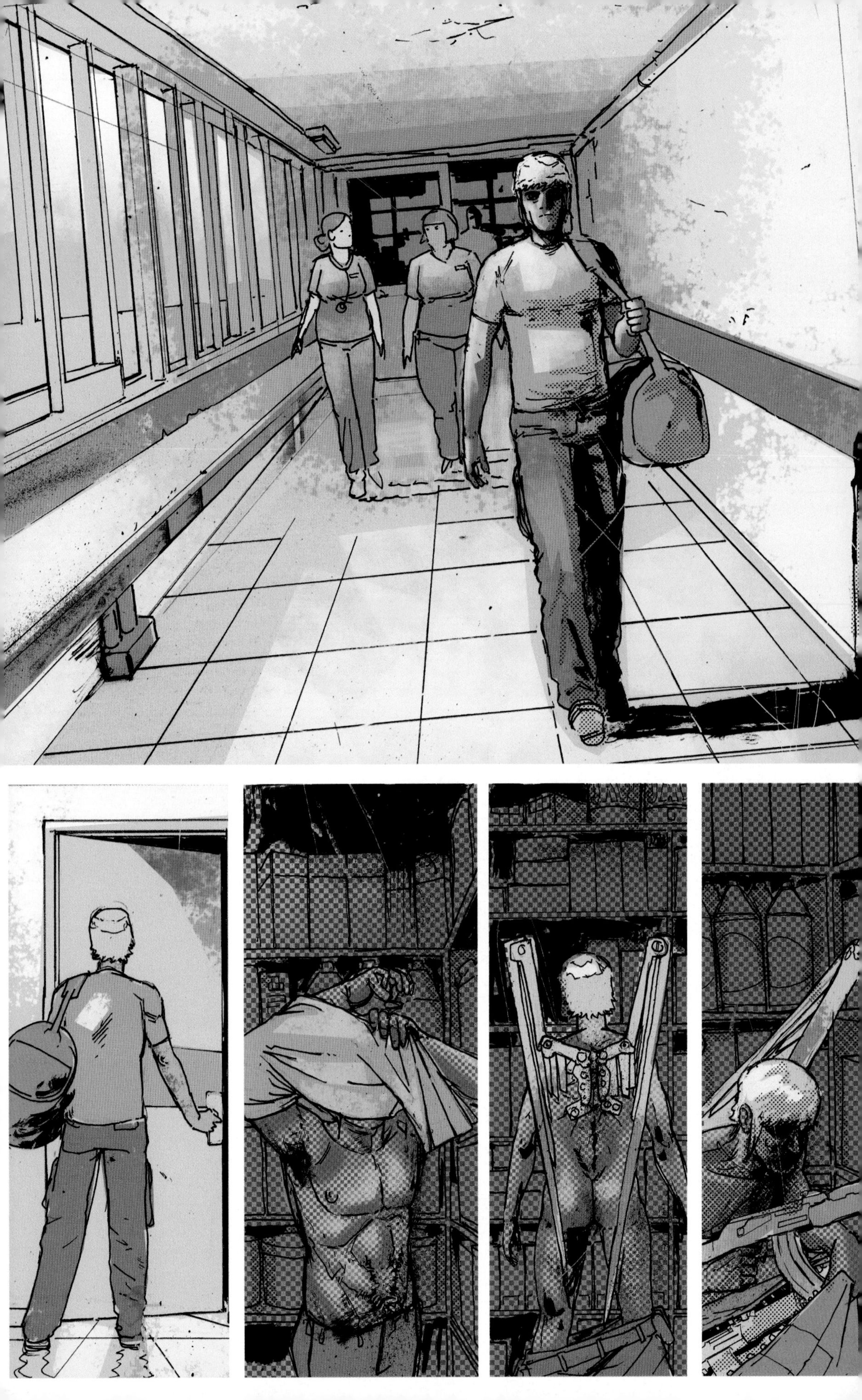

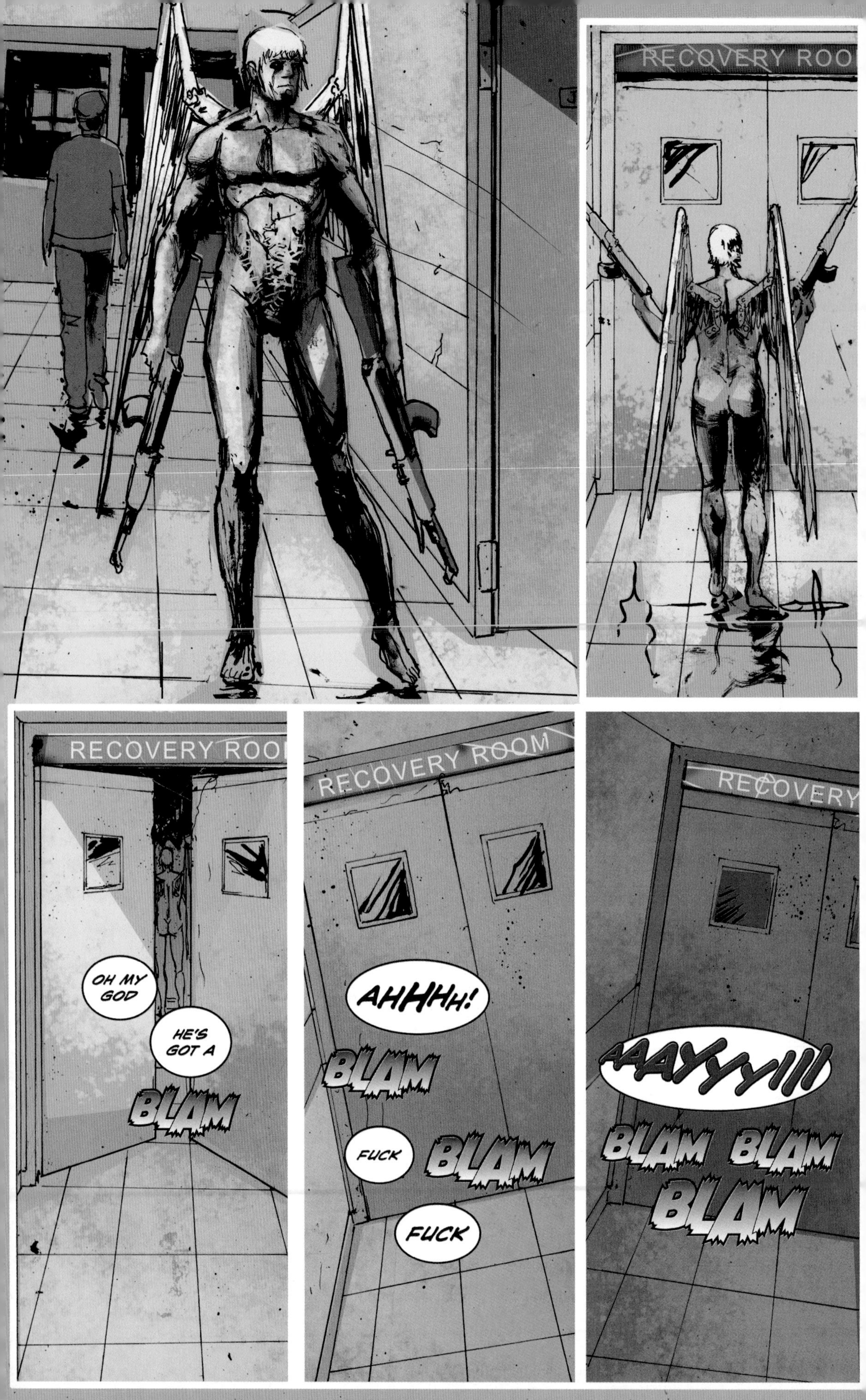
RECOVERY ROO
RECOVERY ROO
OH MY GOD
HE'S GOT A
BLAM
RECOVERY ROOM
AHHHh!
BLAM
FUCK
BLAM
FUCK
RECOVERY
AAAYyyIII
BLAM BLAM
BLAM

5
CHAPTER

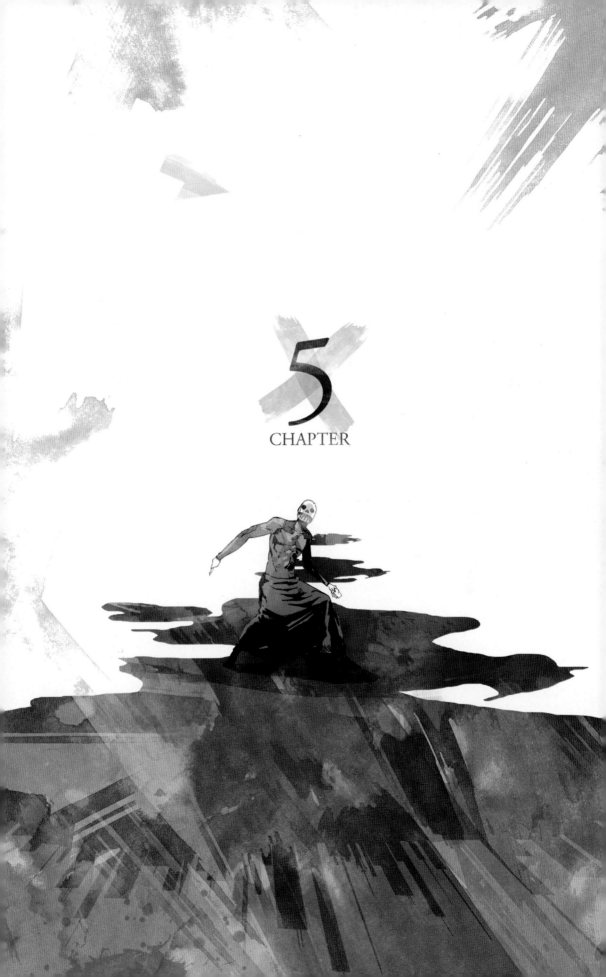

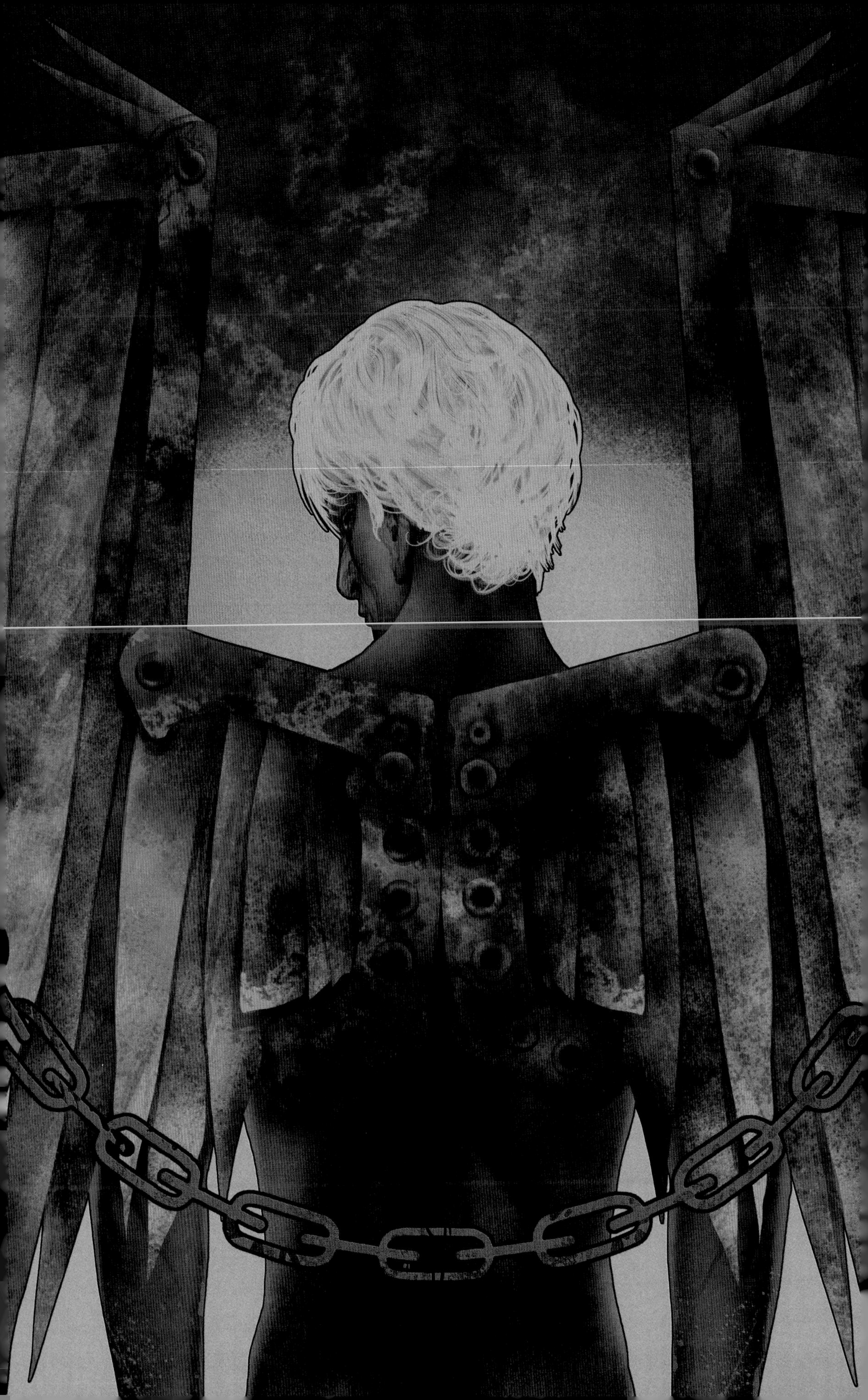

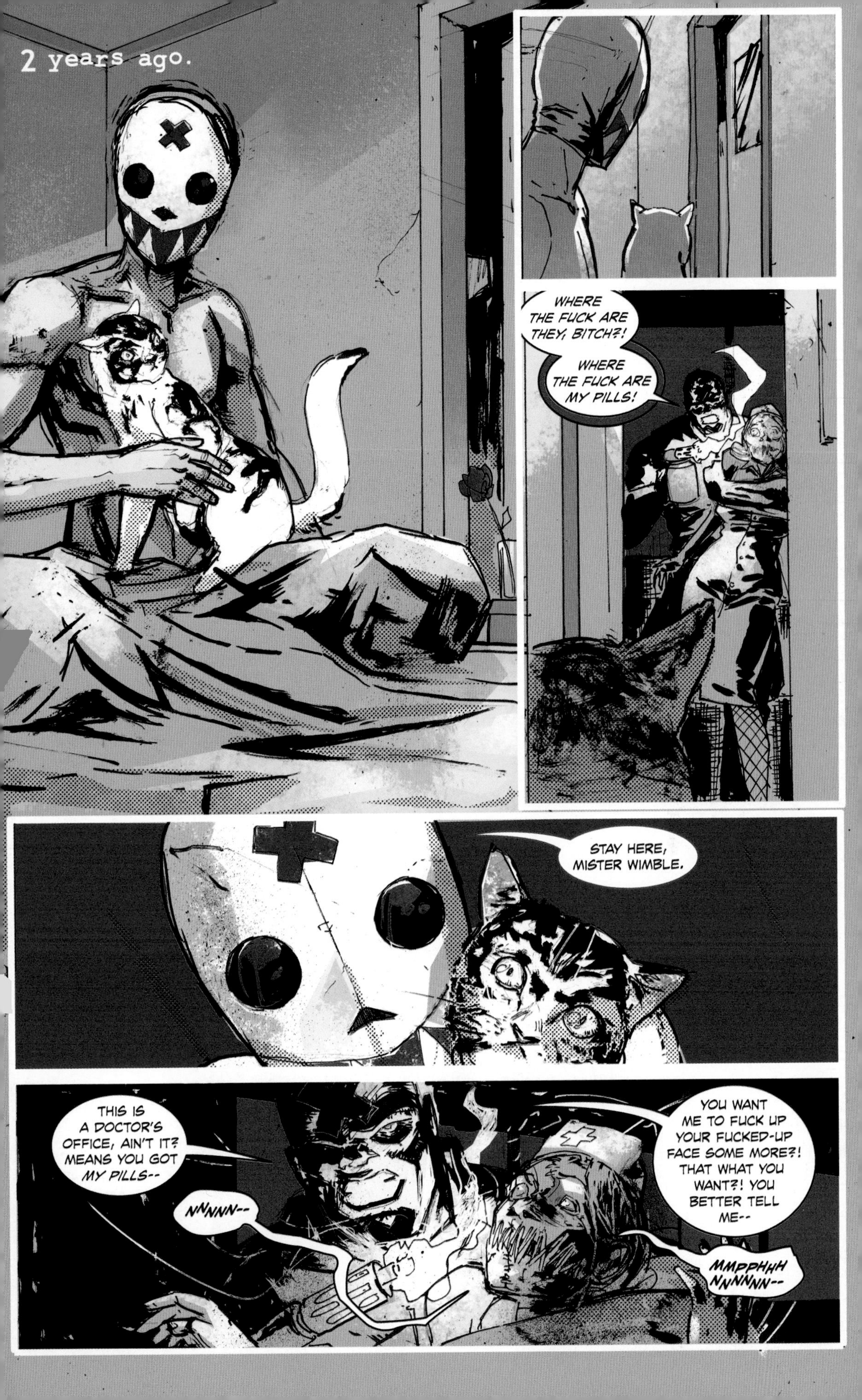
2 years ago.
WHERE THE FUCK ARE THEY, BITCH?!
WHERE THE FUCK ARE MY PILLS!
STAY HERE, MISTER WIMBLE.
THIS IS A DOCTOR'S OFFICE, AIN'T IT? MEANS YOU GOT MY PILLS--
YOU WANT ME TO FUCK UP YOUR FUCKED-UP FACE SOME MORE?! THAT WHAT YOU WANT?! YOU BETTER TELL ME--
NNNNN--
MMPHHH NNNNNN--

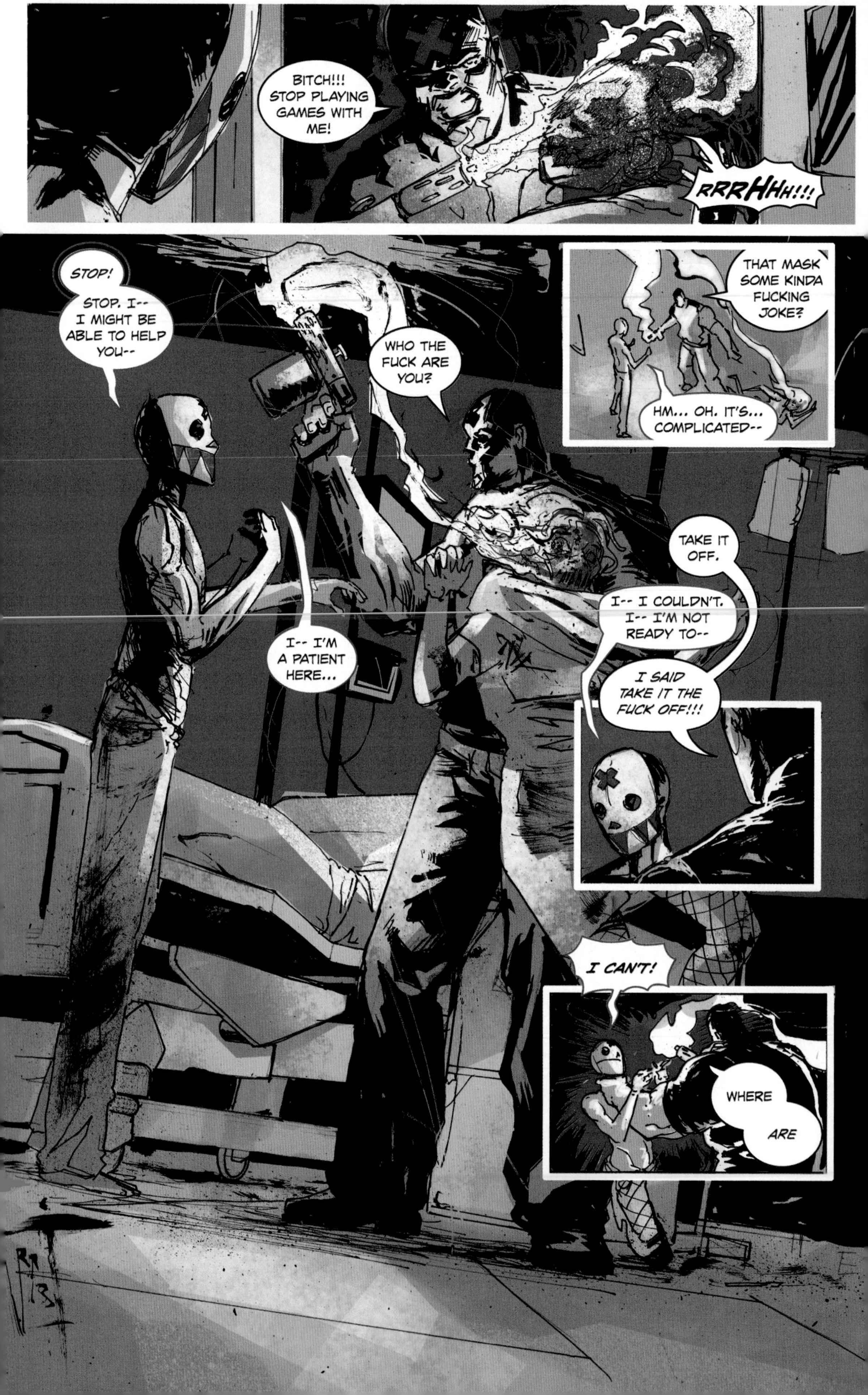
BITCH!!! STOP PLAYING GAMES WITH ME!
RRRHHH!!!
STOP!
STOP. I-- I MIGHT BE ABLE TO HELP YOU--
WHO THE FUCK ARE YOU?
THAT MASK SOME KINDA FUCKING JOKE?
HM... OH. IT'S... COMPLICATED--
I-- I'M A PATIENT HERE...
TAKE IT OFF.
I-- I COULDN'T. I-- I'M NOT READY TO--
I SAID TAKE IT THE FUCK OFF!!!
I CAN'T!
WHERE
ARE

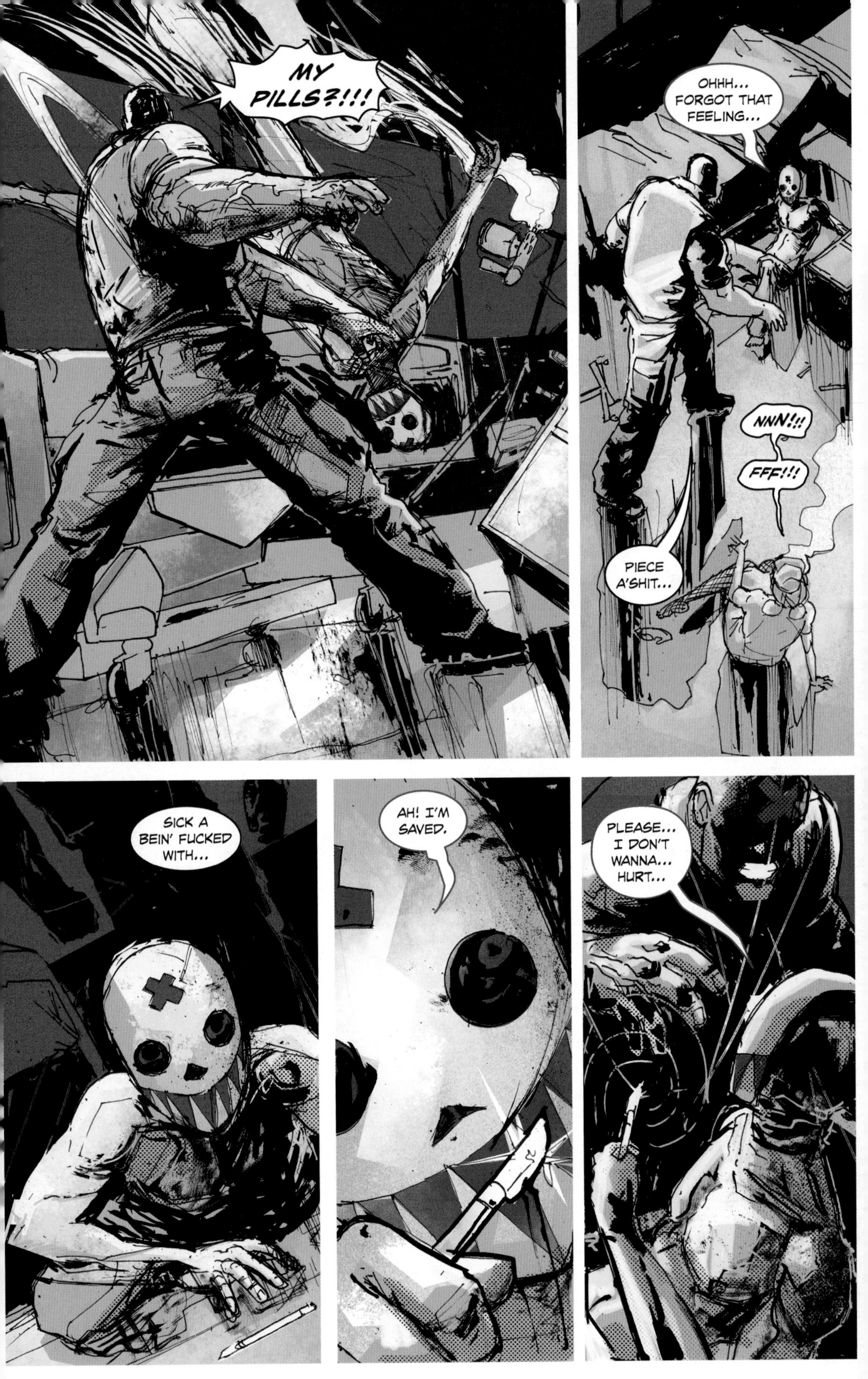
MY PILLS?!!!
OHHH... FORGOT THAT FEELING...
NNN!!!
FFF!!!
PIECE A'SHIT...
SICK A BEIN' FUCKED WITH...
AH! I'M SAVED.
PLEASE... I DON'T WANNA... HURT...

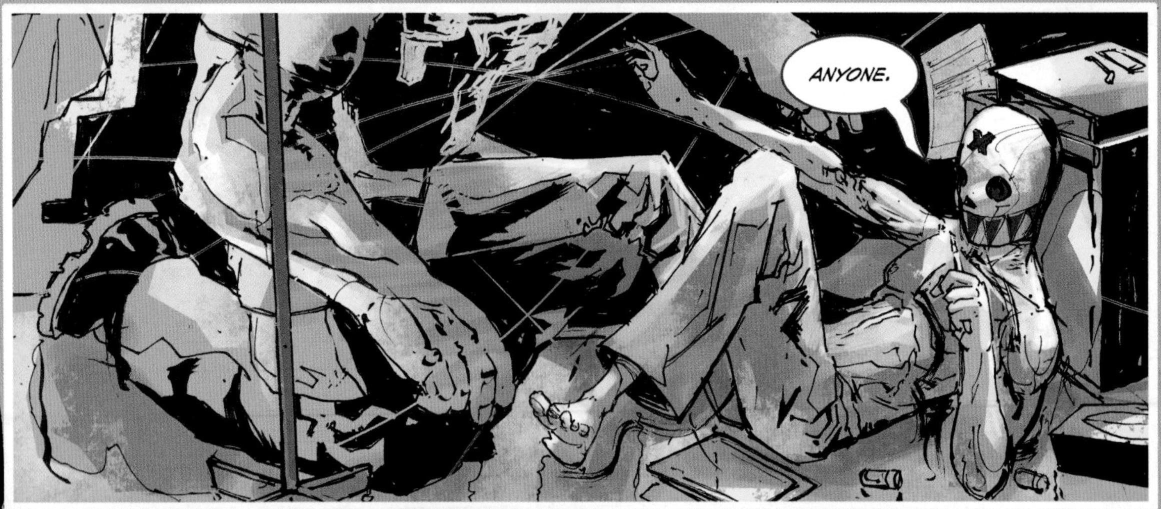
ANYONE.

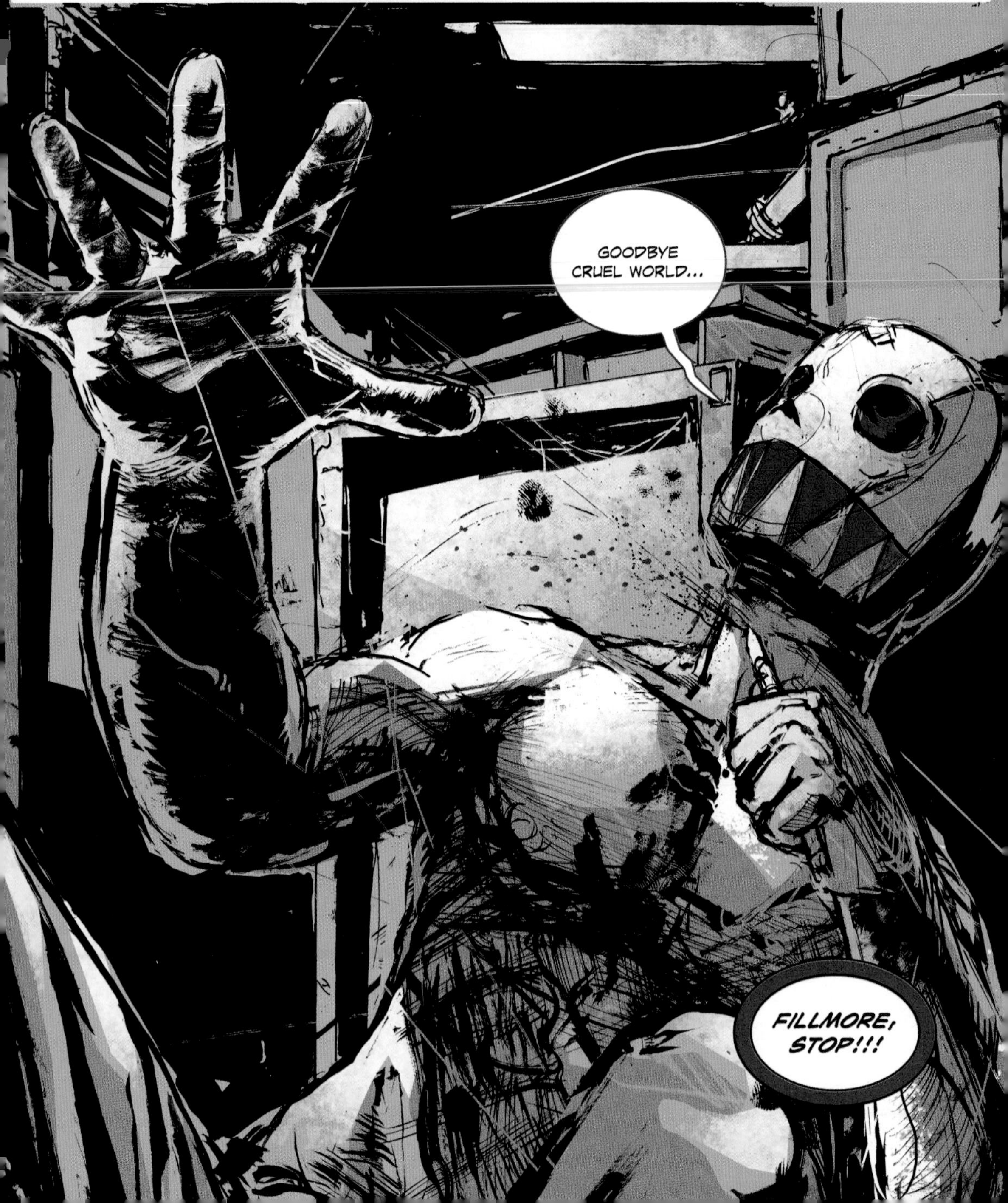
GOODBYE CRUEL WORLD...
FILLMORE, STOP!!!

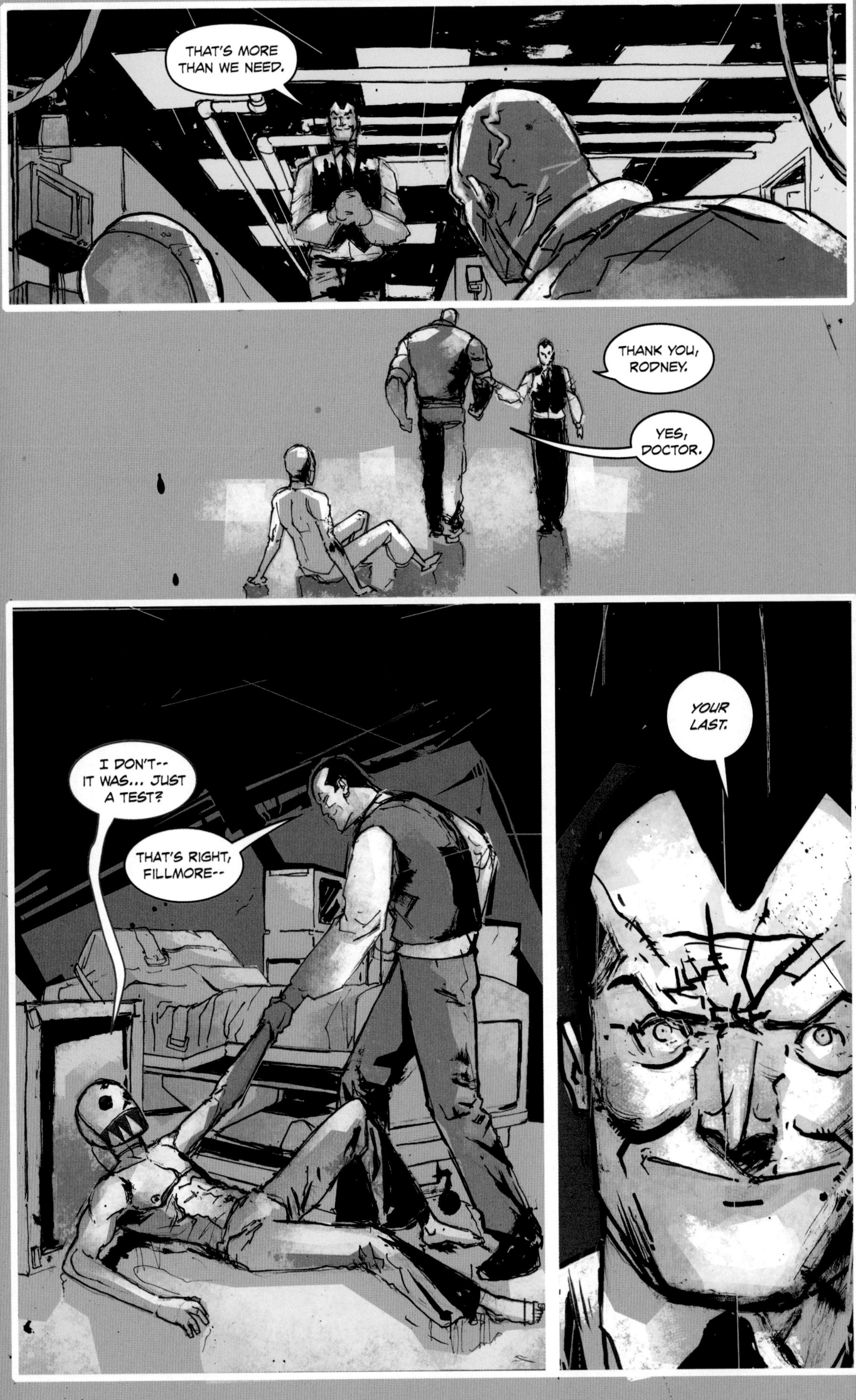
THAT'S MORE THAN WE NEED.
THANK YOU, RODNEY.
YES, DOCTOR.
I DON'T-- IT WAS... JUST A TEST?
THAT'S RIGHT, FILLMORE--
YOUR LAST.

CHAPTER FIVE
TIME TO SET OUR LITTLE BIRD FREE

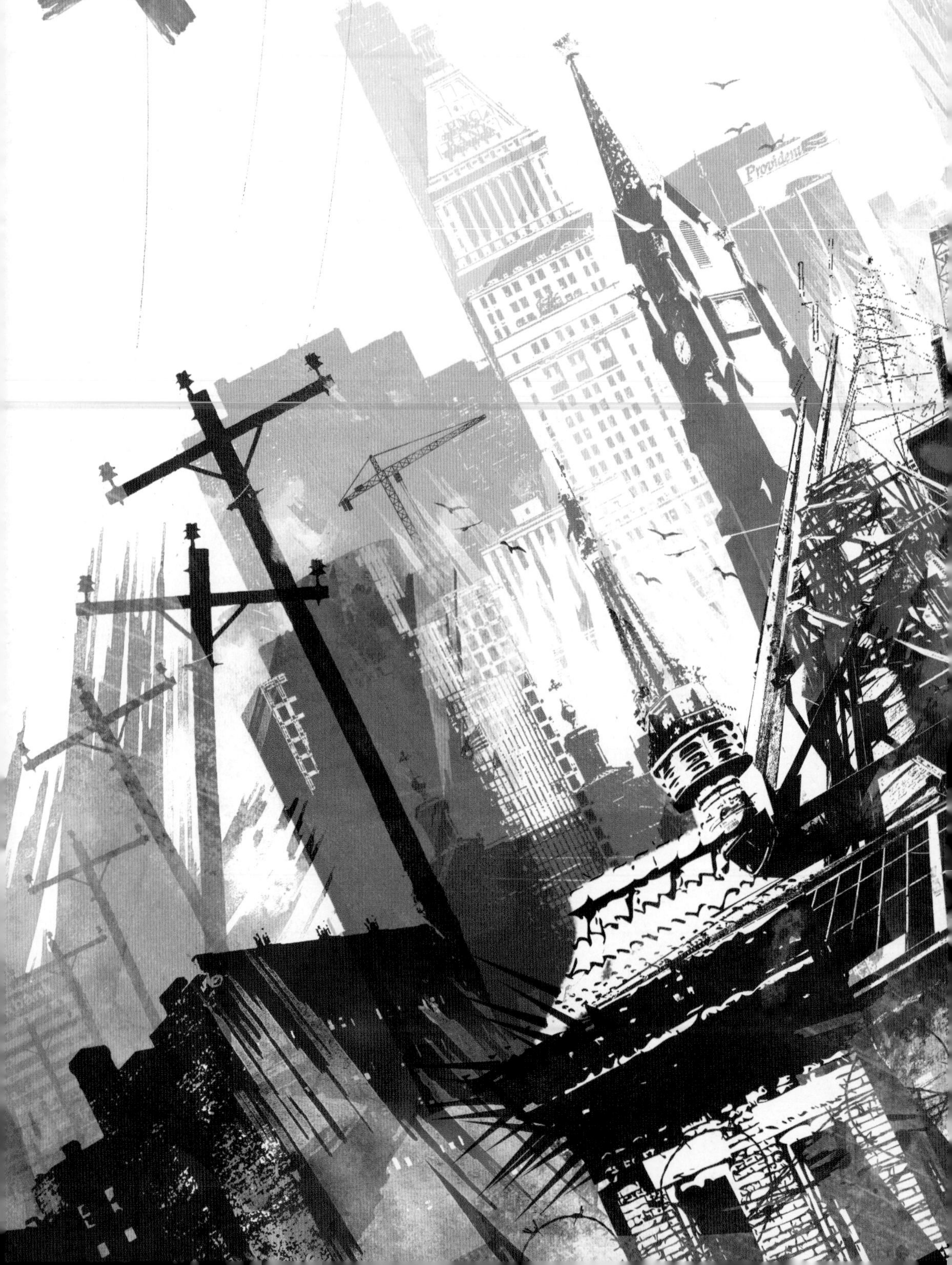

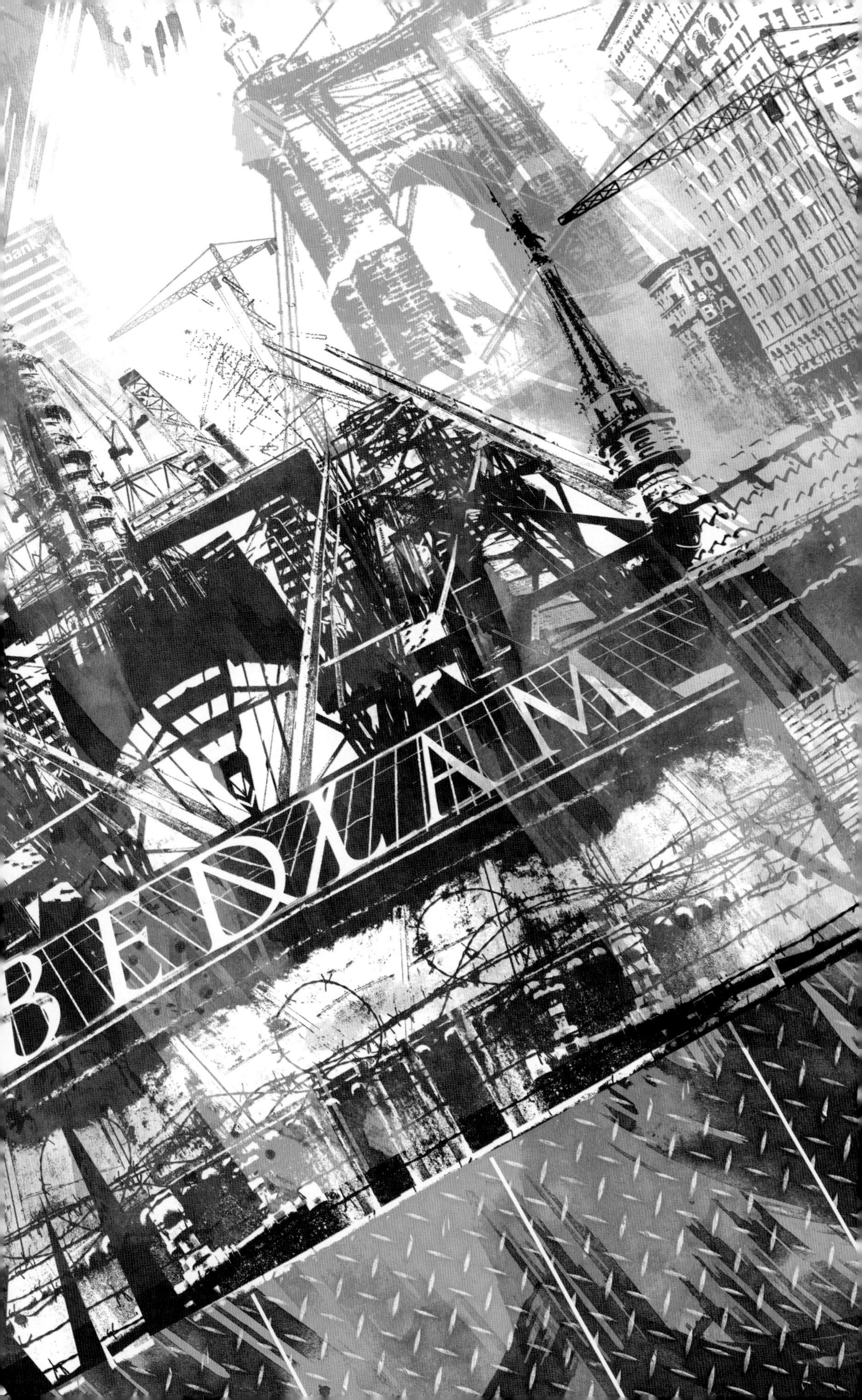
BEDLAM

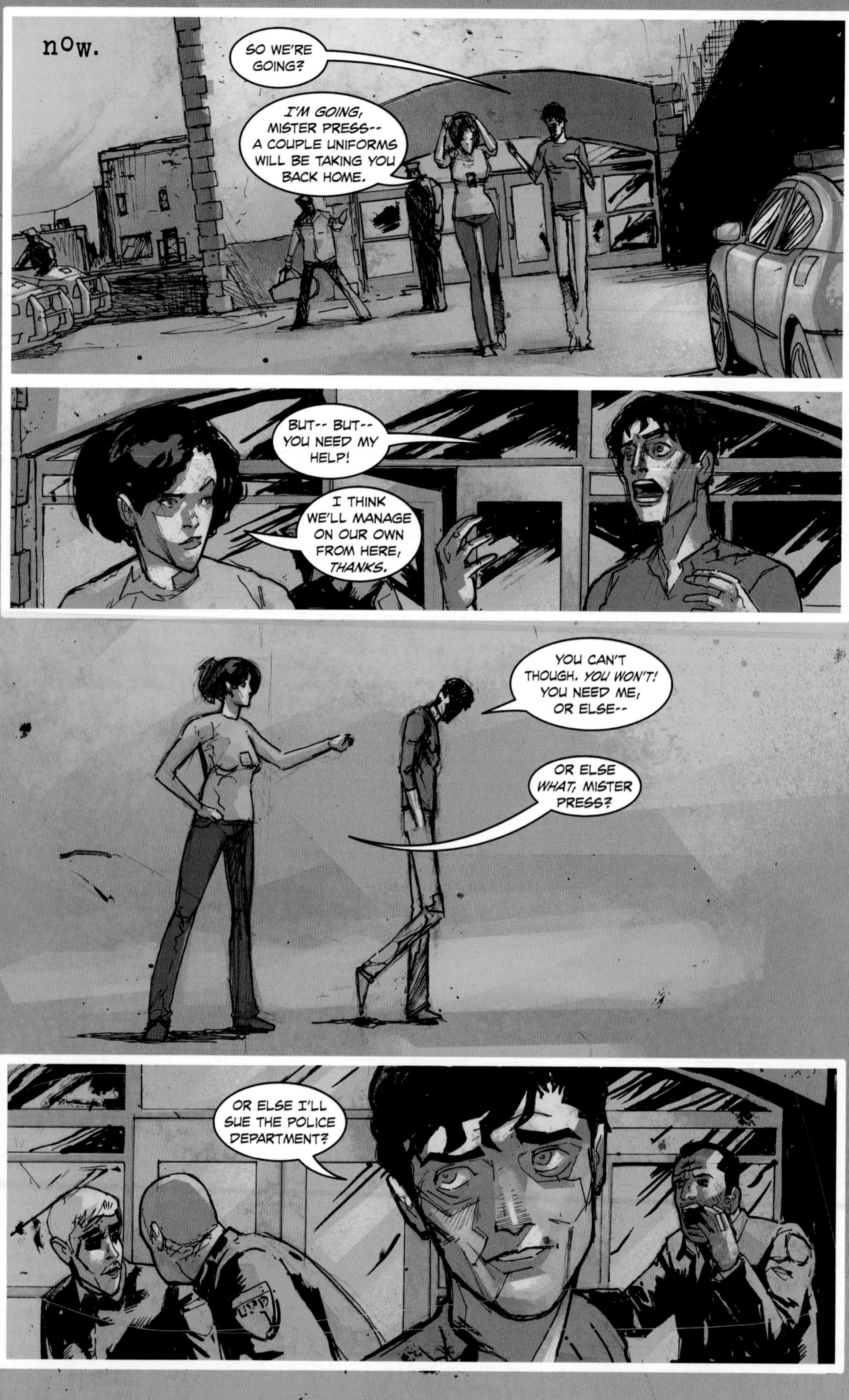
nOw.
SO WE'RE GOING?
I'M GOING, MISTER PRESS-- A COUPLE UNIFORMS WILL BE TAKING YOU BACK HOME.
BUT-- BUT-- YOU NEED MY HELP!
I THINK WE'LL MANAGE ON OUR OWN FROM HERE, THANKS.
YOU CAN'T THOUGH. YOU WON'T! YOU NEED ME, OR ELSE--
OR ELSE WHAT, MISTER PRESS?
OR ELSE I'LL SUE THE POLICE DEPARTMENT?

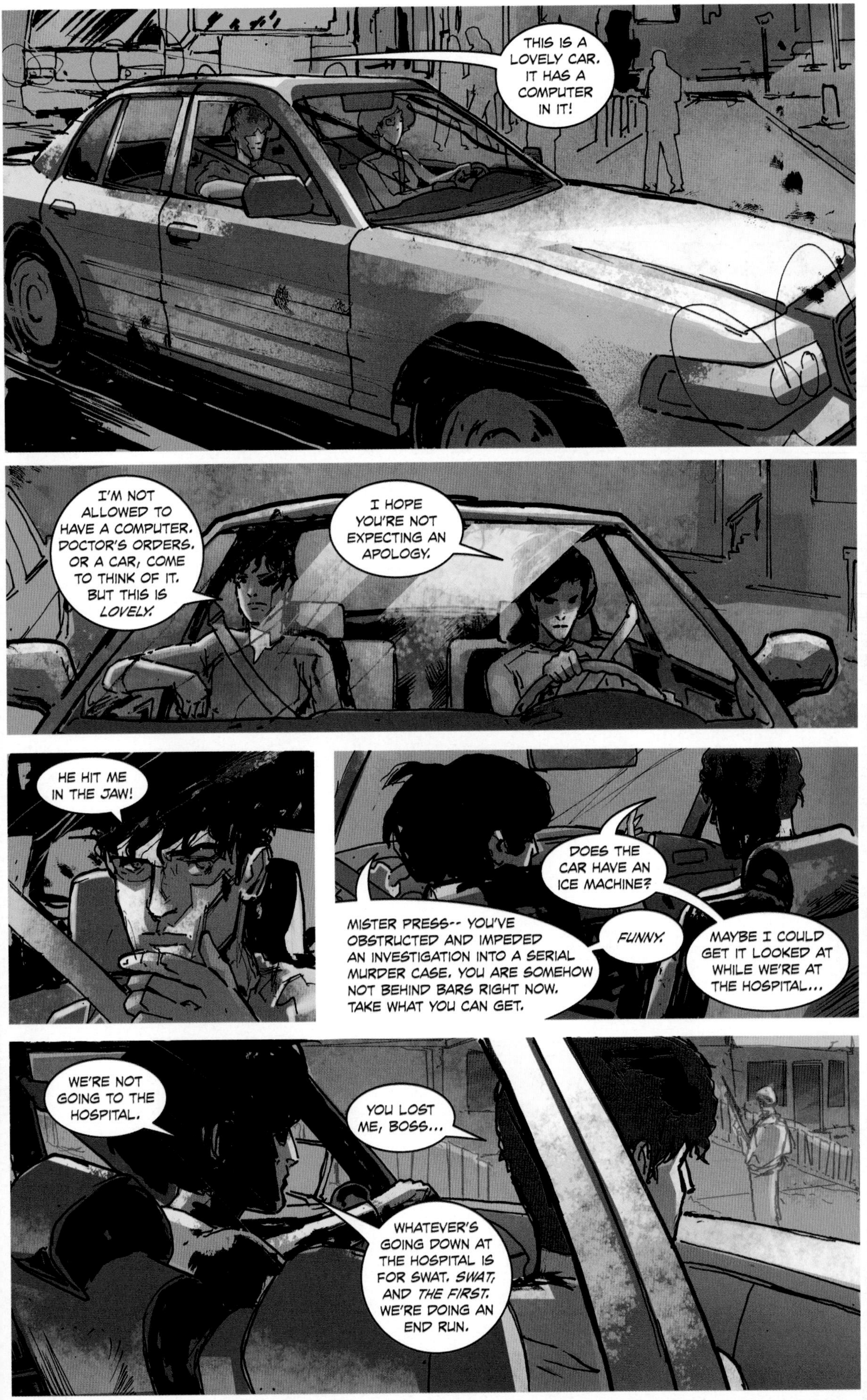
THIS IS A LOVELY CAR. IT HAS A COMPUTER IN IT!
I'M NOT ALLOWED TO HAVE A COMPUTER. DOCTOR'S ORDERS. OR A CAR, COME TO THINK OF IT. BUT THIS IS *LOVELY.*
I HOPE YOU'RE NOT EXPECTING AN APOLOGY.
HE HIT ME IN THE JAW!
DOES THE CAR HAVE AN ICE MACHINE?
MISTER PRESS-- YOU'VE OBSTRUCTED AND IMPEDED AN INVESTIGATION INTO A SERIAL MURDER CASE. YOU ARE SOMEHOW NOT BEHIND BARS RIGHT NOW. TAKE WHAT YOU CAN GET.
FUNNY.
MAYBE I COULD GET IT LOOKED AT WHILE WE'RE AT THE HOSPITAL...
WE'RE NOT GOING TO THE HOSPITAL.
YOU LOST ME, BOSS...
WHATEVER'S GOING DOWN AT THE HOSPITAL IS FOR SWAT. *SWAT,* AND *THE FIRST.* WE'RE DOING AN END RUN.

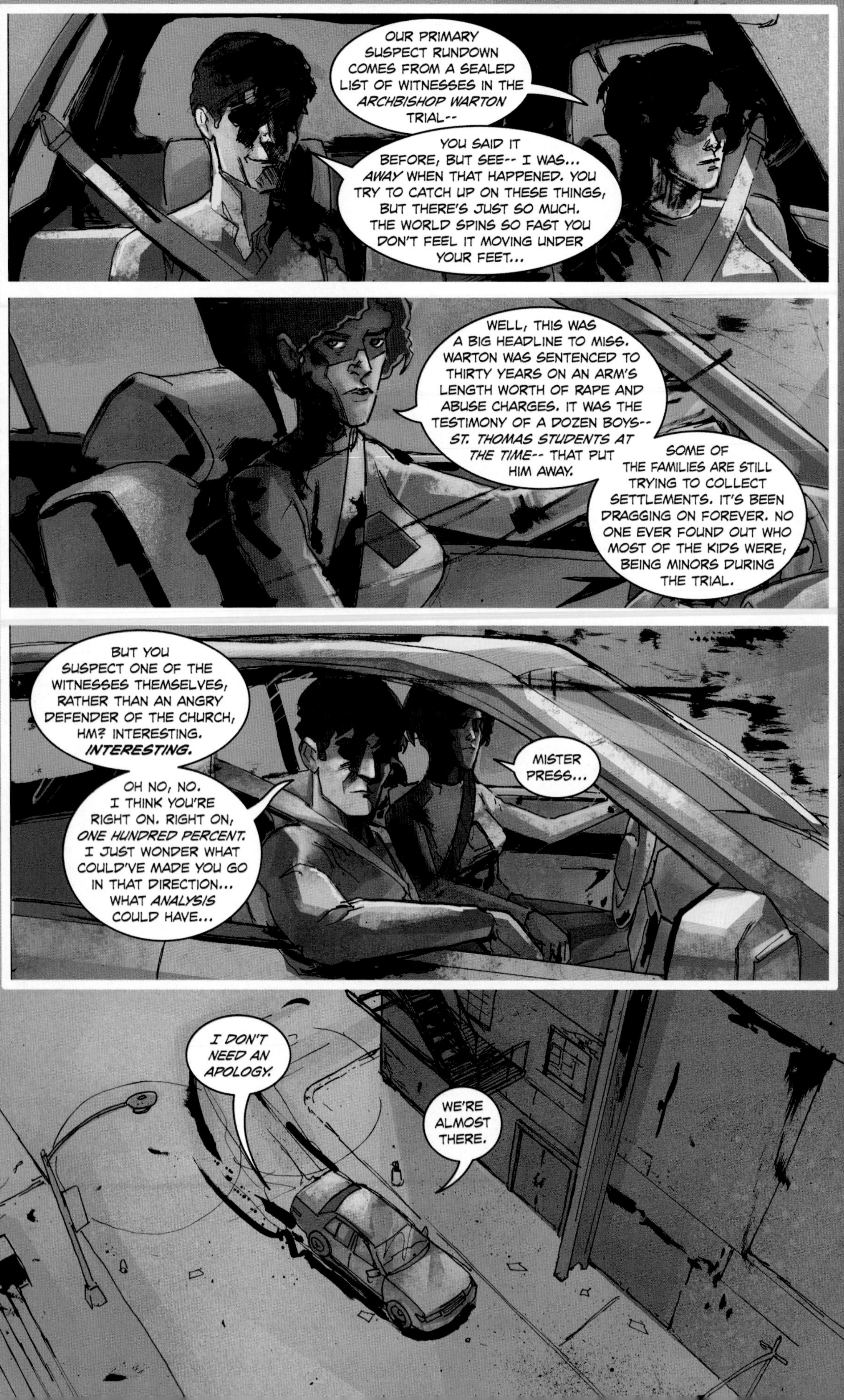
OUR PRIMARY SUSPECT RUNDOWN COMES FROM A SEALED LIST OF WITNESSES IN THE *ARCHBISHOP WARTON* TRIAL--
YOU SAID IT BEFORE, BUT SEE-- I WAS... *AWAY* WHEN THAT HAPPENED. YOU TRY TO CATCH UP ON THESE THINGS, BUT THERE'S JUST SO MUCH. THE WORLD SPINS SO FAST YOU DON'T FEEL IT MOVING UNDER YOUR FEET...
WELL, THIS WAS A BIG HEADLINE TO MISS. WARTON WAS SENTENCED TO THIRTY YEARS ON AN ARM'S LENGTH WORTH OF RAPE AND ABUSE CHARGES. IT WAS THE TESTIMONY OF A DOZEN BOYS-- *ST. THOMAS STUDENTS AT THE TIME*-- THAT PUT HIM AWAY.
SOME OF THE FAMILIES ARE STILL TRYING TO COLLECT SETTLEMENTS. IT'S BEEN DRAGGING ON FOREVER. NO ONE EVER FOUND OUT WHO MOST OF THE KIDS WERE, BEING MINORS DURING THE TRIAL.
BUT YOU SUSPECT ONE OF THE WITNESSES THEMSELVES, RATHER THAN AN ANGRY DEFENDER OF THE CHURCH, HM? INTERESTING. ***INTERESTING.***
MISTER PRESS...
OH NO, NO. I THINK YOU'RE RIGHT ON. RIGHT ON, *ONE HUNDRED PERCENT.* I JUST WONDER WHAT COULD'VE MADE YOU GO IN THAT DIRECTION... WHAT *ANALYSIS* COULD HAVE...
I DON'T NEED AN APOLOGY.
WE'RE ALMOST THERE.

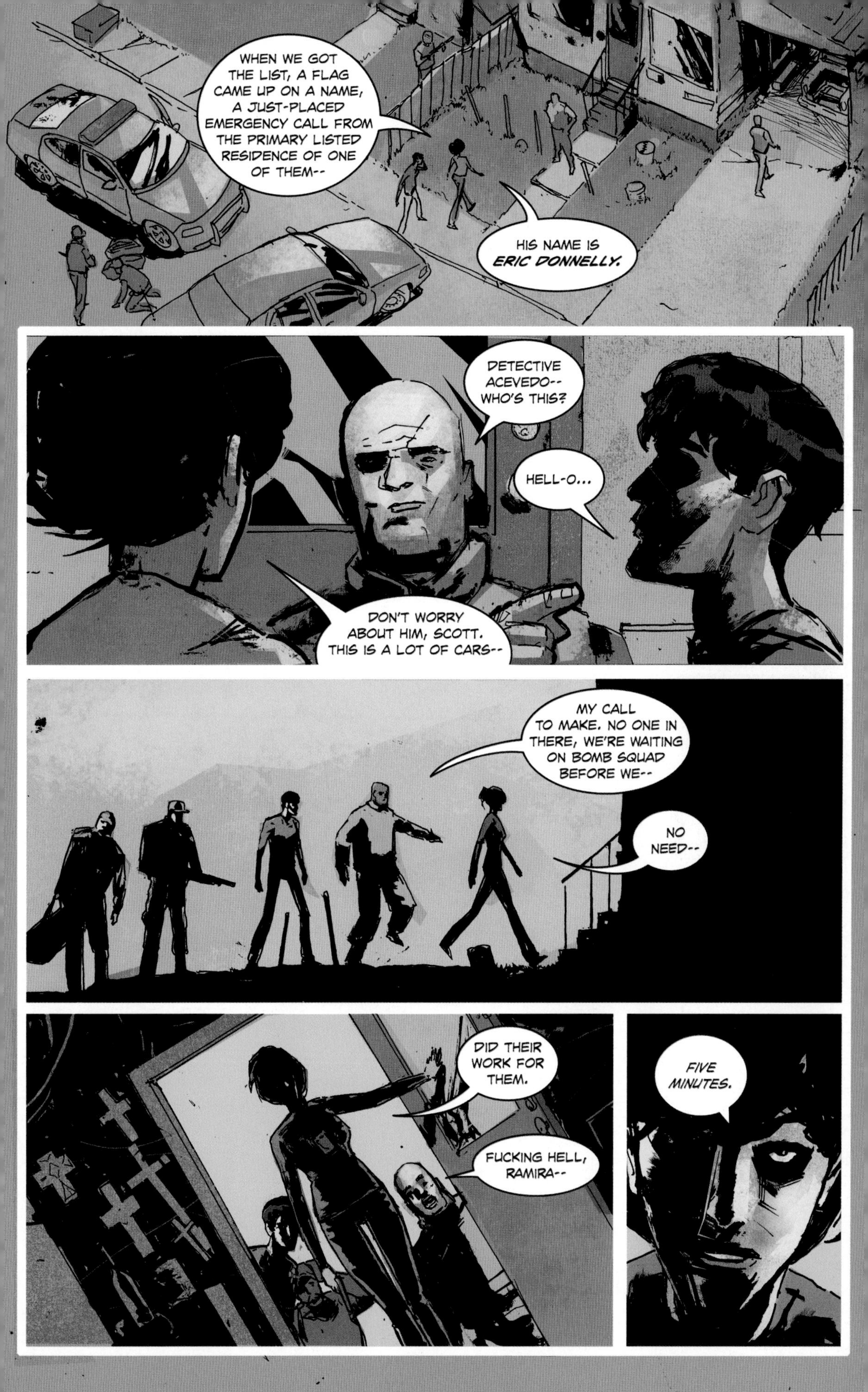
WHEN WE GOT THE LIST, A FLAG CAME UP ON A NAME, A JUST-PLACED EMERGENCY CALL FROM THE PRIMARY LISTED RESIDENCE OF ONE OF THEM--
HIS NAME IS *ERIC DONNELLY.*
DETECTIVE ACEVEDO-- WHO'S THIS?
HELL-O...
DON'T WORRY ABOUT HIM, SCOTT. THIS IS A LOT OF CARS--
MY CALL TO MAKE. NO ONE IN THERE, WE'RE WAITING ON BOMB SQUAD BEFORE WE--
NO NEED--
DID THEIR WORK FOR THEM.
FUCKING HELL, RAMIRA--
FIVE MINUTES.

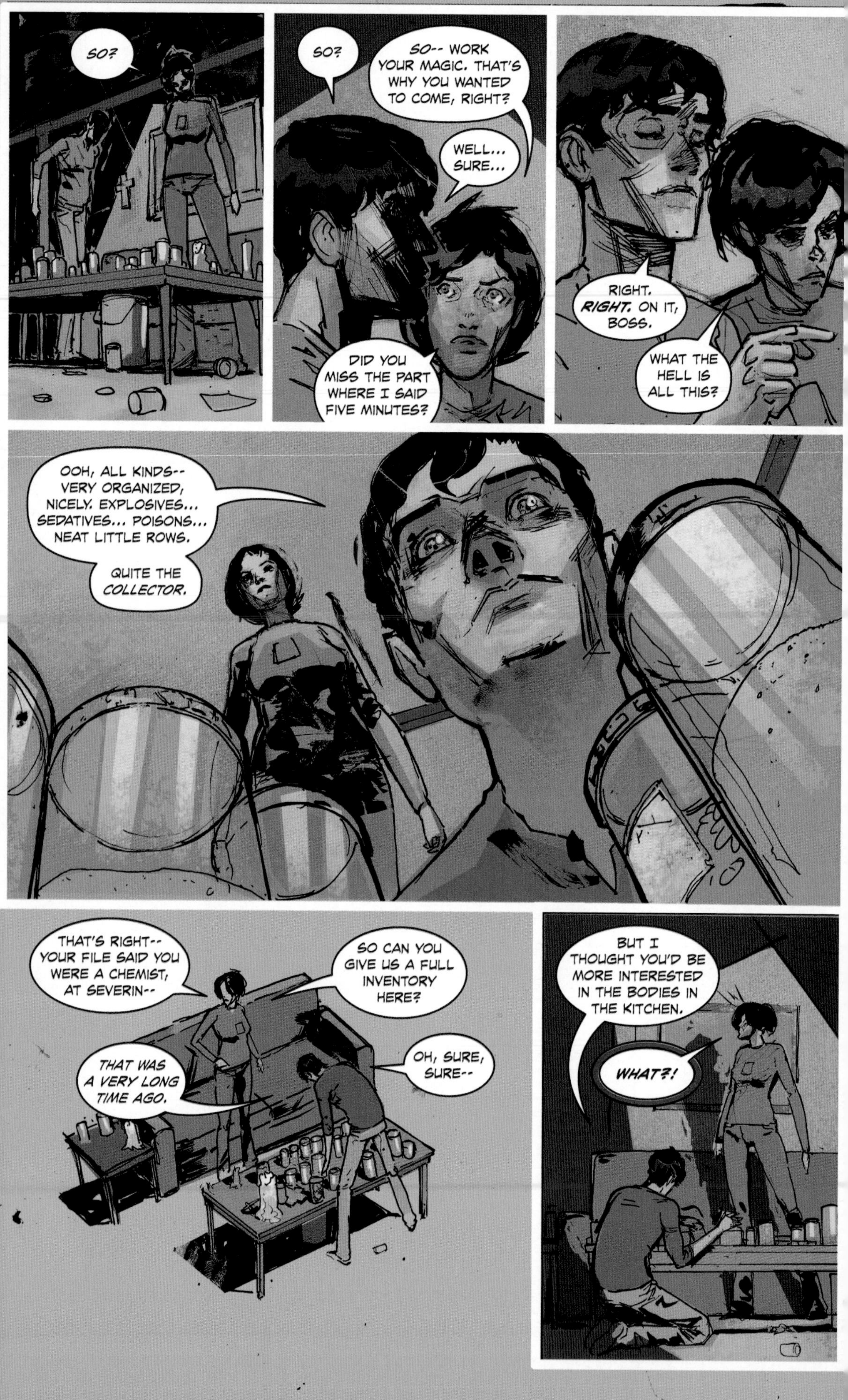
SO?
SO?
SO-- WORK YOUR MAGIC. THAT'S WHY YOU WANTED TO COME, RIGHT?
WELL... SURE...
DID YOU MISS THE PART WHERE I SAID FIVE MINUTES?
RIGHT. RIGHT. ON IT, BOSS.
WHAT THE HELL IS ALL THIS?
OOH, ALL KINDS-- VERY ORGANIZED, NICELY. EXPLOSIVES... SEDATIVES... POISONS... NEAT LITTLE ROWS.
QUITE THE COLLECTOR.
THAT'S RIGHT-- YOUR FILE SAID YOU WERE A CHEMIST, AT SEVERIN--
THAT WAS A VERY LONG TIME AGO.
SO CAN YOU GIVE US A FULL INVENTORY HERE?
OH, SURE, SURE--
BUT I THOUGHT YOU'D BE MORE INTERESTED IN THE BODIES IN THE KITCHEN.
WHAT?!

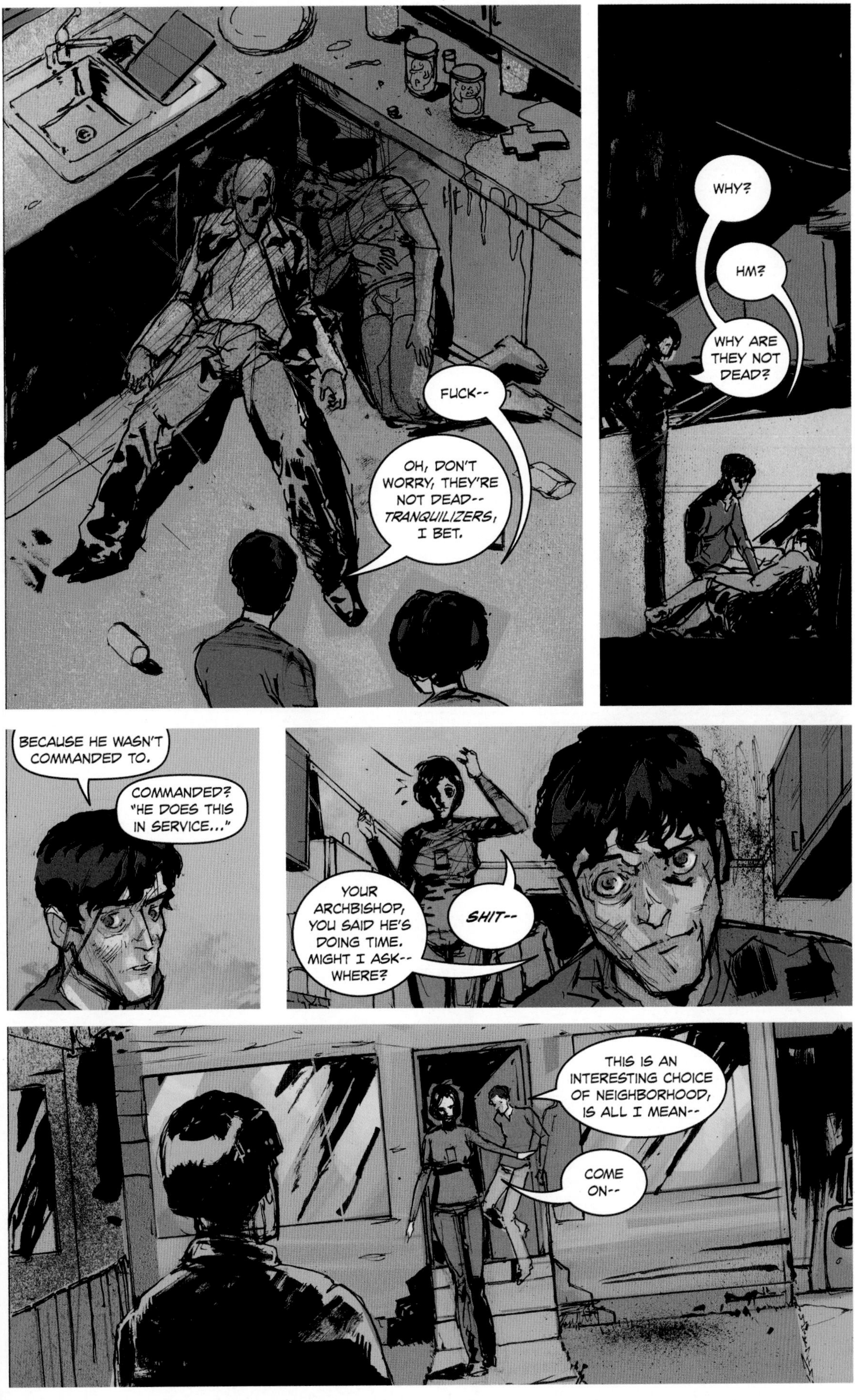
FUCK--
OH, DON'T WORRY, THEY'RE NOT DEAD-- *TRANQUILIZERS*, I BET.
WHY?
HM?
WHY ARE THEY NOT DEAD?
BECAUSE HE WASN'T COMMANDED TO.
COMMANDED? "HE DOES THIS IN SERVICE..."
SHIT--
YOUR ARCHBISHOP, YOU SAID HE'S DOING TIME. MIGHT I ASK-- WHERE?
THIS IS AN INTERESTING CHOICE OF NEIGHBORHOOD, IS ALL I MEAN--
COME ON--

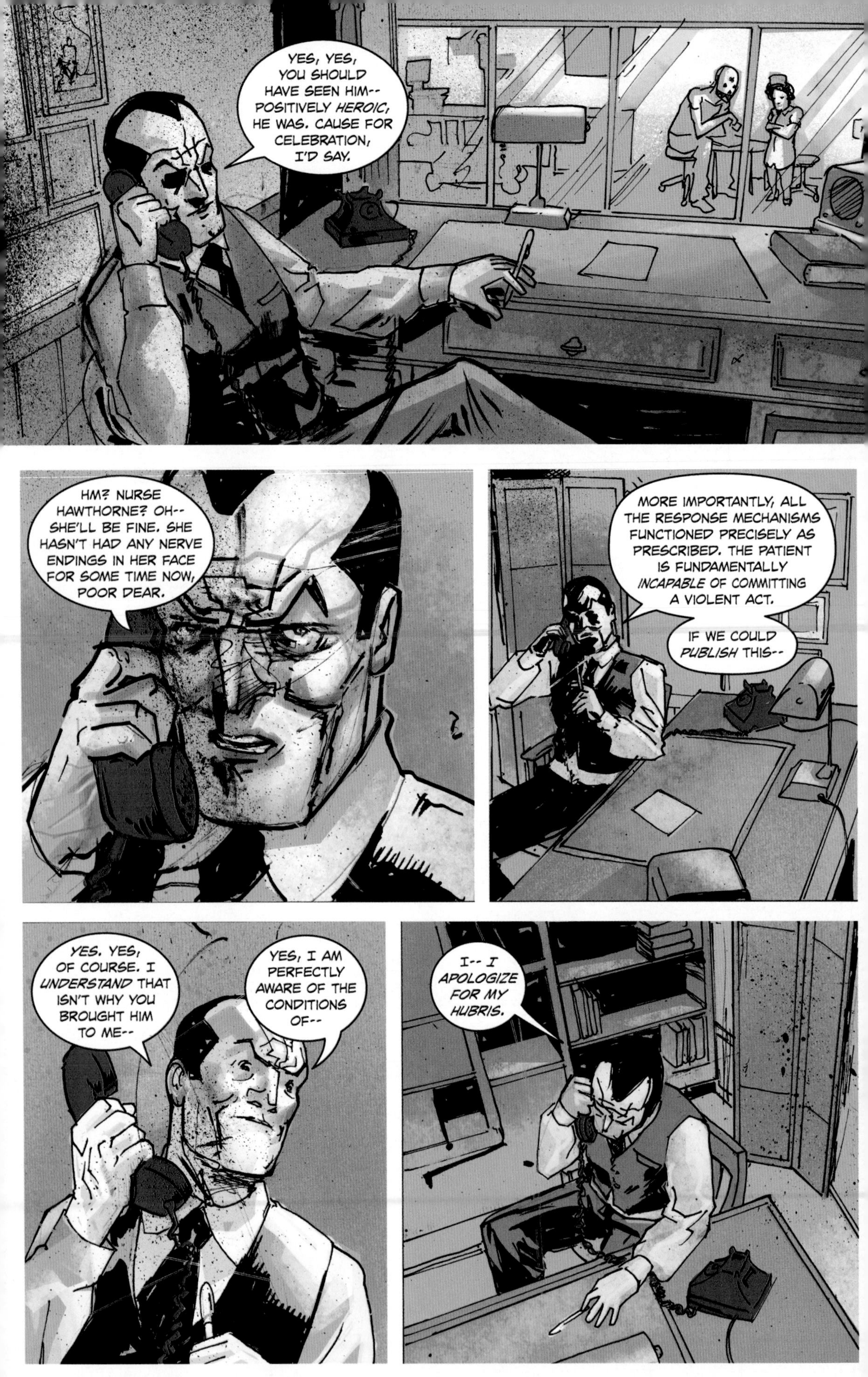
YES, YES, YOU SHOULD HAVE SEEN HIM-- POSITIVELY *HEROIC*, HE WAS. CAUSE FOR CELEBRATION, I'D SAY.
HM? NURSE HAWTHORNE? OH-- SHE'LL BE FINE. SHE HASN'T HAD ANY NERVE ENDINGS IN HER FACE FOR SOME TIME NOW, POOR DEAR.
MORE IMPORTANTLY, ALL THE RESPONSE MECHANISMS FUNCTIONED PRECISELY AS PRESCRIBED. THE PATIENT IS FUNDAMENTALLY *INCAPABLE* OF COMMITTING A VIOLENT ACT.
IF WE COULD *PUBLISH* THIS--
YES. YES, OF COURSE. I *UNDERSTAND* THAT ISN'T WHY YOU BROUGHT HIM TO ME--
YES, I AM PERFECTLY AWARE OF THE CONDITIONS OF--
I-- *I APOLOGIZE FOR MY HUBRIS.*

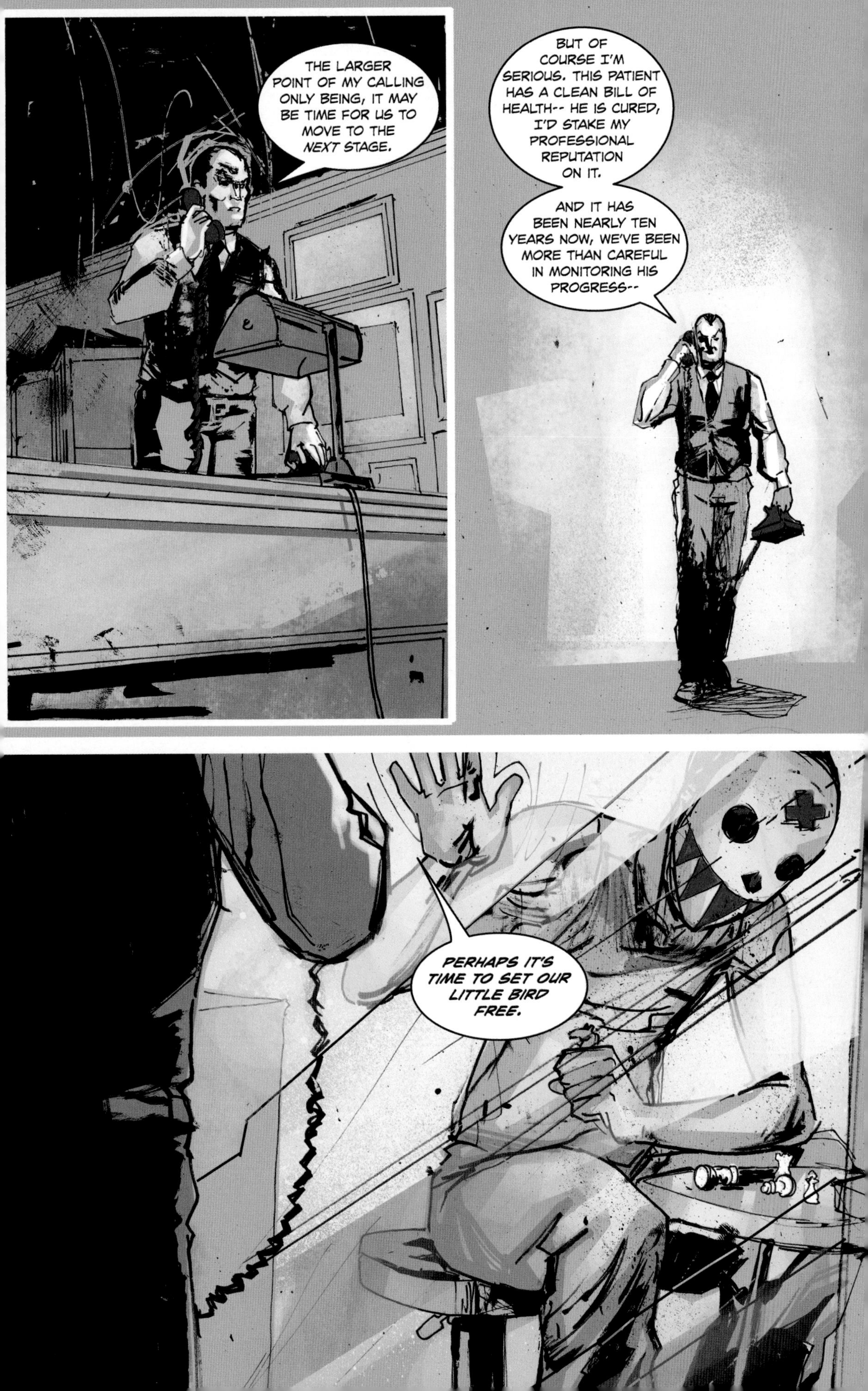
THE LARGER POINT OF MY CALLING ONLY BEING, IT MAY BE TIME FOR US TO MOVE TO THE *NEXT* STAGE.
BUT OF COURSE I'M SERIOUS. THIS PATIENT HAS A CLEAN BILL OF HEALTH-- HE IS CURED, I'D STAKE MY PROFESSIONAL REPUTATION ON IT.
AND IT HAS BEEN NEARLY TEN YEARS NOW, WE'VE BEEN MORE THAN CAREFUL IN MONITORING HIS PROGRESS--
PERHAPS IT'S TIME TO SET OUR LITTLE BIRD FREE.

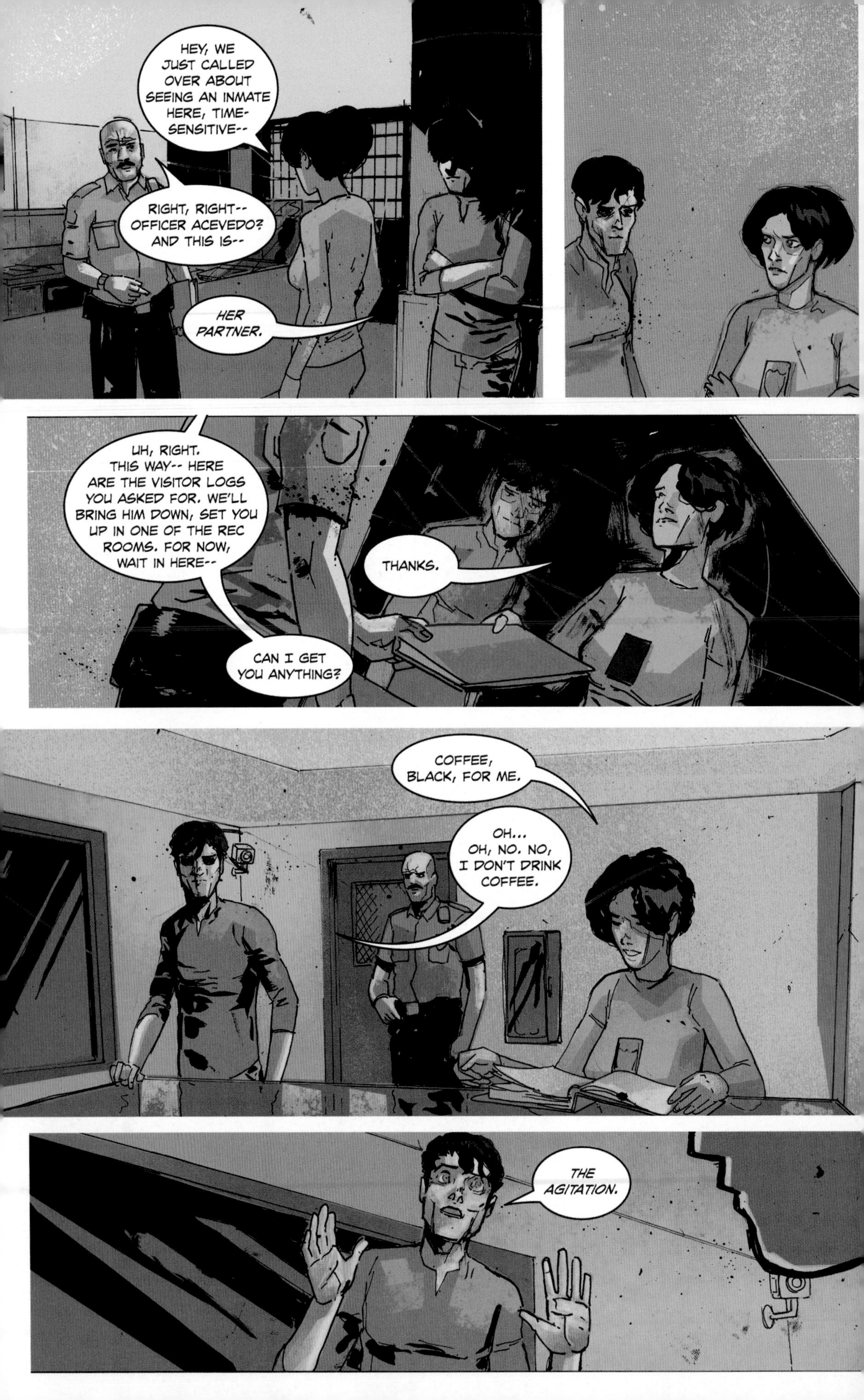
HEY, WE JUST CALLED OVER ABOUT SEEING AN INMATE HERE, TIME-SENSITIVE--
RIGHT, RIGHT-- OFFICER ACEVEDO? AND THIS IS--
HER PARTNER.
UH, RIGHT. THIS WAY-- HERE ARE THE VISITOR LOGS YOU ASKED FOR. WE'LL BRING HIM DOWN, SET YOU UP IN ONE OF THE REC ROOMS. FOR NOW, WAIT IN HERE--
THANKS.
CAN I GET YOU ANYTHING?
COFFEE, BLACK, FOR ME.
OH... OH, NO. NO, I DON'T DRINK COFFEE.
THE AGITATION.

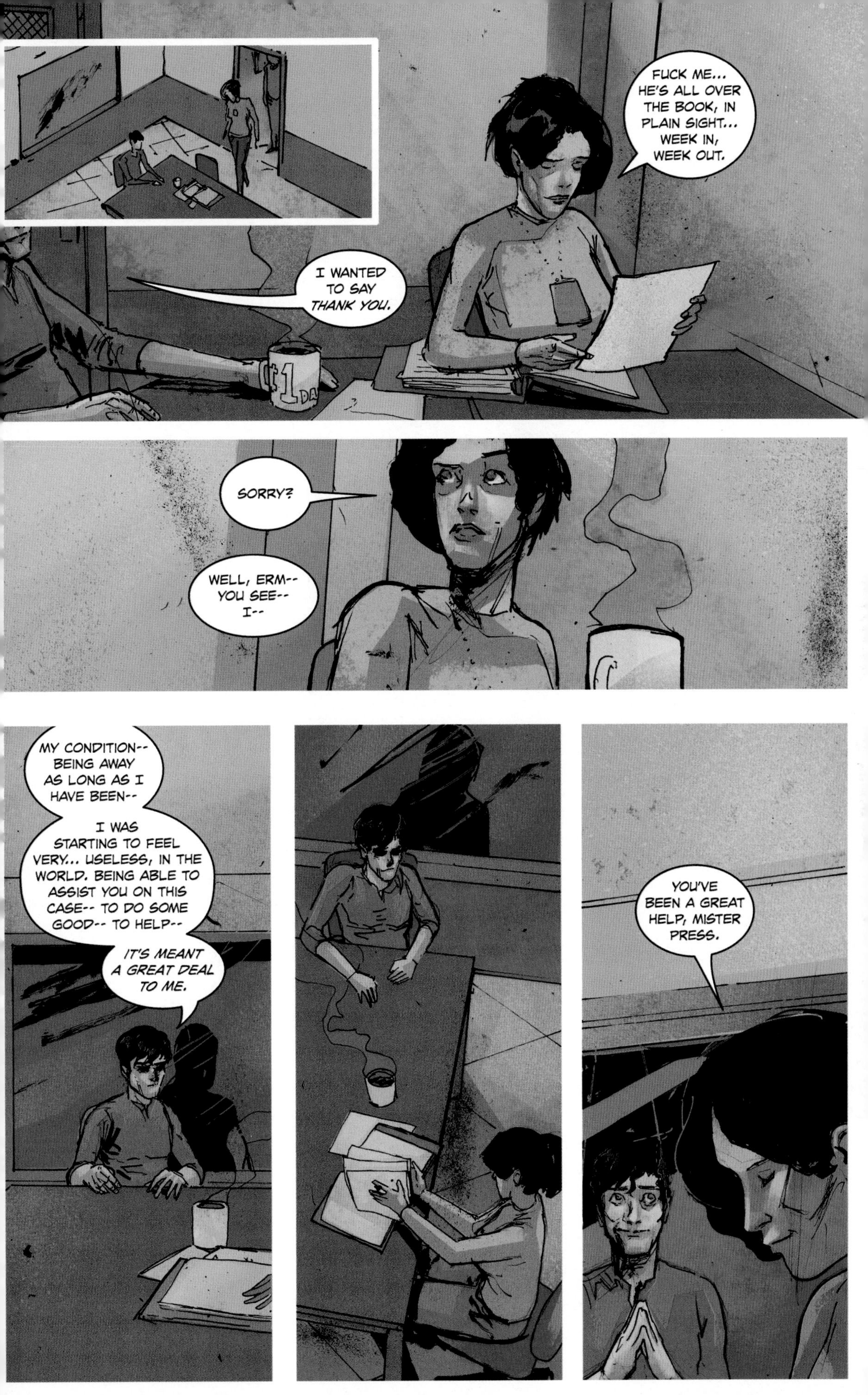
FUCK ME... HE'S ALL OVER THE BOOK, IN PLAIN SIGHT... WEEK IN, WEEK OUT.
I WANTED TO SAY THANK YOU.
SORRY?
WELL, ERM-- YOU SEE-- I--
MY CONDITION-- BEING AWAY AS LONG AS I HAVE BEEN--
I WAS STARTING TO FEEL VERY... USELESS, IN THE WORLD. BEING ABLE TO ASSIST YOU ON THIS CASE-- TO DO SOME GOOD-- TO HELP--
IT'S MEANT A GREAT DEAL TO ME.
YOU'VE BEEN A GREAT HELP, MISTER PRESS.

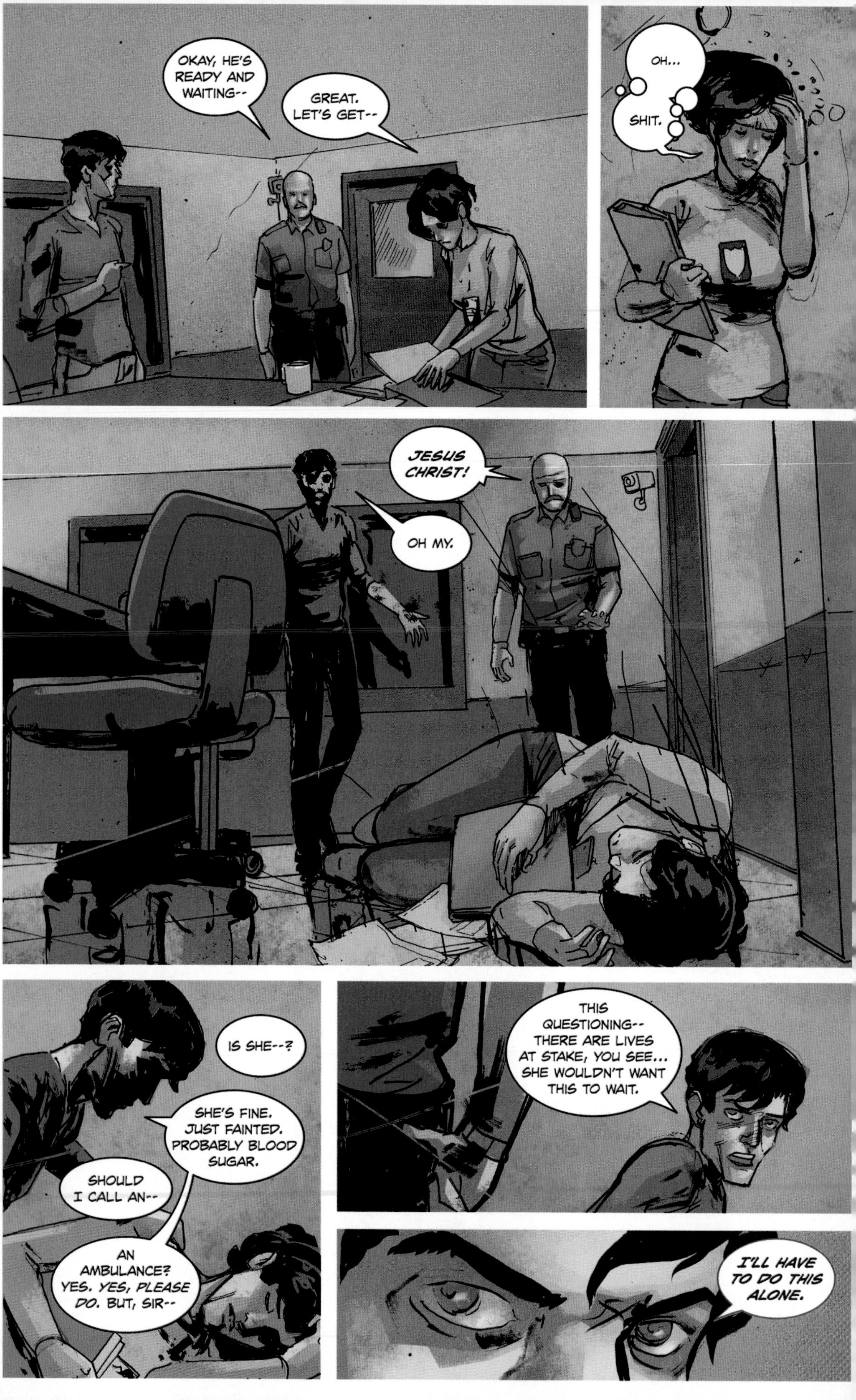
OKAY, HE'S READY AND WAITING--
GREAT. LET'S GET--
OH...
SHIT.
JESUS CHRIST!
OH MY.
IS SHE--?
SHE'S FINE. JUST FAINTED. PROBABLY BLOOD SUGAR.
SHOULD I CALL AN--
AN AMBULANCE? YES. YES, PLEASE DO. BUT, SIR--
THIS QUESTIONING-- THERE ARE LIVES AT STAKE, YOU SEE... SHE WOULDN'T WANT THIS TO WAIT.
I'LL HAVE TO DO THIS ALONE.

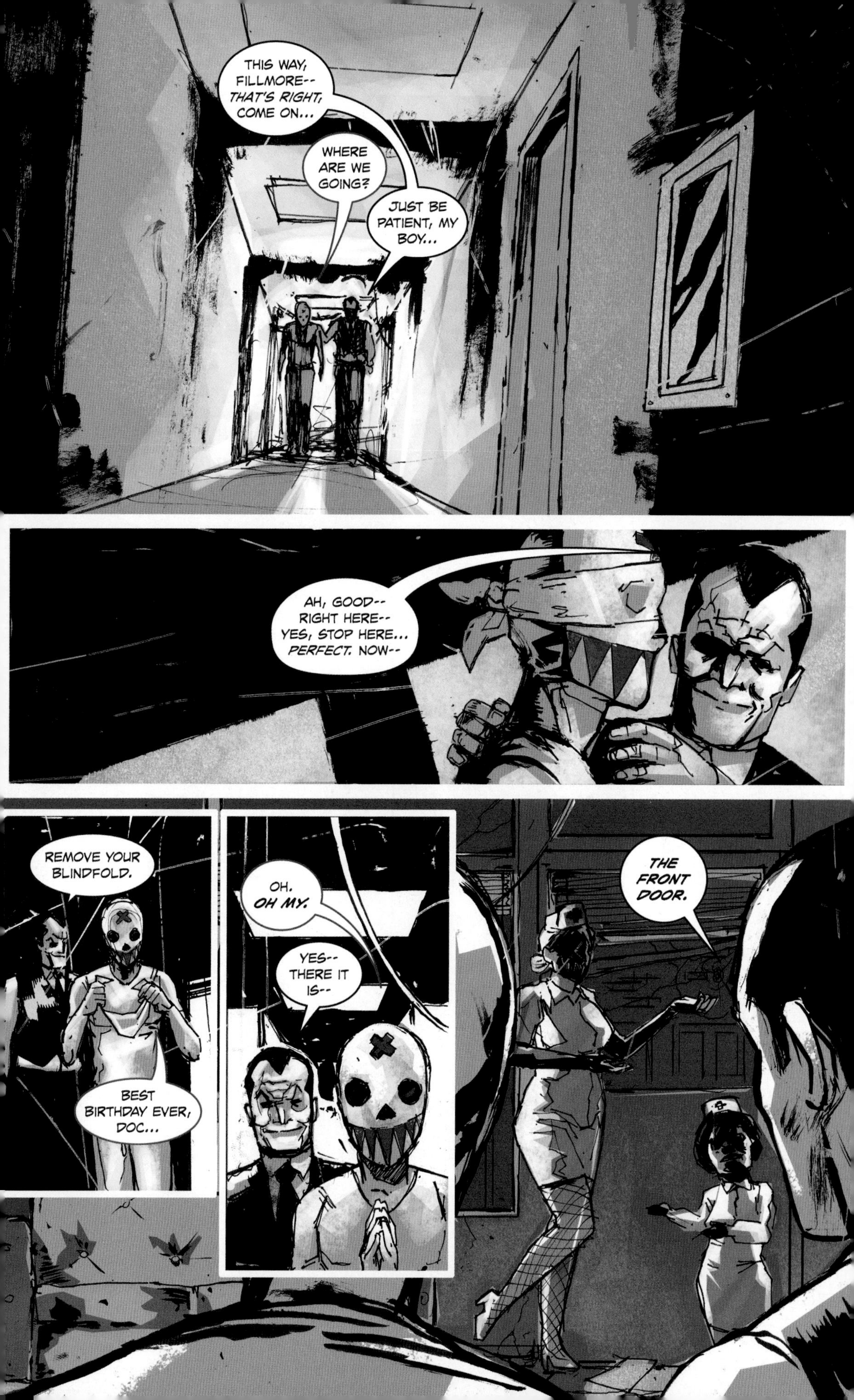
THIS WAY, FILLMORE-- *THAT'S RIGHT,* COME ON...
WHERE ARE WE GOING?
JUST BE PATIENT, MY BOY...
AH, GOOD-- RIGHT HERE-- YES, STOP HERE... *PERFECT.* NOW--
REMOVE YOUR BLINDFOLD.
BEST BIRTHDAY EVER, DOC...
OH. *OH MY.*
YES-- THERE IT IS--
THE FRONT DOOR.

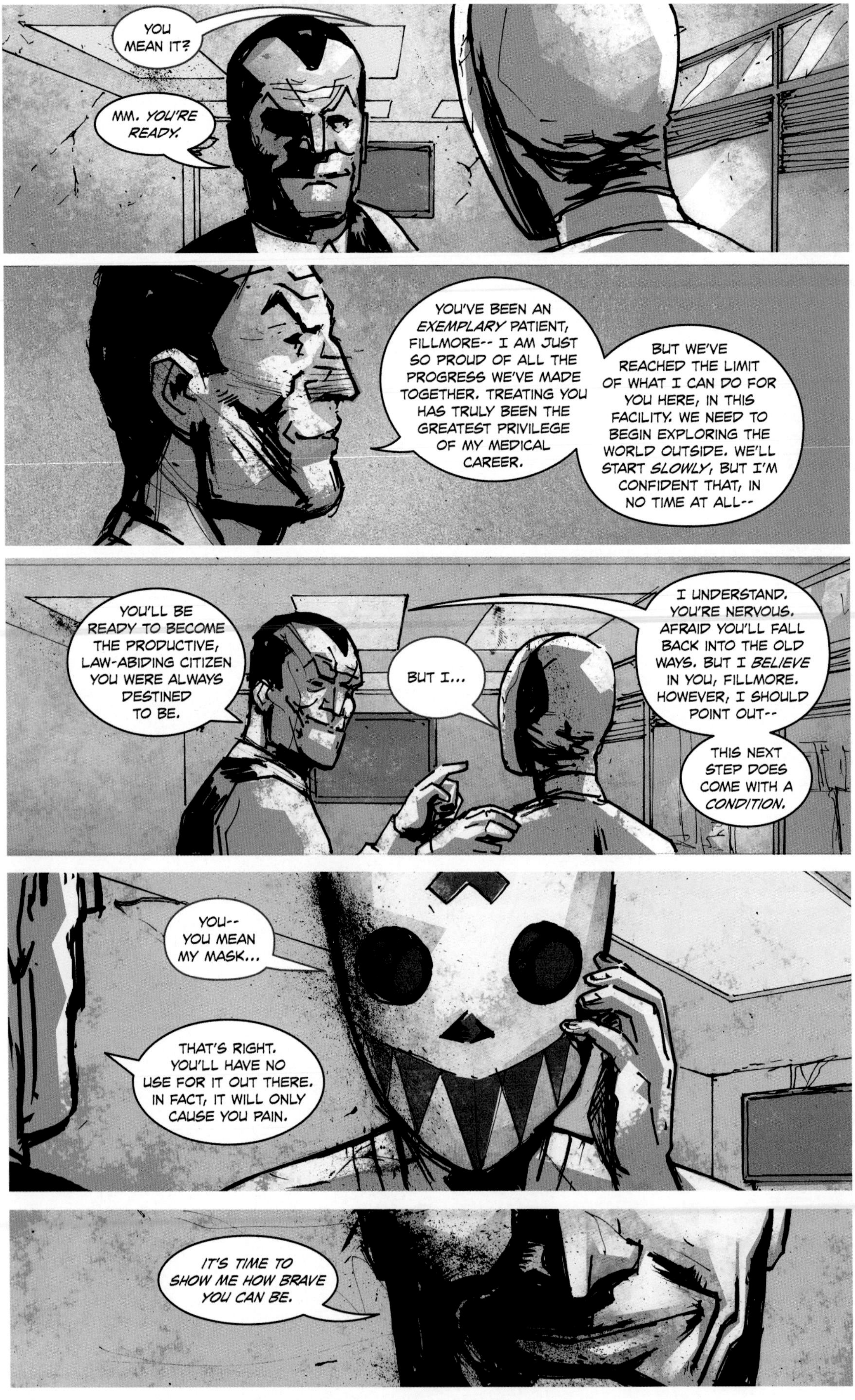
YOU MEAN IT?
MM. YOU'RE READY.
YOU'VE BEEN AN EXEMPLARY PATIENT, FILLMORE-- I AM JUST SO PROUD OF ALL THE PROGRESS WE'VE MADE TOGETHER. TREATING YOU HAS TRULY BEEN THE GREATEST PRIVILEGE OF MY MEDICAL CAREER.
BUT WE'VE REACHED THE LIMIT OF WHAT I CAN DO FOR YOU HERE, IN THIS FACILITY. WE NEED TO BEGIN EXPLORING THE WORLD OUTSIDE. WE'LL START SLOWLY, BUT I'M CONFIDENT THAT, IN NO TIME AT ALL--
YOU'LL BE READY TO BECOME THE PRODUCTIVE, LAW-ABIDING CITIZEN YOU WERE ALWAYS DESTINED TO BE.
BUT I...
I UNDERSTAND. YOU'RE NERVOUS. AFRAID YOU'LL FALL BACK INTO THE OLD WAYS. BUT I BELIEVE IN YOU, FILLMORE. HOWEVER, I SHOULD POINT OUT--
THIS NEXT STEP DOES COME WITH A CONDITION.
YOU-- YOU MEAN MY MASK...
THAT'S RIGHT. YOU'LL HAVE NO USE FOR IT OUT THERE. IN FACT, IT WILL ONLY CAUSE YOU PAIN.
IT'S TIME TO SHOW ME HOW BRAVE YOU CAN BE.

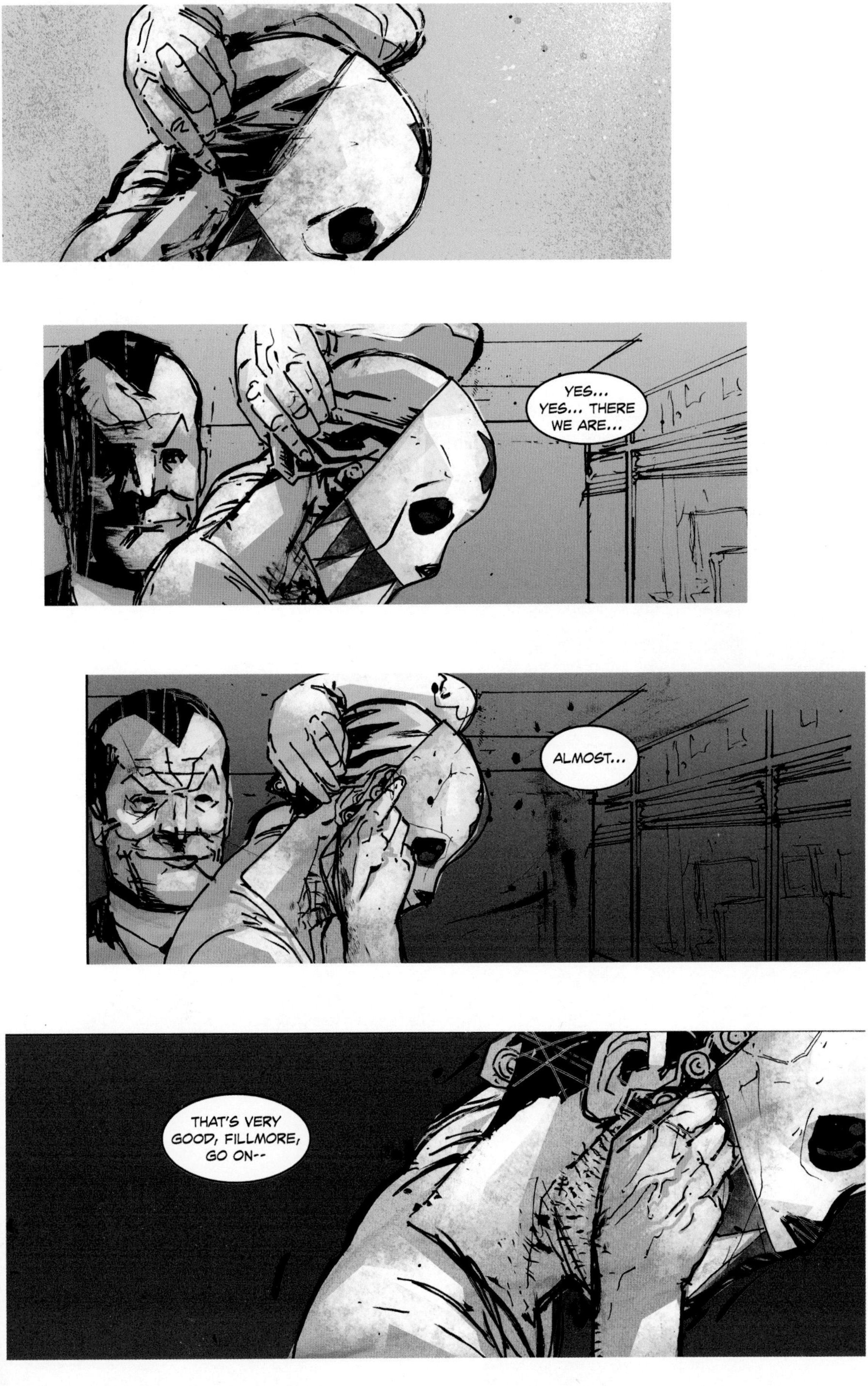
YES... YES... THERE WE ARE...
ALMOST...
THAT'S VERY GOOD, FILLMORE, GO ON--

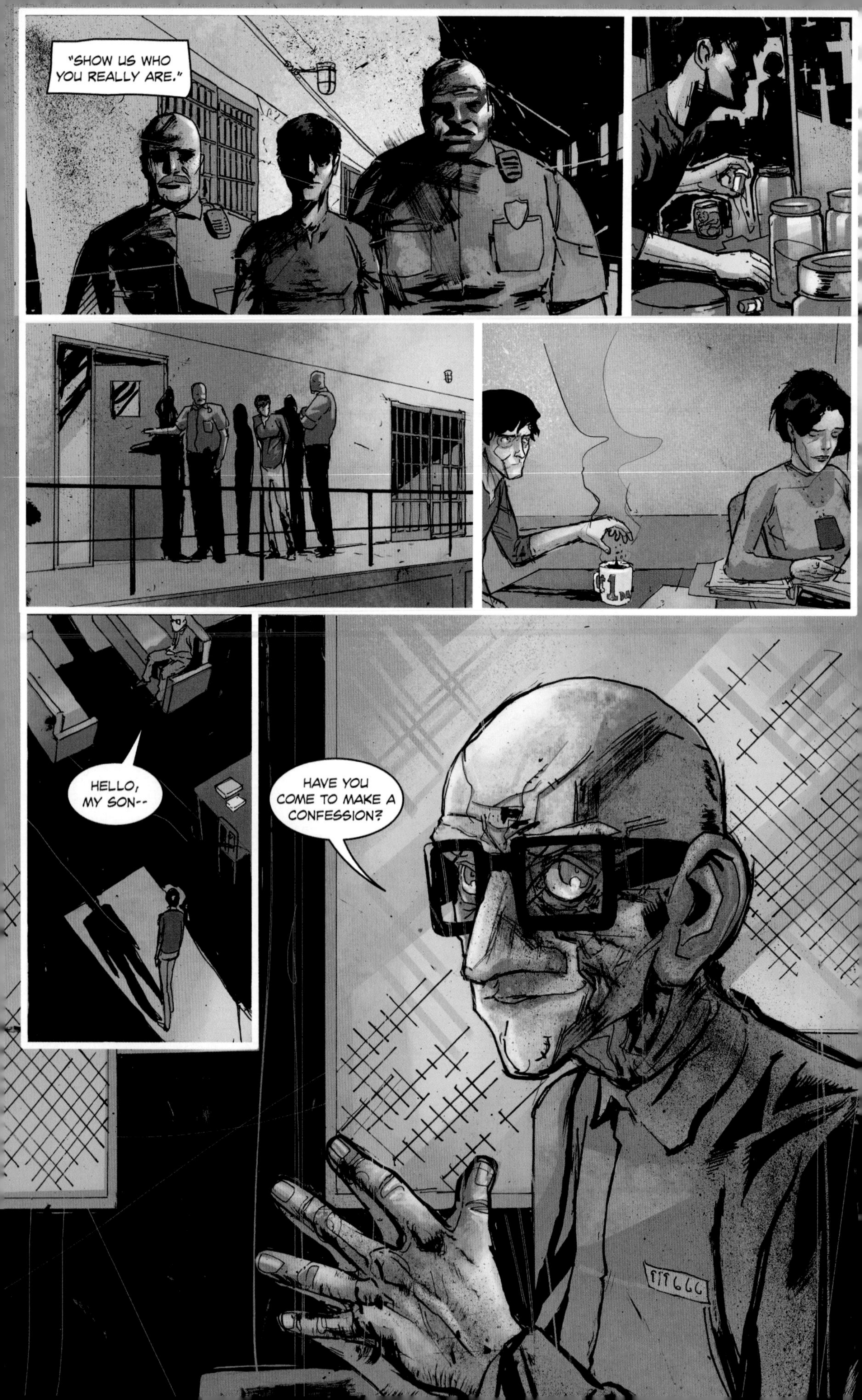
"SHOW US WHO YOU REALLY ARE."
HELLO, MY SON--
HAVE YOU COME TO MAKE A CONFESSION?

6
CHAPTER

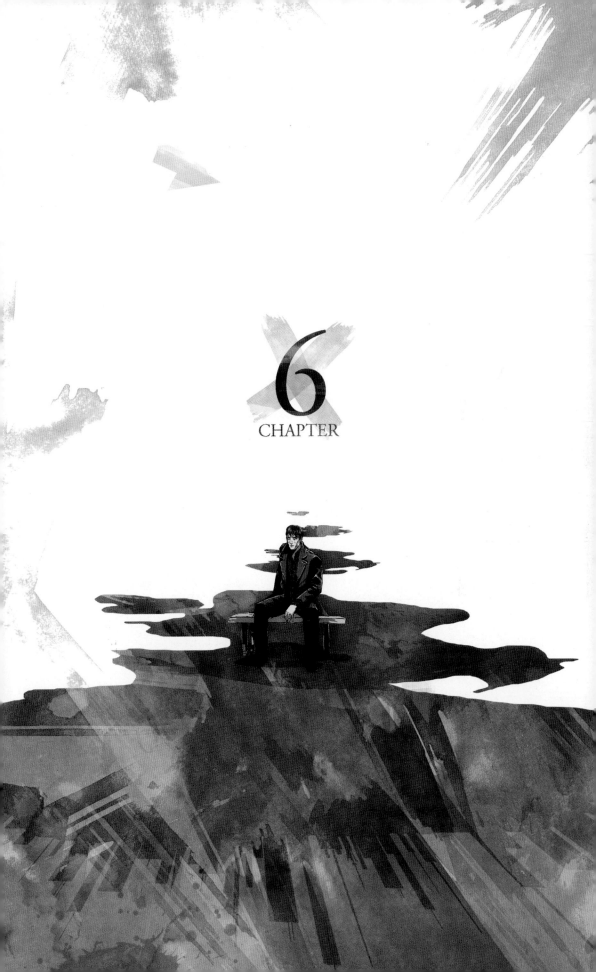

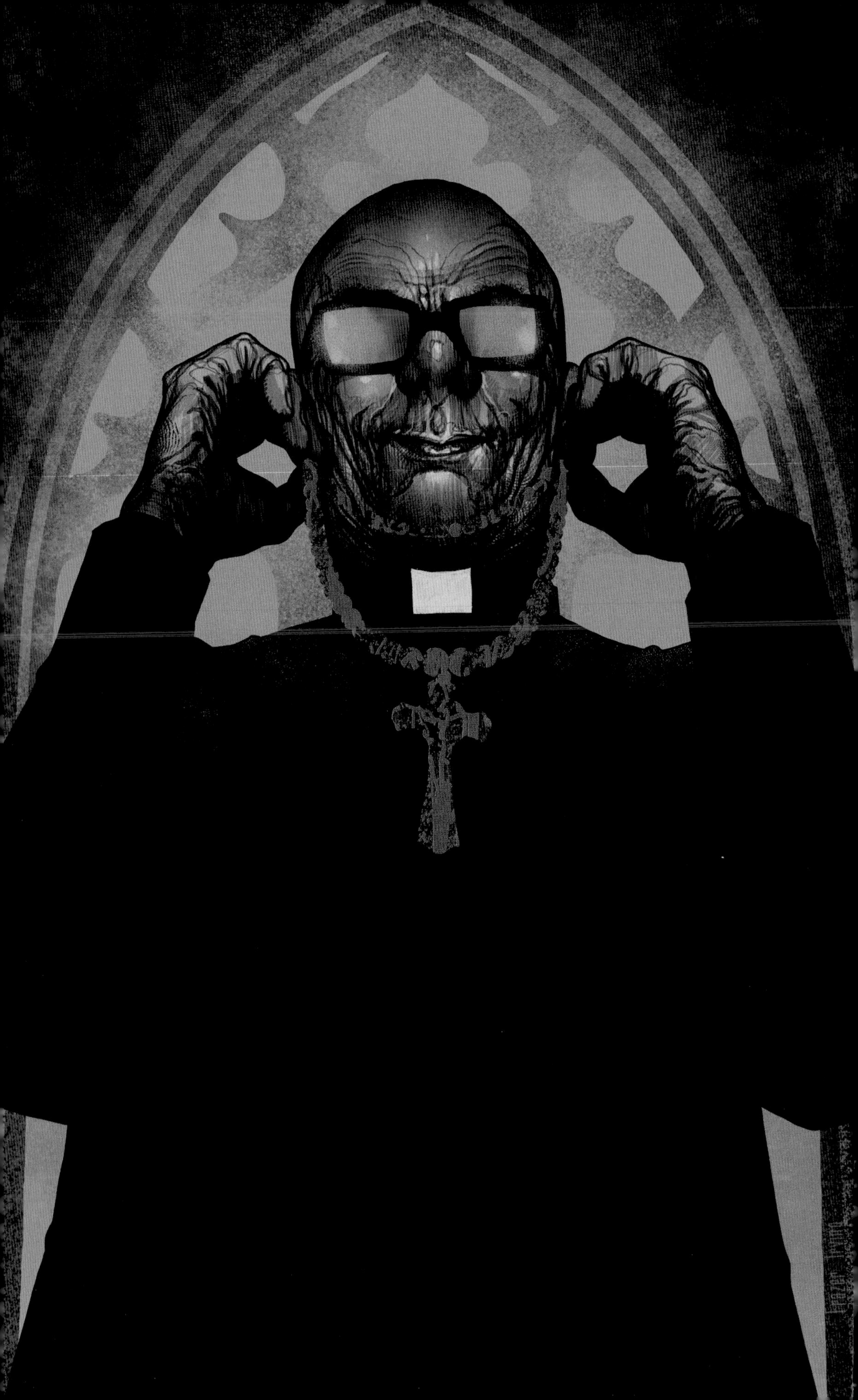

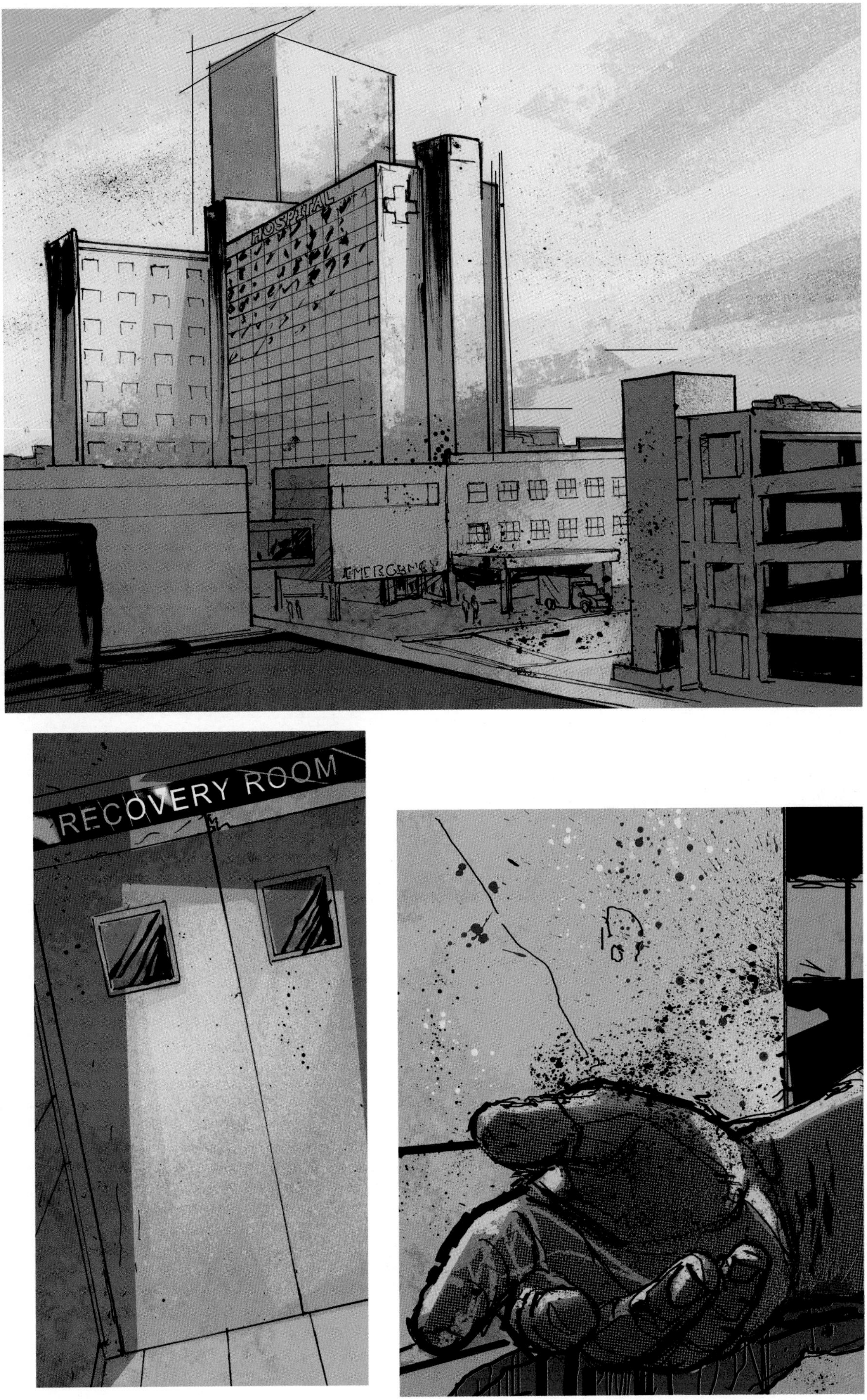
HOSPITAL
EMERGENCY
RECOVERY ROOM

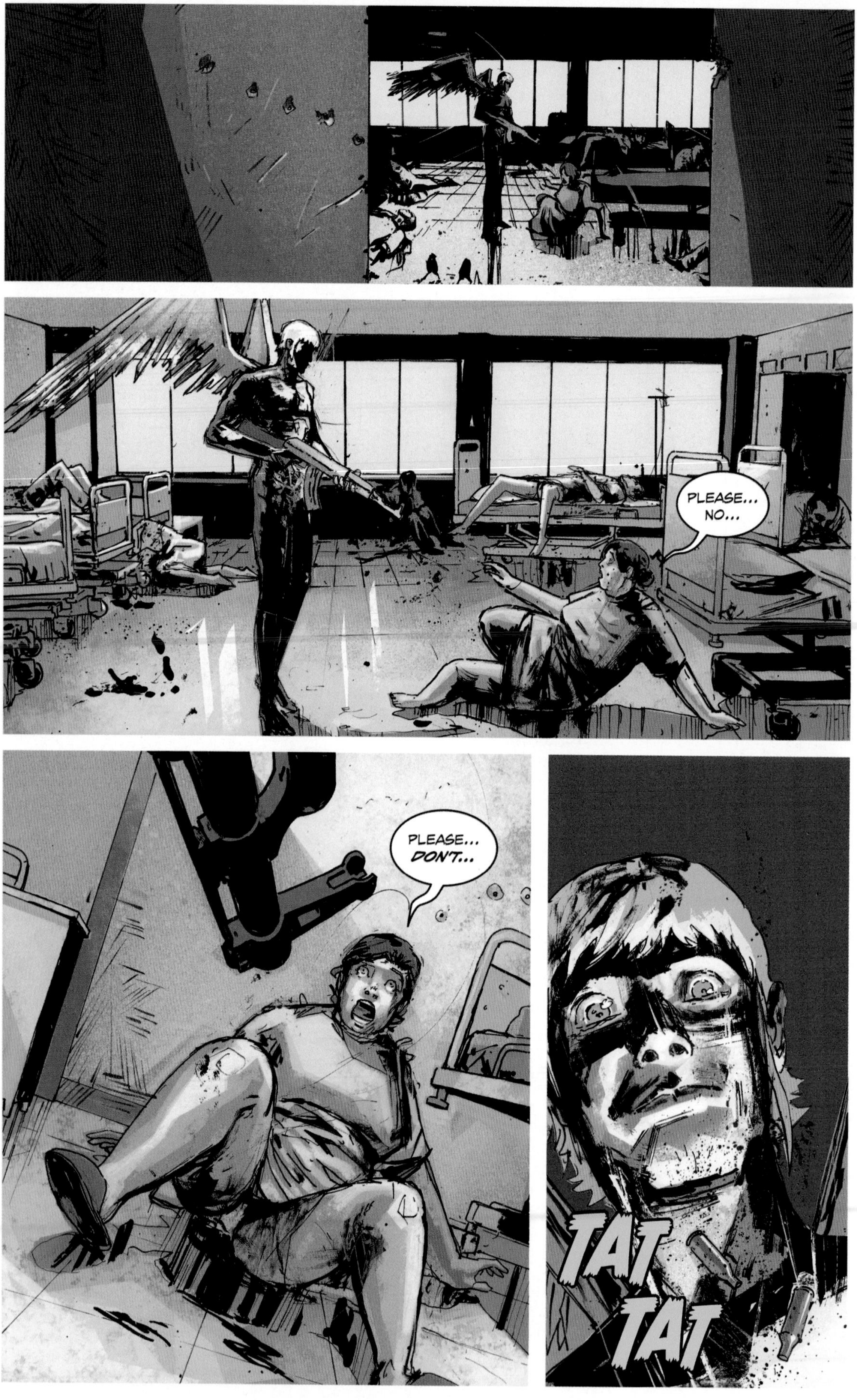
PLEASE... NO...
PLEASE... DON'T...
TAT
TAT

SKLASH

CHAPTER SIX

SOME OF US GOT A LITTLE MORE LOST THAN O

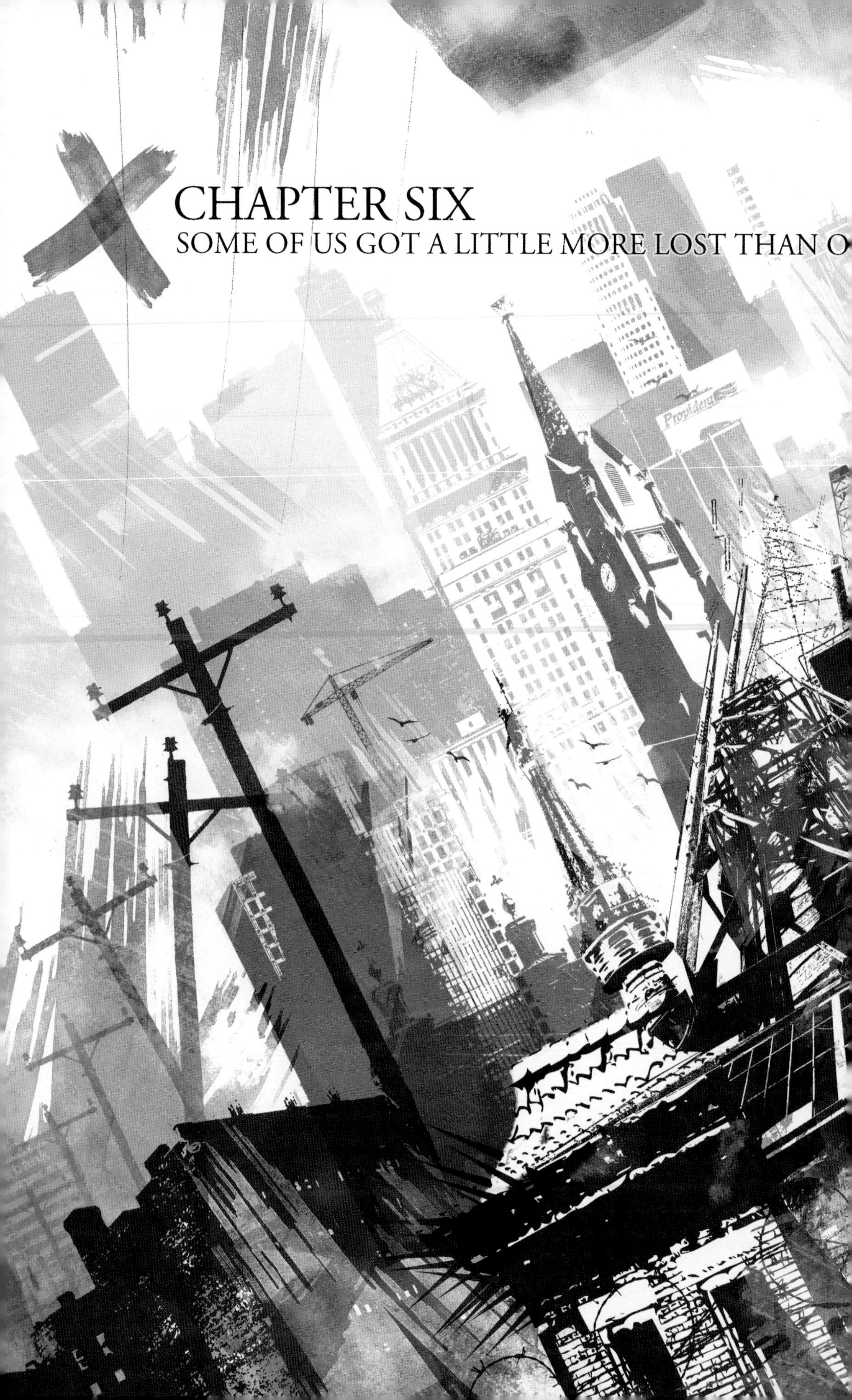

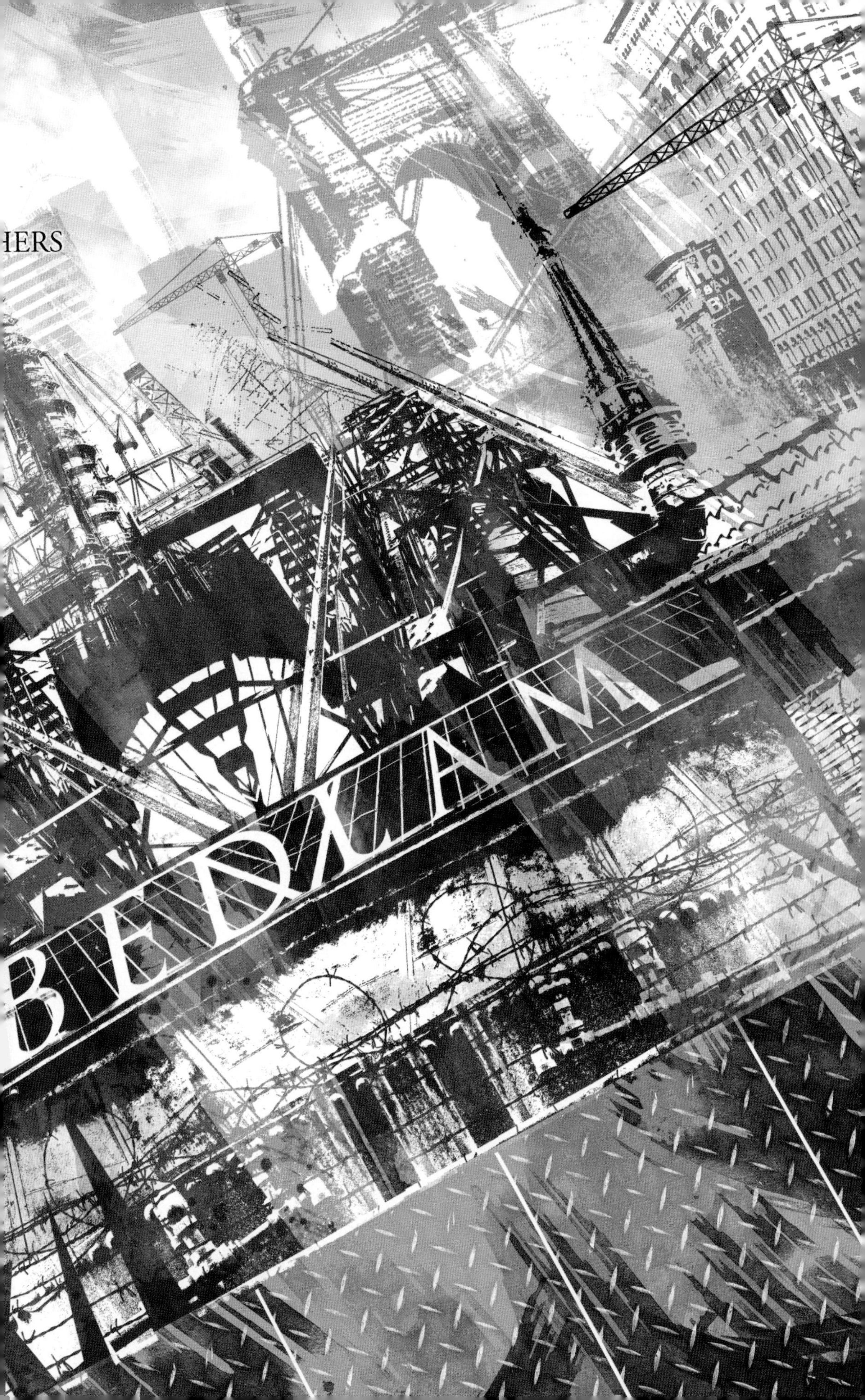
HERS
BEDLAM

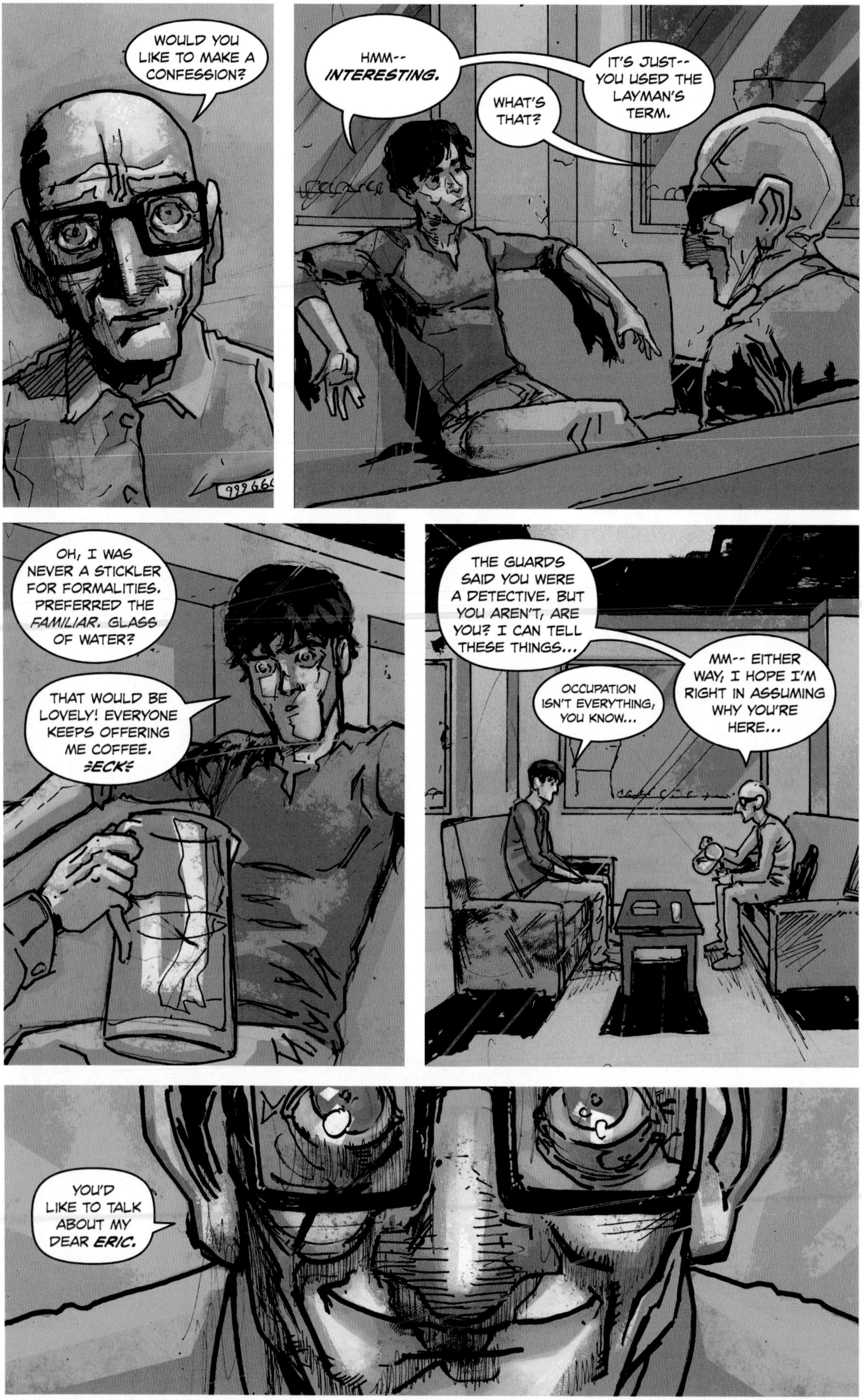
WOULD YOU LIKE TO MAKE A CONFESSION?
HMM-- INTERESTING.
WHAT'S THAT?
IT'S JUST-- YOU USED THE LAYMAN'S TERM.
OH, I WAS NEVER A STICKLER FOR FORMALITIES. PREFERRED THE FAMILIAR. GLASS OF WATER?
THAT WOULD BE LOVELY! EVERYONE KEEPS OFFERING ME COFFEE. ECK
THE GUARDS SAID YOU WERE A DETECTIVE. BUT YOU AREN'T, ARE YOU? I CAN TELL THESE THINGS...
OCCUPATION ISN'T EVERYTHING, YOU KNOW...
MM-- EITHER WAY, I HOPE I'M RIGHT IN ASSUMING WHY YOU'RE HERE...
YOU'D LIKE TO TALK ABOUT MY DEAR ERIC.

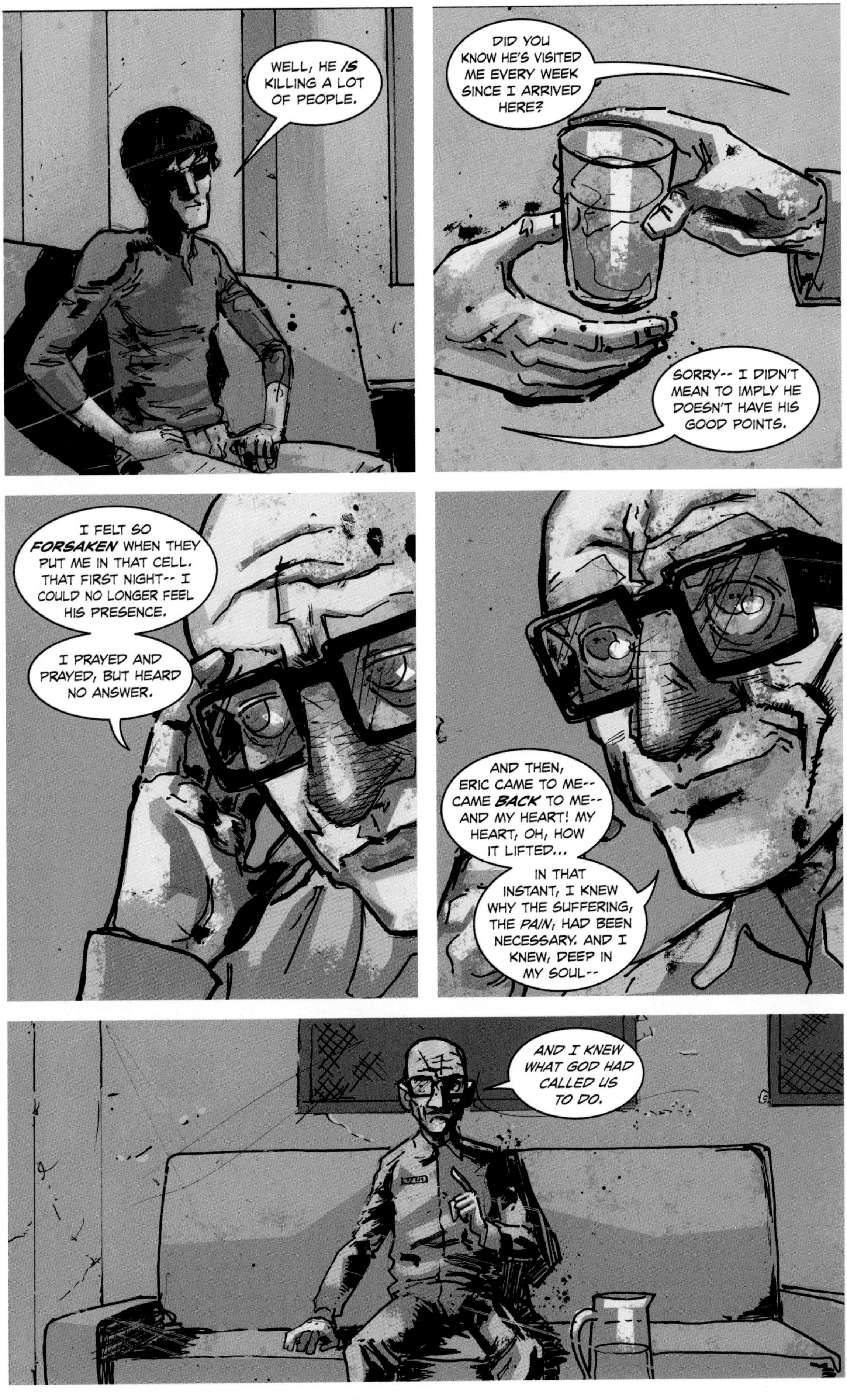
WELL, HE IS KILLING A LOT OF PEOPLE.
DID YOU KNOW HE'S VISITED ME EVERY WEEK SINCE I ARRIVED HERE?
SORRY-- I DIDN'T MEAN TO IMPLY HE DOESN'T HAVE HIS GOOD POINTS.
I FELT SO FORSAKEN WHEN THEY PUT ME IN THAT CELL. THAT FIRST NIGHT-- I COULD NO LONGER FEEL HIS PRESENCE.
I PRAYED AND PRAYED, BUT HEARD NO ANSWER.
AND THEN, ERIC CAME TO ME-- CAME BACK TO ME-- AND MY HEART! MY HEART, OH, HOW IT LIFTED...
IN THAT INSTANT, I KNEW WHY THE SUFFERING, THE PAIN, HAD BEEN NECESSARY. AND I KNEW, DEEP IN MY SOUL--
AND I KNEW WHAT GOD HAD CALLED US TO DO.

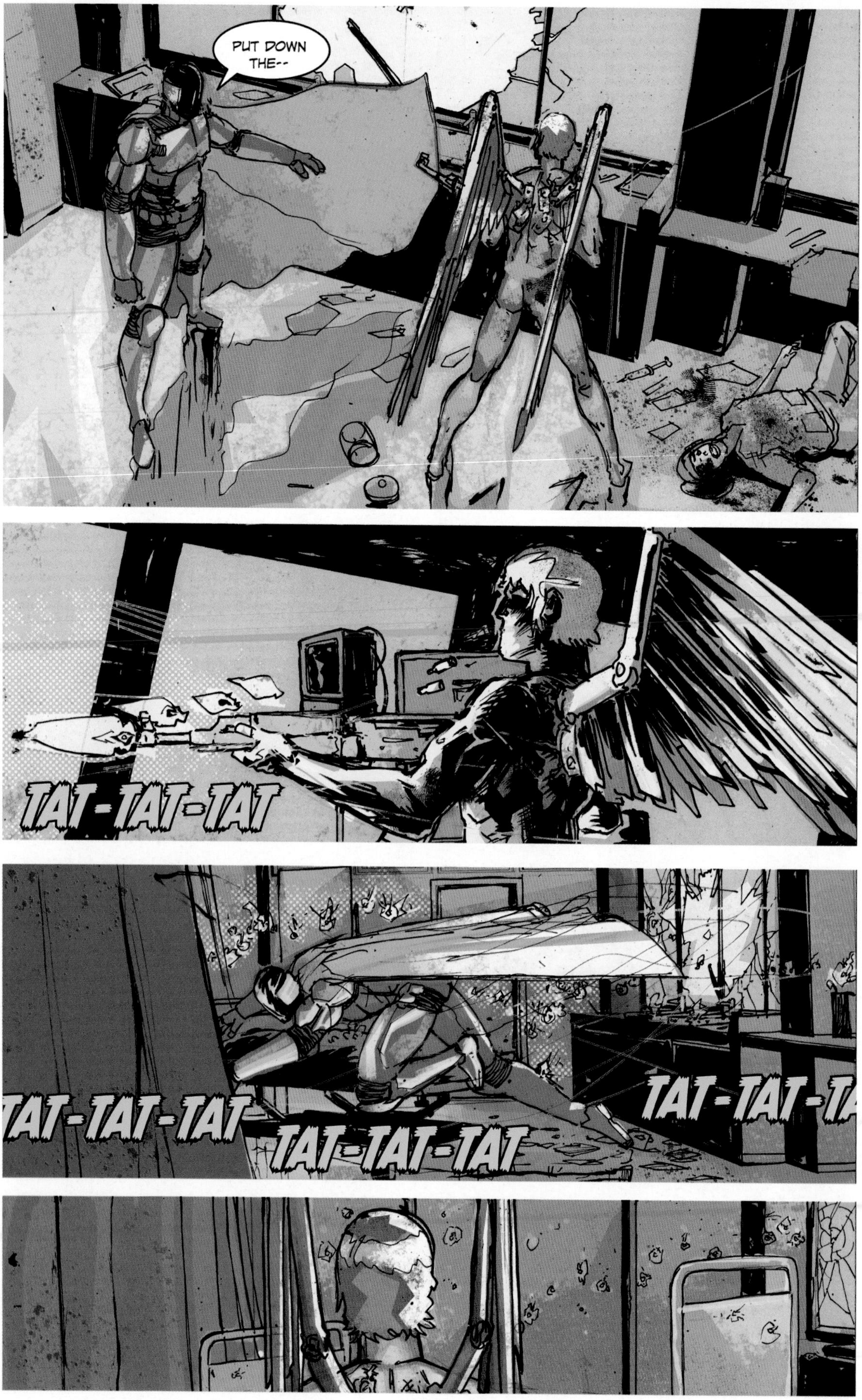
PUT DOWN THE--
TAT-TAT-TAT
TAT-TAT-TAT
TAT-TAT-TAT
TAT-TAT-TA

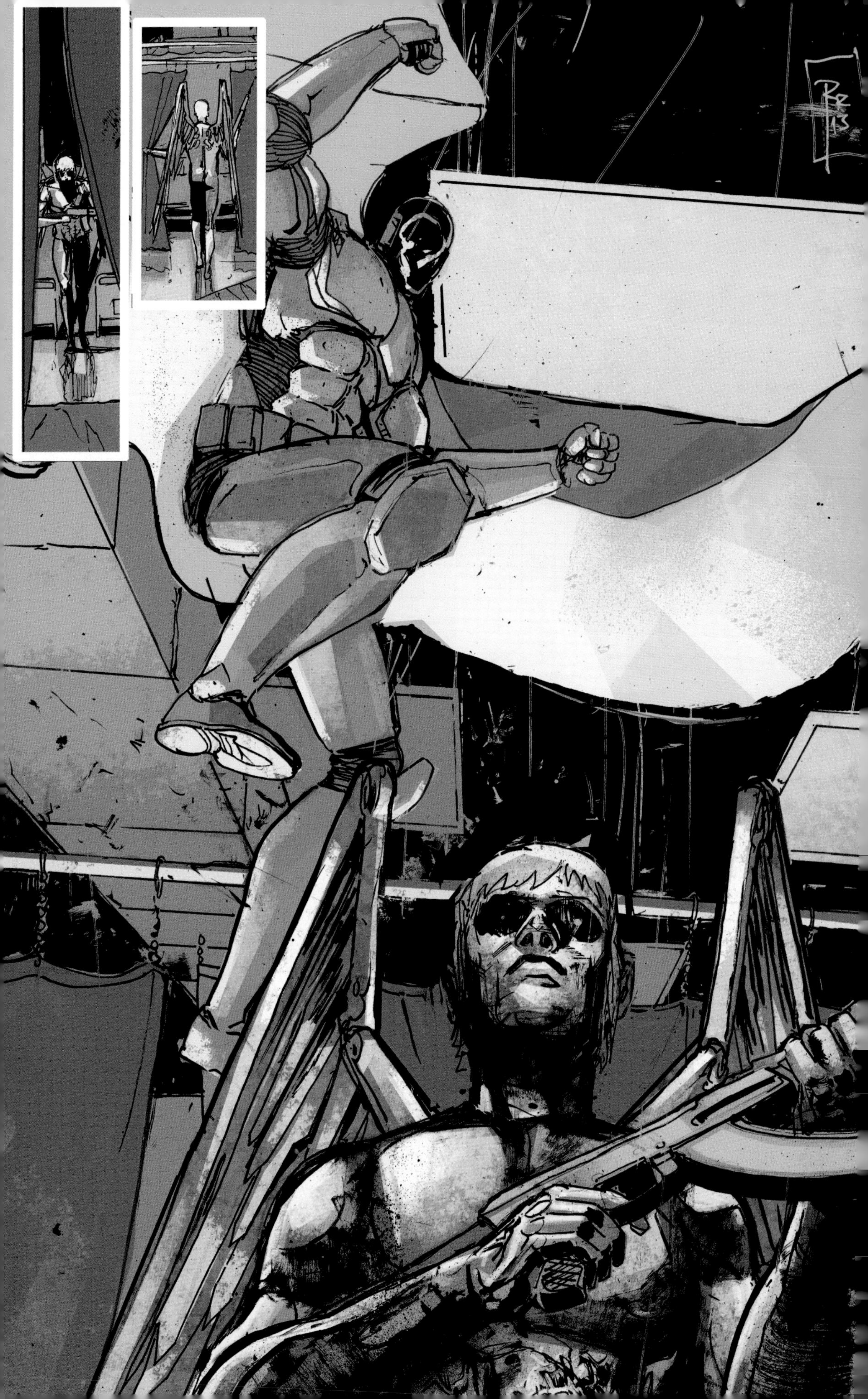

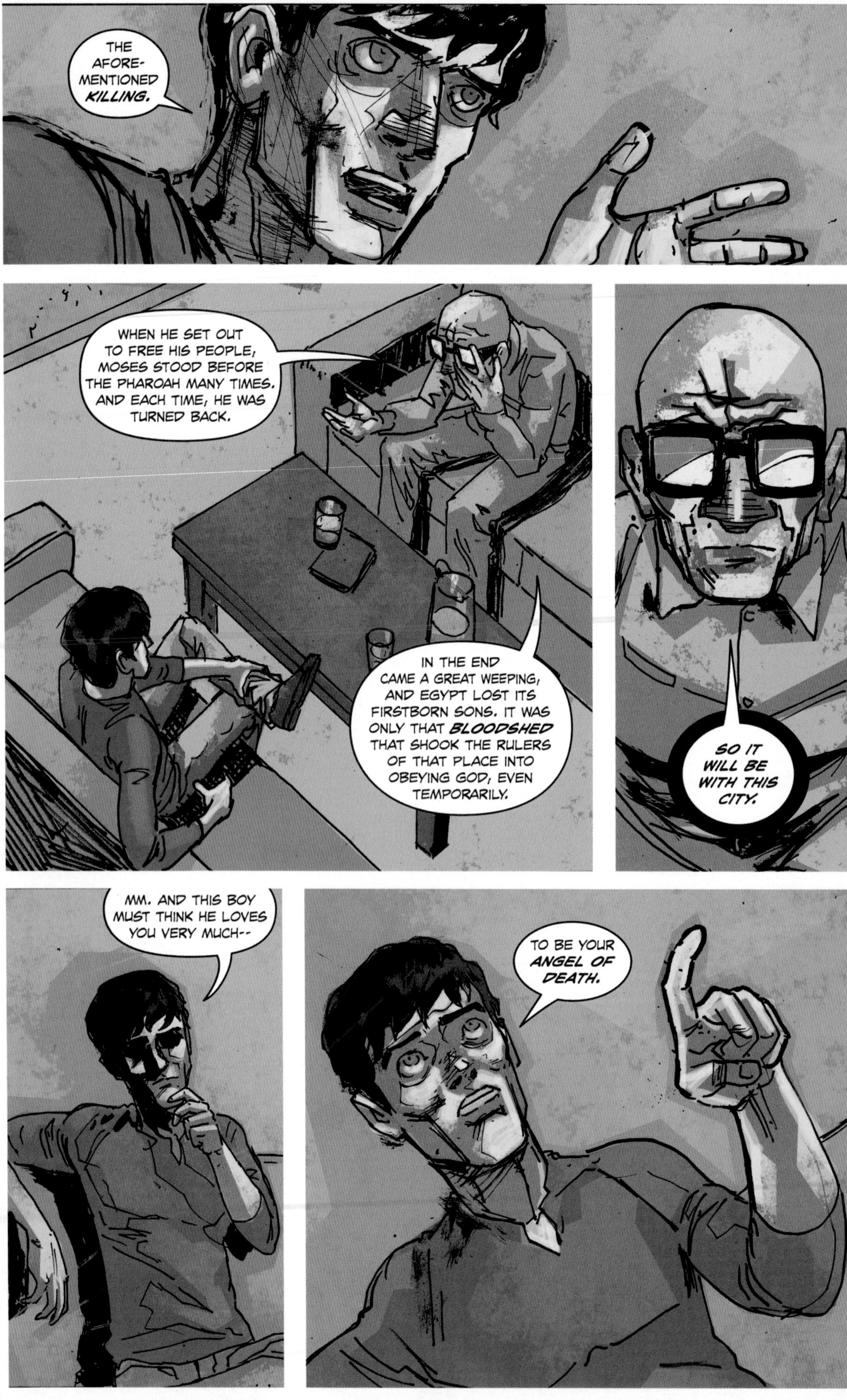
THE AFORE-MENTIONED *KILLING.*
WHEN HE SET OUT TO FREE HIS PEOPLE, MOSES STOOD BEFORE THE PHAROAH MANY TIMES. AND EACH TIME, HE WAS TURNED BACK.
IN THE END CAME A GREAT WEEPING, AND EGYPT LOST ITS FIRSTBORN SONS. IT WAS ONLY THAT *BLOODSHED* THAT SHOOK THE RULERS OF THAT PLACE INTO OBEYING GOD, EVEN TEMPORARILY.
SO IT WILL BE WITH THIS CITY.
MM. AND THIS BOY MUST THINK HE LOVES YOU VERY MUCH--
TO BE YOUR *ANGEL OF DEATH.*

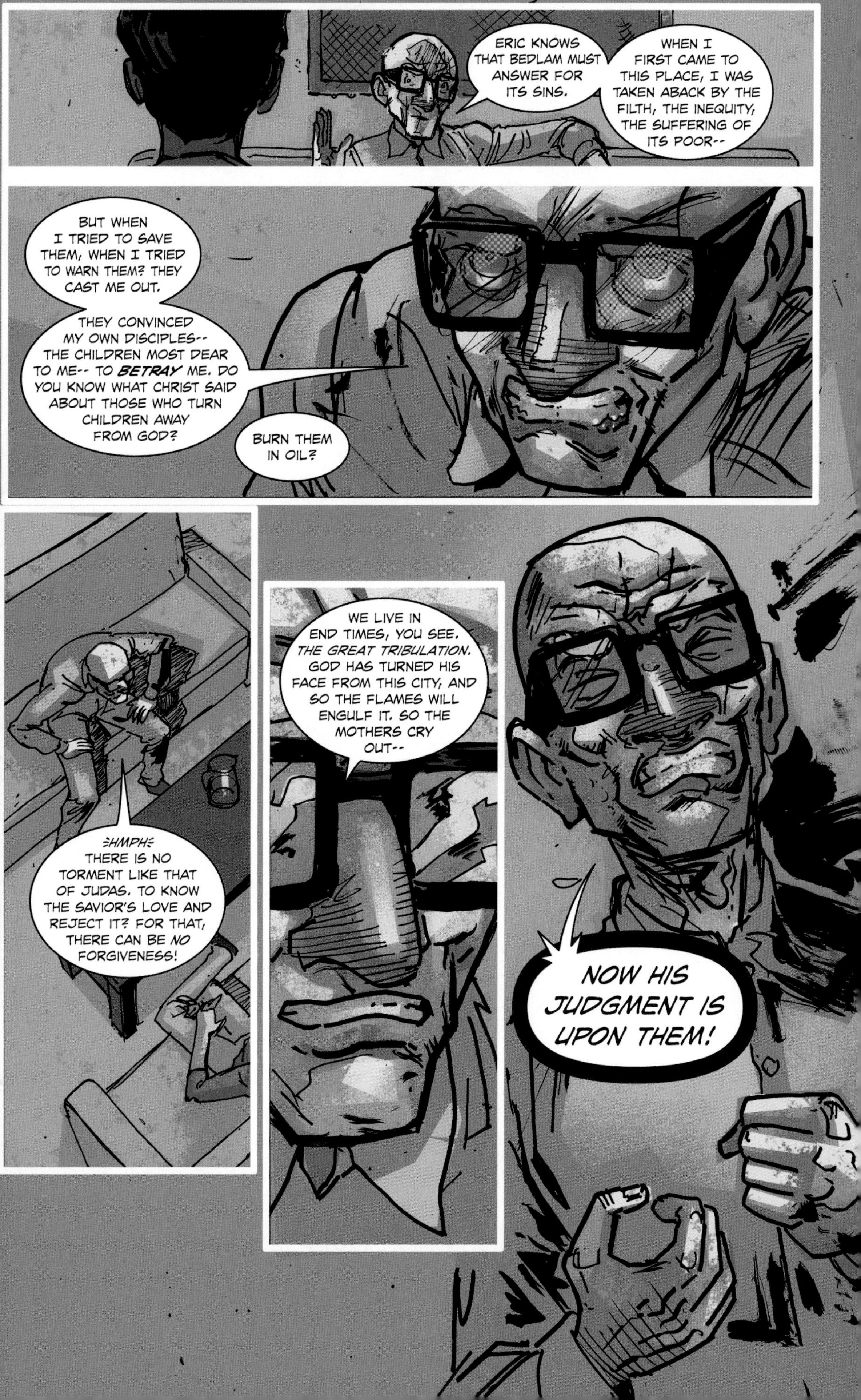
ERIC KNOWS THAT BEDLAM MUST ANSWER FOR ITS SINS.
WHEN I FIRST CAME TO THIS PLACE, I WAS TAKEN ABACK BY THE FILTH, THE INEQUITY, THE SUFFERING OF ITS POOR--
BUT WHEN I TRIED TO SAVE THEM, WHEN I TRIED TO WARN THEM? THEY CAST ME OUT.
THEY CONVINCED MY OWN DISCIPLES-- THE CHILDREN MOST DEAR TO ME-- TO BETRAY ME. DO YOU KNOW WHAT CHRIST SAID ABOUT THOSE WHO TURN CHILDREN AWAY FROM GOD?
BURN THEM IN OIL?
HMPH
THERE IS NO TORMENT LIKE THAT OF JUDAS. TO KNOW THE SAVIOR'S LOVE AND REJECT IT? FOR THAT, THERE CAN BE NO FORGIVENESS!
WE LIVE IN END TIMES, YOU SEE. THE GREAT TRIBULATION. GOD HAS TURNED HIS FACE FROM THIS CITY, AND SO THE FLAMES WILL ENGULF IT. SO THE MOTHERS CRY OUT--
NOW HIS JUDGMENT IS UPON THEM!

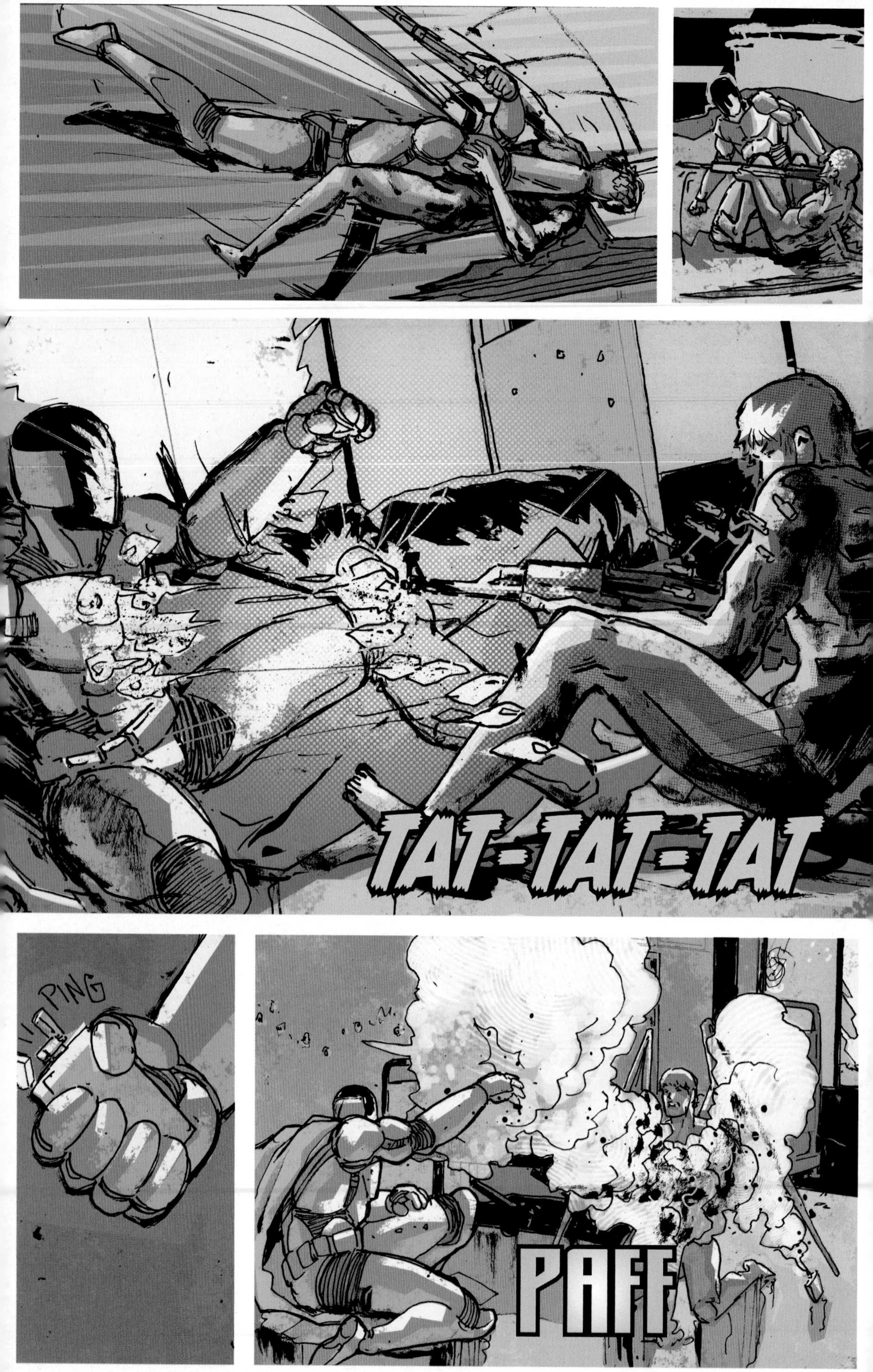
TAT-TAT-TAT
PING
PAFF

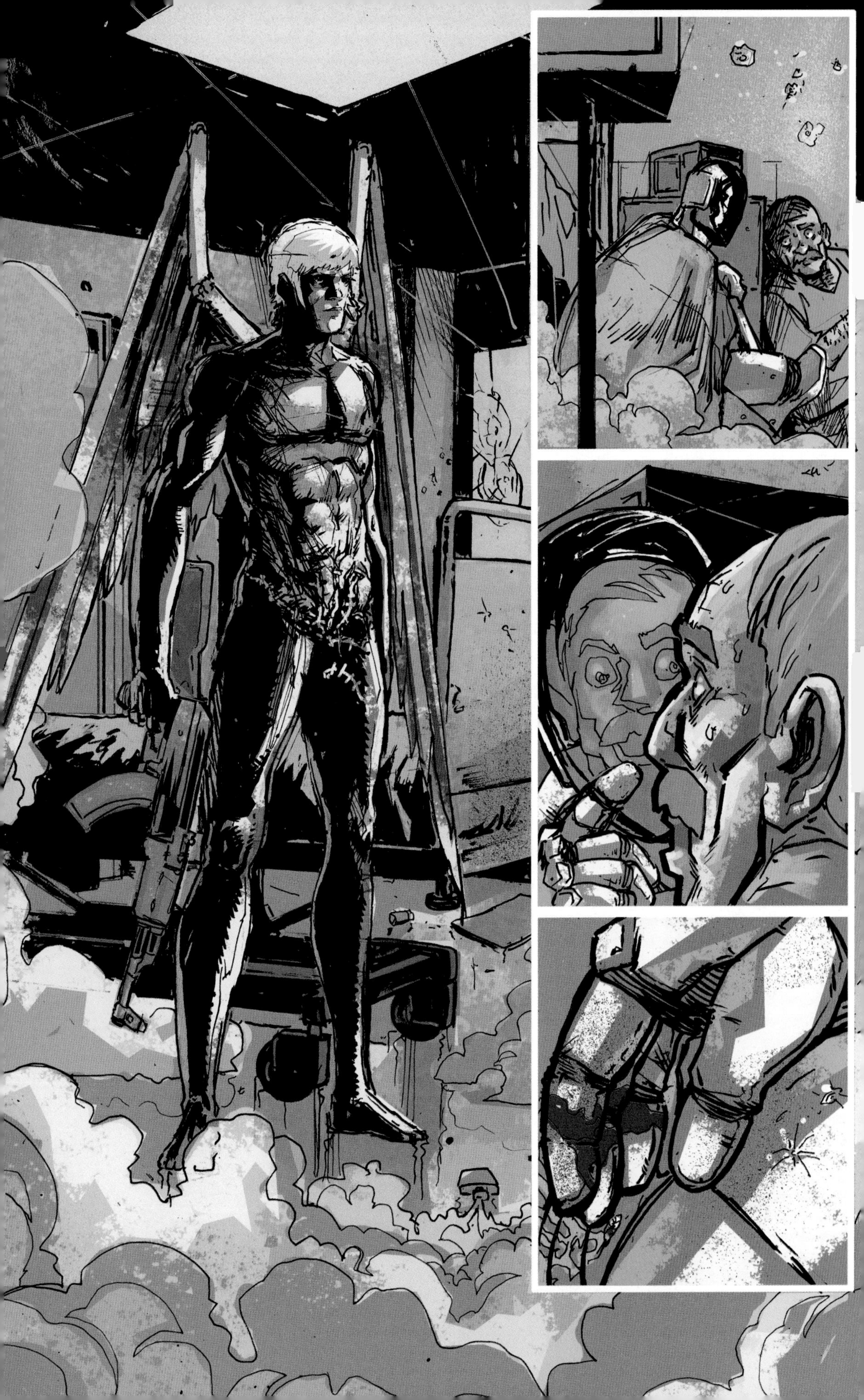

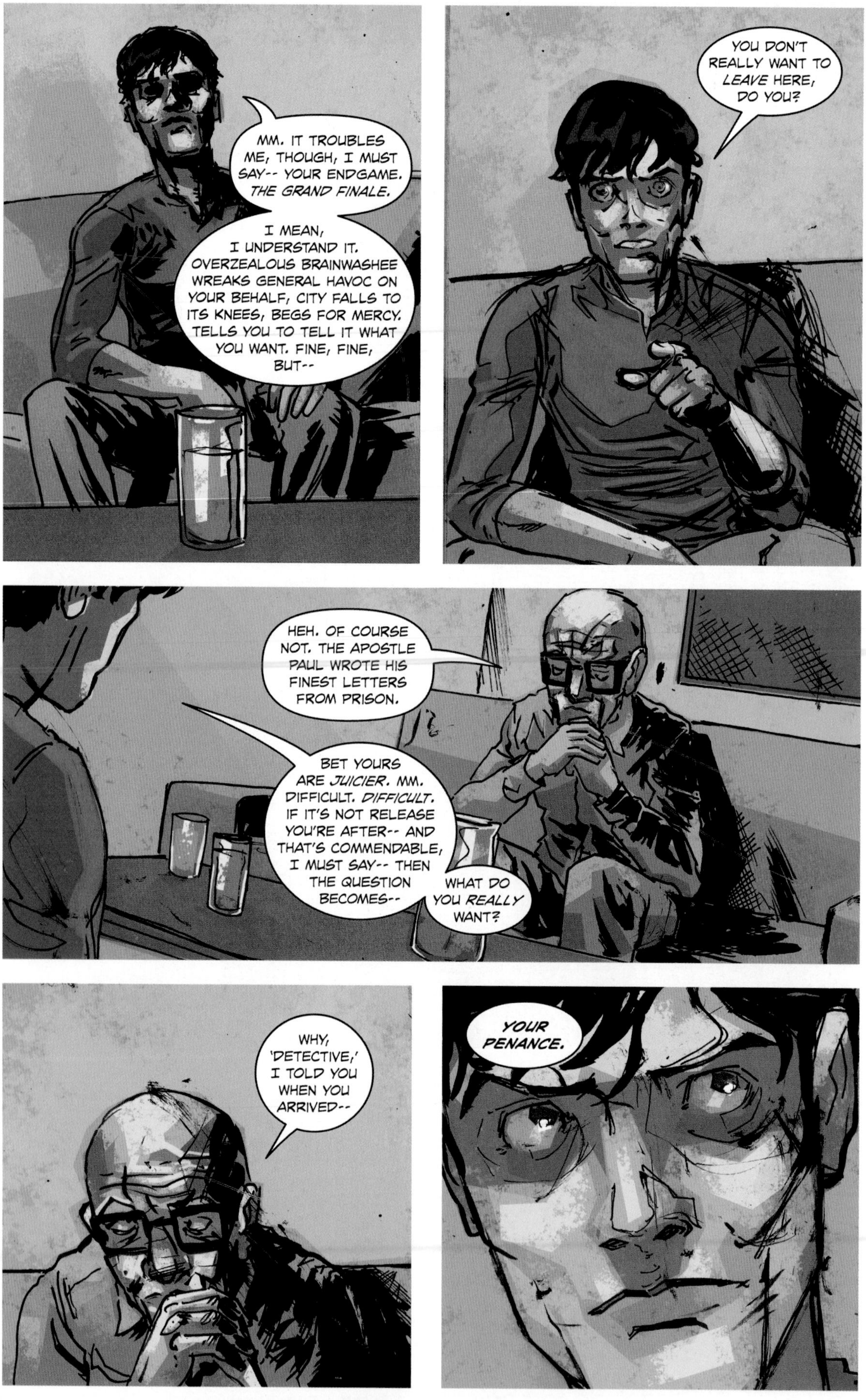
MM. IT TROUBLES ME, THOUGH, I MUST SAY-- YOUR ENDGAME. *THE GRAND FINALE.*
I MEAN, I UNDERSTAND IT. OVERZEALOUS BRAINWASHEE WREAKS GENERAL HAVOC ON YOUR BEHALF, CITY FALLS TO ITS KNEES, BEGS FOR MERCY. TELLS YOU TO TELL IT WHAT YOU WANT. FINE, FINE, BUT--
YOU DON'T REALLY WANT TO *LEAVE* HERE, DO YOU?
HEH. OF COURSE NOT. THE APOSTLE PAUL WROTE HIS FINEST LETTERS FROM PRISON.
BET YOURS ARE *JUICIER*. MM. DIFFICULT. *DIFFICULT.* IF IT'S NOT RELEASE YOU'RE AFTER-- AND THAT'S COMMENDABLE, I MUST SAY-- THEN THE QUESTION BECOMES--
WHAT DO YOU *REALLY* WANT?
WHY, 'DETECTIVE,' I TOLD YOU WHEN YOU ARRIVED--
YOUR PENANCE.

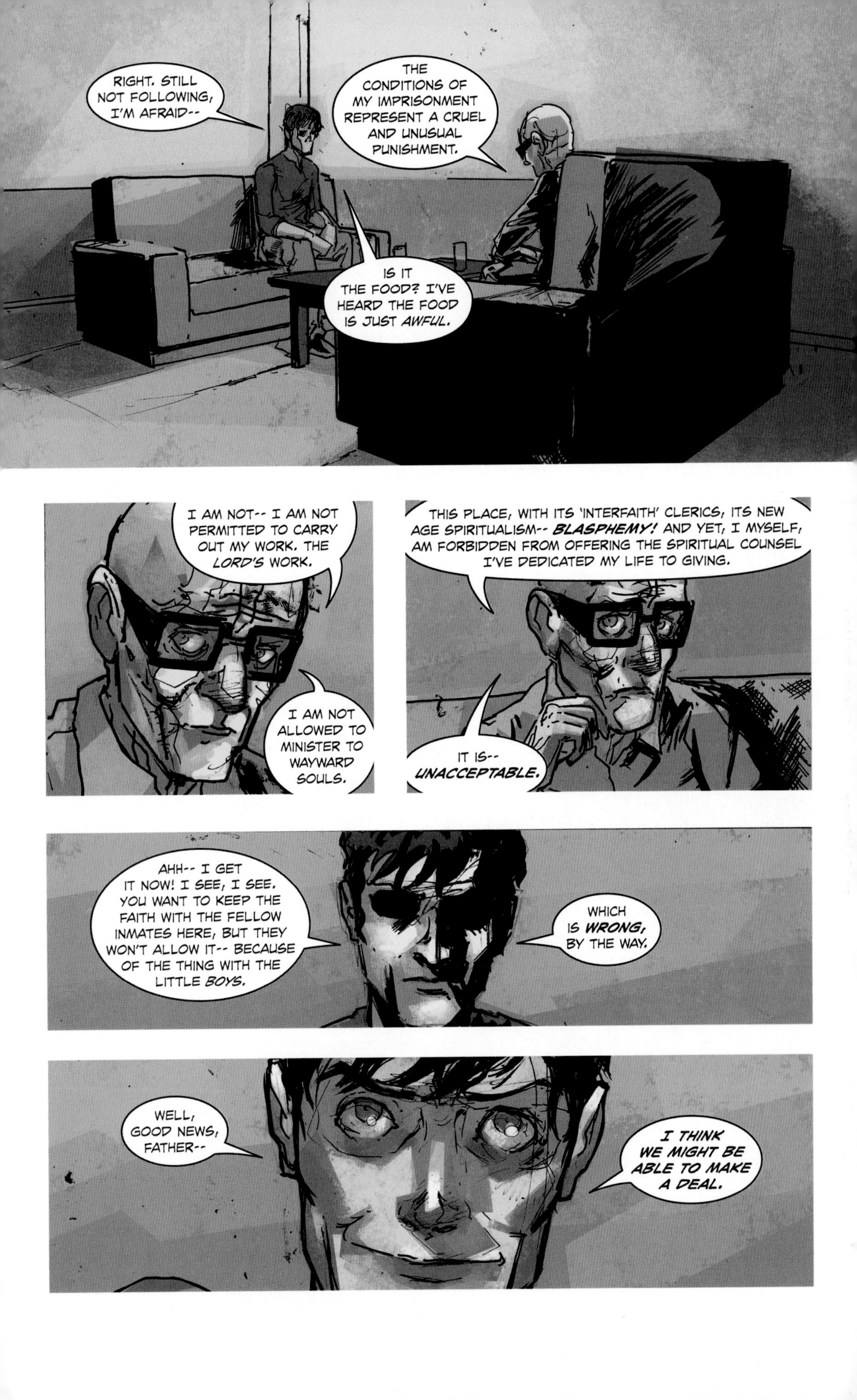

RIGHT. STILL NOT FOLLOWING, I'M AFRAID--
THE CONDITIONS OF MY IMPRISONMENT REPRESENT A CRUEL AND UNUSUAL PUNISHMENT.
IS IT THE FOOD? I'VE HEARD THE FOOD IS JUST *AWFUL.*
I AM NOT-- I AM NOT PERMITTED TO CARRY OUT MY WORK. THE *LORD'S* WORK.
I AM NOT ALLOWED TO MINISTER TO WAYWARD SOULS.
THIS PLACE, WITH ITS 'INTERFAITH' CLERICS, ITS NEW AGE SPIRITUALISM-- ***BLASPHEMY!*** AND YET, I MYSELF, AM FORBIDDEN FROM OFFERING THE SPIRITUAL COUNSEL I'VE DEDICATED MY LIFE TO GIVING.
IT IS-- *UNACCEPTABLE.*
AHH-- I GET IT NOW! I SEE, I SEE. YOU WANT TO KEEP THE FAITH WITH THE FELLOW INMATES HERE, BUT THEY WON'T ALLOW IT-- BECAUSE OF THE THING WITH THE LITTLE *BOYS.*
WHICH IS ***WRONG,*** BY THE WAY.
WELL, GOOD NEWS, FATHER--
I THINK WE MIGHT BE ABLE TO MAKE A DEAL.

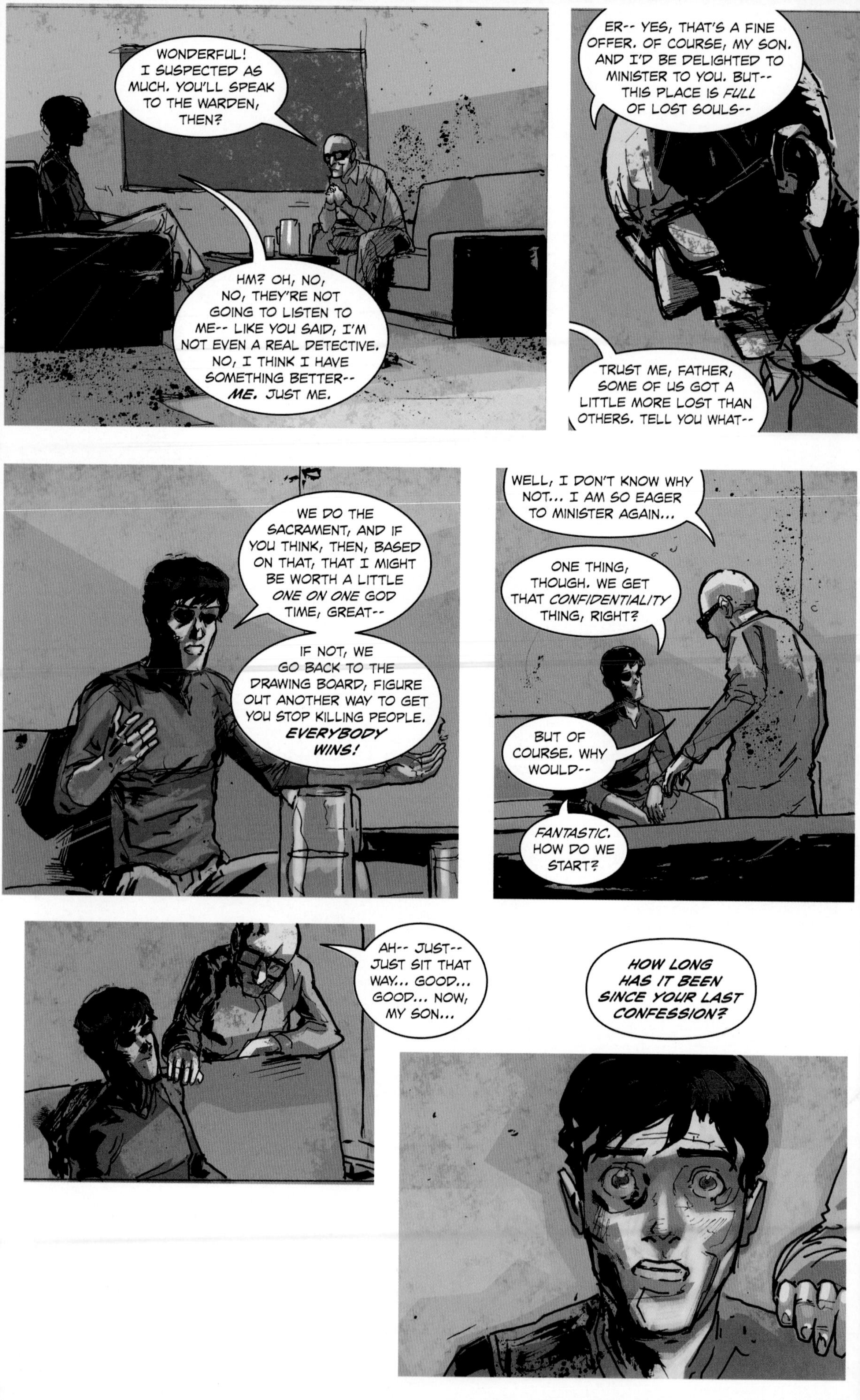
WONDERFUL! I SUSPECTED AS MUCH. YOU'LL SPEAK TO THE WARDEN, THEN?
HM? OH, NO, NO, THEY'RE NOT GOING TO LISTEN TO ME-- LIKE YOU SAID, I'M NOT EVEN A REAL DETECTIVE. NO, I THINK I HAVE SOMETHING BETTER-- ME. JUST ME.
ER-- YES, THAT'S A FINE OFFER. OF COURSE, MY SON. AND I'D BE DELIGHTED TO MINISTER TO YOU. BUT-- THIS PLACE IS FULL OF LOST SOULS--
TRUST ME, FATHER, SOME OF US GOT A LITTLE MORE LOST THAN OTHERS. TELL YOU WHAT--
WE DO THE SACRAMENT, AND IF YOU THINK, THEN, BASED ON THAT, THAT I MIGHT BE WORTH A LITTLE ONE ON ONE GOD TIME, GREAT--
IF NOT, WE GO BACK TO THE DRAWING BOARD, FIGURE OUT ANOTHER WAY TO GET YOU STOP KILLING PEOPLE. EVERYBODY WINS!
WELL, I DON'T KNOW WHY NOT... I AM SO EAGER TO MINISTER AGAIN...
ONE THING, THOUGH. WE GET THAT CONFIDENTIALITY THING, RIGHT?
BUT OF COURSE. WHY WOULD--
FANTASTIC. HOW DO WE START?
AH-- JUST-- JUST SIT THAT WAY... GOOD... GOOD... NOW, MY SON...
HOW LONG HAS IT BEEN SINCE YOUR LAST CONFESSION?

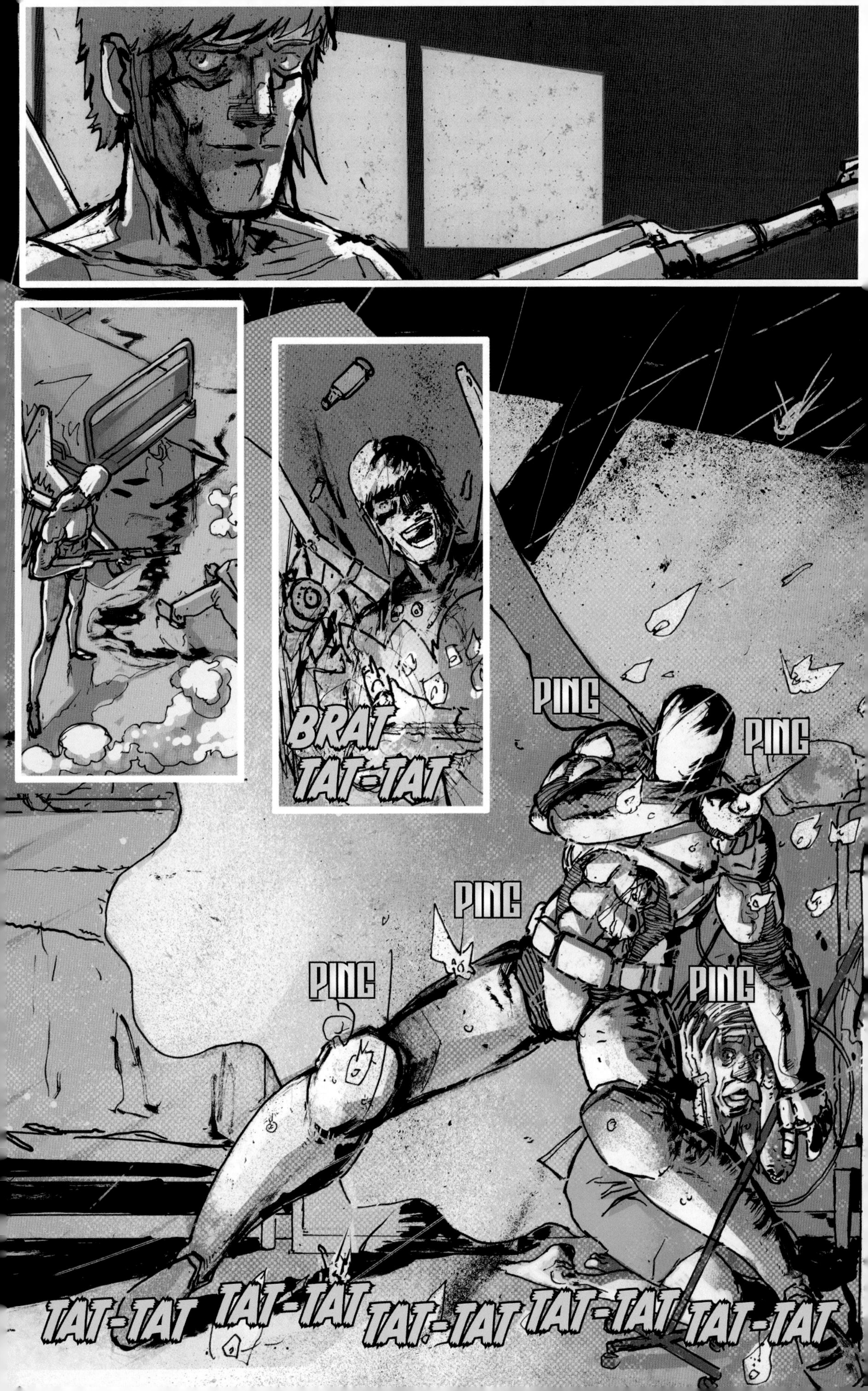
BRAT
TAT-TAT
PING
PING
PING
PING
PING
TAT-TAT TAT-TAT TAT-TAT TAT-TAT TAT-TAT

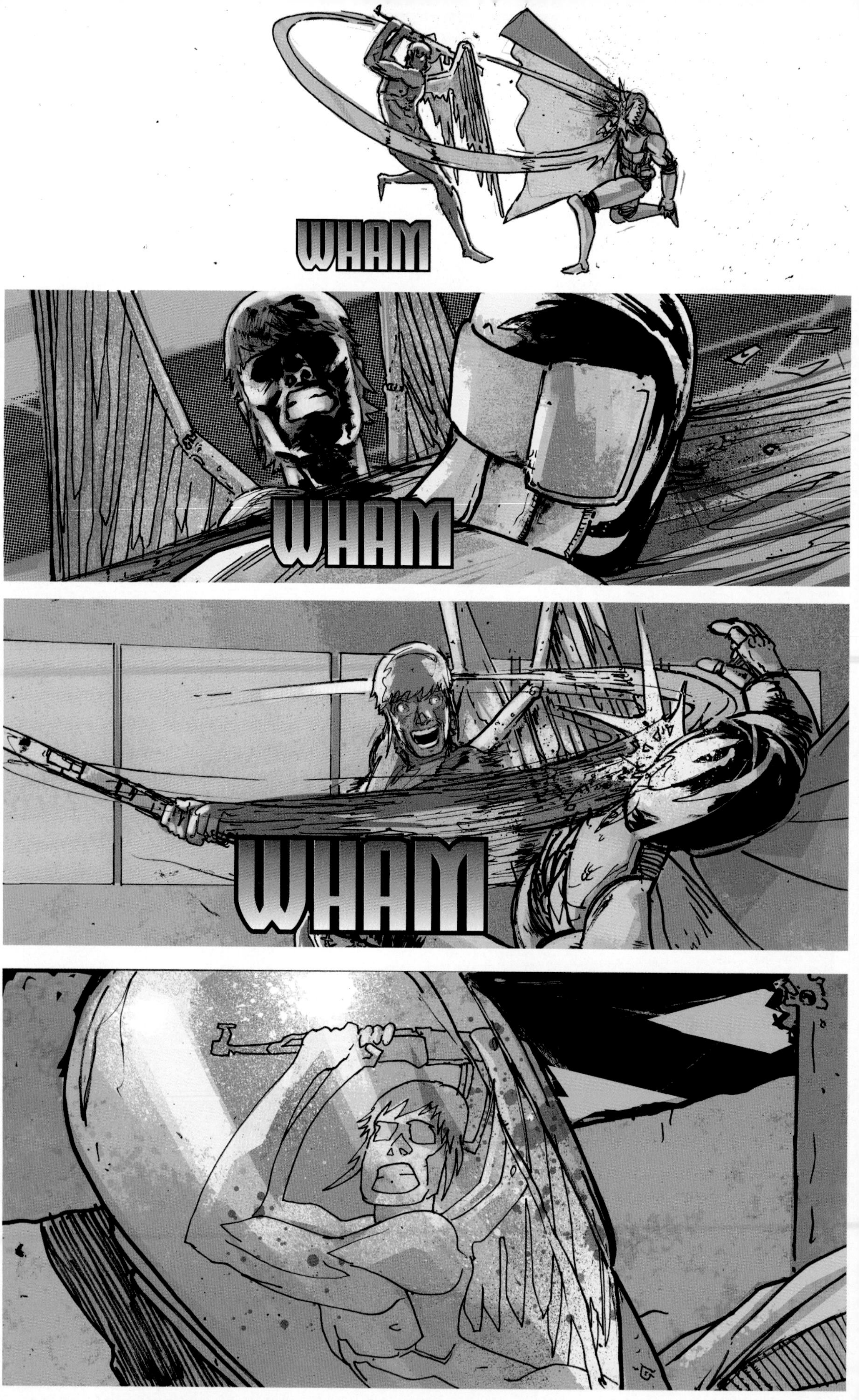
WHAM
WHAM
WHAM

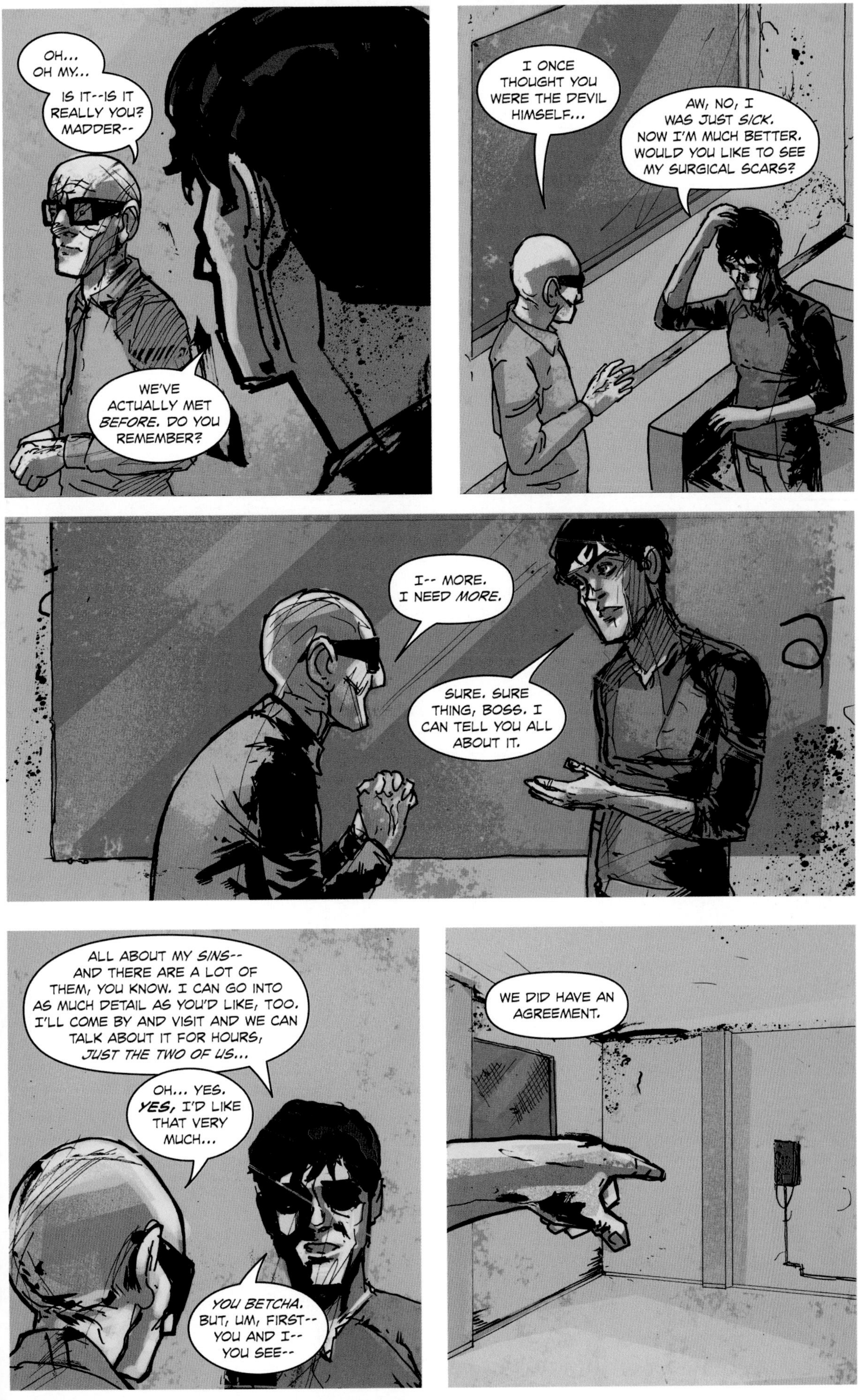
OH... OH MY...
IS IT--IS IT REALLY YOU? MADDER--
WE'VE ACTUALLY MET *BEFORE*. DO YOU REMEMBER?
I ONCE THOUGHT YOU WERE THE DEVIL HIMSELF...
AW, NO, I WAS JUST *SICK*. NOW I'M MUCH BETTER. WOULD YOU LIKE TO SEE MY SURGICAL SCARS?
I-- MORE. I NEED *MORE*.
SURE. SURE THING, BOSS. I CAN TELL YOU ALL ABOUT IT.
ALL ABOUT MY *SINS*-- AND THERE ARE A LOT OF THEM, YOU KNOW. I CAN GO INTO AS MUCH DETAIL AS YOU'D LIKE, TOO. I'LL COME BY AND VISIT AND WE CAN TALK ABOUT IT FOR HOURS, *JUST THE TWO OF US...*
OH... YES. ***YES,*** I'D LIKE THAT VERY MUCH...
YOU BETCHA. BUT, UM, FIRST-- YOU AND I-- YOU SEE--
WE DID HAVE AN AGREEMENT.

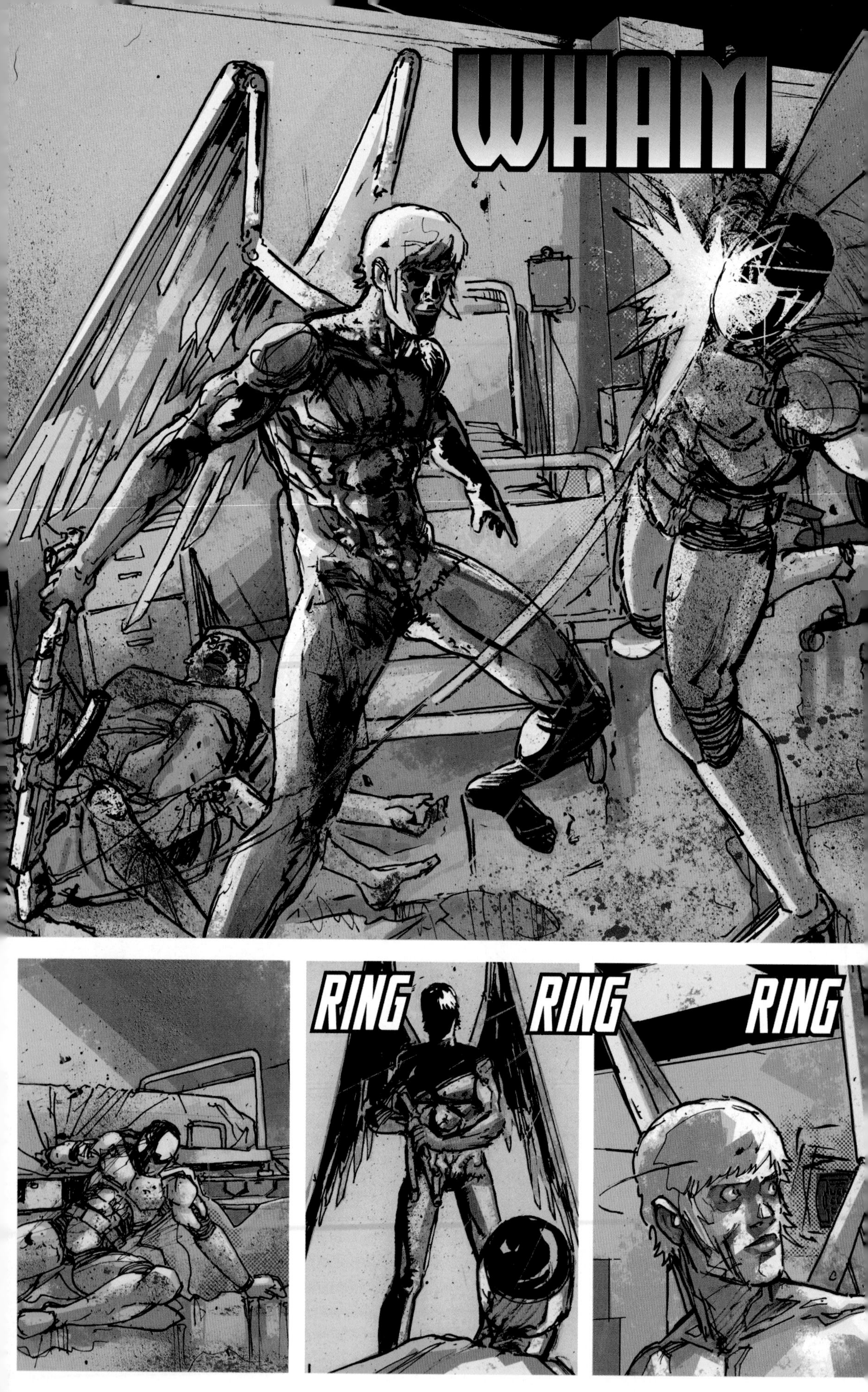
WHAM
RING
RING
RING

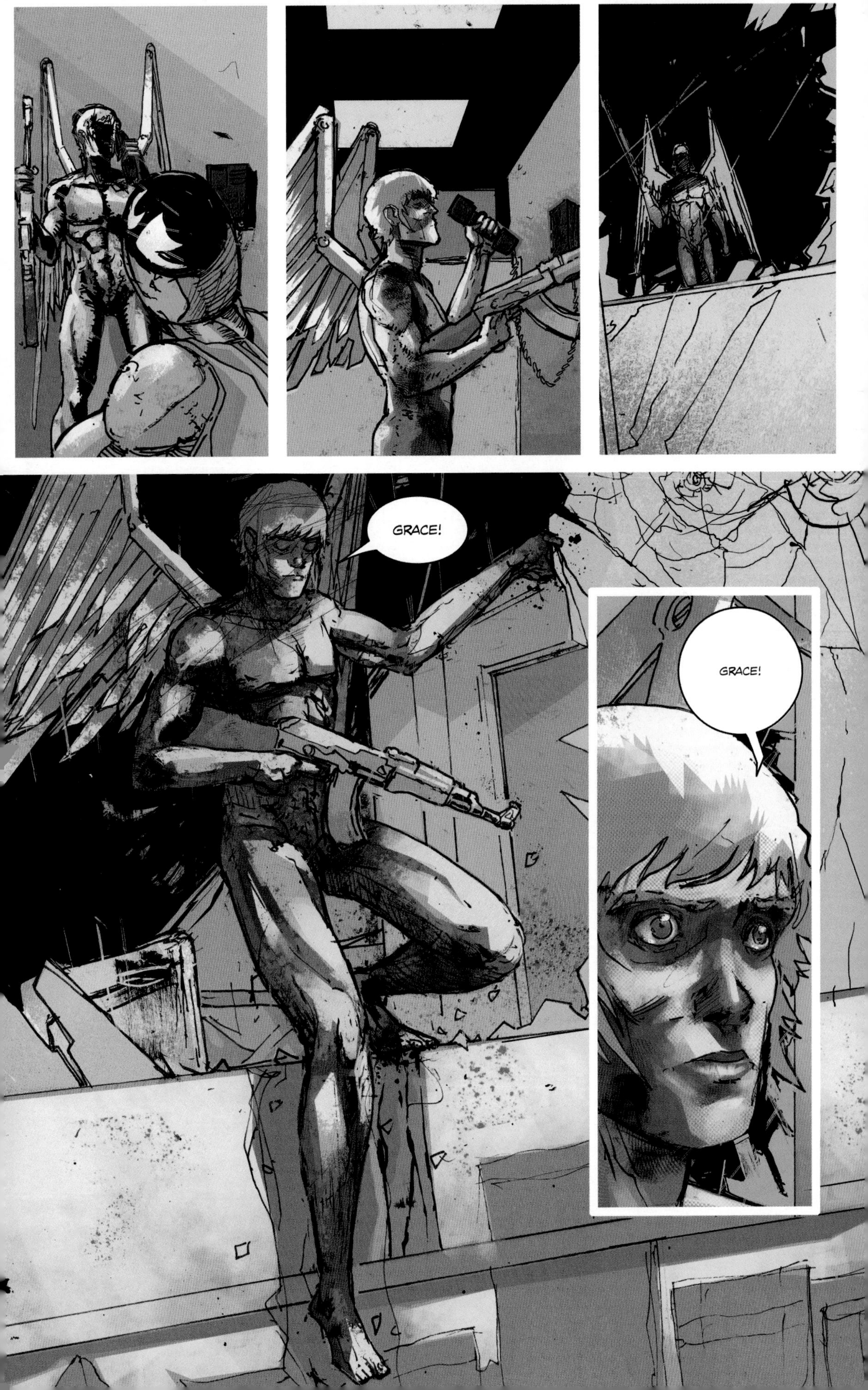
GRACE!
GRACE!

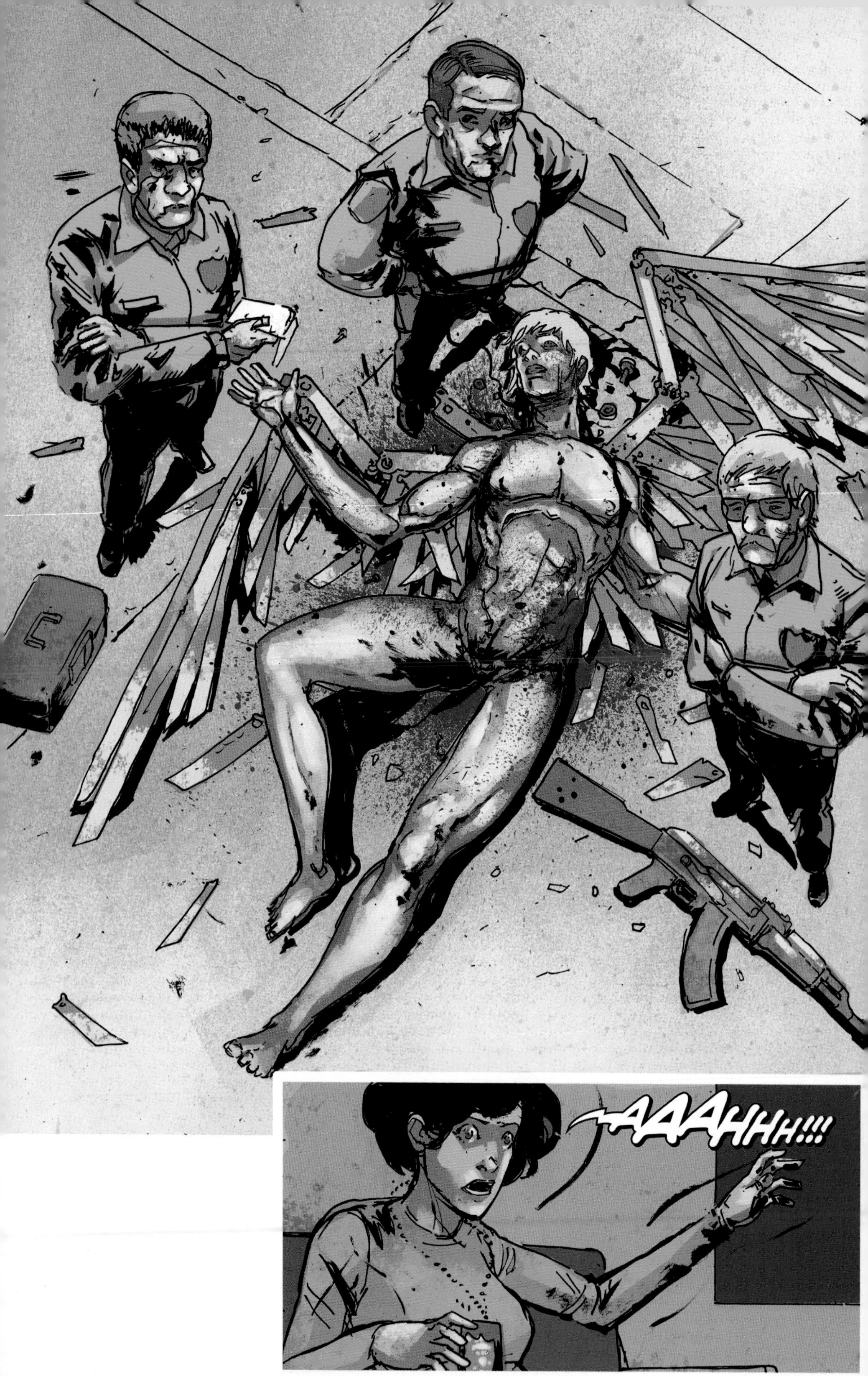
AAAHHH!!!

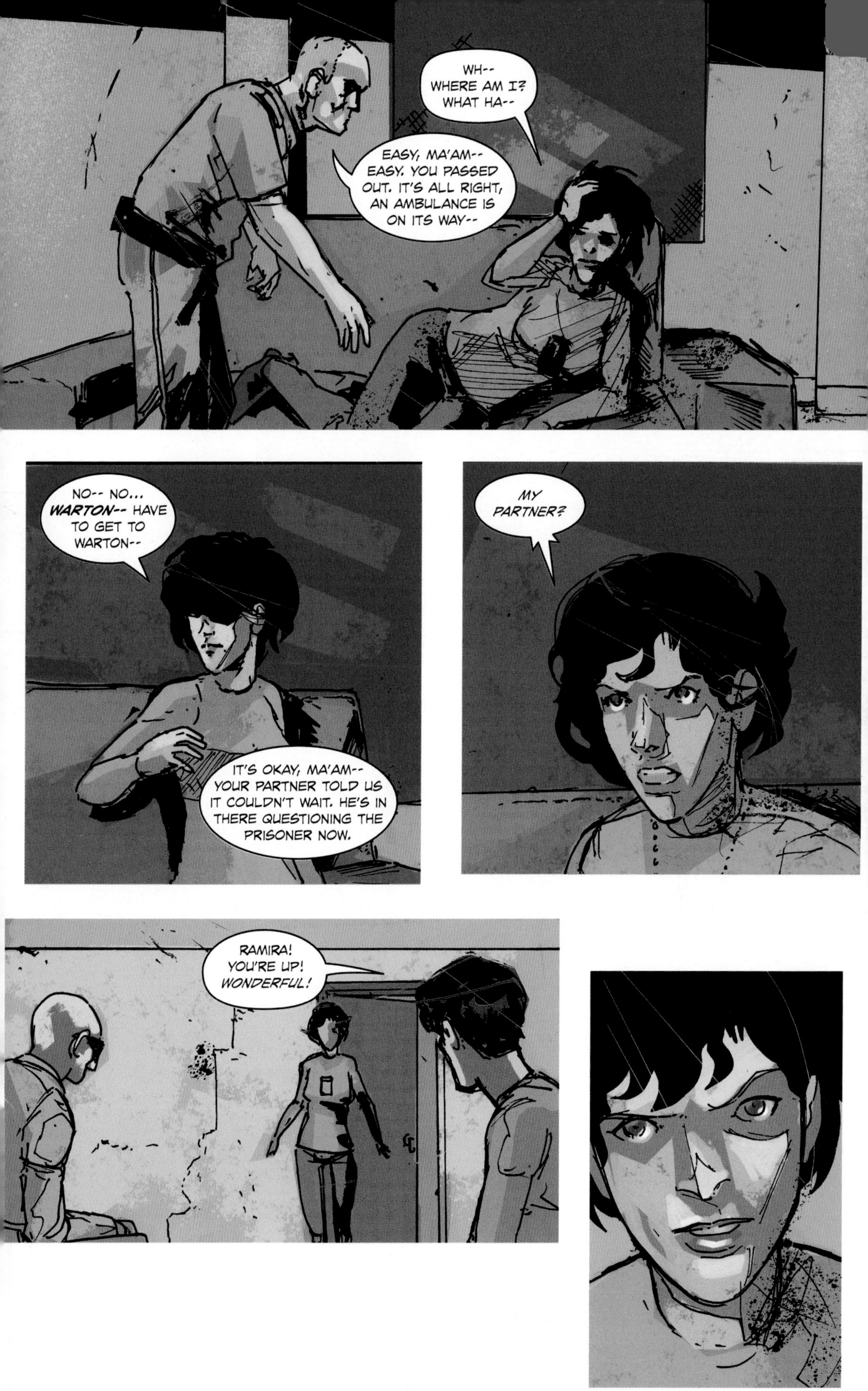
WH--
WHERE AM I?
WHAT HA--
EASY, MA'AM--
EASY. YOU PASSED OUT. IT'S ALL RIGHT, AN AMBULANCE IS ON ITS WAY--
NO-- NO... **WARTON--** HAVE TO GET TO WARTON--
IT'S OKAY, MA'AM-- YOUR PARTNER TOLD US IT COULDN'T WAIT. HE'S IN THERE QUESTIONING THE PRISONER NOW.
MY PARTNER?
RAMIRA! YOU'RE UP! *WONDERFUL!*

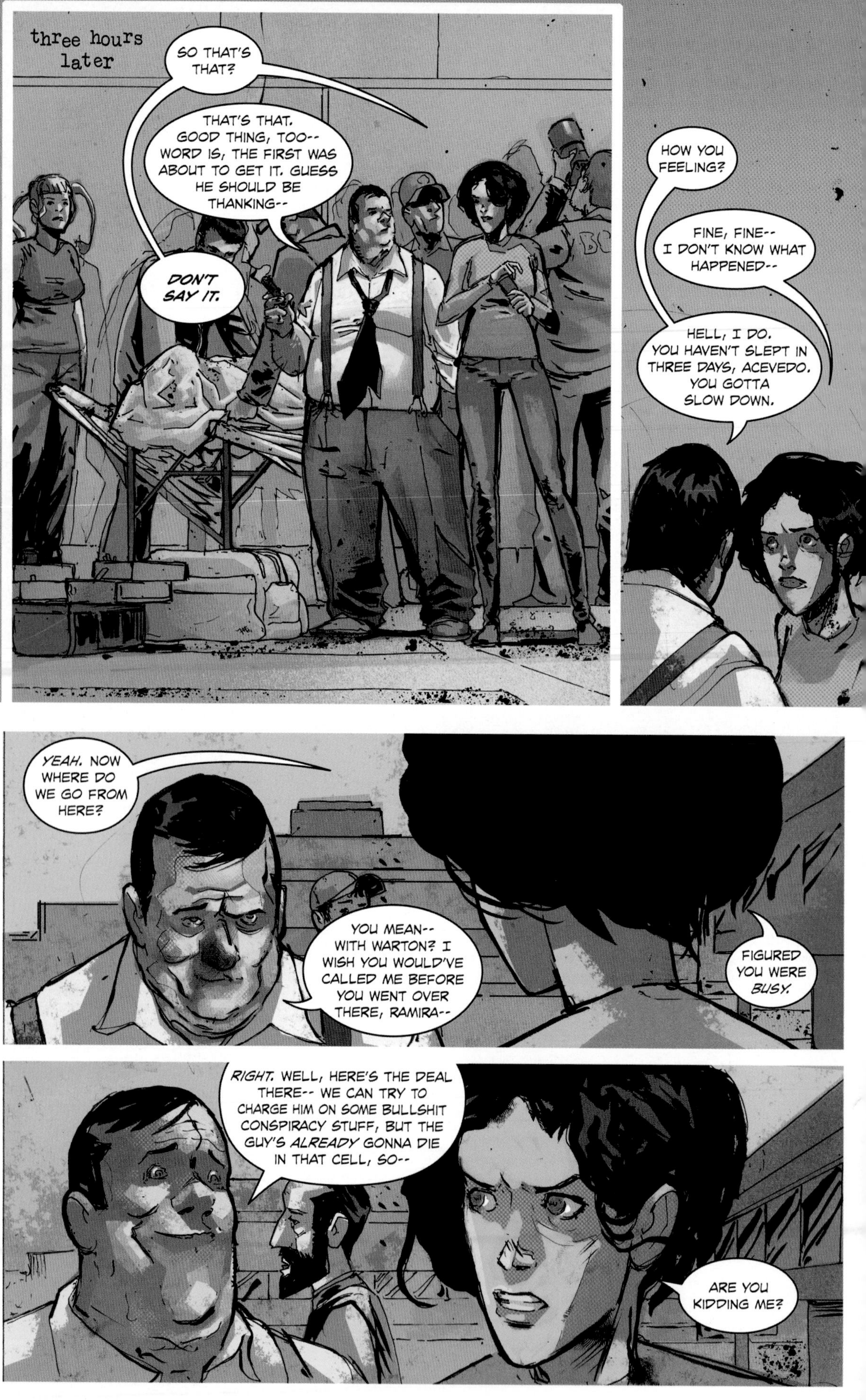
three hours later
SO THAT'S THAT?
THAT'S THAT. GOOD THING, TOO-- WORD IS, THE FIRST WAS ABOUT TO GET IT. GUESS HE SHOULD BE THANKING--
DON'T SAY IT.
HOW YOU FEELING?
FINE, FINE-- I DON'T KNOW WHAT HAPPENED--
HELL, I DO. YOU HAVEN'T SLEPT IN THREE DAYS, ACEVEDO. YOU GOTTA SLOW DOWN.
YEAH. NOW WHERE DO WE GO FROM HERE?
YOU MEAN-- WITH WARTON? I WISH YOU WOULD'VE CALLED ME BEFORE YOU WENT OVER THERE, RAMIRA--
FIGURED YOU WERE BUSY.
RIGHT. WELL, HERE'S THE DEAL THERE-- WE CAN TRY TO CHARGE HIM ON SOME BULLSHIT CONSPIRACY STUFF, BUT THE GUY'S ALREADY GONNA DIE IN THAT CELL, SO--
ARE YOU KIDDING ME?

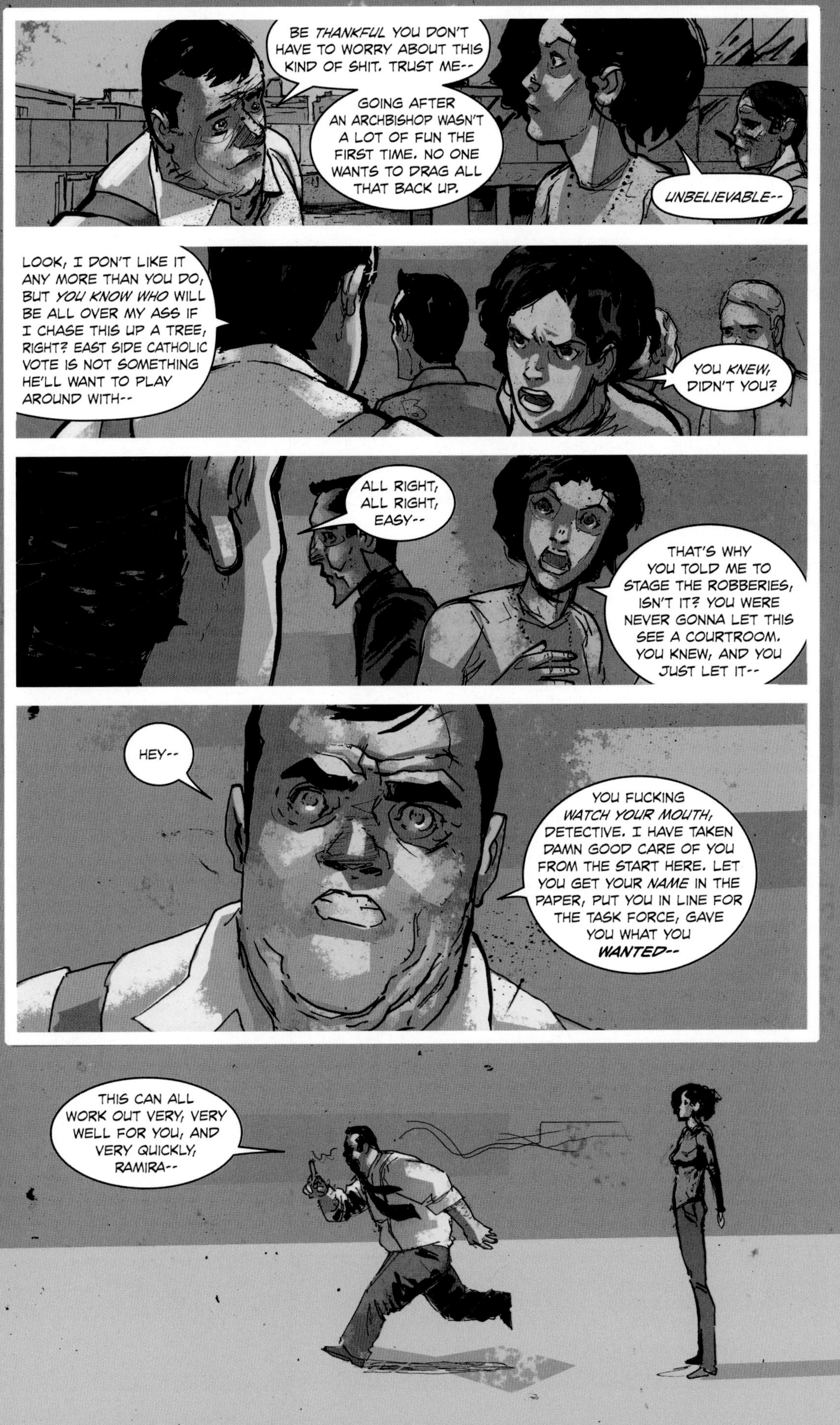
BE *THANKFUL* YOU DON'T HAVE TO WORRY ABOUT THIS KIND OF SHIT. TRUST ME--
GOING AFTER AN ARCHBISHOP WASN'T A LOT OF FUN THE FIRST TIME. NO ONE WANTS TO DRAG ALL THAT BACK UP.
UNBELIEVABLE--
LOOK, I DON'T LIKE IT ANY MORE THAN YOU DO, BUT *YOU KNOW WHO* WILL BE ALL OVER MY ASS IF I CHASE THIS UP A TREE, RIGHT? EAST SIDE CATHOLIC VOTE IS NOT SOMETHING HE'LL WANT TO PLAY AROUND WITH--
YOU *KNEW,* DIDN'T YOU?
ALL RIGHT, ALL RIGHT, EASY--
THAT'S WHY YOU TOLD ME TO STAGE THE ROBBERIES, ISN'T IT? YOU WERE NEVER GONNA LET THIS SEE A COURTROOM. YOU KNEW, AND YOU JUST LET IT--
HEY--
YOU FUCKING *WATCH YOUR MOUTH,* DETECTIVE. I HAVE TAKEN DAMN GOOD CARE OF YOU FROM THE START HERE. LET YOU GET YOUR *NAME* IN THE PAPER, PUT YOU IN LINE FOR THE TASK FORCE, GAVE YOU WHAT YOU ***WANTED--***
THIS CAN ALL WORK OUT VERY, VERY WELL FOR YOU, AND VERY QUICKLY, RAMIRA--

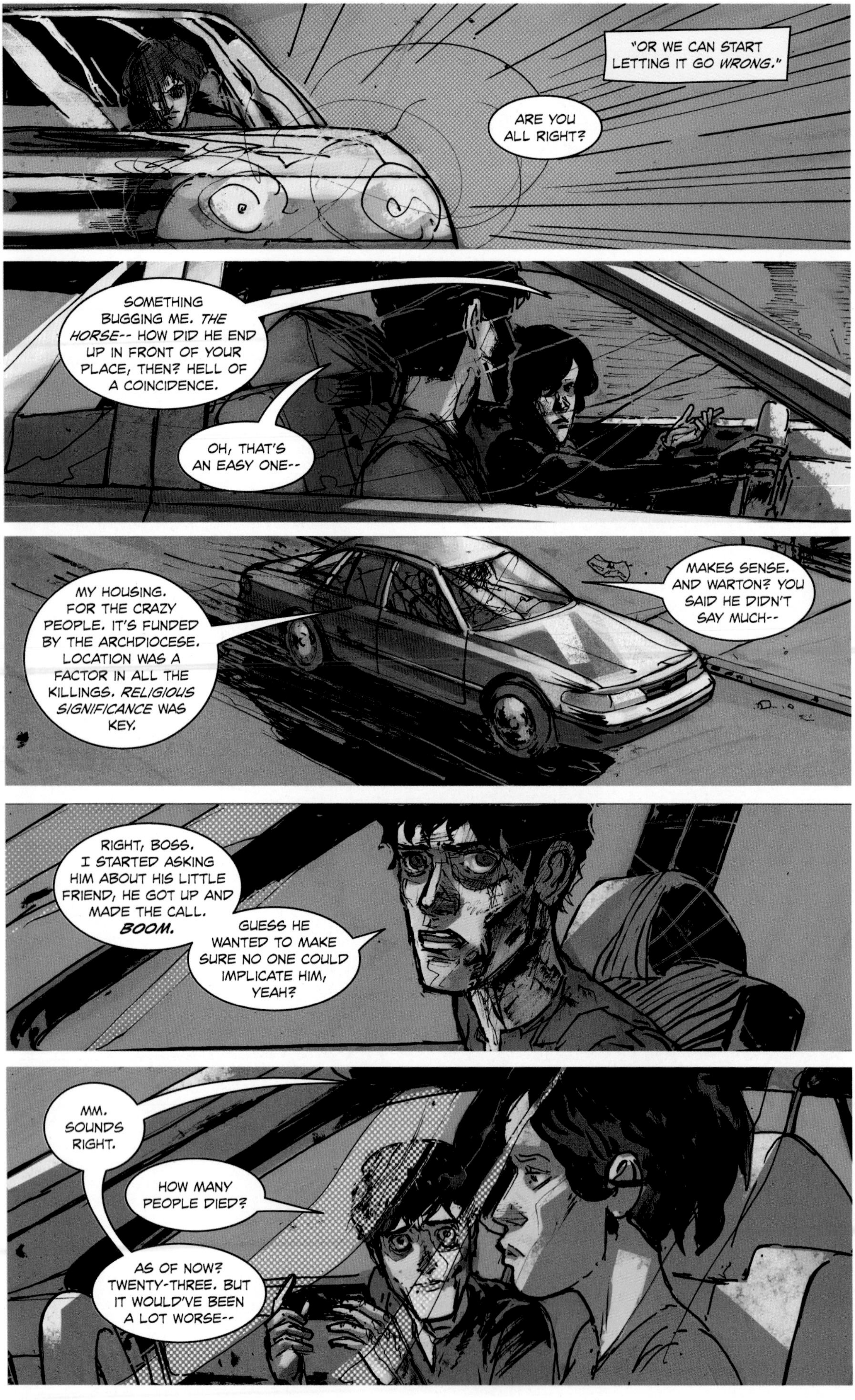
"OR WE CAN START LETTING IT GO *WRONG.*"
ARE YOU ALL RIGHT?
SOMETHING BUGGING ME. *THE HORSE*-- HOW DID HE END UP IN FRONT OF YOUR PLACE, THEN? HELL OF A COINCIDENCE.
OH, THAT'S AN EASY ONE--
MY HOUSING. FOR THE CRAZY PEOPLE. IT'S FUNDED BY THE ARCHDIOCESE. LOCATION WAS A FACTOR IN ALL THE KILLINGS. *RELIGIOUS SIGNIFICANCE* WAS KEY.
MAKES SENSE. AND WARTON? YOU SAID HE DIDN'T SAY MUCH--
RIGHT, BOSS. I STARTED ASKING HIM ABOUT HIS LITTLE FRIEND, HE GOT UP AND MADE THE CALL. ***BOOM.***
GUESS HE WANTED TO MAKE SURE NO ONE COULD IMPLICATE HIM, YEAH?
MM. SOUNDS RIGHT.
HOW MANY PEOPLE DIED?
AS OF NOW? TWENTY-THREE. BUT IT WOULD'VE BEEN A LOT WORSE--

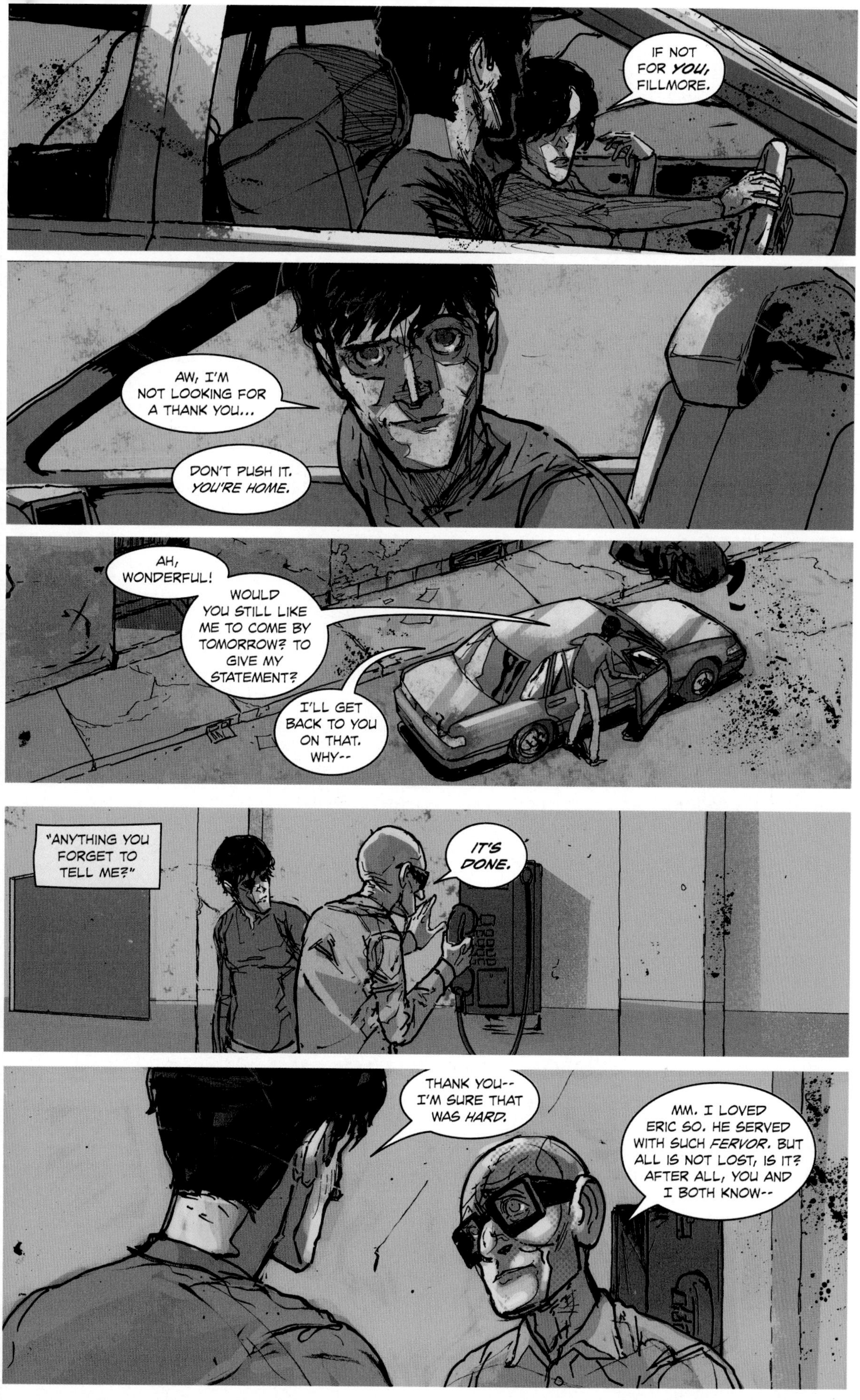
IF NOT FOR *YOU,* FILLMORE.
AW, I'M NOT LOOKING FOR A THANK YOU...
DON'T PUSH IT. *YOU'RE HOME.*
AH, WONDERFUL!
WOULD YOU STILL LIKE ME TO COME BY TOMORROW? TO GIVE MY STATEMENT?
I'LL GET BACK TO YOU ON THAT. WHY--
"ANYTHING YOU FORGET TO TELL ME?"
IT'S DONE.
THANK YOU-- I'M SURE THAT WAS *HARD.*
MM. I LOVED ERIC SO. HE SERVED WITH SUCH *FERVOR.* BUT ALL IS NOT LOST, IS IT? AFTER ALL, YOU AND I BOTH KNOW--

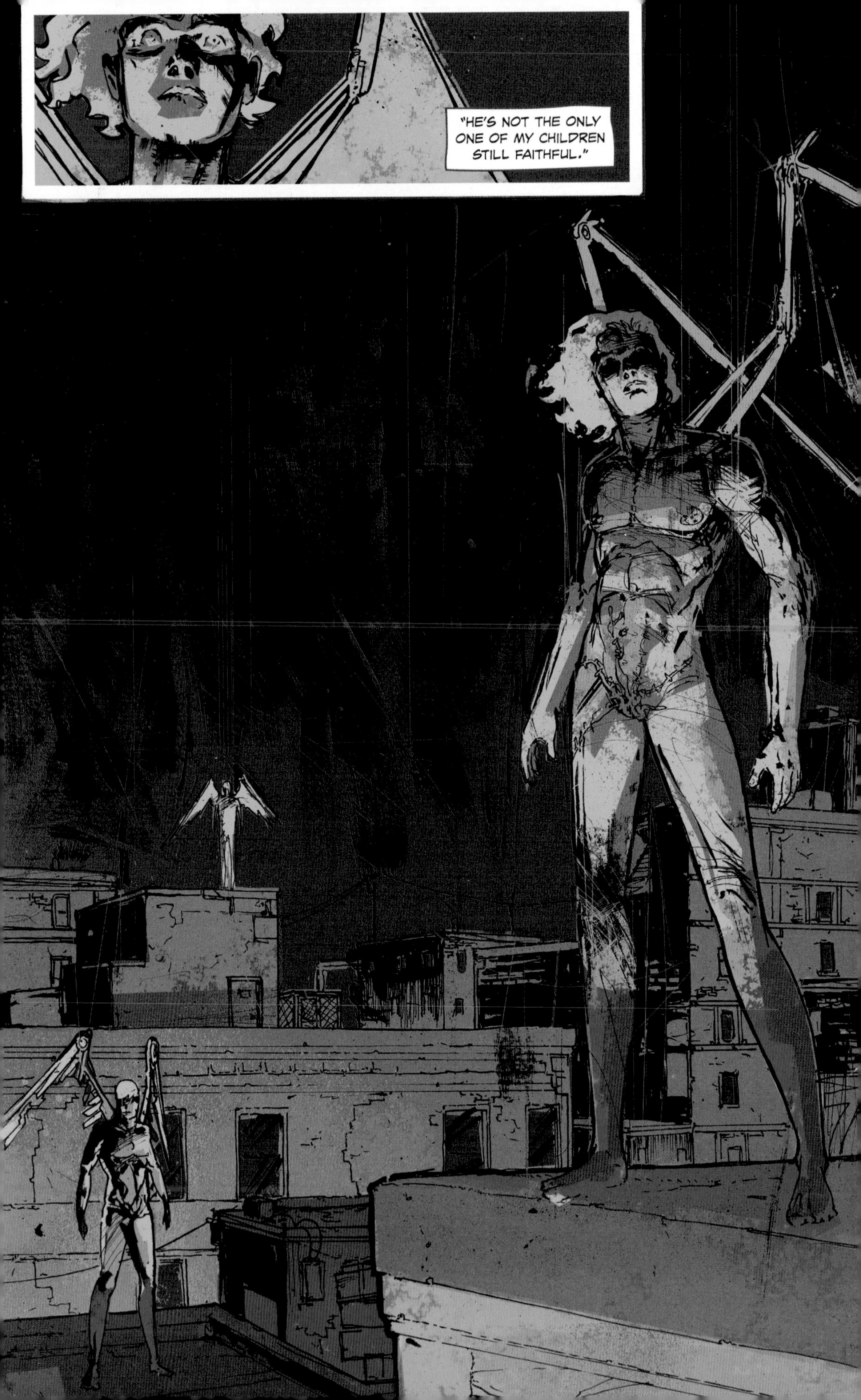
"HE'S NOT THE ONLY ONE OF MY CHILDREN STILL FAITHFUL."